Ethnicity   *Theory and Experience*

Ethnicity Theory and Experience

Edited by Nathan Glazer

and Daniel P. Moynihan

with the assistance of

Corinne Saposs Schelling

Harvard University Press

Cambridge, Massachusetts, 1975

Copyright © 1975 by the President and Fellows of Harvard College
All rights reserved
Library of Congress Catalog Card Number 74-21230
ISBN 0-674-26855-5
Printed in the United States of America

Acknowledgments

This book is the product of a conference, convened with the support of the Ford Foundation at the American Academy of Arts and Sciences in Brookline, Massachusetts, in October 1972. For that conference, we asked several individuals to prepare short papers that might serve as a basis of discussion. Following the conference, we asked those who had prepared papers for the conference to expand them; we asked others, some of whom had been present at the conference, some not, to prepare additional papers. Our intention was to present some (hardly all) theoretical approaches, as well as some more empirical papers describing the variety of situations in which ethnic groups distinguish themselves in different countries of the world. Nothing, we realize, is covered in detail: for Europe outside Russia, we have one chapter covering some developments in Switzerland, Belgium, and the Netherlands (William Petersen). For all of Latin America, we have one chapter dealing with Peru (François Bourricaud); for all of Africa, there is one chapter on an aspect of ethnic relations in Uganda (Ali Mazrui.) One chapter apiece deals with the vast complexities of those three subcontinental realms, Soviet Russia, China, and India (Richard Pipes, Lucian Pye, and Jyotirindra Das Gupta.) Milton Esman reviews the situation in Southeast Asia. Australia, which has recently become ethnically remarkably diversified owing to post-World War II immigration, is unfortunately ignored. One chapter takes up ethnicity in Canada (John Porter); there is one on that amazing museum of ethnicity, the

West Indies, which deals with one of the smaller groups of that area (Orlando Patterson); and two papers touch on different aspects of ethnicity in the United States (Andrew Greeley and William C. McCready and Martin Kilson.) We are all too aware that the conference and the book that followed drew heavily from the banks of the Charles River, and that many other persons unrepresented in this book except in footnotes have been working for many years in developing our understanding of ethnicity.

NG
DPM

Contents

THE OLD WORLD AND THE NEW

THE NEW STATES

THE OLD EMPIRES

Ethnicity *Theory and Experience*

NATHAN GLAZER AND
DANIEL P. MOYNIHAN

Introduction

Ethnicity seems to be a new term. In the sense in which we use it—the character or quality of an ethnic group—it does not appear in the 1933 edition of the *Oxford English Dictionary,* but it makes its appearance in the 1972 *Supplement,* where the first usage recorded is that of David Riesman in 1953. It is included in *Webster's Third New International,* 1961, but did not find its way into the Random House *Dictionary of the English Language* of 1966, nor the *American Heritage Dictionary of the English Language,* 1969. It did, however, make the 1973 edition of the *American Heritage Dictionary,* where it is defined as "1. The condition of belonging to a particular ethnic group; 2. Ethnic pride." One senses a term still on the move. The first of these two definitions fits well with our own: an objective condition. The second, however, is decidedly subjective, that of "pride." How very different from an old meaning, "obs. rare" as the OED has it, "heathendom: heathen superstition." At the very least, a change of relative status is going on here.

All of which may prompt the reader to ask how useful this "new" term is. Any such categorization taken up and given currency by sociologists suffers from a certain presumption of disutility. Does it *mean* anything new, or is it simply a new way of saying something old? Does it make for greater precision in describing the world, or does it merely compound the confusion, fuzz further the fuzziness? Is it the result of insight, or the resort of bewilderment? A reader of this volume for example might well ask any or all of these questions as he encounters this single term applied to phenomena as various as the survival of psychological differences between Italian and Irish Americans in the United States; black politics here; the difficult effort to find a satisfactory place for the French-speaking element in an undivided Canada; the restrained but devastating conflict between Fleming and Walloon in Belgium; the looming nationalities issue in Soviet Russia; the language problem in India; border minorities in China; the status of Indian and *mestizo* in Peru; the all-important issue in Africa of which tribes got recruited for the modern armies there. The phenomenon seems everywhere to be encountered, but somehow, everywhere, also, various. Does a single term help? Would it not be better to describe such varied phenomena as linguistic, national, religious, tribal, racial, and the like, depending on their nature? Would it not be better to separate the very different problems of old nations from those of the new? of the developed world from those of the developing? of heterogeneous empires from homogeneous nation-states? Are these not, in truth, age-old human characteristics and sentiments, expressing themselves, perhaps, in new settings, but in themselves nothing new? Isn't this really what we are dealing with here?

No, it is not. Such, in any event, is our contention. Something new has appeared. The object of this volume—the work of many men no one of whom need subscribe to the views of the editors—is to present certain theoretical explanations for this appearance and to provide a number of concrete illustrations. We cannot hope to be conclusive in our effort, to settle the matter once and for all. The phenomenon is too new and, doubtless, our own range too limited. Hence we do not ask any final assent from the reader. Yet we do hope for a certain openness to the idea that there may indeed be something new here. A reader of the early nineteenth century, encountering the assertion that industrialization was shaping distinctive social classes, could well have shrugged it off with the thought that there had always been social ranks, always different ways of earning a living. Yet to have done so would have been to miss a big event of that age. Similarly, we feel that to see only what is familiar in the ethnicity of our time is to miss the emergence of a new social category as significant for the understanding of the present-day world as that of social class itself. For in the welter of contemporary forms of group expression and group conflict there is both something new and something common: there has been a pronounced and sudden increase in tendencies by people in many countries and in many circumstances to insist on the significance of their group distinctiveness and identity and on new rights that derive from this group character.

Despite the enormous diversity among the groups and situations in which such tendencies have become evident, and among the issues and demands raised by each group, it is possible to explore these various examples of group assertiveness and conflict in terms of what they have in common. Each, of course, arises in a distinctive historical and social setting and must be treated as unique in the sense that everything in human affairs is unique. Yet it is also necessary, we are convinced, to search for common sectors. Perhaps these are deeply felt human needs that have always been present but only recently focused by certain political and social developments that have given rise to new common social circumstances in many countries in the postwar world. Merely to begin speculation is to encounter the range of possibilities.

In other circumstances it would be the task of an introduction to a volume of some half-dozen theoretical essays on a given social phenomenon, and eleven accounts of how the phenomenon expresses itself in a variety of nations and parts of the world, to address key questions, in this case questions concerning ethnic identity, assertiveness, and conflict today: whether they are deeply founded in human needs, or in new social developments, or in the characteristics of modern states, and so forth. The object of this introduction—and of the volume—is more modest: not a theory, but a bundle of partial theories; not an exhaustive source, but an illustrative one; not definitiveness, but merely the assertion that here is a phenomenon that *must* be studied.

The claim is modest but is not unimportant, when one considers how little attention ethnicity as a phenomenon in society and politics has received until the last few years. Thus, in our search for an appropriate definition and characterization we reviewed some available handbooks. G. Duncan Mitchell's *A Dictionary of Sociology*

(Chicago, Aldine, 1968) does not contain an entry for "ethnic groups" or "ethnicity"—although it does contain an entry for "ethnocentrism." (The same is true of the much older *Handbook of Sociology* by Edward Byron Reuter, New York, Dryden Press, 1941.) *A Modern Dictionary of Sociology* by George A. and Achilles G. Theodorson (New York, Thomas Y. Crowell, 1969) does contain an entry for "ethnic group" but one which reflects a somewhat older usage ("a group with a common cultural tradition and a sense of identity which exists as a *subgroup* [our italics] of a larger society"). But do we not now tend increasingly to apply the term "ethnic group" to any group of distinct cultural tradition and origin, even if it is the majority ethnic group within a nation, the *Staatsvolk?* Thus, in the United States we increasingly consider old Americans, descendants of Anglo-Saxons, as themselves an ethnic group—and the odd term WASP, coined one assumes in jest, is often used to describe them.

Admittedly, this is not universal usage, not even in this volume (see the essay by Orlando Patterson). In the carefully prepared *Dictionary of the Social Sciences* by Julius Gould and William L. Kolb (New York, The Free Press of Glencoe-Macmillan, 1964), Melvin Tumin follows the more limited usage also: "a social group which, within a larger cultural and social system, claims or is accorded special status in terms of a complex of traits (ethnic traits) which it exhibits or is believed to exhibit." But the fact that—as we believe—social scientists tend to broaden the use of the term "ethnic group" to refer not only to subgroups, to minorities, but to all the groups of a society characterized by a distinct sense of difference owing to culture and descent, itself reflects the somewhat broader significance that ethnicity has taken up in recent years.

It also to our mind reflects something more important: a shift in the general understanding about ethnic groups. Formerly seen as *survivals* from an earlier age, to be treated variously with annoyance, toleration, or mild celebration, we now have a growing sense that they may be *forms* of social life that are capable of renewing and transforming themselves. As such, perhaps, the hope of doing without ethnicity in a society as its subgroups assimilate to the majority group may be as utopian and as questionable an enterprise as the hope of doing without social classes in a society.

This is not an assertion to be passed lightly. If true, a very great deal of radical and even liberal doctrine of the past century and a half is wrong. To repeat one final time for fear of being misunderstood, we do not assert that it *is* true, although we suspect it to be. In anticipation of a later point, let it also most explicitly and emphatically be stated that we neither welcome nor deplore the phenomenon. When, years ago, Margaret Fuller announced that she accepted the universe, Carlyle commented that she had better. This, and only this, is our purpose, and, for what interest it may have, it is also our view. It is a view we find we have held to with fair consistency for the fifteen years since we first collaborated on *Beyond the Melting Pot*,[1] a study of ethnic groups of New York City which appeared at a time when in theory they were supposed to be disappearing.

We are suggesting that a new word reflects a new reality and a new usage reflects a change in that reality. The new word is "ethnicity," and the new usage is the steady expansion of the term "ethnic group" from minority and marginal subgroups at the edges of society—groups expected to assimilate, to disappear, to continue as survivals, exotic or troublesome—to major elements of a society. Suggestive as usage and language may be, however, they are not an argument. Let us consider some of the questions that are inevitably raised when one tries to make the argument that there is something new afoot in the world, and that we may label it "ethnicity."

1. *What, after all, is new about conflicts between ethnic groups and between "majority" and "minority" ethnic groups, based on demands for prestige, respect, civil rights, political power, access to economic opportunity? Haven't there always been such conflicts?* First of all, we would suggest, there seem of late to be far more of such conflicts, and they are more intense. Walker Connor has undertaken the invaluable task of recording the rise and extent of what he calls "ethnonationalism," which he dates to the French revolution. He reports

1. Nathan Glazer and Daniel P. Moynihan, *Beyond the Melting Pot* (Cambridge, Mass., Harvard University Press and MIT Press, 1963, 1970).

that nearly half of the independent countries of the world have been troubled in recent years by some degree of "ethnically inspired dissonance." [2] We do not have benchmarks for earlier periods, but if we compare some specific known cases, there has clearly also been a rise in *intensity* in given ethnic conflicts in the last decade or so. As some examples, consider the conflicts between Anglophone and Francophone in Canada, Catholic and Protestant in Northern Ireland, Walloon and Fleming in Belgium, Bengali and non-Bengali in Pakistan, Chinese and Malay in Malaysia, Greek and Turk in Cyprus, Jews and other minorities on the one hand and Great Russians on the other in the Soviet Union, and Ibo and Hausa and Yoruba in Nigeria. And, we may add, between black and white in the United States. If we had measurements of intensity we would not necessarily find that *every* ethnic conflict has become uniformly more intense—some of them seem happily to have peaked (sometimes in war and violent conflict), and measures of harmonization and accommodation seem to have had some effect since these peaks were reached (in Nigeria, the United States). In other cases—Pakistan—conflict has reached the point of separation, and has subsequently declined in intensity to be succeeded perhaps by a rise in ethnic discord in the two successor states of Pakistan. But we think it can hardly be disputed that there has been a greater degree of ethnic conflict in the last ten or twenty years than most informed observers expected. If the origins or causes of ethnic conflicts are not new, it is certainly true that their extent, scale and intensity are.

2. *But old lines of division can be found between most of the groups now in conflict, divisions of culture, religion, language, political affiliation. Is there anything about these conflicts that permits us with any legitimacy to give them all a single label, "ethnic"?* We think there is. Perhaps the best way of suggesting what is common is to refer to the *expectations* of most social scientists some time ago and even today as to the course of modern social development. In one of the chapters that follow, Milton Gordon refers to a "liberal expectancy"—the expectation that the kinds of features that divide one group from an-

2. Walker Connor, "The Politics of Ethnonationalism," *Journal of International Affairs*, 27.1 (1973), 1–21.

other would inevitably lose their weight and sharpness in modern and modernizing societies, that there would be increasing emphasis on achievement rather than ascription, that common systems of education and communication would level differences, that nationally uniform economic and political systems would have the same effect. Under these circumstances the "primordial" (or in any case antecedent) differences between groups would be expected to become of lesser significance. The "liberal expectancy" flows into the "radical expectancy"—that class circumstances would become the main line of division between people, erasing the earlier lines of tribe, language, religion, national origin, and that thereafter these *class* divisions would themselves, after revolution, disappear. Thus Karl Marx and his followers reacted with impatience to the heritage of the past, as they saw it, in the form of ethnic attachments. *Interest* should guide rational men—or drive them—in social action; and interest was determined by economic position.

One element thus that is new in the present situation is that *interest* is pursued effectively by *ethnic groups* today as well as by *interest*-defined groups: indeed, perhaps it can be pursued even more effectively. As against class-based forms of social identification and conflict—which of course continue to exist—we have been surprised by the persistence and salience of ethnic-based forms of social identification and conflict.

One of the striking characteristics of the present situation is indeed the extent to which we find the ethnic group defined in terms of interest, *as* an interest group. Thus, whereas in the past a religious conflict, such as that which is tearing Northern Ireland apart, was based on such issues as the free and public practice of a religion, today it is based on the issue of which group shall gain benefits or hold power of a wholly secular sort. Language conflicts—as in India—today have little to do with the right to the public use of the language, as did so many struggles of the nineteenth century when, for example, there were efforts to Russify the Russian empire and Magyarize the Hungarian kingdom. Today they have more to do with which language user shall have the best opportunity to get which job. One should not make the distinction too sharp: certainly the prestige of one's religion and language is involved in conflicts where one advocates the right of public use of religion and language and where one advocates the right to economic or political advantages of the individual adherents of a religion or users of a language. But nevertheless it is clear the weight of these kinds of conflicts has shifted: from an emphasis on culture, language, religion, *as such,* it shifts to an emphasis on the *interests* broadly defined of the members of the group.

It is not easy to know how to interpret this. Talcott Parsons, in a chapter which follows, using a term of David Schneider, refers to the "desocialization" of ethnic groups: the cultural *content* of each ethnic group, in the United States, seems to have become very similar to that of others, but the emotional significance of attachment to the ethnic group seems to persist.[3] In this respect the "liberal expectancy" was right: the cultural differences between groups have been worn down by the institutions and circumstances of modern society. But since each group had a different history, these groups were differentially distributed in the various social positions of society. As a result, the ethnic group *could* become a focus of mobilization for the pursuit of group or individual interests. Perhaps then, in answer to our second question, we might hazard the hypothesis that ethnic conflicts have become one form in which interest conflicts between and within states are pursued.[4]

We would suggest there are two, related explanations that account for this development. The first is the evolution of the welfare state in the more advanced economies of the world and the advent of the socialist state in the underdeveloped economies. In either circumstance, the *state* becomes a crucial and direct arbiter of economic well-being, as well as of political status and whatever flows from that. In such a situation it is not usually enough, or not enough for long enough, to assert claims on behalf of large but loosely aggregated groups such as "workers," "peasants," "white

3. In an essay now more than twenty years old Nathan Glazer, referring to the way in which ethnic groups in the United States were becoming "ghost" nations, had something similar in mind: "Ethnic Groups in America: From National Culture to Ideology," in Morroe Berger, Theodore Abel, and Charles H. Page, eds., *Freedom and Control in Modern Society* (New York, D. Van Nostrand, 1954), pp. 158–173.

4. This was suggested by the authors in Glazer and Moynihan, *Beyond the Melting Pot.*

collar employees." Claims of this order are too general to elicit a very satisfactory response, and even when they do, the benefits are necessarily diffuse and often evanescent, having the quality of an across-the-board wage increase which produces an inflation which leaves everyone about as he was. As a matter of strategic efficacy, it becomes necessary to disaggregate, to make claims for a group small enough to make significant concessions possible and, equally, small enough to produce some gain from the concessions made. A British prime minister who does "something for the workers" probably doesn't do much and almost certainly does even less for his party. Doing something for the Scots, however, becomes an increasingly attractive and real option for Westminster. *That* much in the way of resources can be found, and the Scots are likely to know about it and to consider it a positive gain, at least past the point of the next general election. One can win votes that way, it being a notable quality of ethnicity in our time that it involves itself relatively easily with democratic governmental systems. (It may be noted that nineteenth-century liberalism was at a loss to decide which was the more offensive aspect of the newly risen urban, working-class political "machines": the distribution of governmental largesse *or* the introduction of ethnic categories as a distributive principle. It comes to a matter of strategic efficacy in asserting claims.) The welfare state and the socialist state appear to be especially responsive to ethnic claims. This is everywhere to be encountered: an Indian minister assuring his parliament that "Muslims, Christians and other minorities" will receive their "due and proper share" of railroad jobs; a Czech government choosing a Slovak leader; a Chinese prime minister in Singapore choosing an Indian foreign minister; and so on.[5]

5. Leaders of groups are aware that political skills in pressing such claims vary and occasionally voice their concern, as reported in a recent Associated Press dispatch from Los Angeles:

US–Asians allege exploitation. The Asian-American community leaders have accused the U.S. Department of Labor of exploiting their inexperience in "the political game" to exclude them when allocating federal funds.

"We Asians have always been a quiet minority. We've always been a quiet minority. We've always been taken for granted, and we always get the crumbs," Miss _____ a leader of the Chinese Community Council, told newsmen.

Miss _____ was referring to the distribution of $314,000 in federal funds for career counseling projects. The council leaders accused the U.S. manpower area planning council

The strategic efficacy of ethnicity as a basis for asserting claims against government has its counterpart in the seeming ease whereby government employs ethnic categories as a basis for distributing its rewards. Nothing was more dramatic than the rise of this practice on the part of the American government in the 1960s, *at the very instant when such practice was declared abhorrent and illegal.* The Civil Rights Act of 1964 was the very embodiment of the liberal expectancy. "Race, color, religion, sex, national origin": all such ascriptive categories were *outlawed.* No one was to be classified in such primitive offensive terms. In particular, government was to become color blind. However, within hours of the enactment of the statute, in order to enforce it, the federal government, for the first time, began to require ever more detailed accountings of subgroups of every description—job trainees, kindergarten children, kindergarten teachers, university faculties, front office secretaries—in terms of race, color, and sex. (We seem not yet to have proceeded to religion and national origin. And yet an application form of the Graduate Faculty of Arts and Sciences of Harvard University now states: "It is to your advantage to state if you are a member of an ethnic minority." The question is a fuzzy one—is it advantageous regardless of whether the answer is yes or no—but invites an expansion of reference. Hence, are Catholics an ethnic minority for Harvard purposes? Portuguese? There is, for example, a Portuguese community in Cambridge and in Massachusetts quite undiscovered by equal opportunity offices.) The expectancy that such things would not be known—in the immediate postwar years governments were busy eliminating all references to race and religion from official forms, even forbidding universities to request photographs of applicants for admission—was instantly replaced by the requirement that they not only be known but the facts as to distribution be justified. Skewed distributions

---

of doing "a tremendous wrong" in giving the funds away entirely to Black and Chicano groups, whose project proposals were more professionally drafted.

Not all Asians in the United States are well off, but Americans of Chinese and Japanese descent recurrently come out at the top of census based rankings of American racial groups in terms of social and economic status. No matter: such a claim has a prima facie legitimacy.

would not do: quotas appeared in American society. The instrument of national social policy designed ostensibly to prevent discrimination inevitably went beyond that to positive efforts on behalf of those presumptively discriminated against, a list which in short order commenced to lengthen.

Statutes began to reflect this new strategy. A small example: the Drug Abuse Education Act of 1970 provides "for the use of adequate personnel from similar social, cultural, age, ethnic and racial backgrounds as those of the individuals served under any such program." In other words, the federal government was not only to know the peculiar ethnic patterns of various kinds of drug abuse but was to match the therapists with the patients: Azerbaijani junky, Azerbaijani counsellor. In a variation of folk medicine, it was judged that wherever a malady was found, there, too, would a remedy reside. Which may or may not be nonsense: what is not to be denied is that the statute appropriated many millions of dollars for social services which were going to end up in the pockets of those who dispense them, and these could be concentrated on specific ethnic groups. If government was doing a group a service by providing special therapeutic services, it could compound the favor by concentrating the patronage involved within the same group or groups.

We have suggested there are two related reasons that could account for the degree that ethnic conflicts appear to have become the form in which interest conflicts between and within states are pursued. The first had to do with the strategic efficacy of ethnicity in making legitimate claims on the resources of the modern state. (This is largely an internal matter, as is ethnic conflict itself, but as something like international social policy takes shape in settings such as that of the United Nations, ethnic claims are also made in such fora and with effect.) The second of our two suggestions has to do with the social dynamics that lead to such claims and concerns the fact and the nature of inequality. Men are not equal; neither are ethnic groups. That they should be, or should not be, is, of course, a wholly different question. If one is to describe the way the world is, one describes men everywhere ranked in systems of social stratification where one person is better or worse off than another. This is the empirical fact. As with individuals, so with groups of individuals, with social groups defined by ethnic identity. As to the origins of this inequality, we follow Ralf Dahrendorf in holding that it arises from differential success in achieving social norms.[6] Dahrendorf accounts for individual inequality in these terms: we adapt his thesis to group inequality. His thesis is that every society establishes norms—socially established values— selected from a universe of such values. There seems no end to human ingenuity in thinking of characteristics that can be described as desirable or undesirable. It can be thought a good thing to be wealthy, alternatively to be poor; to be dark or to be light; generous or mean; religious or atheistic; fun-loving or dour; promiscuous or chaste. However, once a selection is made as to what is good and what is bad, individuals—and, we now add, ethnic groups—have different levels of success in attaining the desired condition. Woe to the ectomorph in a society which sets great store on plumpness in the female. Or pity the fat girl in the age of Dior and of blue jeans. Woe to blacks in Rhodesia which sets great store on being white. Pity the white in Uganda. Pity (perhaps) the Nepalese in Bhutan who labors on construction gangs before the eyes of a land-owning peasantry which despises such servility. Woe to the Malay facing the onslaught of Chinese industriousness. A Burmese showing one of the present editors around Mandalay commented that before independence Indians and Chinese had owned all the land. "Do you see," he continued, "why we had to have socialism?" By which he meant simply expelling these settlers who had followed the British.

In Dahrendorf's account the individual encounters the norms of his society *and* the "sanctions designed to enforce these principles" (p. 32). Some do better than others and reap the rewards; some suffer the punishments. This is a dynamic process which forms groups (classes), those who do better and those who do worse. Equally, it can be a process which begins with groups, and helps form them further. Dahrendorf clearly anticipates this: "The selection of norms always involves discrimination, not only against per-

6. Ralf Dahrendorf, "On the Origin of Inequality among Men," in André Béteille, ed., *Social Inequality* (Baltimore, Penguin Books, 1969).

sons holding sociologically random moral convictions, but also against social positions that may debar their incumbents from conformity with established values" (p. 33).

What kind of social positions? Those of social class, perhaps, come quickest to a European mind. (Or did.) Eliza Doolittle is of a social class in which one does not learn the diction of polite English society: only when she has been taught it does the possibility of owning her own florist shop open for her. But an American—and persons in many other parts of the world—is as likely to associate poor diction with ethnicity: first and second generation difficulties with English, and patterns of grammar and pronunciation that persist long after. "Where d'ya worka, John? On the Delaware Lackawan." Similarly, a European might associate wealth with social class. An American—and, again, persons in many other parts of the world—is as likely to associate wealth with ethnicity. To a child of the slums of New York City a generation ago it was "Jews" who were "rich," a point of view that evidently persists in the slums of the present. In Dar es Salaam, in Singapore, in São Paulo the same, but different, perceptions are extraordinarily powerful social facts. And why is this? We suggest it is because so much of the mixture of ethnic groups in the modern world is the result of more or less sharply defined and not infrequently organized movements of people from one part of the world to another to meet new, and, again, often organized demands for labor. The plantation economies of the eighteenth and nineteenth centuries moved Africans and Asians to the farthest reaches of the globe. Other economic forces led to mass European migration to the Western Hemisphere and Asia and Africa. Migration was nothing new, but speed was new. North Africa presumably absorbed the Vandals but presumably because they came over generations. The nineteenth-century French came suddenly and were never absorbed. In the end they were expelled after a bloody ethnic civil war. So equally in dozens and dozens of situations: peoples thrown together quite suddenly and thereafter trying to deal one with the other.

Here the matter of norms comes into play. There are norms within a social group: some individuals are better than others are at achieving them, some are worse. But as between different ethnic groups, which have made quite different selections from the universe of possibilities, the norms of one are likely to be quite different from those of another, such that individuals who are successful by the standards of their own groups will be failures by those of the other. In a situation of mixed ethnic groups where one group is dominant, which is to say that its norms are seen as normal not just for it, but for others also, there follows an almost automatic consignment of other groups to inferior status. But some groups may discover that they are quite good at achieving the norms of the dominant group: even better than the group that laid down those "laws." This is to be encountered almost everywhere: in some instances cheerfully accepted, in others bitterly resented. Africans are traders, so are Indians. In Kenya the Indians were evidently better than the Africans, and so the Indians are being expelled. Jews have known the experience, Japanese, Chinese: which group has not? There are, of course, situations in which no one group is dominant, such that differing norms compete with one another, but this makes if anything for less social peace, as no one is ever quite certain what constitutes success or failure.

We offer these assertions in quest of a theory of ethnicity. They are subject to empirical test, and we believe the chapters that follow offer suggestive evidence from many and varied settings. In the United States, at all events, arguments that follow from this "theory" are increasingly put forward by persons dealing with day to day ethnic issues. Thus, consider this passage in a letter from a U.S. Army colonel, director of Army Equal Opportunity Programs, which appeared in the *Washington Post* of March 21, 1974, and was later distributed by the U.S. Civil Service Commission:

> As a black I do not believe it is fair or meaningful to call [actions to correct racial imbalances] "reverse discrimination." Let's examine what is meant by racial discrimination and then apply the word "reverse" to the term after the examination. Please accept as an operational definition that racial discrimination is the relationship between two groups of people, wherein *one group has defined the rules by which the other group must act.* Such has always been the relationship between the white majority and the minorities in this country. Moreover, the meaningful and political, economic and social power to maintain that relationship in America has been consistently vested in the white majority. (Our italics.)

Herein lies the dynamic element in the system. Dahrendorf writes that inequality "serves to keep social structures alive." This is because "inequality always implies the gain of one group at the expense of others; thus every system of social stratification generates protest against its principles and bears the seeds of its own suppression." It is not perhaps necessary to assert that *every* system of social stratification generates protest against its principles. Some may not. But most that we run into in the twentieth century seem to do so. This is to say that a *different* set of norms is set forth as desirable. Struggle ensues. Changes occur, not infrequently changes that favor those previously unsuccessful. Things *they* are good at come to be labeled good. That at least is the typical object of such struggles.

Here again we come to the strategic efficacy of ethnicity as an organizing principle. Different groups *do* have different norms. In the most natural way the unsuccessful group has the best chance of changing the system if it behaves *as a group*. It is *as a group* that its struggles becomes not merely negative, but positive also, not merely against the norms of some other group, but in favor of the already established norms of its own. One of the difficulties of social class as an organizing principle surely is that there just is not that much conflict of *norm* between most social classes. In the West intellectuals and others at the top of the social stratification will fantasize about the differences between the values of those at the bottom and those in the middle—always to the advantage of the former—but it usually turns out that those at the bottom pretty much share notions of desirable and undesirable with those in the middle. Ethnic differences, however, *are* differences, or at least are seen as such. Marxists thought they would disappear. Why on earth would one wish to be a Pole when one could be a worker? Well, for some reason or set of reasons, there is a desire to be Polish. And not the least of these, to conclude this point, is that being a Pole, or a Sikh, or a *mestizo* frequently involves a distinctive advantage or disadvantage, and that remaining a Pole, or a Sikh, or a *mestizo* is just as frequently a highly effective way either to defend the advantage or to overcome the disadvantage.

Some individuals opt otherwise. They "pass" out of their ethnic (or social, or regional) group into another, typically one that offers greater advantages. This process of absorption is extremely powerful: probably in the United States still quite the most important social process. Americans become more "American" and less ethnic all the time. But in the course of participating in this process, they may also—simultaneously—become more "ethnic." This was most dramatically the experience of Negro Americans during the 1960s—they even changed their name to "blacks" to establish that new assertion of distinctiveness—and other groups followed them, or accompanied them on parallel tracks. As with student activism, this was a phenomenon whole parts of the world were experiencing simultaneously, and any explanation that depends solely on local elements is not likely to remain satisfactory for long. Something larger was going on. Something so large that Ralf Dahrendorf has recently referred to the "refeudalization" of society, the return of ascribed as against achieved characteristics as determinants of social stratification. It may be ethnicity is merely part of this larger development. It is a development worth considering, just as it is worth noting that Dahrendorf took but little pleasure in calling attention to it.

In a most tentative way one further suggestion may be advanced concerning the modernity of ethnicity. Dahrendorf notes that for almost two centuries—"from Locke to Lenin"—"property dominated social and political thought: as a source of everything good or evil, as a principle to be retained or abolished." Yet, he continues, in societies such as those in the Soviet Union, Yugoslavia, Israel, where private property has been reduced to "virtual insignificance," social stratification—class—persists, even flourishes. Further, we would add, the new stratification is to a considerable extent correlated with ethnicity. It probably always was, but the preoccupation with property relations obscured ethnic ones, which, typically, were seen either as derivative of the former, or survivals from a precontractual age. Now, as Yugoslav Communists struggle hopelessly— or so it would seem—to achieve some equity of development and living standard as between Bosnia-Herzegovina, Croatia, Macedonia, Montenegro, Serbia, and Slovenia, as Israeli Socialists look with alarm at the persisting differences in the "social class status" of "European" Jews as against "Oriental" Jews in their homeland, as Great Russians prattle on about the equality of ethnic groups in the Soviet Union, while Ukrainians in Washington rally in protest at the *Russian* Embassy, and Jews in Moscow demand to be allowed to emigrate to Israel, it is *property* that begins to seem derivative, and ethnicity that seems to become a more fundamental source of stratification. Why is this? To repeat, our hypothesis is that ethnic groups bring different norms to bear on common circumstances with consequent different levels of success—hence *group* differences in status. This phenomenon is likely to be as much in evidence in an advanced capitalist society where property relations are attenuated, as in a Communist or Socialist society where they are abolished. A note of caution. As quantitative studies of these issues begin to provide data, they will certainly show that what is common to, say, all Yugoslavians must be accorded much greater weight than what is disparate, but of this it may simply be said that the Croatians don't seem to know the "data."

In any event, Communist nations have shown a concern with ethnic matters far more pronounced than most others, possibly because ethnic reality is so at odds with Marxist-Leninist theory. There are scores of official nationalities in the Soviet Union, and every citizen, at age 16, must opt for one such identity, which he retains for life. Similarly, the Chinese, with their great, central Han culture, find themselves paying considerable heed to "minority nationalities." A recent news dispatch from Peking reads surprisingly like a report of an American political party in the age of New Politics:

China Has More Minority Nationality Communist Party Members—More than 143,000 people of minority nationalities in the autonomous regions of Sinkiang, Tibet, Inner Mongolia, Kwangsi and Ningsia and the Province of Yunnan have been admitted into the Communist Party of China since the Ninth Party Congress in 1969. They include Tibetans, Mongolians, Uighurs, Chuangs, Huis, Koreans, Kazakhs, Yaos and Miaos.

Most of the new party members are workers and former poor and lower-middle peasants or herdsmen. There is a certain number of revolutionary intellectuals. The new members are both men and women and range in age from young to old.

Many of the new party members from national minorities are emancipated slaves or serfs, or children of former slaves or serfs. They warmly love Chairman Mao, the Party and the New Society, and hate the old society.

It may be noted that the flag of the People's Republic of China features one large star, and four smaller ones, representing the Han people and the four principal minority peoples.

But to return to our question: religion, language, and concrete cultural differences did, in our judgment, decline, at least in the West, as specific foci of attachment and concern. But the groups defined by these cultural characteristics were differentially distributed through the social structure. The old bases of distinction, even as their cultural characteristics were modified by modern social trends, became, one may say, increasingly merely "symbolic"— nevertheless they could serve as a basis for mobilization. Thus there is some legitimacy to finding that forms of identification based on social realities as different as religion, language, and national origin all have something in common, such that a new term is coined to refer to all of them—"ethnicity." [7] What they have in common is that they have all become effective foci for group mobilization for concrete political ends challenging the primacy for such mobilization of *class* on the one hand and *nation* on the other. Class was expected in the modern world to become the focus for the mobilization of group interests—it related directly to the rational character of society and the way it generated different interests. Nation was the other great pole around which group interests could be mobilized. We do not in any way suggest that these are not the central categories for understanding modern societies; but it is also true that we must add ethnicity as a new major focus for the mobilization of interests, troublesome both to those who wish to emphasize the primacy of class, and those who wish to emphasize the primacy of nation.

3. *But is not ethnicity more than simply a means of seeking advantage?*

7. For a particularly subtle account and analysis of how this happens, see Michael Hechter, "The Persistence of Regionalism in the British Isles, 1885–1966," *American Journal of Sociology,* 79.2 (September 1973), 319–342; and Hechter, "The Political Economy of Ethnic Change," *American Journal of Sociology,* 79.5 (March 1974), 1151–1178.

groups was *merely* a matter of imitation of blacks, or merely a matter of protective mimicry. Some combination of need and imitation seems to be closer to the reality.

The black movement had as surprising a resonance abroad as at home. A "black power" movement developed in the West Indies, a "civil rights" movement in Northern Ireland, "black panthers" formed in Israel, and some French Canadians explained they were "white niggers." Once again, when we consider the real problems affecting various groups in each of these settings, it would be idle to suggest that what was borrowed was more than a name, a term. Yet in social matters the right name, the right term, is more than terminology. It suggests a comparison of situation, it may propose a similar political course, it may foreshadow similar scenarios of action. The French Canadians did not need the blacks of the United States to teach them that they were conquered and that Anglophones dominated their nation, nor did the Catholics of Northern Ireland need the black example—their miseries go back rather farther in history than even those of American blacks: nor yet did the Oriental Jews of Israel need the black example to remind them something was amiss with their position. In each case, there was a reason for grievance—but there was also the influence, through the ever more pervasive world mass media, of another's example, a teaching.

The exchange is rarely one way only. To the English-speaking peoples of the world, the struggle to put an end to British rule has been a prime source of ethnic invention, adapted by example in widely varied climes by virtue, no doubt, of the sheer inventiveness involved, but also a consequence of the prestige of things British and, by extension, anti-British. (A prestige now largely passed to things American.) The American civil rights movement avowedly and explicitly adopted techniques developed in twentieth-century India. The more recent (and, one hopes, marginal) incidents of urban terrorism in the United States follow, albeit without any evident awareness of the fact, a model of resistance developed by the Irish in the nineteenth century and still present there. (The civil rights movement in Northern Ireland lasted months: in no time the I.R.A. was active again, as were the Orangemen, and the primal struggle resumed, unchanged save for the greater convenience of plastic bombs.) Underground "commandants" in San Francisco issuing "execution" orders against deviant revolutionaries are only acting out the drama of Dublin in 1916. North Africans picked up the technique or else invented it on their own. An Italian made a movie, *The Battle of Algiers*. Soon persons in San Francisco were acting out scenes from *The Informer*. And so exchanges proceed, with, in our time, ever mounting violence. Hijacking was invented we believe by the Palestinians—but American blacks, Croatian workers resident in Sweden, Eritrean dissidents in Ethiopia (to refer only to some of those who have acted out of some ethnic interest) have all made use of it.

We have noted the role of the welfare state in raising the strategic efficacy of ethnic demands, and of international economic developments that led to great migrations of labor in the seventeenth, eighteenth and nineteenth centuries, creating many multi-ethnic states in the process. This process has not stopped. Never in history did Western Europe import as much labor as in the postwar years. A new colored population of West Indians, Indians, and Pakistanis was added to England. One third of the labor force of Switzerland, one eighth of the labor force of Germany, and substantial parts of the labor force of France, Belgium, the Netherlands, Sweden came to be made up of foreign workers. The legal circumstances of each of these waves of new immigrants varied: some were permanent, and had all the rights of citizenship, such as the new colored groups of England. Some were from neighboring members of the European Economic Community, and had claims to full social benefits in any other state of the Community. Some—as the Algerians in France—came from former colonies under special arrangements. But many—e.g., Turks and Yugoslavs in Germany—came under permits that theoretically at least gave no right to any permanent settlement. In other cases, such as Sweden, an egalitarian philosophy of government treated all newcomers, whether Italian or Finnish, generously, as far as social benefits were concerned. The patterns are extremely various, though we see everywhere two different approaches in conflict: on the one hand, the common philosophy of egalitarianism asserts that *all* should be treated alike;

not only those within a nation, but those who come to work and settle there. On the other, Western Europeans have learned that new and permanent settlements of other ethnic groups mean ethnic conflict, and they mean to avoid it if they can. For Great Britain it is too late. Its colored population is permanent, with the full rights of citizenship, and that 2 percent of the population already forms an issue in British politics that far outweighs its proportion. Further immigration has virtually been halted. The North Africans, Spanish, and Portuguese in France, and the Italians, Yugoslavs, and Turks in Germany are not citizens, but one wonders whether they will actually be a less permanent part of those countries. One sees the development of common issues—in conflicts over housing, schooling, jobs. The process of the creation of multiethnic European states through immigration may be slowing down, pursuant to an internal logic of its own. For welfare states are generous to their citizens and tend in that measure to be careful as to who is allowed to become one. But the heritage of the recent period of mass immigration is now being felt, and one wonders whether the new heterogeneity of European nations can really be settled by simple mass expulsions, legal as that may be. In any case, this option exists.

Almost alone among the major nations, the United States continues to accept large numbers of permanent immigrants. Moreover, these immigrants are of quite different "stock" from those of the past. Many are Asian, and the new immigrants are to an unprecedented degree professional, upper middle class persons. What this means is that the process of gaining political influence as a small group, a process which took even the most successful of earlier groups two generations at least, is likely to be rapid for these most recent newcomers. It is odd how little this phenomenon figures in American public discussion: it is neither hailed nor challenged, but simply ignored. Without too much exaggeration it could be stated that the immigration process is the single most important determinant of American foreign policy. This process regulates the ethnic composition of the American electorate. Foreign policy responds to that ethnic composition. It responds to other things as well, but probably *first of all* to the primal facts of ethnicity. In a multi-ethnic society there are often conflicting ethnic loyalties, and our history records sufficient instances of just that, such that no obvious, simple redirecting of foreign policy is in the offing. But our future will record even more such conflicts as Koreans, Filipinos, Indians, Pakistanis, Singaporeans, and dozens more make their interests known. Foreign policy will be affected in diverse and profound ways. Yet oddly, the United States Department of State almost wholly ignores the immigration process. The fact that immigration policy *is* foreign policy is a seemingly inexplicable thought in Foggy Bottom. However much Western Europeans and others may succeed in protecting themselves from the ethnic storms of the twentieth century, we may be sure they will continue to buffet the Great Republic. "Can the Blacks Do for Africa What the Jews Did for Israel?" asks a recent article in *Foreign Policy*. The answer, in the view of the author Martin Weil, is yes, they can, and yes, they ought. The view of the Action Committee on Arab-American Relations, or the recently formed National Association of Arab Americans is unrecorded as of this writing, although they may well welcome the prospect of greater American participation in pan-Islamic adventures. And so round the globe. If other nations wish to lessen ethnic diversity, it is clear that this is not yet the view of Americans, certainly not of Greek-Americans, whose numbers, militance, and congressional strength became evident with the onset of the Cyprus crisis of the summer of 1974.

Nor, of course, can the remaining nation-states easily succeed in avoiding their share of such difficulties. Since World War II almost every new nation, and they far outnumber the older nations, has come into existence with a number of serious ethnic conflicts waiting, as it were, their turn to be the focus of post-independence political life. The old European states, while becoming somewhat more diverse, with the addition of new groups, are still in the process of finding out just how diverse history had already made them. Add to this the fact—still given surprisingly little attention—that in a world in which each society becomes ethnically more diverse, we have had, since World War II, a surprisingly strong prejudice against adjusting any boundary, for any reason. As Samuel Huntington has written, "The twentieth century bias against political divorce, that is, secession, is just about as strong as the nineteenth century bias against marital divorce." [8] Since 1948 remarkably few international frontiers have been altered, and those that have remain very unstable.

Certainly these political realities alone seem to provide a good number of the ingredients for a greater degree of ethnic conflict than, for example, in the world of the Great Depression. Further, as we have suggested, the international mass media network rapidly spreads the story and symbols of ethnic discontent.

Note that this set of reasons that might explain why ethnicity has become a focus for political mobilization—the rise of the welfare state, the conflict between egalitarianism and the differential achievement of norms, the growing heterogeneity of states, the international system of communication—does not easily differentiate new nations from old, or developed from undeveloped ones; and this is why there is reason to consider ethnicity as not only a phenomenon of new states, concerned about "nation-building," but of old states, too.

The foregoing scarcely comprises a "theory" explaining why ethnic identity has become more salient, ethnic self-assertion stronger, ethnic conflict more marked, in the past twenty years. Indeed, we know that the facts assumed in the last sentence themselves can be—and are—disputed: some say that ethnic conflict is simply the *form* that class conflict has been taking on certain occasions in recent decades, and without the motor of class exploitation nothing else would follow. Others say that ethnic conflicts must be decomposed into a variety of elements: colonial conflicts; the uprising of the "internally" colonized; the ambition of individuals organizing followings; fashions and fads; to cite but some assertions ranging from the most serious to the most trivial. Little in this field has been resolved. We are all beginners here. We consider this volume very much an initial contribution in an enterprise to be continued.

It is our hope that this book presents a more catholic view of ethnicity than is generally current: one that extends beyond the more

8. In the foreword to Eric A. Nordlinger, *Conflict Regulation in Divided Societies,* Occasional Papers in International Affairs, no. 29 (Cambridge, Harvard University, Center for International Affairs, January 1972).

limited categories of race, nationality, and minority group; that includes developed as well as developing nations; that presents a variety of theoretical approaches (though scarcely all that could make a case for themselves); and that this approach will suggest to readers that there is a phenomenon here that is, in ways not yet explicated, no mere survival but intimately and organically bound up with major trends of modern societies.

REFERENCES

This volume is only one of a number of recent books which are developing a comparative view of ethnicity. Some of the others from which we have benefited are:

Michael Banton, *Race Relations* (New York, Basic Books, 1967).
Fredrik Barth, ed., *Ethnic Groups and Boundaries: The Social Organization of Culture Difference* (London, George Allen & Unwin, 1969).
Wendell Bell and Walter E. Freeman, eds., *Ethnicity and Nation-Building: Comparative, International and Historical Perspectives* (Beverly Hills, Sage Publications, 1974).
Ernest Q. Campbell, ed., *Racial Tensions and National Identity* (Nashville, Vanderbilt University Press, 1972).
Cynthia H. Enloe, *Ethnic Conflict and Political Development* (Boston, Little, Brown, 1973).
Leo Kuper and M. G. Smith, eds., *Pluralism in Africa* (Berkeley, University of California Press, 1969).
Philip Mason, *Patterns of Dominance* (London, Oxford University Press, 1970).
Eric A. Nordlinger, *Conflict Regulation in Divided Societies,* Occasional Papers in International Affairs, no. 29 (Cambridge, Harvard University, Center for International Affairs, January 1972).
Alvin Rabushka and Kenneth A. Shepsle, *Politics in Plural Societies: A Theory of Democratic Instability* (Columbus, Charles E. Merrill, 1972).
R. A. Schermerhorn, *Comparative Ethnic Relations: A Framework for Theory and Action* (New York, Random House, 1970).
Pierre L. van den Berghe, *Race and Racism: A Comparative Perspective* (New York, John Wiley, 1967); and *Race and Ethnicity: Essays in Comparative Sociology* (New York, Basic Books, 1970).

TOWARD A GENERAL THEORY

1

HAROLD R. ISAACS

Basic Group Identity:
The Idols of the Tribe

Your typical ultra-abstractionist fairly shudders at concreteness: other things equal, he positively prefers the pale and the spectral. If the two universes were offered, he would always choose the skinny outline rather than the rich thicket of reality. It is so much purer, clearer, nobler.

—William James

. . . the unsettled, indecisive character of the situation with which inquiry is compelled to deal affects all of the subject matters that enter into all inquiry. It affects, on the one hand, the observed existing facts . . . On the other side, it affects all of the suggestions, surmises, ideas that are entertained as possible solutions of the problem.

—John Dewey

The Idols of the Tribe have their foundation in human nature itself, and in the tribe or race of men . . . All perceptions, as well as the sense of the mind, are according to the measure of the individual and not according to the measure of the universe. And the human understanding is like a false mirror, which, receiving rays irregularly, distorts and discolors the nature of things by mingling its own nature with it.

—Francis Bacon

The purpose here is to offer a sketch of what is intended to become a full-feature portrait of *basic group identity*. This is the

Note: The material in this chapter has been expanded to book length in *Idols of the Tribe, Group Identity and Political Change* (New York, Harper & Row, 1975).

identity derived from belonging to what is generally and loosely called an "ethnic group." It is composed of what have been called "primordial affinities and attachments." It is the identity made up of what a person is born with or acquires at birth. It is distinct from all the other multiple and secondary identities people acquire because unlike all the others, its elements are what make a group, in Clifford Geertz' phrase, a "candidate for nationhood."

This may sound like a claim to have caught up with the snowman of "ethnicity," whose footprints have been around us for so long but which has been so curiously difficult for academic hunters to track down. But nothing so dramatic is indicated, because the face and form of this creature have been in full view all the time. The difficulty has been to "see" it by itself, to distinguish it from all the other "groups" and "identities" with which it has been so commonly lumped or confused or even covered from view.

In a previous paper I have described the setting and marked the starting points of my own inquiry into this matter.[1] It discussed the present pervasive condition of group fragmentation in all our current politics, post-colonial, post-imperial, post-revolutionary, and—in the United States—post-illusionary. This condition amounts in effect to a massive retribalization running sharply counter to all the globalizing effects of modern technology and communications. The evidence seems strongly to suggest that the House of Muumbi—the home of the progenital mother of the Kikuyu tribe in Kenya, used here as a surrogate name for all the rooms—all the wombs?—in all the tribal mansions—is where human beings still mostly live. It is the refuge to which, in any case, great masses are retreating and withdrawing in the face of the breakdown or inadequacy of all the larger coherences or systems of power and social organization. To get some better understanding of its tremendous power of survival and persistence, it was necessary, I suggested, to detach this basic group identity from the blur

1. Harold R. Isaacs, "Group Identity and Political Change: The Houses of Muumbi," September 1971. Published in part as "The Houses of Muumbi," *Washington Monthly* 3 (December 1971), 10; and as "Group Identity and Political Change: The Politics of Retribalization," *Bulletin of the International House of Japan* 31 (Tokyo, April 1973).

in which so many social scientists and psychologists—unlike the poets, artists, and historians—seem to prefer to leave it, to sort out and examine the elements of which it is made, to see the ways they relate to each other, what functions they perform and what needs they meet, to try to look, in short, at what it is that gives it its extraordinary strength. If this seems elementary, it could be because our past awareness of this phenomenon of basic group identity has clearly not prepared us for the shapes and roles it has assumed in our present affairs and because all that was ever assumed about it as "given" has now been taken away. We have to try to "see" it now, I believe, as if we had never seen it before. The only place to begin, therefore, is at the beginning.

To begin with, then, basic group identity consists of the ready-made set of endowments and identifications which every individual shares with others from the moment of birth by the chance of the family into which he is born at that given time in that given place.

There is first the new baby's body itself, all the shared physical characteristics of the group acquired through the long process of selection, through what René Dubos has called the "biological remembrance of things past," plus whatever else—we still argue about *how* much else—comes through the parental membranes to give each new person the original shape of his or her unique self.[2]

2. Two remarks here regarding the "his" and the "her" of this matter:

a. The only third person singular possessive pronoun in English besides "his" and "hers" is the neuter "its." If the use of "his" when we mean both "his" and "hers"—like the use of "men" when we mean "human beings" or "men *and* women"—does come to be seen simply as male sexist arrogance instead of acceptable surrogate usage and extension of meaning, then, as in the case of the deeply imbedded uses of the word "black," the language may need some revising. Meanwhile, a feminist from way back, who finds sexless neuterism just as offensive as sexist male *or* female chauvinism, must keep on trying to write about these matters without mangling sensibilities or, as far as possible, the prose.

b. Women obviously share common characteristics and some common conditions with other women across many cultures. But that does not mean that they share the same basic group identity as *women* any more than men do as *men,* not in the sense of basic group identity as I am trying to specify it here. The physical and other differences between men and women, marvelous as they are, do not make men and women candidates as such for separate nationhood. Every basic group identity is shared by the men and women in the group, with its particular terms, rules, conditions fixing the relationships between them. The struggle for equality

But even as it draws its first breath, hears its first sound, feels its first touch, the new infant begins to be endowed with everything else that awaits it in that family at that time in that place. These are the common holdings of the group of which the baby becomes a member, the social features, the "shared samenesses" that enter in all their complex ways into the making of the individual ego identity. It is quite a stock of endowments.

The baby acquires a *name,* an individual name, a family name, a group name. He acquires the *history and origins* of the group into which he is born. The group's culture-past automatically endows him, among other things, with his *nationality* or other condition of national, regional, or tribal affiliation, his *language, religion,* and *value system*—the inherited clusters of mores, ethics, aesthetics, and the attributes that come out of the *geography* or *topography* of his birthplace itself, all shaping the outlook and way of life upon which the new individual enters from his first day.

These legacies come to the child bearing the immense weight of the whole past as his family has received it. They shape the only reality in his existence and are made part of him before he has barely any consciousness at all. This is done formally and ritually at or soon after birth, as in baptism, circumcision, and similar rites of entry into the world of the group, and again, after the conditioning of the childhood years, in the varieties of puberty rites or initiations by which young persons become fully admitted members of the group.

The new member of the group comes not only into his inheritance of the past but also into all the shaping circumstances of the present: the conditions of status that come or do not come with these legacies, his family's relative wealth or poverty, its relative position in the larger group to which it belongs, and the group's position relative to other groups in its environment—all the political-social-economic circumstances that impinge on the family and the group, with all the inward and outward effects these conditions

---

of status for women is being fought with different degrees of success in different societies as part of the general current renovation of social and political systems. It has its problems, but as in the fight for racial justice in the American society, separation does not seem to be among the viable solutions.

have on the shaping of the individual's personality and the making of his life. Of these most decisive are the political conditions in which the group identity is held, the measure of power or powerlessness that is attached to it. How dominant or how dominated is the group to which this individual belongs? How static or how changing is this condition, and how, then, is he going to be able to see and bear himself in relation to others? This is the cardinal question and it is essentially the question of the governing politics, the push and pull of power among the groups who share the scene.

Such are the holdings that make up the basic group identity. How they are seen and celebrated has provided the substance of most of what we know as history, mythology, folklore, art, literature, religious beliefs and practices. How the holdings of others are seen has provided most of the unending grimness of the we–they confrontation in human experience. Raised high or held low, these are the idols of all our tribes.

These elements of the basic group identity invite fresh scrutiny, each in itself. For as far as I may dare stretch the prescribed length of this chapter, I will include some additional incomplete notes on two of them—the most symbolic, name, and the most palpable, body—if only for purposes of illustration. But as far as this kind of dissection can take one—quite far—the way invariably leads back to the clustering of all these elements in intimate relation to each other. I will be describing several such clusters of group identity elements as I have found them arranging themselves in different combinations in different settings. My own case study interview material deals with black Americans, American Jews in Israel, Indian ex-Untouchables, English-educated Chinese Malayans, Filipinos, Japanese. The public prints are filled every day with material bearing on other examples from almost everywhere on earth.

Each case, one finds, develops its own shapes, its own dynamics, its own peculiar intensities. There is not much about the study of basic group identity that can be reduced to single formulas or be symmetrically arranged. The various elements show up in different relationships to each other and with quite different specific gravities. Skin color and physical characteristics may be at the heart of the group identity cluster of the black American but only at the margins in the case of the blacker African, the core of whose group identity may lie in his tribal affiliation. History and origins can appear as the most powerfully positive centerpiece, say, for the Chinese with his Great Past, and as the most crushingly negative centerpiece for the ex-Untouchable in India who wants to blot his past out altogether. In Ulster it is being "Catholic" or "Protestant"—with the mix of history and religion that gives these identities their content—that governs everything about the terms on which a person in that country now is going to live or die. The common holding of Islam and fear-hate of the Hindus thrust East Bengal into a nation with the Punjabis, Pathans, Sindis, and other Muslim peoples of India's west: geography, physical differences, language, history parted them a generation later in one of our current history's bloodier amputations.

But varied as such particulars can be, I do believe it is possible to say that in all cases, the function of basic group identity has to do most crucially with two key ingredients in every individual's personality and life experience: his sense of belongingness and the quality of his self-esteem. These come defined in many ways and the needs they serve are met in many degrees of plus-ness and minus-ness in different cases, shaping thereby much of the behavior of the members of the group.

Obviously—and this is precisely the point at which much blurring takes place—these needs can be and often are satisfied in some more purely interpersonal context, or in one or more of the many other multiple and secondary group identities individuals acquire in the course of their lives in all the different collectivities to which they come to belong—class, social, educational, occupational, professional, even recreational. But these secondary sources of belongingness and self-esteem serve only where basic group identity differences do not get in the way. This does occur in some multi-group situations—more today in the American society, for example, than it did only yesterday, as Catholics, Jews, blacks, and others so well know—but takes place most commonly in the enclosure of homogeneous groups, where the basic group identity is a given, shared by all. In most such cases in mixed societies, however, the "outside" is quite nearby and out there it becomes necessary to face what Kurt Lewin called the "uncertainty of belongingness," the challenge to self-esteem, in dealings with members of other groups, be they more powerful or less. Here once more the basic group identity and the conditions of that particular pecking order determine how far these needs are met or not met.

An individual belongs to his basic group in the deepest and most literal sense that here he is not alone, which is what all but a very few human beings most fear to be. He is not only not alone, but here, as long as he chooses to remain in and of it, he cannot be denied or rejected. It is an identity he might want to abandon, but it is the identity that no one can take away from him. It is home in the sense of Robert Frost's line, the place where, when you've got to go there, they've got to take you in—the House of Muumbi, the womb, the emotional handholds of childhood, sometimes the physical place itself. Or, in this age of massive migrations, for great numbers transported great physical and cultural distances, it is the ark they carry with them, the temple of whatever rules one's forebears lived by, the "tradition" or "morality" or whatever form of creed or belief in a given set of answers to the unanswerables.

With this belongingness there goes, all but inseparably, the matter of self-esteem, the supporting measure of self-acceptance, of self-respect, that every individual must have to live a tolerable existence. Some individuals derive sufficient self-esteem out of the stuff of their individual personalities alone. Others have to depend on their group associations to supply what their own individualities may often deny them. Most people, we can probably agree, need all they can get from both sources. Again, like health or money, this matter of self-esteem derived from group identity presents little or no problem when the group identity and the self-acceptance it generates is an assured given, an unquestioned premise of life and therefore not in itself a source of conflict. This can be the case in a tightly homogeneous society or group, or in a stable society in which all groups from top to bottom in the pecking order not only know their place but accept it. All, including the master groups at the top and the lowest at the bottom—for example, the Untouchables in the Hindu caste system—accept themselves as they are told they are and accept the belief system that fixes the conditions of their lives. Such frozen pecking orders have existed for periods of time in different societies. But it is precisely this need for self-esteem, the need to acquire it, feel it, assert it, that has in our own time upset all such orders and become one of the major drives behind all our volcanic politics. The drive to self-assertion, to group pride, has fueled all the nationalist movements that broke the rule of the empires. It stoked up the national/racial chauvinisms that have characterized both the Russian and Chinese revolutions. More than anything else, it generated the power that broke the system of white supremacy in the United States.

We have become familiar with what is called identification with the aggressor, with the patterns of self-rejection and self-hate coming out of negative group identities successfully imposed by stronger on weaker groups. But it is precisely when members of such groups stop submitting to this condition that group identities become a problem both to victimizers and victims and, as all our current affairs show, sooner or later erupt into social and political conflict and crisis. This is the point at which basic group identity and politics meet. It has been the starting point of many notable lives, much notable history, and hardly any more notable than the history of our own time.

This brings us back to the task of making a detailed examination of the elements that make up this basic group identity. For the purposes of this chapter, and to illustrate the beginning of a suggestion of what such an examination involves, here are some notes on just two of these elements, body and name.

BODY

The body is the most palpable element of which identity—individual or group—is made. It is the only ingredient that is unarguably biological in origin, acquired in most of its essential characteristics by inheritance through the genes. Primary as they may be, all the other things that go into the making of group identity are transformable. An individual can change his name, ignore or conceal his origins, disregard or rewrite his history, adopt a different nationality, learn a new language, abandon his family's religion or convert to a new one, embrace new mores, ethics, philosophies, take on new styles of life. But there is not much he can do to change his body.

Some body change can result from cultural change: for example, Japanese are growing taller because of changes in diet. Some aspects of the body's appearance can be changed by cosmetic or other means. This has often been done in the effort to become more "beautiful" or less "ugly" and this has frequently been associated with the effort to shed physical identification with one group or gain closer identification with another group. Hair can be dyed, curled, straightened, weight gained or lost, muscles hardened or laxed, skin can be bleached (up to a point), breasts inflated or flattened, eyelids doubled and noses or other features altered by plastic surgery. But by and large and for most people, the body remains essentially unalterable. The color and texture of its skin and hair, the shape, size, and mutual arrangements of its main features come to us at birth and stay with us until we die. The body is at once the most intimate and inward and most obvious and outward aspect of how we see ourselves, how we see others, how others see us.

Much lore and sacred doctrine has held that the spirit or soul of man is some essence temporarily housed in his body, surviving—indeed, finally freed—when the body wastes away and continuing its independent existence in all the other-worlds that have been created to serve the need not to die. All the ancient religions of India saw life in the body as an interlude of suffering. The body is a stronghold made of bones, an old Buddhist sutra said, "covered with flesh and blood, and there dwell in it old age and death, pride, and deceit." With that more pungent concreteness acquired during its passage through China, Zen Buddhism called the body "a stinking bag of skin." This image and the idea of ascetic mortification that went with it governed much of Indian religiosity but did not get far in China where, as in so much else, earthier notions prevailed. Hajime Nakamura quotes an old Chinese text: "We get our body, hair, and skin from the parents. To keep it from ruin and injury is the beginning of filial piety." [3] For Plato too, the body was

3. Hajime Nakamura, *Ways of Thinking of Eastern People: India–China–Tibet–Japan* (Honolulu, East-West Center Press, 1964), pp. 162–163, 180.

something to be left behind when, high enough up that ladder of love, the human spirit could rise right out of its body and out of the world into the wondrous realm of pure beauty. Aristotle, in his more Chinese-like way, thought that mind and body had to live with each other in a knowable world where pure beauty—perfected man—would not be readily found. In later times, even Descartes, who continued to think he was because he thought, once acknowledged: "I do not only reside in my body (like) a pilot in his ship, but am intimately connected with it and the mixture is so blended that something like a single whole is produced." [4]

It has been more in the modern temper to think of the "single whole"—"the soul is not more than the body," sang Whitman, "the body is not more than the soul"—going on to think of the soul (or "spirit" or "mind" or "personality") as imbedded in a complex of which the self and the body are integral and inseparable parts and joined all but indivisibly to the society of which the individual is part. One student of this matter suggests that the body "plays a fundamental role in our impersonal sense of social identification with 'fellow-citizens' whom we may never have met" and he provocatively calls to witness "the irrepressible metaphor for society as 'the body politic,'" used, he points out, by Plato, Aristotle, St. Thomas, Hobbes, Hegel, and Spencer, suggesting "that the features of civil society may reflect those of our individual body." [5] Coming at this along quite another disciplinary dimension, the psychoanalyst Paul Schilder joins "world, body, and personality," the problem always being to see in every individual case how each relates to the other. "The body image is a social phenomenon. Our own body image is never isolated, always accompanied by the body images of others." Or as extended by Helen Lynd: "One's body image helps to shape one's image of the world and one's image of the world affects the images one has of one's own body; both parts are essential." [6]

4. Quoted by Samuel J. Todes, "The Human Body as the Material Subject of the World," Ph.D. diss., Department of Philosophy, Harvard University, Cambridge, 1963.

5. Ibid., p. 7.

6. Helen Lynd, *On Shame and the Search for Identity* (New York, Harcourt, Brace, 1958), p. 37.

More than any name, physical characteristics serve as a badge of identity. They figure with high visibility and powerful glandular effect in relations between groups, never more so than in our own time when all such relations are being revised as to power, status, and patterns of mutual behavior. The grossest example of this has been the relation between "white" and "nonwhite" in the making and unmaking of European world empire and of the white supremacy system in the American society. In the United States especially, the experience of change has opened a period of acute group identity crisis for blacks who must transform their blackness from the crushing negative the white world made of it into an accepted positive fact in their lives. Similar pressure has come upon some whites—not only in the United States by any means—for whom "whiteness" remains a paramount identification and whose group identity behavior is shaped by their need to maintain their myths about it.

But this is hardly a matter that lies only between "whiteness" and "nonwhiteness" or only between former "white" masters and former "nonwhite" subjects. Now that the mantling mythology of white supremacy has been pulled away and "white" political power rediffused among "nonwhites," long-submerged patterns of attitudes and behavior about skin color have been reappearing in varying intensities along the entire color spectrum and in many different parts of the world. When "racist" behavior erupts sufficiently to come to the world's attention—as it does with poignant and bloody effect in country after country—an effort is often made to explain it away as a legacy of Western white dominance. But evidence of social and aesthetic values attached to "lightness" and "darkness" of skin color appears in the history, art, and literature of numerous cultures widely separated in space and time, in all parts of the globe, and in times long before the spread of the power of white Europeans beyond Europe. Nor, moreover, are the critically effective physical differences confined to skin color. Between the Watutsi and the Hutu, who have been slaughtering each other in Rwanda and Burundi ever since they received their "independence" from the Belgians, the major physical difference is between tallness and shortness, badges of group indentity that can hardly be missed when the groups of killers from both sides seek each other out.[7] A common feature of prejudice patterns built up between groups is the notion that members of other groups are "dirty" or have some peculiarly offensive smell. Also common are attribution of unusual sexual powers or characteristics.

Because the body is the most primordial of all features of basic group identity, extraordinarily powerful taboos and sanctions have been attached in many groups to exogamous unions or marriages that threaten their physical sameness, their "racial purity." Untouchability in India is guessed by some to have had its origin in the imagined efforts of light-skinned "Aryan" invaders to punish and outlaw mixing with the dark-skinned peoples whom they overran. Physical characteristics are almost as important as the Great Past in the makeup of Chinese chauvinism.[8] The Japanese, for their part, hardly needed Spencer's injunction to them a century ago: "Never intermarry!" Among Japanese generally, physical homogeneity is one of the most highly prized of all attributes.[9]

Taboos and sanctions notwithstanding, there are of course large numbers of people in the world who are products of mixed marriages or unions between members of physically quite different

7. "One woman who arrived at a . . . hospital had had both her hands hacked off with a machete. That is a common reprisal, for when the short Hutu find the tall Tutsi, they often cut off their legs at the ankles." *The New York Times,* June 17, 1973.

8. Chinese abroad have intermarried with other groups much more commonly than in the homeland, but even overseas Chinese remain heavily subject to strong feelings about mixing with "outsiders" of almost any description, or more especially about the children of such unions. Chinese vernacular terms for non-Chinese almost always refer to physical features or characteristics.

9. While in some sections of Japanese society during the occupation, popular culture fads and adoption of American beauty standards led to a certain currency for double eyelid operations, most Japanese have guarded themselves jealously against dilution. A glimpse of this appears in the interview account of a young Japanese woman with two impeccably Japanese parents who remembers that as a small girl between the late 1940s and the early '50s, her "big"—that is, somewhat less than almond-shaped—eyes, a faint coppery tint in her black hair, and her slightly-fairer-than-usual skin led classmates to taunt her as an *ainoko,* a mixed child, an experience that brought upon her shame and loathing that she has never forgotten. Cf. Hiroshi Wagatsuma, "The Social Perception of Skin Color in Japan," *Daedalus* 96.2 (Spring 1967), 407–443.

groups. Across color and other assorted lines of distinctiveness, they combine different sets of genes and body characteristics. At the two ends of the given physical spectrum, such individuals could often fade into the physically nearest parental group, if that is what they wanted or were allowed to do. This clearly has been happening for many generations at the margins of all kinds of groups. In some cases, this has actually brought about a change in the physical cast and/or in the range of socially or aesthetically acceptable physical types. This has happened, for example, among the more open and mobile segments of the highly diverse American society, to the extent that some of its racist critics have called it "mongrel." This wide—though never total—acceptance of blending tended to take place, however, within certain limits of difference, for example, north–south European, blonde–brunette. In many other cases, however, the difference remained too wide, usually along the color line, to overcome the governing taboos and sanctions. One result was automatic identification downward into the lower status group—that famous "one drop of Negro blood" that made a person a Negro under the laws and customs of white-supremacy America. Another result was rejection by both parental groups and relegation to a special marginal inbetweenness that often acquired its own legal, social, and group character, for example, the Anglo-Indians in India, the "Coloreds" in South Africa, and other such Eurasian or Eurafrican groups that came into being during the colonial era. In colonial times, such groups were often able, under the patronage of the master race, to move into some narrow place of their own, usually as minor bureaucrats, policemen, jailers, and so on, or, as in British India, as skilled railroad labor. Most of them were left painfully, sometimes tragically placeless when the colonial masters left and the new masters took over. In the more recent and particularly poignant example of the children fathered by American soldiers in Japan, Korea, and Vietnam, especially by black American soldiers, the very common fate has been abandonment and rejection by the local societies, isolation in orphanages ended in only a small number of cases by adoption by American families.

In some instances in the colonial period, the mixed group became the top elite of the lower unmixed or less mixed mass, enjoying social and economic advantages from the greater closeness to the master race, as the so-called "mulattos" or lighter-skinned Negroes did in the Americas and the Caribbean, or even eventually became the elite of the society as a whole, as the mestizos did in most of Latin America and the Philippines after the end of Spanish rule. This invariably took place on the basis of cultural assimilation to the higher status group, the adoption of its styles and its racial attitudes. Such groups usually sooner or later came under the counterattack of their own lower orders, as lighter-skinned Negroes did in America at the hands of Marcus Garvey and his call for "race purity" and again more recently in the tendency of some separationist blacks to identify black nationalism with "race purity" and integrationist ideas with "house niggerism," the "field-hand" versus the "house servant" syndrome carried down from the days of slavery. In Mexico some attempt was made to give the political revolution the color of an Indian reassertion. Some intellectuals, if not the mass of Indians, began trying to restore the pre-Colombian sources of the Mexican identity. In the Philippines similarly, some intellectuals have been urging a new view of the hitherto despised aboriginal hill peoples whose pagan "purity" could be contrasted to the uncertain physical and cultural mixedness of the lowland Filipino Christians.

But whether it takes place through intermarriage or otherwise, the degree of mobility between groups in most societies depends heavily on the degree of physical difference between them. In all societies, some individuals will try to "pass" from one group to another, to bridge status differences, to become more "like" the highly rated group. Where the physical appearances involved are varied enough or similar enough, this kind of passing, never easy, becomes at least possible. It happens all the time, even in caste India. But where plainly visible body differences are a critical feature of the group differences, it remains all but impossible. Even where all other conditions are or can be made equal, the physical characteristics themselves remain the barrier to status and belonging.

This is why, indeed, some groups without distinctive physical features to mark them apart from other groups have deliberately created them. Thus circumcision, scarifying, tattooing, filing teeth, piercing or otherwise changing the shape of nose, ears, tongue, lips, all becoming badges by which to identify those who belong and those who do not, sometimes with highly complicated effect.[10]

Less permanent but hardly less distinctive are the changes made for this same purpose in the body's extensions, beginning with the hair, for example, the scalplock of some North American Indians, the monk's tonsure, the sideburns of the Hasidic Jew, the uncut hair and beard of the Sikh—mirrored more recently, and more transiently, in the adoption of long hair as the badge of the so-called youth counter-culture, the shaved heads of some of London's counter-counterculturists or of some young Americans seeking to be like Hindu holy men, and so on. Then there are all the distinctive marks that can be made on the body's surfaces, caste marks in India, painted patterns on the skin, as in parts of Africa and Oceania. Beyond these come clothes, dress used to distinguish bodies that would all look alike—more or less—undressed, all the "native costumes" which occur from nation to nation, group to group, sometimes from village to nearby village, giving to each one the identifying distinctiveness it needs to feel. Clothes, of course, also become the identifying badge for all kinds of secondary groupings in all cultures, all the special costumes or uniforms worn down through time by the holy and the unholy, priests, judges, lawyers, policemen, firemen, messengers, artisans of every description, and—perhaps most representatively of all—by the soldiers each group dresses in their identifying garb to go out to kill the soldiers of other groups dressed in *their* identifying garb.

Besides serving as the badge of identity in so many groups, the

10. Consider what Shakespeare writes for Othello the Moor to say in his final speech (Act V, Sc. 2):

> . . . In Aleppo once
> Where a malignant and turban'd Turk
> Beat a Venetian and traduced the State,
> I took by the throat the circumcised dog
> and smote him, thus—[stabs himself]

body is for all groups the main basis for its standards of beauty, the main subject by far of most art in most cultures. This begins with what is perceived in any group as sexually attractive. One can find in anthropological literature some remarkable examples of what never pales or withers in the eyes of various beholders in different places. But the portrayal of the idealized human body as an object of art also incorporates all the other complicated perceptions and values that go into the making of any culture's aesthetics. Much waits to be learned from a comparative examination of the body in the art of different cultures, with all that it can tell us about so many aspects of each one and of the points at which they meet or part. These perceptions and values appear in one form or another among all the strands of experience that go into how members of any group anywhere see what they like in the human body—ideal or real—fair or dark, blonde or brunette, tall or short, classic or crude, round or lean, broad or narrow, smooth or craggy, muscular or soft, hairy or bare, large-breasted or small, round-bellied or flat, small buttocks or large. These become, then, the preferred shapes in which "we" see ourselves, and they determine how "we" deal with the negatives of all these positives that "they"—in all those other groups—hold differently in view.

The physical element in basic group identity has to do not only with body but also with place, the land, the soil to which the group is attached, literally, historically, mythically. Octavio Paz identifies solitude not only with the "nostalgic longing for the body from which we were cast out" but also for the place from which the body came or to which in death it will return, seen by many ancients as "the center of the world, the navel of the universe," as "paradise where the spirits of the dead dwell" and as "the group's real or mythical place of origin." He cites from Lévy-Bruhl a primitive belief that to leave one's place is to die, illustrated by an African ritual in which movement from a place is counteracted by carrying and eating every day some of the soil of the place that was home, thus giving the social solidarity of the group "a vital organic character" and making each individual in the group "literally part of a body." Almost all the rites connected with the founding of cities or houses, Paz notes, "allude to a search for that holy center from which we were driven out." Thus "the great sanctuaries—Rome, Jerusalem, Mecca—are at the center of the world or symbolize and prefigure it." [11]

Such is some of the underpinning of "love of country"— scoundrelly love or real love—that gets imbedded in the individual consciousness about one's birthplace. In China—the Chinese name means "central country"—people continue to identify themselves with family birthplaces from which they may actually be many generations removed. In some cases the ancestral homeland, distant in time as well as in space, becomes a critical ingredient in the problem of existence. Blacks in America struggle with the placement of Africa in their redefinition of who and what they are. Martin Buber, who was more concerned with a Jewish state of grace than with the politics of statehood, saw "the physical link with the land" of Israel as crucial to the mystical and historical identity of Jews; this link is of course the mystique on which the state of Israel is based. By some readings the attachment of the group to its "turf" is seen as something that human beings share with animals, and there is little question that the defense or seizure of territory has accounted for some of the most inhuman chapters in human history. Territory is, at the least, a critical factor in maintaining group separateness; without it a nationality has difficulty becoming a nation and a nation cannot become a state.

In all the varieties of this interaction of people and land, it is obvious that the environment itself powerfully shapes the history, mores, and character of the group and the life patterns of its individual members. Thus, all the features attached or attributed to people because they are (or once were) mountain people or plains people or desert people, lake, river, or island people, seacoast or landlocked people, arctic, temperate or tropical zone people, lowland or highland, rural or urban, delta or dry land people, and so on. These differences too, in all their infinitely varied ways, are part of the stuff of which basic group identity is made.

11. Octavio Paz, *The Labyrinth of Solitude* (New York, Grove Press, 1961), pp. 205–206, 208.

NAME

Names seem to be the simplest, most literal, and most obvious of all symbols of identity. But like all simple matters, this is complicated. The quest for the meaning of naming goes back to the first framing of thought, the beginning of language, the first holding of knowledge, and forward again to all its persisting riddles.

Naming, John Dewey has reminded us, *is* knowing, "the distinctive central process of knowledge." [12] All philosophy has wrestled with viewing knowledge as fast or fluid, petrified or plastic, coming—from Heraclitus and the Chinese through to James and Dewey—to the effort to capture the elusive actuality of things by seeing them in constant motion, always being transformed, changing more rapidly than the words—the names—used to describe them. Because of the "many traditional, speculatively evolved applications of the word 'name' . . . many of them still redolent of ancient magic," Dewey looked for greater precision in other terms—designation, cue, characterization, specification, sign, symbol—hoping this would help make it plainer that "we take names always as namings, as living behaviors in an evolving world of men and things." [13] But words and names used to represent "truth" have their own history, successfully imposing themselves on the process and usually growing, as James put it, "stiff with years of veteran service," not easily flexed or displaced.

"One of the difficulties of the history of ideas," wrote Alfred Cobban, "is that names are more permanent than things. Institutions change, but the terms used to describe them remain the same." [14] The same difficulty bothered the Chinese philosophers who some 25 centuries ago belonged to what was called the "School of Names"—*Ming Chia*—so called because it was concerned with the distinctions to be made between "names" and "actualities." There were at least two tendencies, Fung Yu-lan tells us, one "emphasizing the relativity of actual things and the other the abso-

12. John Dewey (with Arthur F. Bentley), *Knowing and the Known* (Boston, Beacon Press, 1949), p. 147. Cf. Anselm Strauss, *Mirrors and Masks* (Glencoe, The Free Press, 1959), chap. 1.

13. Dewey, *Knowing and the Unknown*, pp. 156 ff.

14. Alfred Cobban, *The Nation State and National Self-Determination* (New York, Crowell Co., 1969, 1970), p. 22.

luteness of names." [15] The theme of "rectification of names" recurs through the debates on the issue—which went on for several centuries—having to do essentially with the idea that "things in actual fact should be made to accord with the implication attached to them by names." One of these ancients, Hsun Tzu (ca. 250 B.C.) found three fallacies in the works of the School of Names: "the fallacy of corrupting names with names . . . the fallacy of corrupting names with actualities . . . the fallacy of corrupting actualities with names." [16] Obviously there has been more of the same than of change in these matters in all the time since.

The stretch is not great either between another leader of that ancient School of Names, Lung Kung-Sung (ca. 280 B.C.), who said that he "wished to . . . correct the relations between names and actualities, so as thus to transform the whole world," [17] and this passage from William James: "The universe has always appeared to the natural mind as a kind of enigma, of which the key must be sought in the shape of some illuminating word or name. That word names the universe's principle and to possess it is, after a fashion, to possess the universe itself." [18] Thus the taboo on uttering or even writing the name of Jahveh among the Jews—the founder of the mystical Hasidic sect of Jews in early eighteenth-century Europe called himself "Baal Shem Tov," "Master of the Name." A similar taboo existed on the personal name of the reigning monarch in old China. In the Indian epics, no one of lower rank ever addressed anyone of higher rank by his personal name, or used the personal pronoun when speaking to him. Names themselves over so much time in so many cultures carried with them the power of magic and incantation, the power to solve mysteries, grandly universal or obscurely personal. In the beginning was the word, followed immediately by the tabooed word.[19] "But—" James went on, "if you follow the pragmatic method, you cannot look on any

15. Fung Yu-lan, *Short History of Chinese Philosophy* (New York, Macmillan, 1948), p. 83.
16. Ibid., p. 153.
17. Ibid., p. 92.
18. William James, *Pragmatism: A New Way for Some Old Ways of Thinking* (New York, Longmans, 1907, 1949), p. 52.
19. J. G. Frazer, *The Golden Bough: A Study in Magic and Religion* (Toronto, Macmillan, 1969), chap. 22, "Tabooed Words."

such word as closing your quest. You must bring out of each word its practical cash value, set it at work within the stream of your experience. It appears less as a solution, then, and more particularly as an indication of the ways in which existing realities may be *changed*." [20]

In the stream of our current experience, the cash value of names has clearly been fluctuating with great and unusual violence. The matter of names keeps turning up in one form or another in all the ongoing rediscoveries, revisions, remakings, and reassertions of group identity now taking place all around us. It is clear that quite by itself the name—of individual, of group, of nation, of race— carries a heavy freight of meaning. It is seldom itself the heart of the matter but it often points directly to where the heart can be found. Making our way through the thickets of reality of group identity problems, we can do worse than to follow where the name alone takes us, for it can lead deep into the history, the relationships, the emotions that make up so much of the present tangle of affairs.

Each of my own case studies of particular groups has included a chapter called "A Name to Go By," dealing with the shifting use and meaning of "Negro" and "colored" and "black," and so on, among black Americans, the burdens of shame and pollution carried into every moment of everyday life by group and individual names among emergent Indian ex-Untouchables, the new pools of meaning forming around the terms "Jew" and "Israeli" and the many other terminological ironies and curiosities that turn up so bountifully now in Israel, where Jews from America and Canada become "Anglo-Saxons," Jews from Poland become "Poles," and Jews from Morocco and Yemen become "Moroccans" and "Yemenites." In the Americas, the people called "Indians" by Europeans who thought they had landed in the Indies held to their distinctive tribal names for themselves until they had been wholly conquered and had to submit to the identity imposed on them, along with the name, by their conquerors. In North Carolina quite recently, a nameless and "raceless" group of Indian-Negro-white mixed ori-

20. James, *Pragmatism*, p. 53.

gins, always previously lumped with Negroes for purposes of segregation under the white supremacy system, won recognition as a
distinct "Indian" group by getting the state legislature to give them
a name, the "Haliwas"—made up of syllables of Halifax and Warren counties where many of them live. In India, meanwhile, the effort to give substance and usage to the national identity "Indian"
makes only slow headway against all the separate regional and
linguistic groups bearing the separate names by which most people
in India still identify themselves. The lexicon of vernacular or informal names that groups apply to each other—and sometimes in a
complex transference to themselves—gives the most direct and
pungent expression to the feelings that members of most groups
most commonly have about other groups: contempt, hostility, fear,
envy, hatred. The familiar list in American English—nigger, mick,
wop, kike, chink, jap, spic, honky, polack, gook, and so on—can be
safely assumed to have its counterpart in every tongue in every
place in every culture where differing groups exist or there is any
awareness at all of human differences. But informal or formal, all
group names carry with them a heavy store of past and present history. The term for white men among some Eskimos is "gosseks"
because the first white men they ever saw were Cossacks from Russia. In South Africa there is a heavy cargo of history in the twist of
usages that have gone from "kaffirs" (an Arabic word that originally carried only the meaning of "unbelievers") and "niggers" to
"Natives" and "Nonwhites" and, now, "Bantu." In the Philippines,
there is much to be learned by tracing the passage from the term
"Indio"—the Spanish gave the same name to the people they
found in these islands that Columbus gave to those he found in the
Caribbean—to "Filipino."

The name of the Philippines itself—like every country name—
opens a fruitful vein of inquiry. Similarly in Japan, the use of *Nihon*
or *Nippon* as the style, which in either version identifies it as the
land where the sun rises, in the one case suggesting a certain
softness of spirit and in the other a harsh muscularity. The name
China—*Chung Kuo*—identifies it as the "central country," China
being, as Chinese have always known, the true center of the universe, the only civilized land in a world of barbarians. Some notable

country names, to be sure, have less self-conscious, more accidental origins. America, as every schoolboy knows or used to know, got its name from the explorer Amerigo Vespucci, a contemporary of Christopher Columbus who ventured less, it seems, but wrote more, and who—according to one provocative analysis—had a name that had very special resonances, psychoanalytically speaking, for the man who quite literally first put the name America on the map.[21] In the recent great multiplication of new states in the world, however, the reappearance of long-submerged names—for example, Viet Nam, Ghana, Mali, Zambia, Sri Lanka—marked the self-conscious reopening of veins of identification with the remote past. The different attitudes and usages in North and South Korea involving the ancient name of *Chosen* reflect strongly felt current views about some very old affairs. Or, in quite a different kind of case, consider the synthetic creation of the name Pakistan, made up as an acronym of the names of the main regions from which that remarkably synthetic state was carved—Punjab, Afghanistan, Kashmir, and so on—omitting any initial for Bengal, an omission finally confirmed by reality, 25 years later, by the severance of Bengal from Pakistan and the emergence of a brand new Bengali state with the old name of the Bengali homeland, Bangladesh.

Individual names usually—though not always—also serve as badges of the basic group identity. By language and style, they tell us a great deal about an individual's origins and probable present associations. The individual name, to be sure, remains primarily the symbol for the single and unique person who bears it, that one and only unduplicatable individual who is distinct and different from all other individuals. We have made much of this uniqueness in our own culture, though perhaps not as much as is suggested by the fact that on the island of Truk every single living person has a distinctive name, no duplications allowed. A person's own name in some ways establishes the fact of his existence. The sanction of namelessness imposed on bastardy in our culture is one of the most fearful that a group can impose. Namelessness of any kind, indeed,

21. W. G. Niederland, "The Naming of America—Psychoanalytic Study of an Historic Event," in Mark Kanzer, ed., *The Unconscious Today* (New York, International Universities Press, 1972).

is almost beyond bearing; "nameless fear" is worse than any other kind of fear. Names, like social norms, provide a certain minimum security, bearings that every individual must feel around him or else be lost. As Helen Lynd so acutely put it: "The wood in *Through the Looking Glass* where no creature bears a name is a place of terror." In most, if not all, cultures and languages, we not only have names, but we acquire "good" names or "bad" names. Good names are inherited, won, protected, besmirched, lost, and—worst of all, the poet has told us—filched. Good or bad, we see that they are kept in view on ancestral tablets or graven, as deep as may be, in stone, a desperate effort to keep the name alive to stand for the person who bore it for as long as possible after the person has gone.

But regardless of all that our individual names may come to signify, they do most generally also identify the group to which we belong or from which we come, by nationality, perhaps, or by religion. Where behavior bearing on group status is involved, the name alone can serve as an instant signal for the indicated response—open or closed, welcome or repulse, inclusion or exclusion. Hence, in so many different settings, the familiar business of name-changing by individuals who want to mitigate or conceal inferior status, to be more "like" the more favored group, to gain some more comfortable anonymity by sharing, at least in name, the identity of the dominant group. In the ex-colonial world, the shift in political power relations has brought about a reversal of this process. European given names were in many cases acquired by colonial subjects by baptism, by bestowal, or by choice, reflecting ambition and/or the need to accommodate to the master culture.[22] The shedding of these names, like changing their country names, has been one of the easier, more obvious, and more symbolic ways for ex-colonial subjects to assert their independence and to reassert their own national/cultural identities. In the ex-Belgian Congo now

22. In one case, unique as far as I know, in the Philippines, where Christian given names had long been in use via baptism in the church, Spanish surnames— taken pageful by pageful from a Madrid directory—were simply "given" to large numbers of people by a mid-nineteenth-century Spanish governor for the greater convenience of his tax collectors.

renamed Zaire, President Mobutu recently followed the example of other nationalist leaders, not only by changing his own Christian given names, but legally outlawing all such names in the country and fixing penalties for any priest who baptized a child with any but a Zairian name. Regaining a lost identity takes a particular form in Israel, where the Zionists raised the Hebrew language from the dead and returning Jews often marked the shedding of their Diaspora past by adopting new Hebrew names to fit their new Israeli identities. For some blacks in the United States, the drive to re-establish more prideful self-accepting identities for themselves has involved not only replacing the group name "Negro" and "colored" with "black" or "Afro-American" but also changing individual names, abandoning those acquired from the time of slavery and replacing them with African or—for reasons that invite examination and reflection—Arabic names. Perhaps boldest and harshest of all were the Black Muslims, who shed what they saw as slavemasters' surnames and substituted a plain X, as though to proclaim that while they would no longer go by the names that the hated white world had given them, they did not yet know who they were.

2

TALCOTT PARSONS

Some Theoretical Considerations on the Nature and Trends of Change of Ethnicity

It seems to be generally agreed that what we call ethnicity is a primary focus of group identity, that is, the organization of plural persons into distinctive groups and, second, of solidarity and the loyalties of individual members to such groups. It is, however, an extraordinarily elusive concept and very difficult to define in any precise way.[1] Perhaps the best way to introduce the problem is in terms of a sketch of some of the principal historic and contemporary contexts in which the conception has figured prominently. Following this we will undertake a more careful consideration of the definitional question.

Clearly one primary reference point is to the ideal-type conception of the population of a "nation-state," meaning a politically organized society which has historically enjoyed a legitimate claim to independent existence.[2] The ideal type calls for a coincidence of what in a broad sense we may call common culture and territory of residence. For the typical individual both his residence within the territory and his sharing of the common culture have been conceived as given by birth, that is, he has acquired the ethnic identification of his parents. Ethnicity, then, has very generally been in-

1. See, for example, H. S. Morris, "Ethnic Groups," in D. L. Sills, ed., *International Encyclopedia of the Social Sciences* (New York, Macmillan and the Free Press, 1968), V, 167–172.

2. Cf. Hans Kohn, *The Idea of Nationalism: A Study in Its Origins and Background* (New York, Macmillan, 1944).

terpreted as having a biological base sometimes explicitly stated in terms of racial distinctiveness.[3] If we take, however, the populations of a variety of the classical nation-states, it is to a very varying degree that they can be called racially distinct. But some kind of relative homogeneity has generally been presumed.

On the more specifically cultural side again religious uniformity has historically played an important part, though in the Western world since the Reformation for most nations it has become increasingly problematical.[4] A particularly prominent aspect of cultural identity, then, has been language. Even though what is essentially the same language, as in the case of English, may be spoken in more than one nation, linguistic uniformity has served as one of the primary criteria. Language, in turn, has been closely associated with a relatively diffuse conception of a common cultural tradition. This, of course, has been both oral tradition and in the more evolved societies a tradition embodied in documents of written language; in the broadest sense, a "literature." It is, however, exceedingly difficult to specify such a common cultural tradition more precisely. At a certain common sense level, however, we think we know fairly definitely what is meant by referring to French culture or English culture or Italian culture.

Certainly the development of what we call national states was one of the primary processes involved in the establishment of modern societies, though the European system cannot be said ever to have even come very close to universalizing the ideal type of what in the above imprecise sense would be called an ethnically homogeneous population. The premier classical examples of England and France are perhaps the best approximations, but neither of them has ever been completely pure. Thus the politically organized England has not been confined to "Anglo-Saxon" populations, but has included Celtic components in Wales, Scotland, and, of course, Ireland. In

3. Carleton Coon, with Edward E. Hunt, Jr., *The Living Races of Man* (New York, Knopf, 1965).

4. Wilbur K. Jordan, *The Development of Religious Toleration in England,* 4 vols. (Cambridge, Harvard University Press, 1932–1940). Also, James Hastings, ed., with the assistance of John A. Selbie, *Encyclopedia of Religion and Ethics* (New York, Scribner's Sons, 1908–1915).

the case of France there has been shading off into the German cultural world toward the east, as, for example, in Alsace and Lorraine, and toward the Italian world in the south. At the other extreme, there have been major historical political units, such as the Austro-Hungarian empire, which have never even approached being an ethnically homogeneous entity, but were put together out of a considerable variety of different ethnic groups for the most part, however, territorially concentrated as in the case of German-speaking Austria, Czech-speaking Bohemia and Moravia, and Hungarian-speaking Hungary.

The various components which have figured historically in the ethnic complex have by no means been uniformly involved over time. A notable case has been that of religion. There were, to be sure, many centuries of integrity of Western, that is, Roman Catholicism in Europe, with only very small enclaves of Diaspora Jews who were not Catholics. Since the Reformation, however, that has changed, and though for a time the famous formula of the Peace of Westphalia, *cuis regio eius religio,* held, it has gradually been attenuated and most of the populations of European nation-states have become religiously pluralistic with Protestants, Catholics, and Jews represented in varying proportions. The establishment of the American republic constituted a major step in this process through the institutionalization of the separation of Church and State. In the nineteenth and part of the twentieth centuries there were important attempts to identify ethnicity and nationality with race. The most sensational and disturbing was the attempt of German Nazism to purify the "Aryan" composition of the German people, and to include so far as possible all ethnic Germans in the Reich.[5] By contrast the Jews were also alleged to constitute a distinctive race and cultural characteristics of both groups were held to be derivable from their racial natures. This particular set of views, however, has lost ground most conspicuously.

American society, on the one hand by virtue of its political constitution, on the other hand by virtue of the history of immigration, pioneered in the establishment of a multi-ethnic society. If there is a

5. Stephen H. Roberts, *The House That Hitler Built* (New York and London, Harper and Brothers, 1938).

single formula for ethnic identity in the American population, probably the conception of "national origin" is the most accurate designation for most groups. Certain kinds of exceptions have to be made where color is a major factor, but in the case of the so-called blacks there is the common geographical origin from Subsaharan Africa. The Jews constitute another distinctive case because of the religio-ethnic character of the historic Jewish community.[6] Broadly speaking, ethnic pluralism on something like the American model has been coming to be increasingly characteristic of modern societies.

A notable recent development has taken place in Europe with the establishment of the Common Market and, as one of its primary features, the removal of many previous restrictions on the geographical mobility of labor. Hence, a process of in-migration of "foreign" elements into the most important European industrial societies has occurred on a big scale, creating situations which in some respects are parallel to that of the United States in an earlier period occasioned by mass immigration from diverse European sources.

Finally, with the emergence of the so-called Third World, new nation-states have been created with populations ethnically diverse in one or another sense.

A GENERAL CHARACTERIZATION OF THE ETHNIC GROUP

In spite of the difficulty of being specific about criterial features and components, what social scientists have called ethnic groups do belong to a relatively distinctive sociological type. This is a group the members of which have, both with respect to their own sentiments and those of non-members, a distinctive identity which is rooted in some kind of a distinctive sense of its history. It is, moreover, a diffusely defined group, sociologically quite different from collectivities with specific functions. For the members it character izes what the individual *is* rather than what he *does*. Thus we say, whether resident in Ireland or not, he may be ethnically Irish;

6. Oscar Handlin and Mary Handlin, *A Century of Jewish Immigration to the USA* (New York, American Jewish Committee, 1949).

whether resident in Israel or not, ethnically Jewish; and so on. This is to say it is a primary collective aspect concerning the identity of whole persons, not of any particular aspect of them. Common culture is probably the most important general core, but it is a culture which has some feature of temporal continuity often reaching into an indefinite past. An ethnic group is, of course, always a group consisting of members of all ages and both sexes and ethnicity is always shared by forebears at some level. It is thus a *transgenerational* type of group.

Ethnic groups are traditionally mutually exclusive. This would be rigorously and uniformly the case, however, only insofar as they are consistently endogamous. There are many cases, however, of the marriage of members of different ethnic groups. The question therefore of the ethnic adherence of a married couple can become indefinite and the same is of course true for their children and for their further descendents. Indeed in such cases there may be a certain optional rather than ascriptive character to ethnic identity.

Functionally diffuse time-extended solidary groupings are indeed not exclusively recruited by birth, and this has become conspicuously true of the population of the modern state in the existence of appreciable numbers who have become members or citizens by, to use the American phrase, "naturalization." This points to the fact that national communities share with ethnic groups the involvement of a component of voluntary adherence. This has been classically formulated in social and political theory under the conception of the social contract; a conception which has recently been revived by the philosopher John Rawls in his influential book *A Theory of Justice*.[7] Politically organized societies do have on occasion specific points of origin such as for the United States the combination of independence from Great Britain and the setting up by the recently independent group of a distinctive autonomous constitution of its own.[8] This kind of thing is the nearest to a general social contract establishing a national community which is empirically possible. But as an analytical concept, the es-

7. John Rawls, *A Theory of Justice* (Cambridge, Belknap Press of Harvard University Press, 1971).
8. Seymour M. Lipset, *The First New Nation* (New York, Basic Books, 1963).

tablishment of solidarity by voluntary adherence is an extremely important social phenomenon.

Every social system of the very important type we call a society is in one of its primary aspects what may be called a societal community. At one time this was identified ideally at least with what is called ethnicity—a societal community was almost by definition an ethnic entity. It is exceedingly important to be aware that this is no longer the case even as an ideal type for a number of the important national societies, most conspicuously of course for that of the United States. At the same time it is extremely important that any societal community, so far as it has the central property of solidarity, essentially in Durkheim's sense, is of the same *generic* sociological character as is the ethnic group. This is to say that it is a diffusely defined collectivity which has the property of solidarity and is a major point of reference for defining the identity of its members.[9] To be identified as an American is not to have one's ethnic status identified, but it very definitely is a primary aspect of the "identity" of any given individual so designated.

The generic sociological type to which references here are made has the two primary aspects: first, that of a common distinctive cultural tradition applying to a "population" of members; and second, something of the equivalent of a social contract, that is, a component of membership status which is in some essential respect voluntary. This is to say it is the creation of the members independent of rigid and complete determination by past tradition. The modern community is characterized by a balance between these two vital components, that of tradition and that of "contract."

THE COLLECTIVITY WITH "DIFFUSE ENDURING SOLIDARITY"

We have reached the point of cardinal importance that in the contemporary world what we have been calling societal communi-

9. Talcott Parsons, *Societies: Evolutionary and Comparative Perspectives* (Englewood Cliffs, N.J., Prentice-Hall, 1966), chap. 2, pp. 5–29; and T. Parsons, *The System of Modern Societies* (Englewood Cliffs, N.J., Prentice-Hall, 1971), chap. 2, pp. 4–28. Both chapters reprinted in Talcott Parsons, *Politics and Social Structure* (New York, The Free Press, 1969), as chaps. 1 and 2.

ties or "nations" are to a decreasing degree ethnically homogeneous entities. A significant aspect, however, of the importance of the ethnic group as a social phenomenon lies in the fact that it is one primary example of a large genus of types of social collective organization which might be called the diffusely solidary collectivity.[10] I should like to devote this section to a brief outline of this generic organizational type before returning to some further considerations specifically about ethnicity.

The best single empirical point of reference seems to be what may be called the societal community. This is one primary aspect of the structure and functioning of the extremely important type of social system we call a society. It is that aspect or subsystem which has primarily integrative functions for the society as a whole.[11] The societal community presumes a relatively definable population of membership, which at this level we ordinarily call citizens for the modern case, and presumes as well that the collective organization of reference is politically organized on a territorial basis, that is, it maintains normative order and certain political decision-making processes covering the human events which occur within a defined territorial area.[12] Finally, as a third primary criterion, at some level it is characterized by a common cultural tradition, the nature of which will be further discussed presently.

One of the primary characteristics of a societal community is that it has the property which David Schneider, with special reference to American kinship, has called "diffuse enduring solidarity." We should, however, understand that solidarity in this sense is not a matter of presence or absence, but varies in degree and in type in important ways. Solidarity in this sense should be considered to be

10. See David M. Schneider, *American Kinship: A Cultural Account* (Englewood Cliffs, N.J., Prentice-Hall, 1968); and David M. Schneider, "Kinship, Religion and Nationality," in V. Turner, ed., *Forms of Symbolic Action, Proceedings of the 1969 Spring Meeting of the American Ethnological Society* (Seattle, University of Washington Press, 1969).

11. Talcott Parsons, "Durkheim's Contribution to the Theory of Integration of Social Systems," chap. 1 in *Sociological Theory and Modern Society* (New York, The Free Press, 1967), pp. 3–34.

12. Cf. T. H. Marshall, *Class, Citizenship and Social Development* (Garden City, N.Y., Doubleday & Co., 1964).

a property of the system. The corresponding property of individual members which may be called dispositional or motivational seems best called loyalty. Clearly the solidarity of the collective system is among other things a function of the level and distribution of loyalty of its members but not synonymous with it. Following the cultural structure which Schneider has elucidated for the case of kinship, we may stress two culturally symbolic elements of our generic type of collectivity which correspond to the roles of "blood" and "law" as symbolic definitions of a kinship unit.[13] The equivalent of blood is the transgenerational tradition to which reference has been made above. As I have pointed out, it is exceedingly difficult to specify exact criterial components of its content. It is essential then to consider it first as definitely cultural. Second, it is to be considered as broadly shared in common by the whole population of a societal community. This transgenerational tradition could be broken down down into three primary elements. The first is a common language which has been inherited by the current members of the community from its past and those aspects of the cultural tradition which are most closely associated with language. Language is not, however, an infallible criterion as such cases as the multilingual societal community of Switzerland remind us. A second primary reference may be referred to as the "cultural history" of the community. This concerns a series of events and symbolic outputs of the past which have contemporary significance because those who experienced or produced them were "our" forebears. This sense of a shared history applies to those who themselves or whose immediate forebears have joined the community long after certain other crucial events took place. Thus the American achievement of independence and the establishment of the Constitution involved a population of nearly two centuries ago who were actual ancestors of what is (probably) only a minority of the contemporary population of the American community. Nevertheless, those whose forebears were immigrants much more recently still consider this to be part of "their" history.

Third, the extension of the temporal continuity of tradition is

13. Schneider, *American Kinship*.

operative not only retrospectively with reference to the past, but also prospectively with reference to the future. A major aspect of solidarity in the present sense is the sharing of a common fate by virtue of common membership in the particular societal community. So long as the community itself persists, this continuity will be a central feature of it. A major aspect of the diffuseness of the solidarity system lies in the fact that it is impossible to isolate the symbolic meaningfulness of temporally specific events and prospects from the temporally extended continuum. Just as in the kinship context an individual is ascriptively the child of his parents, so in a societal community the citizen is ascriptively one of the heirs of his forebears in the societal community and will be one of the "progenitors" of the future community so that many of the consequences of the actions of contemporaries cannot be escaped by future members in new generations.

The types of social structure just under discussion belong to a general type the nature and significance of which has recently been substantially clarified in my own mind.[14] This type I have called the "fiduciary association." The adjective fiduciary derives mainly from the element of transgenerational "tradition" that has just been discussed. At any given time the current membership exercises, and is expected to do so, a fiduciary responsibility for the maintenance or development of such a tradition in its place in the larger society, including those inside its boundaries who cannot be expected to assume the highest levels of such responsibility. It becomes a "moral community" in Durkheim's sense.

I hold that, in a highly differentiated society, there are four principal subtypes of fiduciary association, the kinship association, the societal or similar community, the religious association and the educational-cultural association. In the modern type of family, the unit is established by a contract in the above sense, that is, a marriage, but if the couple has children they as parents assume a fiduciary responsibility for their welfare and proper "bringing up." Parties to the marriage also assume such responsibilities for each other and the proper mode of married life, obligations which of

14. See Talcott Parsons and Gerald M. Platt, *The American University* (Cambridge, Harvard University Press, 1973), esp. chaps. 2 and 3.

course obtain even for childless couples. In the communal type special fiduciary responsibilities devolve upon holders of associational office [15] and those members of the community or association who exercise more than the average levels of influence, both for the welfare of less powerful and influential groups and for the integrity of the tradition. In the case of the religious association it is above all what we call the clergy and other specially committed groups on which such responsibility focuses. Finally in referring to the educational-cultural subtype I have had in mind above all the university or other institution of higher education, but various other types of culturally oriented institutions such as museums or musical organizations can also be included. In the university case a particularly conspicuous focus of fiduciary responsibility is members of faculties, both vis-à-vis students who do not yet command the same level of competence and experience, and vis-à-vis the integrity of the tradition itself, in this case with a special concern for the "advancement of knowledge." I have tended to interpret these fiduciary responsibilities of faculties as the set of obligations which underlie and legitimate the elements of special privilege which are often referred to as "academic freedom." [16]

I think of the ethnic group as belonging by and large to this same category of fiduciary association, especially by virtue of the element of continuing tradition which has been emphasized above. It does not seem, however, to belong unequivocally to any one of the above four subtypes. My inclination is to treat it as a kind of "fusion" of the community and kinship types. This would mean that the two have not yet come to be clearly differentiated from each

15. It seems to me that there is a major sense in which the fulfillment of fiduciary responsibilities in the present sense on the part of both elective officials, notably the President, and those holding appointive office, notably those on his staff, constitutes the most important focus of concern in the recent and current activities of the House of Representatives Judiciary Committee, and the office of the Special Prosecutor.

16. On this last point again see Parsons and Platt, *The American University*, esp. chap. 3. I am greatly indebted to David M. Schneider, especially in the course of a collaborative seminar at the University of Chicago, Fall Quarter 1973, for clarification of the nature of what I am here calling fiduciary associations.

other where ethnicity is involved.[17] Such differentiation has clearly been going on in recent times.

SOME PRIMARY FEATURES OF THE CURRENT SITUATION OF ETHNIC GROUPS

In order to drive home the relevance of the above theoretical sketch it may be worthwhile in the remainder of this chapter to speak fairly briefly of three empirical topics. The first concerns certain developments in the relatively advanced modern societies with special reference to ethnic relations in the United States without special concern for the status of the blacks. Second, in light of the fact that a tenth anniversary of the *Daedalus* study entitled *The Negro American* is approaching, it might be worthwhile to undertake a brief stock-taking review of where some of the problems of that study stand in the light of developments since it was made.[18] Finally, third, it seems worthwhile to say something about developments in the so-called "new nations."

I have already strongly emphasized that in spite of its origin as what has sometimes been called a WASP community, the American societal community is no longer in the older sense of its own history and of the classical pattern of the national state an ethnic community. This is not to say that ethnic groups have ceased to have significance. In certain respects quite the contrary is true. The most salient point, however, is that it is an ethnically pluralistic community where even the previous vague and informal stratification of ethnic subgroups has ceased to have its previous importance.[19]

At the same time the complete assimilation leading to the disappearance of ethnic identities and solidarities, which was much dis-

17. As we shall see below, in recent developments the voluntary "contract" element is by no means absent from the current picture of ethnicity.

18. Talcott Parsons and Kenneth Clark, eds., *The Negro American* (Boston, Houghton Mifflin, 1966); first published as *Daedalus* 94.4 (Fall 1965) and 95.1 (Winter 1966).

19. For the situation of the 1920s, see André Siegfried, *America Comes of Age: A French Analysis,* trans. H. H. Hemming and D. Hemming (New York, Harcourt and Co., 1927). The present volume will provide a general review of the current situation.

cussed in the earlier part of the present century and greatly feared
by some groups, has also not in any simple sense taken place. Indeed, full assimilation, in the sense that ethnic identification has virtually disappeared and become absorbed within the single category
of "American," is very little the case. For example, Schneider reports as one of the conspicuous findings of the recent study of families in the Chicago area, on which his theoretical book, *American
Kinship,* is based, that "Almost every family identifies with some
ethnic unit—they were Italians, Jews, Bohemians, Polish, Czechs,
and so on." [20] Those who identified themselves as Anglo-Saxon on
Schneider's and other evidence often also use regional categorization and sometimes that in terms of a type of community as in the
case of being "ordinary Midwestern farmers" or various types of
Southerners.

Schneider goes on to make some exceedingly interesting observations about this situation, saying "It was true that when they [that
is, the interviewers on his project] collected the genealogies of
those who most vehemently and affirmatively claimed they were
Italian, they discovered a succession going backwards of Irish and
Polish mothers and grandmothers. That is, upwardly mobile Italians marry 'blond' Irish and Polish Catholics. This is a well-known
phenomenon. Yet, despite this intermarriage, the affirmation of
Italian identity was quite clear, affirmative, and positive from even
the Irish and Polish mothers and grandmothers. They had 'become' Italian and proved it, for instance, by cooking according to
the Italian style, eating according to distinct Italian traditions
(elbows on tables, eat, eat)."

This seems to be a notable confirmation of the general point we
made earlier in the chapter about the optional and voluntary component of ethnic identification, at least in the United States. It
seems to be especially the family household which tends to adopt

20. Schneider, *American Kinship.* This quotation and the ones that follow are
taken from an informal memorandum written by Professor David Schneider,
Department of Anthropology, University of Chicago (1972) and quoted with his
permission. He and I have also had long discussions and correspondence over
these topics, culminating in a joint seminar on cultural symbolism held at the University of Chicago in the Fall Quarter of 1972.

such an identification and in the process to pass over the actual ethnic origins of various of its members and members of recognized
extended kin groupings.

How, however, is this possible? Schneider goes on to make two
extremely interesting observations. The first of these is that, however strongly affirmative these ethnic identifications are, the ethnic status is conspicuously devoid of "social content." Again, as
Schneider puts it, "It does not require the learning of a totally
new social role for the Irish girl to marry the Italian; they are both
Catholic at least and she picks up some Italian, learns some cooking
styles, and, lo, the symbolic identification is set." He goes on to say,
"The marks of identity are in a very important sense 'empty symbols.' Symbols empty of elaborate social distinctions, and thus they
are able to function freely and smoothly in this multi-ethnic social
system while maintaining a distinct cultural-symbolic identity as
markers." Perhaps it is legitimate to interpret this as saying that the
symbolization of ethnic identification is primarily focused on style
of life distinctiveness within the larger framework of much more
nearly uniform American social structure. This social structure is
differentiated by class, by region, and by type of community, for
example, metropolitan contrasted with small town, but not very
greatly on an ethnic basis. Schneider recounts another example of
a family of Greek origin who were visited by the parents of one
member of the married couple who, after a brief sojourn in the
United States, had returned to Greece. The younger couple, as
Schneider says, "were vehemently, indeed belligerently Greek, and
explained all sorts of special Greek traits and customs to us." The
old couple from Greece, on the other hand, "complained bitterly
that these young people claimed they were Greek and made all
kinds of noises about being true Greek, but they were nothing but
common Americans underneath all that empty talk."

Schneider's second pertinent observation is particularly interesting at the role level. He reports that he and his staff were repeatedly told in respondents' explanations of what underlay their ethnic identity that if the identity was Irish, it could be understood
only if one understood "the Irish mother." The interesting point,
however, is that the assertion about the crucial role of the mother

was repeated for group after group. You could not understand
Jewish family life unless you understood the Jewish mother, similarly with Italian, similarly with Polish, and so on. Whatever the situation with respect to cultural relativity in these respects and,
hence, differences in definition of mother roles in the various ethnic groups, there seems to be a striking uniformity with respect to
focusing on the mother as the symbolic guardian of the ethnic
identity.

These observations clearly indicate that the development of what
we have called ethnic pluralism in American society has involved
major changes in the character of the ethnic groups themselves,
compared to what they were, for example, as embodied in the life
of the first-generation immigrants in question. As Schneider puts
it, there is a certain sense in which they have been "desocialized"
and transformed into primarily cultural-symbolic groups. This
does not preclude solidarity at certain levels such, for example, as
preferences for residential contiguity or, if not that, selective relatedness. Thus, people who identify as Italian in Schneider's sense
may well feel more comfortable in associating in a variety of respects with others who also identify themselves as Italian, whether
or not they reside in predominantly Italian neighborhoods. Similarly, members of such groups may crystallize their solidarities, for
example, about political interests, but here it should be kept clearly
in mind that there is an element of voluntary selectivity. Especially
for the case of the non-Italian mothers and grandmothers to whom
Schneider refers, there is option with respect to what identity to
emphasize for particular purposes. Very important here is the relation between ethnicity and religion. Again, as Schneider notes,
Irish, Italians, and Poles in the current American ethnic sense are
all predominantly Catholic. On questions involving the relation of
Catholicism to other denominational religious groups, obviously
Protestants and Jews, a certain cross-ethnic solidarity is possible. It
should not be forgotten that this applies also to the Jews, since
from the usual point of view, American Jews are far from being
ethnically homogeneous, although they hold special allegiances to
the wider international Jewish community. On such matters as support for Israel they would be likely to be rather highly solidary in

spite of their own internal divisions and differences. Furthermore, there are many distinct Protestant denominations.

The phenomena we have called "desocialization" of ethnic groupings do not stand alone. A good many observers have contended that in recent years, even apart from specifically disadvantaged groups, there has tended to be something like an intensification of ethnic solidarity and a certain tone of militancy in the defense or promotion of what are conceived to be ethnic interests.[21] If such a tendency exists in the United States, two further points need to be made about it. First, it is at least in part of a piece with patterns of the intensification of feelings of both ethnic solidarity and "rights" that have been involved in a number of recent movements in other countries, some of which approach the boundary line of political separatism. Our neighbor, Canada, provides a conspicuous example, though the intensity of the French Canadian movement seemed to have subsided somewhat in the most recent period. Another case of which somewhat similar things may be said has been the conflict between the French-speaking Walloons and the Flemish-speaking population of Belgium, which at certain points has been very acute indeed in recent years. Even though it is less in the international news than it was for some time, recently we had the very striking announcement that the French-speaking sector of the University of Louvain has not only become separated in local operations from the Flemish-speaking sector but has decided actually to move its location to another community. Finally, we are all exceedingly conscious of the situation in Northern Ireland which has seemed so very difficult to cope with.

The second extremely important point is that the accentuation of group solidarity and militancy in insistence on rights has not been confined to ethnic groups. Though trade union movements in general have not been particularly militant in recent times, an interesting problem is created by certain cases among which urban civil service groups seem quite conspicuous. The time when the right to strike was effectively denied to almost all classes of government employees at whatever level seems far behind indeed. Such distur-

21. Cf. Nathan Glazer and Daniel P. Moynihan, *Beyond the Melting Pot* (Cambridge, Harvard University Press and MIT Press, 1963).

bances have, of course, often been connected with ethnic issues, thus in the case of the New York City Teachers Union of a few years ago, the fact that such a large proportion of unionized teachers in the city were Jewish certainly played a part in the situation, producing what many would consider the somewhat bizarre phenomenon of a wave of black anti-Semitism.[22]

We think it important to emphasize that the phenomena under discussion are not related to the political position of members of the groups in question in any simple way. They are probably particularly conspicuous both on the Right and on the Left, but even this identification need not be infallible. Many movements such as that backing Governor Wallace of Alabama in recent presidential elections have a baffling combination of what by ordinary standards would be called radicalism and conservatism. There are many features in common between such movements: the discontent of urban government employees and some of the more militant movements of the Left, particularly in the academic world. The blacks have occupied a very special position on which a special comment will be made.

Finally, in enumerating the above types of groups, those organized about some kind of religious solidarity should not be forgotten. Such phenomena are most conspicuous in the case of Protestant Fundamentalist groups, but the militant right-wing Jewish group led by Rabbi Kahane should not be left out of the picture. Many of the Protestant Fundamentalists who are militant in this sense are in part motivated by a WASP identification and of course the Jewish group just referred to is both ethnic and religious in identification.

A particularly important phenomenon in this whole connection may be considered to be the obverse of the desocialization of ethnic solidarity and identification which I have discussed. Under conditions of rapid social change and certain tendencies to anomic social disorganization and alienation, intensification of "groupism" and the high emotional loading of the status of group membership and identity is one major type of reaction. Like many other such

22. Daniel Bell, *The Coming of Post-Industrial Society: A Venture in Social Forecasting* (New York, Basic Books, 1973).

phenomena it may involve a complex combination of potential and, to a certain degree, actual disruptive consequences for social solidarity and, at the same time, a kind of a constructive mode of reintegration of population elements into structures which are less anomic and alienative than their members might otherwise be exposed to. In attempting to analyze and appraise the forces involved in such phenomena, it is very important not to identify what is found too closely with actual historic antecedent conditions, if by that would be meant for the ethnic case the restoration of a pattern of life and of values and sentiments which is identical with that which the first waves of immigrants brought with them. One would expect some kind of a compromise formation between tendencies to such restorationism and the recognition of many of the facts of current life in modern society which are incompatible with the old patterns.

There does seem to be a common feature which is conspicuous in the ethnic field and also more broadly of social processes which bears a certain analogy to the phenomenon of regression in the psychological sense and which, in terms of motivational dynamics, is undoubtedly associated with regression, but by no means identical to it. I have found it useful to refer to this common factor as "de-differentiation." Its nature and significance should be seen against the background of the very powerful incidence, in recent developments of social structure, of universalistic standards of mobility and of the development of relatively enhanced freedoms, which, however, can easily turn over in anomic directions. Perhaps the most important focus, however, is the pluralization of modern social structure by virtue of which the typical individual plays multiple roles, no one of which can adequately characterize his identification as a "social" personality. The de-differentiating tendency is to select particular criteria and use these as identifying symbols for what the persons who constitute the group actually *are*. This, for example, has been particularly conspicuous in the racial context. But as Daniel Bell adroitly points out, what are we to think of the identity expressed by a reference to a "black woman sociologist"? In some connections the salient feature of her identity would be her racial position, in others it would be her sex, and in still others

it would be her occupational role. For certain subcategories of
each these do go together, but from the point of view of the larger
social structure they are very far from being identical or, in general, ascribed to each other. There are white sociologists and there
are male sociologists as well as black and female, and there are
many blacks and many females who are not sociologists, to say
nothing of there being many females who are white and not black.
These are very elementary considerations, but it is extremely important that their relevance should not be overlooked.

One further general consideration should be commented upon
in the present context. Among various others, Daniel Bell in particular has recently emphasized the problems of the shift in many
quarters from emphasis on equality of opportunity to equality of
result. This is particularly conspicuously manifested in public policy with respect to so-called "affirmative action" in relation to minority groups. In one prominent context, for example, either academic admissions or appointments to teaching positions, there is
strong pressure to assert some kind of quota-defined right of "representation," that is, essentially the same proportion of members of
a minority group in a given status such as students or teachers in a
given institution of higher education as there are in some probably
vaguely defined larger community. The shift is from treating admission or appointment as a selective process guided by criteria of
universalistically defined qualifications individual-by-individual to a
collective group right. Therefore, it gives an enhanced legitimacy
to particularistic criteria.

This tendency seems to us quite definitely to fit in the general
category of processes of de-differentiation. Differentiation of role
and opportunity among the members of a given group on the basis
of universalistically defined qualifications of promise or achievement tends to be played down in favor of some criterion of identity, such as membership in a minority or other such group based
on race, sex, or ethnicity, for example. It can also be extended to
religious groups, community of residence, and other such criteria.

There is an important bearing here on the problem of equality.
Equality is by no means a simple entity which is either present or
absent or which varies only in degree along a linear continuum. It

is a matter of qualitatively different components. As Bell notes, one of these components which is very generally called equality of opportunity is tending to be sacrificed to certain others such as group membership status, as ascertained independently of the universalistic criteria to which we have just referred, so that it comes to be that opportunities should be equal by *groups*, not for individuals.[23]

RECENT DEVELOPMENTS IN THE SITUATION OF AMERICAN BLACKS

Nearly a decade ago I as well as several other contributors to this book was a participant in a major study of what was then called "The Negro American." [24] It seems pertinent to the theme of this chapter to consider briefly the status of my own contribution to that enterprise and perhaps introduce a few considerations which were not taken account of at that time.

First, attention may be called to two interesting and I think significant shifts in symbolism as applied to this particular "minority" group in American society. The first has been introduced on the initiative of members of the group itself but has spread much more widely, namely, the adoption of the term "black" in place of "Negro." The latter term was used not only in the title, *The Negro American,* but pretty consistently throughout the discussion and papers of the project. In going back to my own contribution, I have been struck by the consistency with which I used the term "Negro" and did not use "black." [25] The new term stands in a very frank and explicit contrast, of course, to white, and is a good Anglo-Saxon word in contrast to Negro which has a Latin origin.

The second symbolic change is the introduction of the reference to African origin so that, by sharp contrast with the situation a decade ago, we now have frequent references to "Afro-Americans." This has the interesting effect of introducing a new parallelism be-

23. Daniel Bell, "Meritocracy and Equality," *The Public Interest,* no. 29 (Fall 1972), 29–68.

24. *Daedalus* 94.4 (Fall 1965); *Daedalus* 95.1 (Winter 1966); and Parsons and Clark, *The Negro American.*

25. Talcott Parsons, "Full Citizenship for the Negro American? A Sociological Problem," in Parsons and Clark, *The Negro American,* pp. 709–754.

tween the status of the black group and other ethnic groups in terms of what we have referred to above as "national origin." [26] Thus symmetry is established between the definition of black Americans as an ethnic group and other white Americans. If this interpretation is correct, it is connected with an interesting change of perspective. I recall the frequency with which it has been contended, especially in the discussions at the time of the *Daedalus* study, that the "problem" of the status of the black or Negro American was inherently and fundamentally different from that of white ethnic groups and that any attempt to treat it comparatively with the others under the same general analytical scheme was inherently illegitimate. In my own contribution, I begged to differ with this very prevalent view, and might consider this symbolic change to be a certain straw in the wind of vindication of my own view.

The replacement of the term "Negro" by "black," however, seems in a certain sense to have the opposite significance in that it very explicitly accentuates the *racial* focus of the identity of members of the group as somewhat distinguishable from the greater relative importance of the cultural component in the case of the principal white ethnic groups.

A further interesting change since the older stereotypes of the status of blacks came to be established has been the change of status of one set of groups who are of different racial origin from the predominantly European majority. These are, in the first instance, those whose forebears migrated from East Asia, most prom-

26. At a *Daedalus* conference subsequent to the Negro American enterprise, which was held in Copenhagen in 1965, I distinctly remember raising the question in a discussion of the apparent anomaly that Negro Americans did not refer to themselves nor were they frequently referred to in terms of any equivalent of the concept of national origin. I suggested the possibility that this gap would be filled and that the most likely way of doing so was a reference to Africa as the area of origin. Somewhat to my surprise, this suggestion was not taken seriously by the overwhelming majority of other participants in the conference. I think the feeling was that Africa was an area inhabited predominantly by "primitive" peoples and that black Americans would not wish to be identified with it in this respect. It was not very many years, however, before the identification in fact became common. Not least is the movement which swept the institutions of higher education for the establishment of what have usually been called "Afro-American programs of study." The papers issuing from this conference were published in *Daedalus* 96, no. 2 (Spring 1967), and in John Hope Franklin, ed., *Color and Race* (Boston, Houghton Mifflin, 1968).

inently the Chinese and Japanese. It will be remembered that when they first arrived in substantial numbers, the indigenous American white population showed quite violent antagonism to them with such dramatic episodes as the Chinese Exclusion Act and much later the World War II internment of Japanese-Americans.[27] If I remember correctly, it was in particular Daniel P. Moynihan who in the 1964 *Daedalus* conferences strongly emphasized that being of Chinese or Japanese origin was no longer considered to be a stigma for the most part in this country.[28] There seems to be a certain congruence between this development and the process by which Afro-Americans, if we may use this term, became accepting of an accentuation of the salience of a category of race as the primary identification symbol.[29] There is probably also a certain connection between this and the recent emergence of concern with the American Indians as another minority ethnic group, after a long period of relative neglect by nearly everyone except anthropologists. Thus we may speak of a racial, as well as in more general terms an ethnic, pluralism of the American population consisting of black people, yellow people, red people, and white people.

It also seems clear that these symbolic changes with reference to

27. See Alexander H. Leighton, *The Governing of Men: General Principles and Recommendations Based on Experience at a Japanese Relocation Camp* (Princeton, N.J., Princeton University Press, 1945).

28. D. P. Moynihan in "Transcript of the American Academy Conference on the Negro American, May 14–15, 1965," *Daedalus* 95.1 (Winter 1966), 343.

29. Cf. Talcott Parsons, "The Problem of Polarization on the Axis of Color," in John Hope Franklin, *Color and Race*. This article was written after the *Daedalus* conference in Copenhagen, referred to in note 27 above, and was not included in the issue of the journal which resulted. It is concerned with a rather general analysis of the phenomenon of polarization, with examples from the fields of religion and class as well as race. It is also world-wide in reference and not confined to the United States and is hence particularly pertinent to the concerns of the present volume. One of the principal polemical targets is the paper "Color, Racism and Christianity" by Roger Bastide in *Color and Race*. (The article by Edward Shils in the same volume should also be compared.) As in the present paper I argue there that, while for the short run the American pattern by which a person is *either* black *or* white with no intermediate status category may impede inclusion of blacks, or integration of blacks and whites, for the longer run a case can be made that the American pattern is more favorable. That this is the case is a major argument of the present section of this article.

American ethnic designations where a criterion of race can be relevant have been affected in an important way by events outside the United States. With respect to East Asia, in the case of the Japanese we can speak of a course of American attitudes changing from a kind of indifference mixed with romanticism to a phase of acute hostility culminating in the Second World War and back to a phase of pronounced favorable attitudes strongly reinforced by the great recent economic and social achievements of the Japanese nation. The Chinese case is somewhat different, but the consolidation of revolutionary China in the recent period has made it much less plausible to think of the Chinese in the old terms of a certain kind of social incompetence, as "the sick man of East Asia," comparable with Turkey in the period of the First World War. The consolidation of the revolutionary regime, of course, provoked acute hostility in this country which has only recently given way to a new orientation which seems to be associated with a widespread attitude of respect.

Third, the great development in Subsaharan Africa, of course, has been the achievement of independence by a number of formerly colonial societies. Here also a certain contrast between these predominantly black new nations and the racism of the white minority-dominated Union of South Africa and Southern Rhodesia has tended to give the black African nations something of a good press. Similarly, the case of the American Indian has probably been helped by social changes in Latin America in those countries in which a very large proportion of the population consists of persons of Indian origin who have recently become politically active on new levels.

Finally, with respect to the distinction between race and cultural tradition, it is pertinent to point out that the designations of racial groups by color are themselves cultural symbols.[30] When the four colors just mentioned, black, yellow, red, and white, are used in this connection it is clearly in major part a *cultural* phenomenon. This is true in a sense parallel to that in which the symbol, blood, as

30. Thus Shils (in Franklin, *Color and Race*) is at least partially wrong in designating color as an almost purely "primordial" criterion with the implication that it has virtually *no* other significance than biological characterization.

used by Schneider in the context of kinship analysis, is a cultural symbol and not simply the name for a physiological entity.[31] In this connection it is worth noting that the "blood relationship" par excellence is that of a mother and her own child. Physiologically speaking, however, they do *not* share the same bloodstream; the child's bloodstream develops independently and what passes to it from the maternal organism through the placenta includes a great many other elements, but definitely not blood. "Blood relationship" here is a symbol, not a description, of a physiological relationship.

Precisely in this kind of context the symbol black has certain particularly interesting features. As is true of African populations, a certain proportion of members of the American ethnic group who are now called and call themselves blacks have skin color which is a close approximation to the physical color of black. Unlike Africans, however, the black Americans who approximate this skin color in fact are clearly a minority of the whole group. The predominant reason for this is the history of what used to be called "miscegenation," that is, racial mixing as between black and white people with the offspring as in this sense a hybrid group. In America, however, sociologically the definition of a Negro is not, and has not been historically, in terms of skin color, but in terms of parentage. Any person, one of whose parents was socially classified as Negro or black, has been by *social* ascription Negro or black. Even in South Africa there is a distinctive group called "colored" as distinguished from either white or black. These are descendants of mixed unions of one kind or another; there is no such category on the American scene.[32]

The designation of Negroes or blacks as an ethnic group

31. Schneider, *American Kinship*.

32. One aspect of the meaning of the symbol black came out in classroom discussions held under the impact of the assassination of Martin Luther King, Jr. I had remarked on the emergence of this symbol and asked for suggestions of explanation. A black woman, a member of the class, made the following interesting point: it concerned, she said, the internal stratification of the black community and the correlation between lightness of color and high status. She then said that one of the reasons for identification of all as blacks was to counteract this tendency to stratification and be sure that the least advantaged members of the group were fully included. In a sense this is a case of making a virtue of necessity.

through a symbol designating color is a tag which has made it possible or easier to attribute biologically hereditary characteristics to the group. I think particularly of the allegations, which have been especially prominent in Southern racist ideology, to the effect that blacks are either like children or like animals.[33] Quite apart from the more general question of whether there is a hereditary component in the differences of races which bears on capacity for performance according to the standards of current society, this ideology flies in the face of the massive fact of the heterogeneity of origin, precisely in terms of inherited genes, of the members of the black community. One is reminded in this case of Schneider's comment on the Irish and Polish mothers and grandmothers of ethnic Italians.[34] The black community in a certain sense has chosen to forget or in a symbolic sense to "deny" the relevance of the white component in its ancestry. One might speak of this as "getting back" for the obverse denial of the relevance of parenthood where a white person, notably a father, was a biological parent of a "black" child.

It has, of course, long been known to sociologists and others that even with indelible visibility of skin color, for a certain fraction of members of the black community, there are options of choice of ethnic identity through the phenomenon known as "passing." Cases, for example, have been known where an individual passed as white in an employment situation, but with reference to residential associations functioned as a member of the black community.[35]

It has been almost a sociological commonplace, and was strongly emphasized in my own *Daedalus* paper, that a primary feature of the status ascribed to the blacks has been the stigma of somehow inherent inferiority.[36] That there should be a group thus stigmatized seems in turn to be to an important degree a function of a society in which the achievement complex, with its inherent competi-

---

33. Thomas Pettigrew, *A Profile of the Negro American* (Princeton, N.J., D. Van Nostrand, 1964).

34. D. Schneider, informal memo. See note 22.

35. The obverse is also known to occur, namely, the "passing" of whites as black. This has been true by marriage, but also otherwise.

36. Parsons, "Full Citizenship for the Negro American?"

tive aspects, has been so prominent. This also goes a considerable distance toward making it understandable that racial prejudice has centered rather more in the lower ranges of the stratification of the white community than in the upper. No matter how relatively "unsuccessful" such people may seem to be and think of themselves as, this view provides a floor below which they cannot fall, that is, they cannot be identified with the lowest group of all, the blacks. In order to maintain this fiction of black inferiority it can be seen that it has been exceedingly important to maintain the salience of a *single* identifying characteristic of the group which is both visible and indelible, namely, color.[37] This has not, however, prevented a certain amount of differentiation among other things because the color characteristic is, as we have just noted, empirically not uniform.

Inferiority of status, however, has been to a substantial degree a self-fulfilling prophecy. The allegation that blacks as such were incapable of the higher orders of achievement has been a major factor in preventing them from having the opportunity for such achievement. In American society, at least, actual development of what is usually called upward social mobility, which is linked with personal achievement, therefore becomes particularly important in breaking the symbolic rigidity of the old stereotypes. It is, therefore, a matter of profound interest that, in spite of a good deal of unevenness, the last decade or so since the Civil Rights Movement gathered force has seen a pretty massive process of upward mobility among blacks. Among specialists there is considerable skepticism of the statements made by Wattenberg and Scammon in their recent article in *Commentary* that it can now be said that slightly over half of the black population (52 percent) should be classified as middle class.[38] For example, a very knowledgeable and judicious student of the problem, Thomas F. Pettigrew, has es-

37. See Edward Shils, "Color, the Universal Intellectual Community, and the Afro-Asian Intellectual," in *Daedalus* 96.2 (Spring 1967), 279–295; this article also appears in Franklin, *Color and Race.*

38. Ben J. Wattenberg and Richard M. Scammon, "Black Progress and Liberal Rhetoric," *Commentary* (April 1973). Also, "Letters, An Exchange on Black Progress: Ben J. Wattenberg and Richard M. Scammon and Critics," *Commentary*, 56.2 (August 1973), 4–22.

timated (by personal communication) that the proportion is closer
to 35 percent. However this may be, there seems to be no question
but that a strong current of upward mobility has been underway,
including a shift in the distribution of income, of occupational status, of educational levels, and a variety of such criteria resulting in
an increasingly large cohort of the more successful blacks.

It seems that this change either already has or soon will reach the
point of making a very fundamental difference to the symbolic impact of the success of a select number of outstanding blacks like Justice Thurgood Marshall, the late Whitney Young, or Senator
Brooke. There will be the impact of the familiarity of very substantial numbers whose social characteristics, apart from their color or
status as blacks, are very similar to those of the majority of non-
black middle-class Americans. It may thus turn out in the longer
run that acceptance of the more radical symbol of identity, black,
will have favored rather than hindered the process of inclusion in
the American societal community on a basis of something like
parity with other ethnic groups, the inclusion of which has preceded that of the blacks in time.[39]

In spite of such indications, however, the situation should not be
oversimplified. The symbolic change around which this discussion
has been organized has also underlain and in part been caused by a
tendency to militant separatism on the part of a substantial proportion of the politically activistic blacks, finding its extreme manifestations in such phenomena as the Black Panthers and the Black Muslims; escalating polarization of the separation has occurred at many
points and been highly visible. It is clear, however, that this polarization trend does not stand by itself, but that the inclusion-
pluralization trend is also present to an important degree. Again,
following Schneider, we would like to reemphasize that insofar as
these latter tendencies become more prominent, there will tend to
be a considerable process of desocialization of black ethnicity which
is parallel to that which has occurred with other American ethnic
groups.

39. Cf. Talcott Parsons, "The Problem of Polarization on the Axis of Color,"
and Roger Bastide, "Color, Racism and Christianity," in Franklin, *Color and Race*.

Insofar as this does take place, it will have the interesting implication that the status of the ghetto blacks becomes increasingly
anomalous. There has been an understandable tendency to assume
that the ghetto pattern of existence was the "natural" mode of living for urban blacks. With, however, a substantial decrease in the
proportion of those identified as blacks found in the ghetto pattern
of life, it will become increasingly difficult to maintain this attitude.
It may be said that during the critical period of the Civil Rights
change, non-ghetto blacks have tended to be more or less ignored
and pushed out of the center of national awareness. In a comparable sense the non-black poor have had a similar fate, though it has
always been well known to experts that though a very large proportion of blacks relatively speaking have been counted among the
poor, in fact they have been a minority of the poor, the substantial
majority of whom have been white.[40] Perhaps with these developments the problem of poverty as one cutting entirely across ethnic
lines will undergo a certain reinstatement which should eliminate a
good deal of confusion.[41]

A WORD ON ETHNICITY AND
THE NEW NATIONS

A disproportionate amount of the space of this chapter may have
been devoted to American and other Western-type modern societies. I have, however, a firm conviction that the kind of theoretical
analysis which has been used here can legitimately be tested by its
relevance to quite different empirical conditions. I should therefore like to illustrate this by rounding out the discussion with a few
points about the so-called new-nation world. I think the same fundamental problems of the relation between the diffuse transgenerational solidarities of ethnic and other groups and their place in

40. Cf. Daniel P. Moynihan, ed., *On Understanding Poverty,* Perspectives on Poverty Series (New York, Basic Books, 1968); and Herman P. Miller, *Rich Man, Poor
Man* (New York, The New American Company, 1964).

41. This is not to say that I am unaware of the salience of many "backlash" phenomena such as the appeal of anti-busing slogans in the current situation. It
seems, however, unlikely that these will prevail in the longer run.

the structure of the total society are to be found in different form with the same components occurring in different combinations in other types of society.[42]

We may emphasize in this area three aspects of the problem field. The first has to do with the fact that it is rare that a new nation is composed of a population that in any simple sense approaches ethnic homogeneity. The commonest formula used to describe the lack of such homogeneity is "tribal" diversity. Second, for the most part the definition of national boundaries which has resulted from independence from the colonial powers has failed to coincide with territorial-ethnic boundaries and has tended to include diverse tribal groups and to cut many important such groups in two or more pieces by placing them on different sides of a political boundary.

Tribal diversity, to continue, is in turn associated with a good deal of diversity with reference to a number of the factors I have discussed which tend to be used to define ethnic identity. A prominent case is language and it is notorious that a large proportion of these societies have very complicated language problems. The linguistic diversity of the "common people" is apt to be so great that the most convenient medium of communication for the leading strata involved in government and other such affairs has continued on a large scale to be the language of the former colonial power. Central Africa is thus very broadly divided into areas where the "elite" are English-speaking on the one hand, French-speaking on the other. Naturally, this dependence on the language of a previously hated colonial power creates substantial ambivalence.

This is compounded by the fact that the culture of the elites has been, in respects other than language, strongly influenced by the colonizing nation, and as one important manifestation, many of the generation which have taken political and other responsibility in the new nation have been educated in the "metropolitan" country, to use the French term. It should thus not be forgotten that the two great emancipating heroes of Indian independence, Gandhi and Nehru, were both British-educated. India has been a focus of

42. Cf. Reinhard Bendix, *Nation-Building and Citizenship* (New York, Wiley and Sons, 1964).

intense conflict over language problems with an attempt to institutionalize the general usage of indigenous languages which, however, has run into very severe difficulties. English remains the lingua franca of the substantial majority of the upper groups.[43]

To stress the third problem, it is clear that the problem of ethnic diversity and the threats it poses to some kind of "national unity" is a ubiquitous problem in almost all the new nations. Though certain personnel who have, as it were, inherited their status from previous colonial regimes have retained some kind of residence and functions in many of these societies. In Africa and India, for example, the racial factor is not a primary one in this diversity. It is simply a consequence of the particularistic localism of so much of the indigenous society.

The obverse problem derives from the historically arbitrary division of ethnic groups as between two or in some cases even more politically organized societies. This clearly is a phenomenon which has also been exceedingly prominent in European history. In a national solidarity sense are the French-speaking components of Swit-

43. That these problems do not operate only at political and governmental levels is illustrated by an interesting phenomenon. Dr. Bennetta Jules-Rosette in her recently submitted doctoral dissertation analyzed a new religious movement called the Apostles, which, from a Protestant missionary background, has spread in Zaire, the former Belgian Congo, and certain neighboring countries, notably Kenya. The boundary with which Dr. Jules-Rosette was most concerned was between the former Belgian Congo and a neighboring former British colony which cut across ethnic lines. She observed and described, however, an exceedingly interesting linguistic phenomenon. In certain of the rituals of the Apostles there is alternate "preaching" and "singing" introduced by various members of the group participating. The interesting point is that the ritual is conducted in several different languages. Some of the participants chose to speak or sing in French; others used not one, but several, different indigenous tribal languages, most of which are, however, sufficiently closely related as to be with some approximation mutually understandable. The religious movement, as such, is clearly a cross-tribal phenomenon which is forming links of solidarity independent of tribal affiliations. It is, however, as it were, paying its respects to tribal identities by institutionalizing the use of plural tribal languages in the same ritual performance. It seems legitimate to interpret this as a case of maintaining a delicate balance between the creation of new solidarities and respectful recognition of tribal diversity. See Bennetta Jules-Rosette, "Ritual Contexts and Social Action: A Study of the Apostolic Church of John Marangue." Unpublished doctoral thesis, Harvard University, Cambridge, Mass., June 1973.

zerland or Belgium members of the French nation or not? Or are the German-speaking Swiss members of the "German nation"? It is clear from the historical record that the answers to these questions are seldom simple. Even where geographical location is very distant indeed, the same problem has arisen with respect to what significantly is called the "Francophone" group in Canada. Some of the separatist-oriented French Canadians, egged on by de Gaulle, have made a great deal of the definition of their ethnic identity as French and thus in some symbolic sense as inherently part of the same French ethnic community as metropolitan France, and hence to be separated from "Anglophone" Canada.

Political realities, however, are such that it is no more likely in the new nations than it has been in European history that neat correspondences between traditional ethnicity and political allegiance can be worked out for the system as a whole.

There are, therefore, powerful incentives toward commitment to ethnically pluralistic national societal communities in a sense which involves at least some resemblances to the problem of the evolution of a type of community like the recently emerged America. It is almost a commonplace that an important factor underlying the intensity of "nationalistic" sentiments in many new nations is a function of the tensions occasioned by this diversity and the fact that the new nation is incompatible with many of the traditional conceptions of sub-ethnic independence. I suppose it could be said that the recent civil war in Nigeria, which was structured mainly on this kind of basis, is a classic example from the field of the new nations, but, of course, there are many others.[44]

It is an important fact bearing on the possibilities of development in pluralistic directions that, important as race and color have been in many instances, this symbolic focus of ethnic identity is very widely cross-cut with others, thus producing, even from the beginning, the kind of structural pluralism which in the long run strongly inhibits polarization.

44. Robin Luckham, *The Nigerian Military: A Sociological Analysis of Authority and Revolt* (Cambridge, England, Cambridge University Press, 1971).

CONCLUSION

It is quite clear that in this chapter it was possible to deal with only a small part of the problems and topics which are relevant to the theme of ethnicity on a world-wide basis. I hope, however, that it has been helpful to try to show not only how deep-rooted are the forces which make for stress on an ethnic type of solidarity, but also some of the relations of ethnicity to different but related modes of establishing solidary groupings. Finally, I hope that the differences between the various relevant groups in the United States, notably white and black, and the differences and similarities between American developments and those going on in other parts of the world will prove illuminating. It is hoped that this chapter can serve as a modest contribution to the development of a more general theory of the nature, variety, and functions of groups in which diffuse enduring, that is, transgenerational, solidarity is a salient characteristic. If so, comparative sociology in this area would be greatly facilitated and the resort to the mere assertion of uniqueness less necessary or tempting.

3

MILTON M. GORDON

Toward a General Theory of Racial and Ethnic Group Relations

In *Assimilation in American Life,* published in 1964,[1] I presented a multidimensional model of the assimilation process and applied it to the American scene historically and contemporaneously. This model distinguished seven assimilation dimensions or variables: cultural, structural, marital, identificational, attitude receptional (absence of prejudice), behavior receptional (absence of discrimination), and civic (absence of value and power conflict). Certain hypotheses about the relationship of these variables were advanced; these were (1) that in majority–minority group contact cultural assimilation or acculturation would occur first; (2) that acculturation may take place even when none of the other types of assimilation has occurred; and this situation of "acculturation only" may continue indefinitely; and (3) that if structural assimilation occurs along with or subsequent to acculturation, all the other types of assimilation will inevitably follow. This theoretical model of variables and propositions was used to analyze the meaning of the tradi-

Note: I wish to thank W. Clark Roof for a careful reading of an earlier draft of this paper and for some useful suggestions.

1. Milton M. Gordon, *Assimilation in American Life* (New York, Oxford University Press, 1964). In two earlier publications, one going back to 1954, I had made the distinction between cultural and structural assimilation which is basic to the model. See my "Social Structure and Goals in Group Relations," in Morroe Berger, Theodore Abel, and Charles H. Page, eds., *Freedom and Control in Modern Society* (New York, D. Van Nostrand Co., Inc., 1954), pp. 141–157; and "Assimilation in America: Theory and Reality," *Daedalus* (Spring 1961), 263–285.

tional American ideologies of "Anglo-conformity," the "melting pot," and "cultural pluralism," and the historical and current realities of American racial and ethnic group life. It was concluded that massive (although not complete nor uniform) acculturation to Anglo-Saxon norms and patterns had in fact taken place historically, while structural separation of racial and religious groups, and to some degree national origins groups, still remained. One important exception to this generalization were intellectuals and artists among whom a new subsociety appeared to be forming which largely ignored ethnic considerations in the formation of primary group relationships and organizational membership. To this overall picture of American racial and ethnic relations in the early 1960s, which it seemed to me would continue indefinitely, I applied the term "structural pluralism." This analysis contributed to the unfolding realization among students of race and ethnicity that the optimism of an earlier generation of sociologists concerning the inevitable assimilation or "melting" of American minority groups into some common framework which would effect their disappearance was distinctly unwarranted and that, in the words of Glazer and Moynihan, "the persisting facts of ethnicity demand attention, understanding, and accommodation." [2]

Subsequent events in American intergroup relations during the latter half of the 1960s and into the 1970s, the deepening of racial and ethnic conflicts throughout the world during this period, and my concurrence in the cogency of the call to both comparative research and the formulation of more general theories of intergroup relations by such writers as van den Berghe, Blalock, and Schermerhorn have led me to reexamine the assimilation process in a context somewhat more expanded than that of my previous formulation.[3] The domestic events referred to above center particularly on the rise of the "black power" movement, Afro-American

2. Nathan Glazer and Daniel Patrick Moynihan, *Beyond the Melting Pot* (Cambridge, Mass., Harvard University Press and MIT Press, 1963), p. v.

3. Pierre L. van den Berghe, *Race and Racism: A Comparative Perspective* (New York, John Wiley and Sons, Inc., 1967); H. M. Blalock, Jr., *Toward a Theory of Minority-Group Relations* (New York, John Wiley and Sons, Inc., 1967); R. A. Schermerhorn, *Comparative Ethnic Relations* (New York, Random House, 1970).

cultural nationalism, rioting by blacks in major American cities, efforts to institute community control over public institutions in black neighborhoods, and the presumed effects of these developments on the heightening of group consciousness and collective action among Mexican-Americans and Puerto Ricans, and possibly "white ethnic" groups as well.

The balance of this paper will first consider the relationship of assimilation analysis to the concepts of power and conflict which were relatively ignored (or, more accurately, perhaps, taken for granted) in my previous study, and second, will attempt to place considerations of assimilation, pluralism, power, and the like, into the more general framework of a multi-causal model for the prediction of particular outcomes in majority–minority group relations. The assimilation paradigm itself and its application to the American historical experience up until the early 1960s I find no reason to materially alter.

Blalock has made a useful distinction between competitive resources and pressure resources and, drawing upon social psychological theory, has conceptualized power as a product of resources and the mobilization of those resources.[4] We may, then, speak of competitive power—the ability to compete as individuals in the rewards system of the society—and pressure power—the power to effect change in the society in a collective fashion. I find it additionally useful to subdivide pressure power into two subtypes: (1) political pressure, narrowly defined, in the form of action by means of voting and litigation to induce favorable action on the part of the legislature, the courts, and the executive branches of government, and (2) disruptive pressure, consisting of acts which disrupt normal and expected routines of social intercourse; these could range from peaceful nonviolent demonstrations at one end of the spectrum through angry and violence-threatening confrontations, up to sporadic rioting, and finally to the ultimate extreme of violent revolution.

With these distinctions in mind, I turn now to a reconstruction of the expectancies about the manner of social change in the area of

4. Blalock, *Toward a Theory of Minority-Group Relations*, chap. 4.

racial and ethnic relations in the United States which prevailed in this country around the middle of the twentieth century among the liberal leadership of the movement for racial equality, both Negro and white, and among men of good will generally. These expectations were approximately as follows: that because of what appeared to be overwhelming white dominance, demographically, economically, and politically, the attempt to improve the lot of racial and ethnic minorities would have to be made by a massive effort to activate the consciences of white Americans to implement the American creed of democracy and equalitarianism, to eliminate Jim Crow laws in the South through litigation at the Supreme Court level, to fight for legislation in the North (and nationally) to legally bar discrimination in employment and housing, to break down the extralegal barriers to voting by Negroes in the South and to encourage the use of the ballot by minority group members generally for the achievement of equal rights, and finally to work for federal and other governmental efforts to deal effectively with poverty and urban blight in a manner which would benefit all the poor in the population impartially, but which would, clearly, have particular impact, because of generations of past discrimination, on submerged racial groups.

Even the peaceful demonstrations of civil disobedience which became a part of the civil rights movement in the early sixties did not, on the whole, challenge these expectancies. The demonstrations, while often drawing violent reactions from hostile whites, were, at least so far as the demonstrators were concerned, generally nonviolent and were aimed at obtaining rights for Negroes which had already been granted by law in the wake of the Supreme Court decision against segregated public education in 1954, or were otherwise well within the boundary of practices sanctioned by American democratic values.

In summary, the proclaimed goal of both blacks and white liberals was equal treatment by the law, integration, the raising of the competitive resources of blacks by the corrective means of governmental aid programs and the opening up of white institutions to all, regardless of race, who could now or later qualify by meeting universalistic standards—in short, the use of competitive resources plus political resources, with nonviolent demonstrations viewed not so much in terms of disruption as a call to the conscience of America, and with the pace of progress seen as inevitably determined by the overwhelmingly greater power of the white majority. Within this context, the prediction of indefinitely continuing structural separation, or structural pluralism, was seen as a concession to the realities of both existing (though hopefully lessening) attitudes of prejudice and avoidance, and the factual presence of an already built-up institutional structure within the communities of racial minorities.

What actually happened, of course, in the subsequent period was not only an intensification of structural separatism, but, along with *some* of the developments mentioned above in what might be called "the liberal expectancy," the generally unanticipated emergence of the black power movement, black cultural nationalism, sporadic rioting in the black ghettoes, and the gradual supplanting (though not completely) of old-style liberal black leadership by a more militant type advocating and using disruptive pressure resources. Thus, there has developed, in a pluralist context, something close to a real power struggle with both potential and actual outbreaks of conflict signifying the uneasy race relations climate of the current American scene and which could conceivably, although not inevitably, reach the stage of what Lewis Killian has called "the impossible revolution." [5] At the same time, some of the processes encompassed in the "liberal expectancy" also continue to operate so that the picture is a mixed one. For an analysis of this complex situation the variables of power and conflict must be attached or built into assimilation theory. This, however, is only another way of saying that *assimilation theory must, for purposes of achieving greater explanatory power, be placed in the framework of a larger theoretical context which helps explain the general processes of racial and ethnic group relations.* [6]

5. Lewis M. Killian, *The Impossible Revolution?* (New York, Random House, 1968).

6. It should go without saying that assimilation theory, as presented in my earlier model, was never meant to advance the thesis that complete assimilation inevitably occurred in contact between ethnically diverse population groups—quite the contrary: the multidimensional approach to assimilation provided by my model allowed the various subtypes of assimilation to be conceptually distinguished from

What is required, then, is a more general theory of intergroup or racial and ethnic group relations, one which includes not only sociological but also psychological variables, a consideration of power relationships, and an examination of relevant basic social-psychological processes of human interaction. In the next portion of this chapter, I shall attempt to suggest the outlines of what, as it seems to me, such a theory should contain.

The first task in constructing a causal theory is to designate the effect, or dependent variable. While this attempt to extract such a temporarily static phenomenon from the ceaseless ebb and flow of human interaction is bound to be less than perfectly successful because of both "chain" and "feedback" effects, such an attempt must, clearly, be made if any theory at all is to be developed. The problem is also made more difficult by the fact that often the effect we are interested in is not a single or unfactorable variable but a complex of variables, whose total variation is a function of varying combinations of positions of its components. In such a situation, it is entirely possible that no overall quantitative measure of position on a unidimensional scale is possible at all, and the varying possible outcomes must be designated as a qualitative typology in which the subtypes of effects are separated not by quantitative units but by differences in kind. Such must certainly be the case in a first ap-proximation of the designation of the dependent variable in a theory of intergroup relations.[7]

My thesis, then, is that the most useful dependent variable or at-tribute in a theory of racial and ethnic intergroup relations is a construct which consists of four subvariables. These are: (1) *Type of*

---

each other, advanced hypotheses about the interrelationships of these subtypes, allowed for the possibility of varying rates of progress toward assimilation among the various dimensions, or on some dimensions virtually no progress at all, and, in fact, predicted the indefinite continuance of structurally separate ethnic groups on the American scene. Nor did my discussion of assimilation assign absolute positive valuation to either the assimilationist or pluralist ends of the continuum. It did, however, present the hypothesis that there were boundaries to the process of sep-aration of ethnic groups within the same society beyond which disfunctional ef-fects were likely to occur.

7. See, for instance, the typology developed by Schermerhorn in R. A. Scher-merhorn, *Comparative Ethnic Relations*.

assimilation, with the major distinction being that between cultural and structural assimilation. Each type can, in theory, of course, be thought of as quantifiable along a single scale or dimension ranging from complete assimilation on one end of the scale to complete pluralism on the other. (2) *Degree of total assimilation.* This variable would consist of an index combining scores for each subtype of assimilation. Theoretically, such scores could be assigned for each of the seven assimilation subtypes in my original assimilation model. For purposes of research economy, cultural and structural subtypes alone might be used, or more desirably, four subtypes: cultural, structural, marital, and identificational. There might be good theoretical reasons for assigning variable weights to scores on the different types, although this is not an issue that need concern us here. (3) *Degree of conflict* existing in the society between the minority group or groups in the society and the majority group and among each other. (4) *Degree of access to societal rewards*—economic, political, institutional, and so on—for the minority group or groups in comparison with the majority group. This is an equality dimension.

For purposes of expository economy, we may arbitrarily trichotomize each of the continuous variables in this complex into high, moderate, and low to illustrate some possible outcomes. One outcome for minority group *A* might be high cultural assimilation, low structural assimilation, moderate degree of total assimilation, high degree of conflict, and low degree of access to societal rewards. Another outcome for minority group *B* might be high cultural assimilation, moderate structural assimilation, moderate total assimilation, low degree of conflict, and high degree of access to societal rewards. This type of constellation or profile, in my opinion, identifies the essential features of the minority group's position in the society at a given time. The research strategies for obtaining the requisite measures, while posing difficulties, offer no insuperable theoretical obstacles. Their discussion, however, is not within the scope of this chapter. It will be noted that this scheme, while it incorporates the variable of conflict in the dependent variable complex, by implication places power on the independent variable side of the causal equation.

Let us turn now to a consideration of the more important independent variables relevant for a general theory of racial and ethnic group relations. In fact, what I shall attempt to do is to make a classification of the types of appropriate variables, list some that belong in each type, and discuss one or two from each list that seem to deserve particular attention. Finally, on the basis of the foregoing, I shall attempt to illustrate the possible nature of such a general theory by suggesting several hypotheses and questions which would properly derive from it.

I would classify the relevant independent variables under three rubrics: *bio-social development variables, interaction process variables,* and *societal variables.* Bio-social development variables refer to those relating to the biological organism which is man, and the shaping of that biological organism, within conceivable limits, by the social environment in the process of attaining adulthood. Interaction process variables refer to social psychological processes of interaction among adults, and societal variables refer to collective structures and phenomena pertaining to the demographic, ecological, institutional, valuational, cultural, and stratificational features of a society which are the sociologists' stock in trade and need no further definition here.[8]

Bio-social development variables. The biological organism of man contains capacities, indeed imperatives, for acting on three levels: the satisfaction of physiological desires, cognition, and emotional or affective response. This bundle of imperatives is acted upon by the social environment in the attempt to effect a socialization which will allow the developed person to function within the bounds of societal and subsocietal demands. This process, I believe, is rarely completely successful and the resulting tensions and dynamics both make and record the relation of man to his social milieu. In this ongoing process the human organism develops a sense of self. Since society is constantly and, in my opinion, inevitably evaluative and value-giving, the protection of the self, not only in the physical and physiological sense, but at least as importantly, in the social-

8. Obviously, interaction processes take place among children and adolescents, as well. The distinction made here is for the purpose of separating out the developmental stage from a later stage.

psychological sense, becomes the dominating theme of personality development and human interaction. The capacities to be both co-operative and aggressive, altruistic and selfish, are all contained within this framework. The significance of this viewpoint for intergroup relations is that the sense of ethnicity (in the larger definition of racial, religious, or national origins identification), because it cannot be shed by social mobility, as for instance social class background can, since society insists on its inalienable ascription from cradle to grave, *becomes incorporated into the self.* This process would appear to account for the widespread, perhaps ubiquitous presence of ethnocentrism, and perhaps even more crucially means that injury to the ethnic group is seen as injury to the self, and the intensity of the passions engendered by ethnic conflict becomes of a magnitude comparable to those engendered by threats to the individual.[9] In other words, man defending the honor or welfare of his ethnic group is man defending himself.

A consideration of the role of self in the process of bio-social development inevitably raises questions about the concept of "human nature" and its potential connection to a theory of racial and ethnic intergroup relations. Virtually since its inception, the discipline of sociology, attempting to carve out a distinct field of inquiry for itself, reacting against a naive biological determinism that had traditionally dominated man's thinking about human behavior, and, later, rejecting the proliferating "instinct" theories of some early psychologists, has with few exceptions resolutely turned its back on the question of human nature, assuming implicitly or explicitly either that man was infinitely plastic and malleable, and thus basically formed for better or worse by the particular social and cultural environment in which he was socialized, or alternately, that the question was not relevant.[10]

It has become more and more apparent, however, that the question of human nature is relevant—that it must be faced—since any

9. See the role of ethnocentrism in Donald L. Noel's paper, "A Theory of the Origin of Ethnic Stratification," *Social Problems*, 16 (Fall 1968), 157–172.

10. An early critic of alleged overemphasis on cultural conditioning in the sociological discipline was A. H. Hobbs in *The Claims of Sociology* (Harrisburg, Pa., The Stackpole Co., 1951). See, particularly, his chapter 3 on "Personality."

theory of social action must inevitably deal with the nature of the social actor, however formed; and some observers, including myself, have become increasingly struck by the persistent similarities in human behavior across cultural lines and historical epochs and have begun to wonder whether there are not biological constants or propensities in human behavior which fall short of the "instinct" category but which predispose the actor to certain kinds of behavior in a more forceful fashion than the tenets of conventional cultural determinism would allow. Thus a pair of contemporary anthropologists speak of a biologically programmed "behavioral infrastructure of human societies," and point out that "This view of human behavior . . . makes the organism an active, searching, and stubborn participant in the learning process, rather than just a receiver; it suggests that the teacher is as moved to teach in a certain way as the pupil is to learn. The slate [the familiar *tabula rasa*] here is not blank at all; it is doing a lot of its own writing." [11]

At least two important sociological works of the past few years, in which the authors dealt with standard theoretical issues in sociology, have recognized the necessary link between the problems they were respectively dealing with and the question of human nature. Gerhard Lenski in *Power and Privilege: A Theory of Social Stratification* integrates in his theory of why social stratification exists and at what magnitude it exists under varying conditions a variety of cultural, social, and environmental variables with certain postulates or "constants" concerning man and society.[12] One of these postulates is that man is predominantly selfish or self-seeking when it comes to areas of choice of large importance to himself or his group.[13] This postulate plays a decisive part in Lenski's theory, since he conceives of it as the major motivational force in the dif-

11. Lionel Tiger and Robin Fox, *The Imperial Animal* (New York, Holt, Rinehart and Winston, 1971), pp. 13, 15.

12. New York, McGraw-Hill, 1966.

13. Lenski's exact statement reads as follows: "Thus, when one surveys the human scene, one is forced to conclude that when men are confronted with important decisions where they are obliged to choose between their own, or their group's, interests and the interests of others, they nearly always choose the former—though often seeking to hide this fact from themselves and others." (*Power and Privilege*, p. 30; partly italicized in original.)

ferential appropriation of economic surplus which produces social stratification.

Similarly, Tausky, in his analysis of major theoretical perspectives about the behavior of men in work organizations,[14] compares the classical or scientific management theory of Frederic Taylor, based on a conception of man as motivated by self-interest, with the "human relations perspective" which focuses the worker's motivation by means of affective relationships and "self-actualizing" on organizational goals, and himself opts for the "structuralism perspective," a somewhat intermediate view which, he notes, is "closer to that of scientific management than to human relations." Which view one takes, Tausky points out, is predicated to a considerable extent upon one's conception of human nature as either based primarily on self-interest and thus essentially indifferent to organizational needs, or the contrary. "Try as I might," Tausky states, "I remain skeptical about human relations. Research which attempts to validate the human relations perspective has not, in my judgment, successfully done so. Let me state baldly the basis for my skepticism. It is simply that I do not share the optimism about human nature embedded in human relations writings." [15]

Any attempt to formulate a conception of human nature which can be used as a primary building block in a theory of social action must deal not only with a selfish-altruistic dimension but also with the crucial and ubiquitous phenomenon of human aggression. Psychoanalysts, psychiatrists, psychologists, and sociologists have struggled with this issue for several generations with indecisive results. Some see man as basically non-aggressive but seduced into aggressive behavior by corrupt institutions and defective socialization. Others, following Freud, find aggression to be deeply embedded in the early development of the psyche as a result of incorporation into a "death wish" or through a relationship with sexuality. Some ethologists posit a specific instinct for aggression as a function of man's close evolutionary relationship to other animal species (this assumes, of course, the presence of an instinct for aggression in

14. Curt Tausky, *Work Organizations* (Itasca, Ill., F. E. Peacock Publishers, 1970).
15. Ibid., p. viii.

these other species). Still others, in a thematic development which goes back to the work, a generation ago, of John Dollard, and also has roots in Freudian psychology, consider aggression among human beings to be a likely response to situations of frustration. The theory of the origins of aggression in man, however, which I find most persuasive and congruent with my own observations has recently been brilliantly stated in a new book by the psychiatrist Gregory Rochlin.[16] In a sense, Rochlin's formulation appears to be closely related to the frustration–aggression theory mentioned above; however in Rochlin's hand the frustration–aggression mechanism is put into a larger framework with an organizing principle of its own.

Briefly stated, Rochlin's thesis is that aggressive behavior among human beings is not instinctive, but rather derives from the fact that man, unlike other animal species, has a distinct psychological concept of self; that love of the self, or narcissism, is the most basic human feeling; and that injuries or threats to the self, which are omnipresent in human life, evoke aggressive responses. In short, aggression is the inexorable response to continually embattled narcissism. "Neither metaphor nor a mere label," writes Rochlin, "narcissism, this love of self, is the human psychological process through which preserving the self is assured. In infancy, childhood, maturity and old age, the necessity of protecting the self may require all our capabilities. And, when narcissism is threatened, we are humiliated, *our self-esteem is injured,* and *aggression appears.*" [17] And in a more rhetorical vein he declares:

The compelling imperative for self-preservation is self-love. It expresses itself in an endless lust for a rewarding image of oneself, whether that image is seen in a glass or in another's eye. The further passion for praise, honor and glory makes for an endless marathon. We enter it remarkably early in our existence and leave it only when we expire. Self-love . . . is a governing tyrannical principle of human experience, to which aggression responds as a bonded servant.[18]

16. *Man's Aggression: The Defense of the Self* (Boston, Gambit, 1973).
17. Ibid., p. 1. Italics as in original.
18. Ibid. Rochlin, like most social scientists, acknowledges that human aggression is not always destructive—that, in fact, it can play a creative role in societal af-

Another area of human functioning, as we have mentioned before, is the cognitive one. While emotional tendencies and predispositions may well be of greater importance in the formation of racial and ethnic prejudice, still it would appear that the ability to avoid stereotyping by noting distinctions among people in an out-group, to discern connections between historico-cultural experience and group behavior, to think of groups in terms of the distribution of individuals along the normal or bell-shaped curve, to imagine the functional value of cultural diversity, to foresee the disfunctional consequences of unchecked and exacerbated conflict—are all characteristics related in some measure to level of intellectual functioning. We should all like to believe that the general or average level of human intellectual capacity is quite sufficient to encompass all these tasks; but the dominant role of racism and intergroup conflict in the Western world in the several centuries ushered in by the Enlightenment should give us at least some pause before making this assumption with extreme confidence.

To hypothesize or to assert as postulates that man is basically selfish, narcissistic and perpetually poised on the edge of aggression, and intellectually somewhat wanting, is not, of course, to prove these conceptions of the human condition. Numerous illustrative examples in life, literature, and history can be quickly adduced, but so can some examples on the other side. We are clearly dealing here with matters of statistical frequency, central tendency, more or less, mostly or partly, differences of degree, and so on. Moreover, as I have mentioned before, there are socializing forces and institutions in society which begin the process of controlling, taming, and shaping man from the day of his birth onward designed to predispose him to display cooperation, altruism, and socially beneficial behavior toward his fellow human beings and to develop attitudes of sympathy, concern, and responsibility which would make such behavior a function of internal attitudes as well as external sanctions. Even here, however, one must reckon with certain capacities of the individual, classically identified in the psychological literature, for (among others) rationalization, self-

fairs. Nevertheless, it is the destructive aspects of aggression which occupy most of his attention.

delusion, selective perception, and hysterical repression, which allow, in Freudian terms, the id to outwit the superego while ostensibly accepting the socially certified comfort of the latter's hegemony.

In any event, the process is a dialectic one. Where to categorize the presumed statistical result determines one's judgment about the character of the individual actor whose multiple interactions make up the social process. Unfounded optimism in this matter will do no service for the cause of improved intergroup relations and will inhibit the scientific understanding on which true and lasting progress must be based. Total pessimism would foreclose all actions designed to alleviate racial and ethnic tensions, and seems to me also unjustified as a scientific judgment. It is my view, however, that the conception of man as basically motivated by self-interest, irresistibly narcissistic and protective of the self, ready to defend the self by aggressive behavior (however defined and however circumscribed), and possessed of not unlimited intellectual capacity, is a more plausible portrait of the human being than any others which have as yet been advanced. When we add to this conception of the resolute defender of the self and the vigilant watcher over its well-being the hypothesis which I stated earlier—namely, that the sense of ethnicity, by virtue of its totally ascriptive nature, becomes incorporated into the self—we are then ready to insert into a theory of racial and ethnic contact the actor who, with his fellow actors, is at one time part of the cause and at another time, or perhaps simultaneously, part of the effect in the ever recurrent drama of intergroup relations.

Interaction process variables. Those that seem particularly important with regard to intergroup relations would include stereotyping, which stems from what would appear to be rather widespread cognitive inadequacies reinforced by affective tendencies and lack of equal-status primary group contact between groups; frustration-aggression mechanisms in which aggression is easily produced by frustration and directed, depending upon accessibility, either toward the perceived source or toward scapegoats; felt dissatisfaction phenomena based on the mechanisms of relative deprivation, rising expectations, status inconsistency, and cognitive dissonance (it is this cluster which has been most successfully adduced to date to explain the rise of the Negro Protest and Black Power movement in the late 1960s); [19] calculation of success chances in goal-attainment based on conflict—an intellectual or cognitive phenomenon which is not unaffected by emotional considerations but which also operates in the context of estimation of the amount and kind of restraint or punitive forces which are likely to be brought to bear; and, finally, a process which appears to me to be well-nigh universal in human interaction, namely, that of conflict escalation—the tendency for parties in conflict to react to each other's threats and reprisals by escalating the level of aggression, punishment, and revenge unless checked by either overwhelming power, exhaustion, or conflict-reducing mechanisms which we at present know too little about. [20]

Stereotyping and the frustration-aggression dynamic have received considerable attention in the sociological and psychological literature on intergroup relations. [21] It is the last three processes: felt dissatisfaction phenomena, calculation of success chances, and conflict escalation—and particularly their interrelationships—which I should like to explore in greater detail in this chapter.

19. See the excellent and groundbreaking discussion of these phenomena in James A. Geschwender, "Explorations in the Theory of Social Movements and Revolutions," *Social Forces,* 47 (December 1968), 127–135.

20. See Lewis Coser's comment that "In the state of nature, to use Hobbesian terminology, conflict, whether it be waged for gain, for safety, or for glory, 'ceaseth only in death.' Hobbes' philosophical vision can be translated into modern sociological terminology when we note that social conflicts tend to continue or to escalate, and to end with the total destruction of at least one of the antagonists, when unchecked by societal regulation and by deliberate actions of the contenders. Social structures always contain or create mechanisms that help control and channel conflicts through normative regulation. Yet the degree to which conflicts are so regulated varies considerably." *Continuities in the Study of Social Conflict* (New York, The Free Press, 1967), p. 37.

There is a growing and interesting literature that embraces conflict escalation from the point of view of game theory and/or the analysis of war and international relations. See, for example, Herman Kahn, *On Escalation* (New York, Praeger, 1965); Thomas C. Schelling, *The Strategy of Conflict* (Cambridge, Harvard University Press, 1960); and Amitai Etzioni, *The Hard Way to Peace* (New York, Collier Books, 1962).

21. For a classic statement, see Gordon W. Allport, *The Nature of Prejudice* (Cambridge, Addison-Wesley, 1954).

Man is apparently and irretrievably a comparer.[22] That is, he makes judgments about his own needs and their satisfaction not only on the basis of absolute criteria—I am hungry; I am fed and thus satisfied—but on the basis of comparisons with others—he is better fed than I; or I am better fed than he. This mechanism applies, of course, not only to material satisfactions, but also to status issues where the range of possible positions is virtually limitless. The points of reference in this endless process may be not only the individual and other individuals, but his group or groups and other groups. Empirically, the individual and group referents are likely to become inextricably intertwined. Thus the individual is potentially in the situation of comparing the material or status position of himself and his ethnic group with the material and status achievements of members of other ethnic groups and of the other ethnic groups as entities.

With the issue posed in this way, the question we need to ask is why such endless invidious comparisons and their implicit strivings do not produce a level of conflict among individuals and groups which bursts the bonds of societies asunder. The answer, it seems to me, is that the transmuting of felt dissatisfaction into conflict depends on three other factors, two of which play a strong role in determining the level of felt dissatisfaction itself, and the third of which powerfully determines whether felt dissatisfaction will actually turn into overt conflict. Let us examine these stages in the process serially.

The two factors which produce the level of felt dissatisfaction itself are the value system, and the attendant ideologies, of the respective comparing individuals or groups and the actual nature or profile of the reward system. Even these two factors interact with each other in myriad ways, since the values and ideologies concerning the just distribution of rewards will influence feelings about the reward system, whatever it may be. An individual in a low economic and status position in a caste or estate form of society may accept his position with equanimity as foreordained by the gods or

22. See Robert K. Merton, chaps. 8 and 9 on reference group behavior in *Social Theory and Social Structure* (Glencoe, The Free Press, 1957). (Chap. 8 was written in collaboration with Alice S. Rossi.)

the divinity. Or one in an open class society may believe that he has a sturdy chance for upward mobility if he is industrious and thrifty or acquires the requisite educational skills. In these two instances felt dissatisfaction is kept at a low level by acceptance of the prevailing ideology by all parties. And in the latter case where the reward system actually provides perceived cases of upward mobility, this perception adds to the forces which minimize felt dissatisfaction. Translated into group terms, a suppressed ethnic group in a racist society which accepted the usually prevalent ideology in such a society which stigmatized it as inferior would conceivably have a low degree of dissatisfaction (scholars are coming to question the actual substantive existence of such acceptance historically, but here we are for the moment concerned with theoretical possibilities in a model), or a suppressed ethnic group in a somewhat open society with substantial upward mobility opportunities which in practice were continually being exercised by members of all groups would presumably also have relatively low rates of dissatisfaction.

If the value systems of the respective individuals and groups do not simultaneously legitimate the given rewards system, however, or if the rewards system is so extreme in its manifestations of inequality that any value consensus would be continually thwarted by the sheer pressure of lack of satisfaction of human needs at a bearable level, then the third factor, if present in the situation, will come into play to reduce overt conflict; that factor is the system of perceived sanctions based on force or power aimed at suppressing revolt, threatening physical attacks on the system, disruptive demonstrations, and so on. In other words, there is, to use my previously suggested phrase, a "calculation of success chances" prior to the projected action which will play a powerful role in determining whether the action will, in fact, be undertaken. The entire process of combining value impetus with a judgment of the probability of carrying out the action without incurring prohibitive punishment is somewhat similar to the concept of the "dynamic assessment" immediately prior to the initiation of action which was advanced by MacIver a generation ago in his analysis of action and causality.[23]

23. R. M. MacIver, *Social Causation* (Boston, Ginn and Co., 1942). See particularly chaps. 11 and 12.

There is a pronounced tendency in recent sociological writings to minimize the role of perceived sanctions in human action and to conceive of the human actor as responding largely to valuations, ideology, and emotional forces in actualizing behavior. While these forces clearly do make up a significant portion of the field of stimuli which propel behavioral responses, given the perpetual tension between human desires and societal restraints, it seems illusory to me to ignore the important role which perceived power sanctions play in governing the passions of men.[24] This formula applies, I believe, both at the micro level of individual action and the macro level of group action. It is certainly true that both individuals and groups may at times under situations of extreme stress act violently or disruptively to relieve their anger or frustrations, or their sense of being unfairly treated, regardless of perceived probable consequences. But our hypothesis is that, statistically speaking, perceived power sanctions substantially reduce the level of overt violent conflict between competing or potentially conflicting individuals and groups. It should go without saying that this is a sociological statement, not a value judgment bearing on the question of the desirability or undesirability of using violence or disruption to redress grievances under particular circumstances. The attempt here is to suggest a processual model of human behavior which actually has application to both micro and macro situations of human contact and to many fields besides that of racial and ethnic relations.

If conflict does erupt between contending individuals or groups, it has a distinct tendency to escalate, all other things being equal. This proposition follows from our discussion of the overriding nature of the propensity to defend the self—and the ethnic group which becomes incorporated into the self. Conflict, virtually by definition, is viewed, usually quite correctly, by each of the contending parties as either a physical attack on the self, a threat of physical attack on the self, or a psychological attack on the self. The emotional anger engendered by this attack syndrome dictates a coun-

24. These sanctions may, of course, be either legal or illegal. For an important recent and more extensive statement of a similar viewpoint, see William J. Goode, "The Place of Force in Human Society," *American Sociological Review*, 37.5 (October 1972), 507–519.

terattack of some kind, which is then viewed by the other of the
contending parties as an attack on *his* sense of selfhood. This first
party will then reattack with even greater vehemence. And so the
escalation of conflict proceeds. If escalating conflict is not to reach
the point of annihilation of one or both of the contending parties,
some conflict-reducing mechanism or mechanisms must be brought
into play. Such mechanisms consist of institutional arrangements
supported by societal power for the resolution of certain kinds of
conflict—for instance, legal adjudication, arbitration, decision by
the rules, so to speak (but the rules supported by authority, or legal
power), internal controls in the personality implanted by the socialization process, or by the signalized retreat or submission, however
temporary, of one of the contesting parties in the face of power
"calculated" to be for the time being insurmountable and even
more threatening to the self, physically or psychologically, than
continuance of the conflict.

   In the case of disadvantaged ethnic groups in a given society, understandably dissatisfied with their disadvantaged position, if they
can count on a favorable ideological climate and operate through
legitimated parliamentary channels to press their claims for an end
to discrimination and prejudice and for special programs of aid to
effect their normal distribution into the economic and political institutions of the society, the eruption of overt power conflict with
its escalating tendencies can probably be avoided. If the dominant
tendency in ethnic relations becomes an overt power struggle,
however, the escalating tendencies in such a struggle project a
precarious future—one in which the costs are unknown and the
benefits uncertain.

   Societal variables. These variables include a cluster of demographic phenomena such as absolute size of the majority and
minority groups, their relative size, and their comparative rates of
natural increase. Included in this group are also territorial dispersion
and concentration of minority groups by region, rural-urban residence, and section of city.[25] Another cluster of societal variables

   25. See, for instance, Karl E. Taeuber and Alma F. Taeuber, *Negroes in Cities*
(Chicago, Aldine Publishing Co., 1965); Stanley Lieberson, "The Impact of Residential Segregation on Ethnic Assimilation," *Social Forces,* 40 (October 1961),

consists of value consensus or dissensus between the majority and minority groups and specifies the particular areas where such consensus or dissensus exists. This cluster has already been examined in connection with its role in felt dissatisfaction phenomena. Still a third group of variables is made up of cultural differences between the majority and minority groups existing at the time of initial contact. For instance, differences in language or religion which existed at the time of first meeting presumably would have a cumulative influence on the extent of cultural assimilation conceptualized as a dependent variable at the time of study. A fourth variable is the nature of ideologies about racial, religious, and ethnic groups present in the general population and concerns the degree of equalitarianism and humanitarianism present in these ideological systems and also the degree and type of assimilation or pluralism desired. A fifth major group of variables devolves around the distribution of power between majority and minority groups. The distribution of competitive power, political power, and disruptive power quite clearly affects the outcome of our designated dependent variable profile. Here, however, the analysis becomes even more complex, since the mobilization of power resources does not operate in a structural vacuum but depends on the perception of threatened restraints, punishment, and application of countervailing power which help to make up what might be called "the field of power vectors." Frustration and perceived need provide the motive power for action toward desired goals, but such action, as I have pointed out, also has a cognitive component of estimation of the probable degree of negative sanctions.

Sixth, the degree of access to societal rewards (the equality-inequality dimension) available to the minority ethnic group affects the degree of felt dissatisfaction of the group and thus affects the dynamics of social change which determine the outcome at any given time. That this variable thus appears on both the dependent and independent variable sides of the causal chain should produce no great methodological disquietude, since this simply attests to the

52–57; and W. Clark Roof, "Residential Segregation of Blacks and Racial Inequality in Southern Cities: Toward a Causal Model," *Social Problems*, 19 (Winter 1972), 393–407.

constant feedback and interaction effects of factors in societal processes.

Seventh, the political nature of the society with regard to the democratic-totalitarian scale or dimension should be recognized as an important variable for outcomes in intergroup relations.[26] This variable interacts with the power variable, since its position determines whether ideological and value positions and their behavioral implications for ethnic group relations can be fought out in the legislative and public opinion arenas by concerned citizens' groups, or whether such decisions are made by a small group of rulers at the top and handed down and enforced by the concentrated power of governmental control in the hands of the totalitarian state.

I have already discussed the "distribution of power" variable at several points and noted its useful categorization into competitive, political, and disruptive subtypes. Another dimension of power which it is necessary to isolate and subclassify, with regard to the ethnic group context, is whether the power of the group, whatever its degree, comes exclusively from inside the society in which it is located (either from its own power base or with internal allies), or whether its power is augmented by allies from outside the sovereign host society. Many or most ethnic groups within a given society or state have ancestral ties of language, religion, race, or national origins with some other sovereign state. If the ancestral sovereign state is militarily powerful, or has strategic interests or ideology in common with the host sovereign society, the latter may be constrained to attenuate or eliminate discriminatory measures against the minority ethnic group within its borders. In other words, ethnic group relations in the modern interconnected world operate within an international as well as an internal context (under conditions of actual international conflict—that is, war—this fact can operate, of course, to hinder as well as help a given minority—in this case one which is ancestrally derived from the now defined "enemy"). We may thus distinguish between "inside power" derived from the minority's own power position plus that of internal allies, if any, and "outside power"—that augmentation

26. See Schermerhorn, *Comparative Ethnic Relations*, chap. 5, and particularly pp. 186–187.

of power stemming from the friendly interest in the minority's welfare of another sovereign state, or, conceivably, an international body (for example, the United Nations), the degree of such augmentation being a function of the actual power such a state or body has and is willing to use in order to influence relevant events in the host society.

The final point which I should like to raise and discuss briefly in this consideration of societal variables takes us back to the issue of ideologies about racial and ethnic group relations present in the society and held respectively by the majority and the minority groups. As I have indicated, these can be categorized along an equality-inequality dimension. In this sense, we can distinguish very roughly between ideologies which are essentially inequalitarian or racist and those which are essentially equalitarian and non-racist. Within the latter group, however, three subtypes seem to have particular relevance in the contemporary world. One is an assimilationist structure in which the presumed logical goal would be eventual complete assimilation along the various dimensions previously distinguished in the assimilation process. The two others are essentially pluralist structures which need to be carefully distinguished from each other, since their differences constitute crucial points of current controversy in many pluralistic settings over the world, and their actual respective implementations could well have differential consequences for outcomes in intergroup relations.[27]

The first type I would call "liberal pluralism." It is characterized by the absence, even prohibition, of any legal or governmental recognition of racial, religious, language, or national origins groups as corporate entities with a standing in the legal or governmental process, and a prohibition of the use of ethnic criteria of any type for discriminatory purposes, or conversely for special or favored treatment. Many members of such groups would, of course, receive benefits provided by legislation aimed at the general population in connection with problems produced by lack of effective economic participation in the society: for example, anti-poverty measures,

27. Some of the distinctions noted below are insightfully discussed by Daniel Bell in his essay "On Meritocracy and Equality," *The Public Interest*, no. 29 (Fall 1972), 29–68.

housing, education and welfare measures, and so on. Members of disadvantaged ethnic groups would thus benefit as individuals under social programs in relation to their individual eligibility, but not in a corporate sense as a function of their ethnic background. Structural pluralism under these circumstances would exist voluntarily, as an unofficial societal reality in communal life, as would also some measure of cultural pluralism, at the will of the ethnic group members, and subject to the pressures toward conformity to general societal norms implicit in whatever degree of industrialization and urbanization was present in the society. Equalitarian norms in such a society would emphasize equality of opportunity and the evaluation of individuals on the basis of universalistic standards of performance. Such a model of society is very close, it will be recognized, to that implicitly envisaged by the "liberal expectancy" mentioned earlier in this chapter.

The contrasting pluralistic structure may be called "corporate pluralism." Under corporate pluralism racial and ethnic groups are formally recognized as legally constituted entities with official standing in the society. Economic and political rewards, whether in the public or private sector, are allocated on the basis of numerical quotas which in turn rest on relative numerical strength in the population or on some other formula emanating from the political process. Equalitarian emphasis is on equality of condition rather than equality of opportunity, and universalistic criteria of reward operate only in restricted spheres themselves determined in a more particularistic manner. Structural pluralism is officially encouraged, and indeed becomes the necessary setting for individual action, and cultural pluralism tends to be reinforced even in urban and in industrial settings.

Putting together the equality dimension with the structural dimension, we may thus distinguish four types of societies with regard to ethnic orientation: (1) racist, (2) assimilationist, (3) liberal pluralist, and (4) corporate pluralist. In practice, of course, elements of several types may exist at any given time in combination. Nevertheless, in a theoretical sense, these four types need to be distinguished from each other. Both as ideological goals of either minority or majority, and as actual conditions of given societies in a particular period, they may influence the outcome of racial and ethnic group relations in the next stage of the society's existence.

APPLICATIONS: SOME THEORETICAL PROPOSITIONS

Within the appropriate limits of this chapter, I shall be able to select only a few major variables which seem to me most salient and construct some plausible causal chains. As an initial strategy, I shall consider some actual historical situations of intergroup relations and apply the variables previously adumbrated. Most observers would agree that the two most devastating and horrendous examples of intergroup relations in the past four hundred years were the enslavement of four million Negroes of African descent in the American colonies and American state prior to the Civil War and the murder of six million Jews by the Nazis in the twentieth century. We begin with the bio-social development variables (or relative constants, if one prefers) of the human being conceived as essentially a narcissistic defender of the self, aggressively ready to defend the self, incorporating the sense of ethnicity into the self and displaying the usual ethnocentrism. In the interaction process we focus on the tendency to compare the self invidiously with others, the tendency to conflict escalation, and the potential tempering of this process by the field of power vectors which produces a calculation of success chances prior to the initiation of a given contemplated action. These relative "givens" may be thought of as present in all the causal chains I shall adduce below, although for purposes of conserving space I shall not necessarily refer to them again in the formal propositions.

Within the American colonies, from an ideological point of view, although democratic and relatively equalitarian values applied to whites, they distinctly were not considered relevant to blacks. The overwhelmingly prevalent view of whites toward blacks was racist. With regard to power, the blacks had virtually none. Internally, they were fragmented, socially and culturally, carefully kept uneducated, and unable to acquire by virtue of their bondage the military technology which would have enabled them to revolt with any possibility of success against their masters. Externally, the societies in Africa from which they had been seized had neither the organizational unity nor the military technology with which to even attempt the mounting of a power threat against the technologically advanced white civilization. The use of black slave labor in the South was economically advantageous. Thus we might say in summation: American colonial whites, infused with a racist ideology (equalitarian and democratic values applying to whites only), finding it economically advantageous and thus self-enhancing to enslave blacks, unopposed by countervailing power on this issue from the outside world, moved inexorably into the enslavement of the black population. In propositional terms, this historical example suggests the following:

Racist ideology pervading the majority group plus low degree of "inside" minority ethnic power, plus low degree of "outside" minority ethnic power plus felt opportunity to enhance the self through economic means by massive discrimination *leads to* low degree of access to societal rewards by the minority ethnic group ranging from second class citizenship to slavery plus minimal conflict (at least, in the short run).

In the case of the Jews in Nazi Germany, we note the presence of an endemic racism (anti-Semitism), again a minority relatively powerless internally in either a numerical or potentially military sense, a quickly emerging totalitarian state, and no threat of effective countervailing military sanctions from the outside (World War II did not begin until Germany invaded Poland). In this situation, a genocidal ideology was promulgated by totalitarian rulers who made use of both endemic anti-Semitism and the overwhelmingly effective social control mechanisms and institutions of the modern industrialized totalitarian state to engender support and terrorize any potential opposition to their policy of extermination of the Jews. In propositional terms, we emerge with the following:

Intermediate degree of racist ideology permeating the majority group plus low degree of "inside" minority ethnic group power plus low degree of "outside" minority ethnic group power plus totalitarian government *leads to* low degree of access to societal rewards by the minority ethnic group, quick and intense mobilization of hatred toward the minority group at governmental will, plus massive and quickly terminated conflict ranging in outcome to the point of expulsion or extermination.

It will be noticed that for the purpose of brief exposition here I have chosen to focus, among the dependent variables, on access to societal rewards and degree of conflict, and among the independent variables on ideology, power (both "inside" and "outside"), and the political nature of the society on the democratic-totalitarian scale. I should like to add a further comment on the individual and simultaneous effects of ideology and power on particular outcomes in intergroup relations. In both examples I have used to suggest theoretical propositions, the minority had low "inside" power. In the face of a distinctly racist ideology converted into action on the part of a highly discriminatory majority, an ethnic minority clearly needs augmented power in order to redress the balance and secure its rightful opportunity for an equitable distribution of rewards and respect. It might be inferred from this that I am suggesting that an optimal situation in all pluralistic societies is an equal distribution of power among all groups, majority and minority. I do not, in fact, advance this hypothesis for the following reason, or complex of reasons. In a pluralistic society which operates in a democratic ethos and with equalitarian ideals, albeit with ever present modest degrees of ethnocentrism, a situation of equal power for all groups in the society, given the volatile and escalating nature of ethnic passions, will probably be inherently unstable and conflict producing. The optimal situation in a democratic-egalitarian pluralistic society, I would hypothesize, is one in which the minority group has an *intermediate degree of power*—less than that of the majority, so that it cannot disrupt the society completely, but enough so that it can levy strategic influence to protect its rights—"cause trouble," so to speak, in areas of discriminatory treatment, and in which it is supported by "outside" power in the face of a violent threat of attack by the majority on its existence and legitimate aspirations. "Outside" power—that is, power wielded by another sovereign entity—cannot, in the very nature of things, be wielded often or indiscriminately, or on every or even most day-to-day issues of potential conflict inevitably arising in a pluralistic society. It can serve, however, as a "backup" threat in the face of extraordinary danger to the minority, and, perhaps more usually, in the form of special diplomatic negotiations relating to specific issues of unusually grave concern. A latter recent case in point would be the presumptive influence of American détente and trade relations with the Soviet Union on that country's relaxation of emigration restrictions on its Jewish population.

One final point. I have deliberately refrained from inserting into any causal hypothesis which I have hitherto advanced the influence of the type of pluralism ideologically supported by either majority or minority group, or experienced by the society to date. These two types, in the equalitarian setting, are the liberal type and the corporate type. Most nations in the world either are now or are becoming pluralistic in nature. Even if the battle against outright and overt racism can be won, a conflict between policy choices tending toward either liberal pluralism or corporate pluralism will constitute a significant portion of the dynamics of racial and ethnic group relations in the decades ahead. Which type produces better outcomes in terms of the general welfare—the welfare of all—we do not as yet know. Not enough of the data has yet transpired, much less been studied. My own guess—and it is only a guess—is that, for reasons I do not have space to elucidate here, the liberal variety promises better results. But I may be wrong. History will write its answer. Sociologists will read it, one hopes, correctly. Or, as is said, time will tell.

4

DONALD L. HOROWITZ

Ethnic Identity

In the foothills of the western Himalaya, in the Indian state of Himachal Pradesh, three ethnic groups are caught in a process of close interaction. The Chamialis are centered on the town of Chamba; they are, as Frances L. Nitzberg describes them,[1] more highly educated, more urbanized, and more orthodox in Hindu caste and marriage ritual than the other two groups of concern here. Their advanced and urban position is reflected in their domination of government employment. East of Chamba live the Brahmauris, pastoralists and seasonal migrants in close contact with the Chamialis. The Brahmauris are under stress. Their land is over-populated, there is less of it available, and what is available is of declining quality. Many Brahmauris have taken to employment in Chamba Town. But, within the Brahmauri community, the impact of employment in town has been differential. The Brahmauri Brahmans have been involved more than the Brahmauri Gaddis, a group that is actually an amalgam of several high-caste subgroups. The result is that the Gaddis, despite their high status, are increasingly a depressed community. The term "Gaddis" has become pejorative in Chamba Town, and the Gaddis seem to be reverting more and more to their subcaste identities.

Note: I am indebted to Martin Doornbos for comments on this paper.
1. "Changing Patterns of Multiethnic Interaction in the Western Himalaya," unpublished paper presented at the Annual Meeting of the American Anthropological Association, November 20, 1971. The description that follows is drawn from this paper. Responsibility for the subsequent interpretation is mine.

At the same time, the Brahmauri Brahmans, who were formerly on terms of virtual equality with the Gaddis, have begun to sever their ties with their depressed cousins. They are no longer willing to dine with Gaddis, and have begun to adopt orthodox practices, such as abstention from meat and hard drink, that distinguish them from the Gaddis and identify them with the urban Chamialis. Dependence on Chamba Town has led, on the one hand, to increasing assimilation by the Brahmans and, on the other, to their differentiation from the Gaddis, as well as to heightened internal Gaddis cleavages previously declining in significance.

If these are the consequences of severe dependence, more modest dependence seems to have produced the opposite result for the third ethnic group, the Churahi, largely sedentary folk who live in the hills north of Chamba. The Churahi have suffered fewer population pressures, and those only recently. They have had crop failures and other economic problems, and they have experienced greater contact with Chamba. But their response has been to solidify their group identity and decrease the importance of intra-Churahi differences. Intercaste marriage, even high caste–low caste marriage, occasionally occurs and is tolerated. For the Churahi, dependence has not been a spur to group disintegration and emulation of an external model, as it has for the Brahmauris, but instead has generated greater solidarity and ethnocentrism.

The extent of the emerging shifts in group boundaries in Chamba is worth underscoring. Group identities are in flux now and were in the past. The Gaddis, for instance, are an amalgam of discernible, formerly separate segments. Moreover, the present movement goes in no fewer than five different directions. The Brahmauris are losing internal cohesion and dividing into component parts. Some of these parts are accepting a new identity model, the Chamiali identity, while others, the Gaddis, are further subdividing into ancient subgroups. At the same time, the Chamiali are expanding their boundaries to absorb the Brahmauri Brahmans, provided they in turn render their practices more orthodox. The Churahi, for their part, steadfastly refuse to allow dependence to diminish their identity, but instead heighten their boundaries while reducing their internal cleavages.

This, then, is a capsule of the complexity that prevails among only three out of seven ethnic groups in only one district in only one state in North India. The example is parochial, but there is no reason to think it is unique. Quite the contrary. Group boundaries are often fluid.[2] Yet most research in ethnic relations has tended to take the groups as it finds them, as if they all existed in their present form since time out of mind.

I do not say that the fluidity of boundaries is some new "discovery": it is not. The point is rather that the extent and importance of boundary change have generally been underrated. The matter is of more than purely scholastic significance. How, for example, might anyone evaluate the prospects for assimilationist solutions to ethnic conflict—the kind implied in the once-fashionable phrase "nation-building"—without some systematic understanding of the conditions under which groups obliterate the lines between them?

Nor do I propose to set the matter aright in a short essay. What I aim to do is merely to identify some of the directions boundary change can take, some of the forces that seem to influence those directions, and some of the other movements that may accompany boundary change.

VARIETIES OF ETHNIC CHANGE

Ethnic groups can become larger or smaller, more or less exclusive. "Membership in an ethnic group is a matter of social definition, an interplay of the self-definition of members and the definition of other groups."[3] Most groups change their boundaries slowly and imperceptibly, but some change quickly, deliberately, and noticeably. Ascription is, of course, the key characteristic that distinguishes ethnicity from voluntary affiliation. Ethnic identity is generally acquired at birth. But this is a matter of degree. In the first place, in greater or lesser measure, there are possibilities for changing individual identity. Linguistic or religious conversion will

2. For examples of some analogous trends in Uganda, see May Edel, "African Tribalism: Some Reflections on Uganda," *Political Science Quarterly*, 80.3 (September 1965), 367–370.

3. Immanuel Wallerstein, "Ethnicity and National Integration," *Cahiers d'Etudes Africaines*, 1.3 (July 1960), 131.

suffice in some cases, but in others the changes may require a generation or more to accomplish by means of intermarriage and procreation. In the second place, collective action, in the sense of conscious modification of group behavior and identification, may effect shifts of boundaries, as in the Chamba case. It is, therefore, a putative ascription, rather than an absolute one, that we are dealing with. There are fictions about, and exceptions to, the birth principle for most ethnic groups. Ethnicity thus differs from voluntary affiliation, not because the two are dichotomous, but because they occupy different positions on a continuum.

There are so many related processes of ethnic change that it becomes important to specify exactly the phenomena in question, distinguishing them from others. Here we are focusing on changes in *group boundaries*—changes not in individual but collective identity. A group may become more or less ascriptive in its criteria for membership, more or less acculturated to the norms of some other group, more or less internally cohesive, and more or less ethnocentric or hostile to other groups. Although all these possible changes may bear on questions of group boundaries,[4] they are not quite the same thing.[5]

Also confused frequently with boundary expansion and contraction are changes in the social status of groups arranged in an ascriptive hierarchy. In India, status change and boundary change have often gone together and often been confused. A portion of a caste may find itself more prosperous than the remainder and then proceed to sever its ties in the interest of advancing its collective position, thereby producing two groups where before there was one.[6] Unification, as well as separation, has occurred within the

4. For example, if a group loses its internal cohesion, it may at some point divide into components. If it consistently becomes less ascriptive in its criteria for membership, it is likely to widen its boundaries considerably, as well as to expand its numbers.

5. Cf. Erich Rosenthal, "Acculturation without Assimilation?" *American Journal of Sociology*, 66.3 (November 1960), 275–288. I discuss some of the relations between cultural change and identity change below.

6. David G. Mandelbaum, *Society in India* (Berkeley, University of California Press, 1970), II, 488.

caste system. Some formerly separate castes have merged, and the new unit has often sought upward mobility by discarding the attributes of inferior rank.[7] As a matter of fact, collective mobility is often a motive for merger, in the hope that a larger unit will stand a better chance of attaining higher ritual and social status.[8] While boundary change is sometimes associated with attempted rank change, it is important to note here that neither process is necessary to the other.

As we have already suggested, group boundaries can become either wider or narrower. Some group identities may be lost by *assimilation,* the process of erasing the boundary between one group and another. There are two principal varieties of assimilation. Two or more groups may unite to form a new group, larger and different from any of the component parts. This we refer to as *amalgamation.* In Chamba, the Brahmauris and their subgroup, the Gaddis, are both amalgams that resulted from such a process. Alternatively, one group may lose its identity by merging into another group, which retains its identity. This we call *incorporation.* The Brahmauri Brahmans in Chamba are apparently in the process of being absorbed in this way by the Chamialis.

Differentiation is the narrowing of boundaries by the creation of additional groups. A group may separate into its component parts. This, obviously, is *division.* In Chamba, the Brahmauris were dividing into component parts, one of which, the Gaddis, was further subdividing into *its* component parts. On the other hand, there is the possibility of *proliferation:* a new group comes into existence without its "parent group" (or groups) losing its (or their) identity. There is no case of this reported for Chamba, but the phenomenon exists elsewhere. In certain West Indian societies under slavery, "whites" and "blacks" (themselves amalgams) produced sepa-

7. F. G. Bailey, "Closed Social Stratification in India," *European Journal of Sociology,* 4 (1963), 107–124; Robert L. Hardgrave, "Caste: Fission and Fusion," *Economic and Political Weekly* (Bombay), Special Number (July 1968), 1065–1070.

8. Mandelbaum, *Society in India,* II, 496–499; cf. Mahadev L. Apte, "Voluntary Associations and Problems of Fusion and Fission in a Minority Community in South India," unpublished paper presented at the Annual Meeting of the American Anthropological Association, November 1972, p. 5.

rate "mulatto" or "brown" groups through procreation.[9] In contemporary Bosnia, in Yugoslavia, there is said to be an emerging "Muslim" ethnic group.[10] Those now beginning to be called Muslims were formerly identified as either Serb or Croat (or some combination). But most Serbs are Orthodox Christians, and most Croats are Roman Catholics; heavy emphasis on these religious affiliations as attributes defining ethnic identity has begun to generate a new identity on the part of those who do not possess the same religious attributes.[11] These possible boundary changes are summarized in the following table.

Processes of Ethnic Fusion and Fission

Assimilation		Differentiation	
Amalgamation	Incorporation	Division	Proliferation
			$A \rightarrow A + B$
$A + B \rightarrow C$	$A + B \rightarrow A$	$A \rightarrow B + C$	$(A + B \rightarrow A + B + C)$
Two or more groups unite to form a new, larger group	One group assumes the identity of another	One group divides into two or more component parts	One or more groups (often two) produce an additional group from within their ranks

Despite the manifold possibilities for changes in group identity, some groups seem able to retain their traditional identity more or less intact over long periods of time. The Samaale and Sab of Somalia, with their historical antipathies and their clan subdivisions, seem to be groups of rather early vintage.[12] The Sinha-

9. Donald L. Horowitz, "Color Differentiation in the American Systems of Slavery," *Journal of Interdisciplinary History*, 3.3 (Winter 1973), 509–541.

10. To be distinguished from the Albanian Muslims in Kosovo.

11. Compare the emergence of a "Jurassien" identity among Swiss of the Jura region who are both French-speaking and Roman Catholic. Manfred W. Wenner, "A Comparative Analysis of Modern Separatist Movements: Examples from Western Europe and the Middle East," unpublished paper presented at the Annual Meeting of the American Political Science Association, September 2–6, 1969. For the relation between the Yugoslav Muslim identity and census categories and official policy, see *New York Times*, April 8, 1974, p. 2.

12. See I. M. Lewis, "Integration in the Somali Republic," in Arthur Hazelwood, ed., *African Integration and Disintegration* (London, Oxford University Press, 1967), pp. 251–284.

lese kingdoms of Sri Lanka (Ceylon) embraced a variety of caste subgroups and from time to time absorbed new migrant groups from India, such as the Salagama.[13] The result was an overarching Sinhalese identity which has persisted for a considerable time. The sheer longevity of such groups, however, does not mean that their inclusiveness remains constant. Some groups whose corporate history is measured in centuries are not now the highly open and absorptive entities they once were. The Tonga of Zambia and the Baganda of Uganda customarily welcomed and incorporated ethnic strangers on a considerable scale; neither does, at least to the same extent, any longer.[14] The group identity is traditional, but there have been subtle changes in the solidity of the boundaries and the extent to which membership can be acquired only by birth.

Other groups are simply new. Until relatively recently, the Sikhs, many of whose members were the sons of Hindu families, could hardly be called a distinct ethnic group at all. Sikhism was an offshoot of Hinduism, a religious and military protest against Muslim rule in the Punjab.[15] In the terms of the table, the Sikhs are the product of proliferation. The Kikuyu likewise had no real group coherence in pre-colonial Kenya, and strong subgroup loyalties remain important.[16] The Kikuyu are an amalgam. Many other ethnic groups in Africa and Asia have also been called "artificial," in that they had little or no sense of collective consciousness 50 or 100 years ago. Among these are some of the most clearly identifiable and cohesive actors in the contemporary politics of their respective states—groups like the Ibo of Nigeria and the Malays of Malaysia. It seems somewhat inappropriate to use the frequently employed

13. B. H. Farmer, *Ceylon: A Divided Nation* (London, Oxford University Press, 1963), pp. 26, 31.

14. Elizabeth Colson, "The Assimilation of Aliens among Zambian Tonga," in Ronald Cohen and John Middleton, eds., *From Tribe to Nation in Africa: Studies in Incorporation Processes* (Scranton, Chandler Publishing Co., 1970), pp. 39, 51–52; Edel, "African Tribalism," p. 368; cf. A. I. Richards, "The Assimilation of the Immigrants," in Richards, ed., *Economic Development and Tribal Change* (Cambridge, England, W. Heffer & Son, 1954), pp. 161–188.

15. Baldev Raj Nayar, *Minority Politics in the Punjab* (Princeton, Princeton University Press, 1966), pp. 57–74.

16. P. H. Gulliver, Introduction to Gulliver, ed., *Tradition and Transition in East Africa* (Berkeley, University of California Press, 1969), p. 22.

term "primordial" to describe groups that are products of such recent fission or fusion or, for that matter, groups which have become far more ascriptive than they ever were before.[17]

I have spoken of these processes of expanding or contracting identity as if a person could hold membership in only one such group at a time. Naturally, this is not so. Many old identities are in the process of slowly being abandoned for new, and for this reason more than one identity is often claimed. Even without such a transitional situation, multiple ascriptive identities are the rule, particularly where the several identities are at different levels of generality. A person who identifies himself as a member of a small kin-group or clan for some purposes may also consider himself a member of a larger ethnic aggregation or "nationality" or "race" for others.[18]

Ascriptive identity is heavily contextual. It embraces multiple levels or tiers, and it changes with the environment. An African student in France will identify himself in one way; at home, in another.[19] Under some circumstances, a Lebanese will content himself with his sectarian affiliation (Maronite or Orthodox, Sunnite or Shiite, for example); under other circumstances, he will be compelled to consider himself broadly as a Christian or Muslim.[20] Notwithstanding the multiplicity of ascriptive identities, all levels do not remain equally significant, if only because all contexts do not remain so.

What, then, determines which are the most significant memberships or, to put it more accurately, which of many potential identities will be activated most frequently? More or less perma-

17. The term "primordial" has been subjected to a searching examination by Martin R. Doornbos, "Some Conceptual Problems Concerning Ethnicity in Integration Analysis," *Civilisations*, 22.2 (1972), 268–283. See also his comments on the new categories, "Bantu" and "Nilotic," in Uganda. Ibid., p. 281.

18. These layers of identity are well explored by Charles W. Anderson, Fred R. von der Mehden, and Crawford Young, *Issues of Political Development* (Englewood Cliffs, Prentice-Hall, 1967), chap. 3. For a survey of potential units of identity in Africa, see Elliott P. Skinner, "Processes of Political Incorporation in Mossi Society," in Cohen and Middleton, eds., *From Tribe to Nation*, pp. 177–180.

19. See Otto Klineberg and Marisa Zavalloni, *Nationalism and Tribalism among African Students: A Study of Social Identity* (The Hague, Mouton, 1969), pp. 24–25.

20. Michael C. Hudson, *The Precarious Republic: Political Modernization in Lebanon* (New York, Random House, 1968), p. 21.

nent shifts in the "center of gravity" of ethnic identity seem related to the persistence of certain external stimuli. (What kinds of stimuli we shall consider shortly.) As the stimuli at a certain level persist and outweigh those at other levels, one can begin to think of himself as primarily an Ibo but also an Onitsha Ibo and also a Nigerian, or primarily a Tamil but also a member of the Vellala caste and also a Ceylonese. There is, then, the possibility of a "spillover effect." At a certain point, an identity may become independent or "functionally autonomous" of the stimuli that produced it and may become so internalized as to be invoked even in contexts quite different from the one in which it was formed.[21] These spillover effects or functional autonomies constitute a limitation on the general proposition that identities vary with changes in the context. The fact that ethnic identity is formed by a process of learning provides a brake on the rapidity with which it can change.

There is an additional distinction that must be drawn before considering the dynamics of boundary change. The distinction is between the *criteria* of identity, on which judgments of collective likeness and unlikeness are based, and the operational *indicia* of identity, on which ready judgments of individual membership are made. If the slightest degree of known African ancestry renders a person a "Negro" in the United States, that is the criterion of membership. The indicia are, of course, color, physiognomy, and so on—no one or even all of these being determinative of the criterial question of ancestry. Likewise, in Northern Ireland, group membership is based on Irish (and Catholic) versus Scottish or English (and Protestant) origin. As in many other cases, however, surnames are frequently employed indicia of membership, reliable for the vast majority of group members.[22]

The distinction, clear in principle, is elusive in practice. Indicia

21. On functional autonomy, see K. B. Madsen, *Theories of Motivation* (Kent, Kent State University Press, 1968), pp. 121–122. Cf. Muzafer Sherif and Carl I. Hovland, *Social Judgment: Assimilation and Contrast Effects in Communication and Attitude Change* (New Haven, Yale University Press, 1961), p. 78. See also Henry Teune, "The Learning of Integrative Habits," in Philip E. Jacob and James V. Toscano, eds., *The Integration of Political Communities* (Philadelphia, J.B. Lippincott Co., 1964), pp. 247–282.

22. See Walker Connor, "Nation-Building or Nation-Destroying?" *World Politics,* 24.3 (April 1972), 340.

are evidence of identity; unlike criteria, they do not define it. They are shorthand; they develop after criteria have been adopted (however tacitly). As surrogates, indicia of identity are probabilistic and subject to contradiction, much as the wearing of a uniform or the insignia of an organization can be contradicted by reference to the authoritative roster of members.[23] The confusion between the two arises in part because long usage of an indicium may result in its being treated increasingly as criterial, a possibility that the emergence of the new "Muslim" group in Bosnia may exemplify.

As new identities take hold, then, judgments of individual membership are generally made on the basis of symbols that permit discriminations with a significant degree of reliability, the degree of reliability varying with the importance of the memberships and the extent to which they are tightly ascriptive. The less important the boundaries between ethnic groups, the less reliable the indicia need be and the easier it may be to falsify or mistake membership.[24]

Identities thus tend to crystallize or, in Gordon Allport's language, "condense" around symbols or cues.[25] Allport has suggested that the cues are usually visible. Indeed, they often are, for visual cues have considerable reliability and relative immutability, especially if they are bodily cues. Yet the cues or indicia need not be visible. If the difference is specially significant, there is "increased efficiency in the detection of identifying cues," [26] whether or not those cues are visible. Furthermore, the symbols employed to differentiate group from group may be of widely divergent characters at different levels of identity. An overarching identity may be indicated by language, while a lesser one may be evidenced by a behav-

23. For the use of marks of identity in delineating organizational boundaries, see Herbert Kaufman, *Why Organizations Behave as They Do: An Outline of a Theory* (Austin, University of Texas, 1961), p. 40.

24. See, e.g., the flexible indicia of group membership for "Indians" and "ladinos" in Andean America. Marvin Harris, *Patterns of Race in the Americas* (New York, Walker & Co., 1964), pp. 38–39.

25. Gordon W. Allport, *The Nature of Prejudice* (Cambridge, Addison-Wesley, 1954).

26. Henri Tajfel, "Perception: Social Perception," in David Sills, ed., *International Encyclopedia of the Social Sciences* (New York, Macmillan, 1968), XI, 570. For examples of such efficiency, see Donald L. Horowitz, "Three Dimensions of Ethnic Politics," *World Politics*, 23.2 (January 1971), 240–244.

ioral trait and a still lesser one by a visual one.[27] Finally, it almost goes without saying that a symbol of identity that is of the highest importance in one society may be ignored or interpreted quite differently in the next, depending on the shape and significance of the underlying criteria of identity.

IDENTITY, EXPANDED AND CONTRACTED

On what precise basis previously unrelated groups come to regard themselves as possessing a common identity while excluding others from sharing it remains an essentially unresearched question. Put starkly, we may know that the indicia of identity tend to follow the criteria of identity, but what do the criteria follow?

Generally, two types of variable seem to be most influential in shaping and altering group boundaries. The first is contact with ethnic strangers perceived as possessing varying degrees of likeness and difference. The second is the size and importance of the political unit within which groups find themselves.

These two are, of course, related. Political boundaries tend to set the dimensions of the field within which group contact occurs. That contact, in turn, renders it necessary for groups to sort out affinities and disparities.

It is not really accurate to describe this sifting process as one of "choice" in the sense that one chooses friends or allies,[28] for the end result of the process is the conclusion that some groups are alike by virtue of imputed common ancestry. That is not to rule out instrumental or strategic considerations entirely, but, where these are involved, they are heavily entangled with perceptual judgments of the relatedness of some groups (but not others) within the series encountered in a specific context.

27. Cf. Michael Moerman, "Ethnic Identity in a Complex Civilization: Who Are the Lue?" *American Anthropologist*, 67.4 (October 1965), 1225.

28. This discussion does not, therefore, refer to the kinds of deliberate, instrumental, usually temporary, coalitions described by William H. Riker, *The Theory of Political Coalitions* (New Haven, Yale University Press, 1962), or, for that matter, by Lloyd I. Rudolph and Susanne H. Rudolph, *The Modernity of Tradition: Political Development in India* (Chicago, University of Chicago Press, 1967), pp. 98–101, who use the terms "fusion" and "fission" for short-term allegiances not necessarily regarded as ascriptive.

As this way of putting the problem suggests, what is entailed is an aspect of the general study of social perception and the specific phenomena of assimilation and contrast effects.[29] In matters of social as well as physical judgment, scales of judgment tend to develop, and stimuli are placed on the scale in positions relative to those already in the series. If, for example, a subject is presented with a series of weights, he begins to assign them values relative to each other. The end values of the series serve as "anchors." That is, they exert greater influence on judgment than do the other values on the scale, and judgments tend to be more accurate (where the values are objectively verifiable) and less variable the nearer the stimuli are to these anchors. Shifts in judgment are associated with changes in the range of stimuli (which is to say, changes in the location of the anchors) and in the frequency distribution of the stimuli (which is to say, changes in the median of the stimuli). When the differences between an anchor and a series of stimuli are great, contrast effects are observable: the differences tend to be exaggerated beyond the range of the actual discrepancy, producing a sharp contrast. However, when some items in a series begin to approximate the location of an anchor, assimilation effects are observable: the differences tend to be minimized to a point beneath the range of the actual discrepancy, producing a merger.

The relevance of these phenomena to the emergence of new identities seems clear enough. Here the scale relates to group likeness and unlikeness rather than weight or size. The end points or anchors refer to the range of groups represented; the groups in the particular context constitute the series; and the judgmental question is where particular groups will be placed on the scale. Not merely the range but the frequency distribution—that is, the numbers of particular groups represented at various points in the series—influences the placement process. And assimilation and contrast effects are likely to occur. What looks like a major characterological or behavioral deviation in a parochial environment with

29. For the most thorough treatment of this subject, see Sherif and Hovland, *Social Judgment*. A summary, critique, and updating are contained in Charles A. Kiesler, Barry E. Collins, and Norman Miller, *Attitude Change: A Critical Analysis of Theoretical Approaches* (New York, John Wiley, 1969), chap. 6.

a restricted range of difference may begin to look trivial when the range is expanded. Groups which may have been separate and even mutually hostile in one environment may be identified or identify themselves as one in a new environment of greater heterogeneity. The underlying mechanism is the general perceptual tendency to simplify nuances of difference, ignoring small differences and exaggerating large ones, when these begin to assume an unmanageable degree of complexity. In short, assimilation and differentiation, as we have referred to them, may simply be special cases of assimilation and contrast effects.

If this is a model of the general process of identity change, it still leaves the major substantive questions unanswered. Research on scales of judgment has always proceeded with the stimulus property (weight, size, and so on) specified in advance, but that is the thing most at issue in boundary change: what are the *criteria* of likeness and unlikeness? Furthermore, social judgment is heavily influenced by internalized reference scales, those developed earlier through learning. What kinds of collective experience are likely to have an impact on judgments of identity in a new milieu? These, it seems to me, are two of the principal questions for research investigation.[30]

Despite these crucial omissions, some clues to the bases of identity change are provided by social judgment theory. For one thing, judgments tend to shift toward rewarded values in a series.[31] On this basis, it is reasonable to suppose that somewhat more prestigious ethnic groups will act as magnets for incorporation. This, of course, has been the case for prestigious groups like the Baganda. Moreover, in an ambiguous series, the evidence is strong that the judgments of others become specially influential; the more ambiguous the stimuli, the more suggestible the subjects of experiments are to the views of those around them.[32] This confirms the interplay of self-definition and other-definition in boundary change, and

30. It should perhaps be added that the laboratory seems less well adapted to judgments of ethnic boundaries than to areas of social perception where the responses of casual groups are to be examined.

31. Sherif and Hovland, *Social Judgment*, pp. 74–75.

32. Ibid., pp. 86–87.

focuses attention on the question of who those others are. Finally, casting the problem in the relativistic terms of shifting scales, series, and anchors plants the seeds of doubt about conventional formulations of group boundaries in terms of cultural content or isomorphism. Cultural change may follow or accompany, rather than precede, identity change. If so, the significance of a certain cultural mix as a determinant of identity has probably been vastly overemphasized.[33]

Assimilation may thus not always be dependent on prior acculturation, as has so often been suggested. The relation of cultural change to identity change, and especially the sequencing of the two, may depend on the type of assimilation involved. Because of the frequent assertions that one of the characteristics that *defines* an ethnic group is a distinctive culture, this point is worthy of elaboration.

With respect to cultural conformity, there may be a substantial difference between incorporation and amalgamation. To be "eligible" for incorporation, the group to be merged (group B in the second cell of the table) will probably be required to demonstrate its acceptability by modifying its behavior in advance so as increasingly to assume the modal attributes of members of the incorporating group. That is what the Brahmauri Brahmans in Chamba have in fact been doing. At least some acculturation, therefore, may be a precondition of incorporation.

The same may not be true for amalgamation. To the extent that a new identity is emerging for all the component groups, no one subgroup is in the same position as an incorporating group to impose its own characteristic patterns of belief and behavior. In this situation, therefore, the inclusive, emerging identity may subsequently be threatened by significant cultural deviations as some of the merged subgroups discover at closer range traits among other subgroups which they regard as highly unusual and in need of change. To prevent disruption of the new identity, centripetal forces begin to bring cultural variations into basic harmony.

That is not to say that no differences are tolerated. There is

33. Cf. Fredrik Barth, Introduction to Barth, ed., *Ethnic Groups and Boundaries* (Boston, Little, Brown, 1969), pp. 14, 18, 32–33; Doornbos, "Some Conceptual Problems Concerning Ethnicity," p. 279.

every reason to think that amalgams have little power to force the same kinds of homogeneity on component parts as incorporating groups do. What seems to emerge is a "least common denominator" culture of the amalgam. The grossest deviations are filtered out, and certain modal traits, that may or may not have been associated prominently with particular subgroups, seem to become prominent. Thus, the Islam of Muslims in Mauritius is heavily "sunnified"; "local and sectarian practices" have been abandoned "in favor of a uniform orthodox practice" [34]—this very much the result of the amalgamation of sectarian subgroups. Similarly, Muslims from the Noakhali district of East Bengal are often regarded as especially pious, certainly more so than men of other East Bengal districts. Evidence of religious practices and values among Noakhali cultivators supports the image. But experienced urban factory workers from Noakhali show no especially religious orientation. Howard Schuman concludes that rural-to-urban migrants from Noakhali may be less religious than those who stay behind, but he also suggests that "once in the city they respond to norms that encourage still more relaxation. As the 'deviant' group in piety, the Noakhali men would be most likely to change in an urban work situation where transethnic norms come to prevail." [35]

Other significant deviations are probably also minimized. The Malays of Negri Sembilan, West Malaysia, are often members of the Minangkabau subgroup; this group is atypical in that it practices matrilineality. Other Malays see this "as an odd deviation from the 'normal' Malay pattern." M. G. Swift surmises that, in the course of interaction, "Negri Sembilan Malays tend to accommodate to majority cultural standards." [36] In Nigeria, too, it has been observed:

The cultural renaissance, an integral part of the nationalist movement, has tended to produce greater uniformity within each ethnic group and so differentiate it more sharply from neighboring groups. Thus among

34. Burton Benedict, *Mauritius: The Problems of a Plural Society* (London, Pall Mall Press, 1965), pp. 38–39.

35. "Social Change and the Validity of Regional Stereotypes in East Pakistan," *Sociometry,* 24.4 (December 1966), 436–437.

36. *Malay Peasant Society in Jelebu* (London, Athlone Press, 1965), p. 134. For an example of Negri Sembilan Malays who brought majority standards back to their village, see ibid., pp. 96–98.

the Yoruba, for instance, a standard dialect is emerging and dress styles, both for rich and poor, have a similarity that did not exist a century or two ago. There is in fact a consciousness of being Yoruba which is recent—the term Yoruba applied formerly only to the Oyo Kingdom.[37]

There thus seems to be a general tendency to smooth off rough edges in the behavior of subgroups as amalgamation proceeds.[38]

In amalgamation, as in incorporation, cultural change is fostered. But in the former it is likely to be a lesser conformity that is demanded, and it is likely to be demanded at a later time—not as a prerequisite to identity change, but as an outcome of it. If this is so, it again casts into question the role of perceptions of cultural affinities in boundary change. Aspects of group culture (we do not know which) may certainly be criterial, but, once judgments of likeness and unlikeness are made, cultural adjustments may then be effected to suit the new boundaries.

Let us now look more closely at the impact of changes in the "series" and of the interaction of self- and other-definitions of group identity on ethnic boundary change. All else being equal, the wider the series, the wider the boundaries of groups within it. Students of Africa have often called attention to the importance of migration and urbanization in widening ethnic identities. The growth of small, previously discrete ethnic groups into larger agglomerations, sometimes called "super-tribes," has been well documented.[39] These newer identifications grew as rural-to-urban migrants interacted with stranger-groups for the first time in the towns, discovered commonalities that had not been evident back

37. P. C. Lloyd, "The Ethnic Background to the Nigerian Crisis," in S. K. Panter-Brick, ed., *Nigerian Politics and Military Rule: Prelude to the Civil War* (London, University of London Press, 1970), p. 12.

38. For another example of cultural synthesis, see Abner Cohen, *Custom and Politics in Urban Africa: A Study of Hausa Migrants to Yoruba Towns* (London, Routledge, 1969), p. 159.

39. See Anderson, von der Mehden, and Young, *Issues of Political Development*, chap. 2. See also Crawford Young, *Politics in the Congo* (Princeton, Princeton University Press, 1965), chap. 11; John N. Paden, "Urban Pluralism, Integration, and Adaptation of Communal Identity in Kano, Nigeria," in Cohen and Middleton, eds., *From Tribe to Nation*, pp. 245–246; Immanuel Wallerstein, "Migration in West Africa: The Political Perspective," in Hilda Kuper, ed., *Urbanization and Migration in West Africa* (Berkeley, University of California Press, 1965), p. 156.

home, and then returned to their rural areas of origin to popularize the newly discovered collectivity, to put rural group members
into "vicarious contact" [40] with members of other groups, and often
to reinforce the new identification by political organization designed to embrace the entire group.

That the towns have been the crucibles of group enlargement in
much of Africa does not mean that specifically *urban* contact is necessary for the expansion of group boundaries. The heterogeneous
urban setting merely expands the ethnic series, paving the way for
the blurring of distinctions between some groups and the sharpening of distinctions between others. That this is so can be seen from
similar results in rural or territory-wide settings. As exhibits, three
cases—one African, one Asian, and one Caribbean—can be cited.

The first is the widening of boundaries of the "Shirazi" group in
Zanzibar.[41] The Shirazi were formerly composed of those Zan-
zibaris who claimed mixed Afro-Persian ancestry; hence they did
not include Africans resident in Zanzibar. With a large influx of
mainland Africans, however, the group definition expanded. As
the contrasts with the mainlanders became apparent, Shirazi became a term applied to all "indigenous" (that is, long resident) Africans on Zanzibar, regardless of claims to Persian ancestry. The
Shirazi–mainlander cleavage that developed has had considerable
political significance, manifested, for example, in party politics before the overthrow of the parliamentary regime in 1964.

A second example comes from Malaya (now West Malaysia). At
the time of the British intervention in Malaya in the 1870s, the
"Malay" population was exceedingly varied, comprising groups
that originated from as far afield as Sumatra, the Celebes, Borneo,
and Java, as well as a sprinkling of Arabs. These groups tended to
speak separate languages, to be endogamous and often mutually
hostile and violent.[42] The Chinese who arrived on the scene, in

40. G. William Skinner, "The Nature of Loyalties in Rural Indonesia," in Skinner, ed., *Local, Ethnic, and National Loyalties in Village Indonesia* (New Haven, Yale
University, Southeast Asia Studies, 1959), pp. 7–8.

41. Michael F. Lofchie, *Zanzibar: Background to Revolution* (Princeton, Princeton
University Press, 1965), pp. 81–82.

42. J. M. Gullick, *Indigenous Political Systems of Western Malaya* (London, Athlone
Press, 1958).

especially large numbers after the advent of large-scale tin mining in the nineteenth century, were themselves no less divided by place of origin. So-called dialect differences defined the principal lines of contrast among Chinese, as well as the lines of internecine strife.[43] Within several decades, however—and certainly by the end of World War II—strong, coherent Malay and Chinese identities had, for most purposes, superseded these lesser loyalties.[44] This development was prompted by the juxtaposition of these groups throughout most of the Malay Peninsula.

The third illustration of non-urban group fusion involves the evolution of overriding identities among the African slaves and, later, the indentured East Indian laborers in the former colonial territories of British Guiana (now Guyana) and Trinidad. As is well known, a wide array of ethnic groups was represented among the Africans who were transported to the New World. In spite of the continuing infusion from Africa for two centuries, as well as suggestions that the white planters considered intra-African hostility to be useful for their own security by impeding concerted efforts to revolt,[45] this formidable diversity was homogenized into a single identity. Principally, this was due to the overriding labor requirements of the estates, which made it impossible to perpetuate ethnic differences deriving from Africa, and to the tremendous brutality of the plantation experience, which made it inescapable that the slaves would accept the ethnic definitions of the masters.

A similar, though less complete, fusion occurred among the East Indians imported to work on the estates after the emancipation of the slaves in 1834. For the white planters, the most significant group distinctions were between those who were vital to the sugar

43. For the Chinese divisions, see Victor Purcell, *The Chinese in Southeast Asia* (London, Oxford University Press, 1968), pp. 269–272.

44. As is attested by any general study of Malaysian politics. Nevertheless, intra-Malay and intra-Chinese divisions still have some force. On the Chinese side, see ibid. On the Malay side, see Swift, *Malay Peasant Society in Jelebu*, pp. 22, 88; Peter J. Wilson, *A Malay Village and Malaysia* (New Haven, HRAF Press, 1967), pp. 18–24.

45. See Charles Leslie, *A New History of Jamaica* (London, J. Hodges, 1740), pp. 310–311. Compare Winthrop D. Jordan, *White over Black: American Attitudes toward the Negro, 1550–1812* (Baltimore, Penguin Books, 1969), pp. 111, 185.

economy and those who were not. The personal qualities that were thought by local whites to be associated with effective performance of estate labor (at very low wages) were imputed to Indians as a group. The opposite attributes were ascribed to the African ex-slaves. Despite religious, linguistic, and caste heterogeneity among the Indian immigrants, the Indian population was treated as if it were composed of essentially fungible entities, with no significant ascriptive differences recognized.[46] This was the treatment most compatible with the requirements of managing a relatively undifferentiated labor force. Colonial policies and stereotypes thus helped to solidify the Indian identity as against competing sub-group identities and to demarcate it sharply from the Negro or Creole identity.

Even the division between Hindus and Muslims lost much of its significance in the process. Elsewhere in overseas Indian communities, the partition of India instantly divided the immigrants into "Indians" and "Pakistanis." In East Africa, the entire group was neutrally renamed the "Asian" community.[47] By contrast, Guyanese and Trinidadian Indians came to regard Hinduism and Islam as appropriate alternatives to the Creole religion, Christianity, and so merely as "alternative ways of being Indian." [48] Such divisions elsewhere were partly a product of the closer and continuing contact those Indian communities had with India. But, in large measure, the relatively undivided Indian identity in Guyana and Trinidad can be attributed to the leveling effects of the brutal and intense West Indian plantation experience.

The Malayan and West Indian examples of amalgamation illustrate, not merely the role of new group juxtapositions in producing new groups, but also the role of third-party judgments of affinities and disparities in defining the emerging situation. In both, the

46. See, e.g., Edward Jenkins, *The Coolie: His Rights and Wrongs* (New York, George Routledge & Sons, 1871).

47. See George Delf, *Asians in East Africa* (London, Oxford University Press, 1963).

48. Chandra Jayawardena, *Conflict and Solidarity in a Guianese Plantation* (London, Athlone Press, 1963), p. 23. See also Morton Klass, *East Indians in Trinidad: A Study of Cultural Persistence* (New York, Columbia University Press, 1961), pp. 156, 178–179.

British were heavily influential in the process of fusion. In a significant way, it was the colonial perception of group boundaries that prevailed. Rather crude stereotypes were employed in decision making even in the relatively late colonialism of Malaya. Indians and Ceylonese (who had also immigrated to Malaya) were felt to be indispensable to the management of the railways and post and telegraph offices. "Subordinate posts requiring intelligence and financial skill in the holders were best filled by Chinese." [49] The Malays were said to be "unquestionably opposed to steady continuous work"; [50] hence the encouragement given to immigration. By channeling motivation and recruitment in preconceived directions, colonial policy gave the existence of the emerging groups a firmer basis in the groups' own perceptions than it might otherwise have had. The result was to make each group increasingly conscious of the aptitudes and disabilities, virtues and vices it supposedly held in common.

If this was true in Malaya, it was, of course, many times more true in the West Indies. Although the initial disparities within the African and Indian groups in Guyana and Trinidad may have been greater than the comparable disparities were in Malaya, far more complete fusion was produced in the former than the latter. While Malays and Chinese still evidence their incomplete amalgamation, Caribbean Creoles and Indians are each more firmly bonded. For this result, the more thoroughgoing and oppressive colonialism of the West Indies must be cited. The views of the Europeans and their unimpeded ability to act on them were surely an important reason for the greater assimilation within the Caribbean groups.

This squares very well with experience elsewhere and with social judgment theory. For the Congo, Crawford Young has richly documented the central role of Belgian missionaries, military commanders, and colonial administrators in forging, among others, the Bangala and Mongo communities among colonized peoples lacking a previous sense of commonality. [51] I pointed out earlier that, in

49. Frank Swettenham, *British Malaya* (London, George Allen & Unwin, Ltd., 1948), p. 247.
50. Ibid., p. 139.
51. *Politics in the Congo*, pp. 242–245, 247–249.

judging ambiguous stimuli, the views of others are particularly influential. There is additional experimental evidence that the influence of the others varies with their prestige; the higher their status and power, the less variance in the judgment scales that emerge.[52] On this basis, we would certainly expect ethnically differentiated superiors (in these cases, the colonialists) to exercise a formidable impact on the definition of group boundaries. The more rigidly ranked the system, the greater the influence of ranked superiors.[53]

Two further points regarding changing group boundary perceptions should be noted here. The first relates to the interaction of self- and other-definitions; the second involves spillover effects.

Self-definitions and other-definitions do not necessarily adjust at the same rate, simultaneously producing a new identity. Especially if the new identity is wider than the old, other-definitions are likely to be "ahead of" (that is, wider than) self-definitions for some time. The existence of internalized reference scales often means that an emerging group in a new context may still be psychologically tied to the old, narrower context. If, however, others have had little previous experience with the emerging group, their judgments will be less hampered by knowledge of the old context, and hence they will blur subgroups together more readily.

What often happens, therefore, is that there is a lag in identifications. Others at first perceive the emerging group as more homogeneous than it sees itself. Examples of this are not lacking. "Thus the Fon, Sav, and Popo people who went to the Ivory Coast were not distinguished one from another by the Ivory Coast people, but were lumped together as Dahomeyans and treated as such. Likewise, the Mossi and related but distinct groups from the north such as the Busani and Gurunsi were often lumped together as 'Moshi' by the Ghanaians." [54] The "Biharis" of East Bengal were by no means all from Bihar; they were Muslim migrants from several states in North India whose collective identity the Bengalis had

52. Sherif and Hovland, *Social Judgment,* pp. 89–90.
53. For an example of a highly ranked system, see Horowitz, "Color Differentiation."
54. Elliott P. Skinner, "Strangers in West African Societies," *Africa,* 33.4 (October 1963), 315.

compressed.[55] The same tendency has been observed among Batak in Bandung, Java.[56] Back home in Sumatra, the Muslim Mandailing Batak differentiate themselves from the Christian Toba Batak. In Bandung, however, the Sundanese fail to observe the distinction and merge the two into the category of Batak. This leads the Mandailing to reemphasize what separates them from the Toba, but they have also come to realize that, in the new context, the wider identity has some validity or at least utility; and, on occasion, they, too, have begun to employ it.

Once self-definitions "catch up," however, the same internalized scales have a different effect. The new identity may be invoked even where the context is not quite the same as the new context in which boundaries were re-formed. Whereas earlier the effect of learned identities was to retard change, now its effect is to accelerate and complete it. In Malaya, for example, as the Malay identity superseded the identities of the component subgroups, it was invoked even in areas where contact with the Chinese was of a relatively low order of magnitude.

POLITICAL BOUNDARIES AND IDENTITY CHANGE

Territorial boundaries define the "social space" in which group contact occurs. In terms of social judgment theory, they tend to set the range of the ethnic series within which groups are "placed." Their breadth or narrowness may also suggest some of the rewards of expanded or contracted identities.[57]

The case of the Ibo underscores the importance of formal political boundaries and provides a rather clear instance of the grafting of new layers of identity into old, each available to be invoked as the context seems to require. While the Ibo have operated rather cohesively *as Ibo* at the national level of Nigerian politics, they have divided up at lower levels along lines determined variously by

55. See A. F. A. Husain and A. Farouk, *The Social Integration of Industrial Workers in Khulna* (Dacca, Bureau of Economic Research, University of Dacca, 1963).

56. Edward Bruner, "The Expression of Ethnicity in Indonesia," unpublished paper, Southeast Asia Development Advisory Group, New York, 1972, p. 21. See also Young, *Politics in the Congo,* pp. 240–241.

57. Bailey, "Closed Social Stratification," 121–122; Mandelbaum, *Society in India,* II, chap. 26.

region of origin, lineage, and so on. In the former Eastern Region of Nigeria, colonial administrative units generated new identities that became increasingly relevant as migrants from these areas met in the urban setting of Port Harcourt, an Ibo-majority town. In this contracted context, the Ibo identified themselves by reference to place of origin—this defined by the colonially imposed "intermediate communities of administrative division and province," even though, it should be emphasized, these units were distinguished from each other "primarily by the arbitrary placement of colonial boundaries and only secondarily by cultural variations." [58]

Survey data from pre-Bangladesh East Bengal reveal equally strong district-level allegiances. Asked to name their "country," two thirds of an East Bengali sample named their district.[59] Among the Tonga of southern Zambia, local identities based largely on kinship have gradually given way to an inclusive Tonga identity. However, the "new sense of Tongahood has clashed on occasion with the existence of the three political divisions created by the administration: Plateau Tonga, Valley Tonga, and Toka Leya then view one another as threatening aliens." [60] In Sarawak, East Malaysia, a significant cleavage among the numerically predominant Ibans is based on rivalries between "divisions." During the early years of independence, a person's party loyalties were determined to some extent by whether he was a Second Division Iban or a Third Division Iban; the competition was sometimes frenetic. The five divisions were administrative units imposed by the colonial regime.[61] And in Kinshasa, Zaire (then Leopoldville, the Congo), some of the major ethnic associations of the pre-independence period were actually based on rural administrative divisions.[62]

Despite the "arbitrariness" and "artificiality" of these territorial boundaries, they have come to constitute internalized anchors for

58. Howard Wolpe, "Port Harcourt: Ibo Politics in Microcosm," *Journal of Modern African Studies*, 7.3 (September 1969), 486.

59. Schuman, "Social Change and the Validity of Regional Stereotypes," pp. 429–430.

60. Colson, "The Assimilation of Aliens Among Zambian Tonga," p. 37.

61. See R. S. Milne, *Government and Politics in Malaysia* (Boston, Little, Brown, 1967), p. 100.

62. Young, *Politics in the Congo*, pp. 245–246.

group identity. A colonial administrative unit is not too superficial
a basis for ethnic identity. Interpreting his survey data on East
Bengal, Howard Schuman comments that to an outside observer
the districts seem to be merely administrative units, but to the
Bengalis

they also represent distinct regions, and a man tends to identify and be
identified in terms of the District he "belongs to"—meaning the one from
which he originates . . . From a theoretical standpoint, the Districts can
usefully be regarded as "ethnic groups" in the generic sense of "peoplehood," similar in nature (though less sharply and deeply defined) to nationality groups in the West and to many of the so-called tribal groups in
Africa.[63]

The tenacity of the intra-Ibo provincial rivalries of the same kind,
both before and after the Nigerian civil war,[64] reinforces the same
interpretation.

So far we have been chiefly concerned with the expansion of
group identity, with new and higher levels being superimposed on
old and lower levels. It is quite true, of course, that in the developing world during the colonial period, as in Europe much earlier,
the principal thrust of group contact and colonywide boundaries
was to create larger ethnic groups, many capable of acting with a
considerable measure of cohesion even at the colonial (later the national) level of politics. But it is also true, as I have indicated, that
the more inclusive identities did not always displace entirely or
render vestigial the less inclusive identities. With the multiplication
of contexts, there was typically a multiplication of levels, and some
of the lower levels of identity often remained quite powerful.[65]

Though the general thrust was upward, that was neither the universal nor the exclusive tendency for any given country. Some of

63. Schuman, "Social Change and the Validity of Regional Stereotypes," pp.
429–430 (footnotes omitted).

64. Following the civil war, the federal official appointed to administer the
former secessionist state was accused of favoring his own "subgroup," the Onitsha
Ibo. *Washington Post,* Nov. 30, 1970, p. A-20.

65. For a deadly example, see the role of the southern Tutsi preceding the mas-
sacre of Hutu in Burundi. Victor D. DuBois, "To Die in Burundi—Part I: The
Eruption of Intertribal Strife: Spring 1972," American Universities Field Staff
Reports, Central & Southern Africa Series, 16.3 (September 1972), 4–5.

the most significant ethnic interactions in the post-colonial period in Asia and Africa, and the post-World War II period in the West as well, have involved downward shifts in the focus of group identity. Even during the colonial period some groups were differentiating themselves from others who had earlier been regarded as members of the same group. In nineteenth century India, for example, one of the effects of religious revival movements was to sharpen the lines between Hindus and Muslims.[66] A side-effect was to differentiate Sikhs from Hindus. The reformism of the Hindu Arya Samaj was not very different in content from the Sikhs' own movement, the Singh Sabha. But the Arya Samaj emphasized Hindi as the language of a revitalized Hindu culture, whereas the Sikhs were attached to the Punjabi language. Gradually, the Sikh movement sought to "purify" Sikhism by excising Hindu influences, thereby creating a sense of a distinctive Sikh identity.[67] This, it should be said, was a development that proceeded in the face of centuries of ritual and social interaction, as well as intermarriage and conversion, between Sikhs and Hindus. In short, the earlier boundary was exceedingly fluid, and now, for the first time, an ascriptive Sikh identity emerged.

The alacrity with which groups are able to adjust their identity downward as well as upward demonstrates that changing contexts can work for fission as easily as for fusion. Indeed, in some ways more so, for the availability of lower or "subethnic" levels of identity provides a convenient, preexisting basis of cohesion to which a group can repair if the context in which it operates seems to shrink. Hardly had the Indo-Pakistani subcontinent been partitioned along what were thought to be hard-and-fast Hindu–Muslim lines when, in 1948, Mohammed Ali Jinnah, who had done so much to foster subnational identities in undivided India, ironically found it necessary to warn against the "curse of provincialism" in undivided Pakistan.[68]

The Pakistan case, in fact, exemplifies what appears in retrospect to

66. Hugh Tinker, *India and Pakistan* (New York, Praeger, 1968), pp. 10–12.

67. Nayar, *Minority Politics in the Punjab,* pp. 62–63, 71–73.

68. Quoted in the *Far Eastern Economic Review* (Hong Kong), May 15, 1969, p. 375.

have been a striking pattern of downward shifts in the central focus of ethnic identity in a score or more countries around the time of independence. It is sometimes said that the colonial powers "contained," "suppressed," or "muted" ethnic animosities—though it is also asserted that they "used" ethnic differences to "divide and rule." Although it is difficult to have it both ways, it is not necessary here to pause over these contrasting interpretations. For the more theoretically interesting point about the rising incidence of ethnic conflict as colonial rule neared its end is that it reflected the increasing importance of the local context.[69] While colonial domination lasted, the colony-wide unit was a level of identification of some importance. A man might be an Ibo, but, so far as the Europeans were concerned, he was also a Nigerian, and, in consequence, both identities were significant under different circumstances. The nationalist movements, while they did not always embrace all ethnic groups proportionately, attempted to reinforce the wider identity by emphasizing the common condition of subordination which the colonial powers had imposed. As long as the external context retained its importance, both levels of identity were salient. When the colonial powers retreated, the external context lost much of its meaning, and the duality in levels of identity declined.

How dramatically this occurred could be observed in the events that transpired in the first few Asian and African states to receive independence. With the precipitous partition of India in 1947, several hundred thousand lives were lost in an outbreak of communal murder that spread from Baluchistan in the west to Bengal in the east. The blood was barely dry when, with the new territorial boundaries fixed, a further contraction of identity occurred, and the "provincialism" deplored by Jinnah set in, not only in Pakistan, but also in India. Burma, granted independence a year later, slid into civil and secessionist wars from which, more than a quarter century later, it has not yet fully emerged; while Ceylon, also independent in 1948, took eight years to reach an upsurge of hostility between Sinhalese and Tamils, but when it came, it was exceedingly brutal. The Sudan,

69. It should be made clear that there was surely ethnic antipathy and violence even at the height of colonial rule, but there was much more after the first small steps were taken toward decolonization.

one of the first of the African states to be decolonized, followed the Burmese path. On the eve of independence, Southern troops mutinied, extensive rioting occurred, and a war of secession followed.

At the time, each of these and other cases was viewed as *sui generis*. Of course, each case has its own variations, but each also illustrates a general and powerful tendency: as identity tends to expand with an expanding context, often shaped by expanding territorial boundaries, it tends to contract with a contracting context, again often defined by contracting territorial boundaries.[70] Self-determination, by definition, renders the contracted context the important one. Self-determination thus raises the question of the "self"—it determines very little.

The moving force of assimilation and differentiation is the sense of similarity and difference from others sharing the same space. As the importance of a given political unit increases, so does the importance of the highest available level of identification immediately *beneath* the level of that unit, for that is the level at which judgments of likeness are made and contrasts take hold. There seems to be a kind of "Parkinson's Law" at work, by which group identity tends to expand or contract to fill the political space available for its expression.

CONCLUSION

There are many questions about ethnic boundary change to which there are not, as things now stand, even rudimentary answers. Not only is the formulation of the criteria by which groups

70. It is the significance, as much as the location, of territorial boundaries that affects the relative importance attached to various levels of identity. For some newly independent states, the external context remained important even after the colonialists left. In Somalia, for instance, the first several years of independence were marked by irredentism as the Somalis sought to retrieve their brothers in Ethiopia and Kenya. Even during this period, Somali politics was heavily influenced by the interests of contending ascriptive groups, but a policy of external détente really opened the way for internal disintegration. In 1969 the precarious ethnic balance was destroyed in an election marked by violence, the subsequent assassination of the president, and a coup which brought to power a Supreme Military Council chosen carefully to reconstruct the balance of ethnic groups. See E. A. Bayne, "Somalia's Myths Are Tested," American Universities Field Staff *Reports*, Northeast Africa Series, 16.1 (1969).

judge likeness and unlikeness a wholly unexplored process, but even the basic distinctions between amalgamation and incorporation or division and proliferation remain in doubt.

One suspects, for example, that amalgamation and division may be more "mechanical" processes than incorporation and proliferation. That is, specific collective goals—such as economic or prestige gains—almost purposefully espoused, often seem to be of considerable importance in incorporation and proliferation, whereas amalgamation and division may be more dependent upon purely external circumstances, such as abrupt changes in the size and significance of political boundaries. It is interesting that incorporation and proliferation, once accomplished, usually entail a renunciation of the earlier identity—perhaps because instrumental considerations are often involved [71]—while amalgamation and division tend to involve a multiplication of identities, rather than a mere exchange of one identity for another.[72] This may leave the latter processes more flexible for a potential revision downward or upward as new contexts impinge on perceptions. That, at least, is a plausible hypothesis.

Equally uncertain are the determinants of variations within particular processes. Why did the Baganda qualify their practice of incorporating less prestigious migrants to Buganda, whereas a similar process underway in western Uganda was terminated, not by the prestigious incorporating group, the Batoro, but by the Bakonjo, who had been actively abandoning their own customs, practices (including circumcision), and language in favor of the Batoro model? [73] What variables will determine whether the Chamialis

71. For an example, see Barth, "Pathan Identity and Its Maintenance," in Barth, ed., *Ethnic Groups and Boundaries,* pp. 124–125.

Of course, instrumental calculations are not necessarily always excluded from amalgamation and division. See notes 6–8 and accompanying text, above.

72. To take account of the full range of possibilities, Herbert Kaufman proposes a threefold, rather than twofold, typology of boundary expansion for organizations, by dividing amalgamation into merger and federation; in the latter, "the participating organizations retain their own identity and boundaries, but by agreement establish another organization whose boundaries encompass them all." *Why Organizations Behave as They Do,* p. 55.

73. Martin R. Doornbos, "Kumanyana and Rwenzururu: Two Responses to Ethnic Inequality," in Robert I. Rotberg and Ali A. Mazrui, eds., *Protest and Power*

continue to receive the Brahmauri Brahmans or whether the Brahmans will continue to pursue their relatively recent proclivity to move toward the Chamiali identity? Here are three cases of partial incorporation with no apparent explanation for divergence in "outcome."

It is perhaps curious, in view of these basic gaps in our understanding, that there are clues in the study of identity change to some larger issues of policy in ethnically divided societies. I shall touch briefly—and broadly—on three such issues.

First of all, we noted at various points that the general effect of amalgamation was to superimpose new layers of identity on old, without displacing the old levels. Only rarely and only over very long periods of time has amalgamation succeeded in producing so complete a fusion as to obliterate the component subgroups. The destruction of diversity within the Creole and Indian ethnic groups in the West Indies took a heavy human toll and was possible only because these were slave or, later, semi-slave societies. Few states today can reproduce the degree of subordination, coercion, and pressure on the component groups which made the West Indian fusion possible, and few will find the method appealing in any case. The brutality of the West Indian experience points to the high costs of assimilationist or, more accurately, amalgamationist policies of "nation-building" in either the new states or the old. Within present political boundaries, most will have to content themselves with at best incomplete results if fusion is the goal.

Second, at least equal doubt is cast on secessionist or partitionist "solutions" to ethnic conflict. If the aim is to excise ethnic diversity by dividing one state into two or more, the contextual character of ethnic identity will have to be faced. To the extent that there are residual subgroups, a region that appears to be homogeneous while it is part of a larger entity is not likely to remain so if it is

---

in Black Africa (London, Oxford University Press, 1970); Doornbos, "Protest Movements in Western Uganda: Some Parallels and Contrasts," *Kroniek van Afrika* (1970/3), pp. 213–229. It should be said that the Bakonjo most involved in the emulation and later rejection of Batoro custom were largely members of an aspiring elite. This is not surprising, since movements for incorporation often begin at the elite level.

carved out and set on its own. Most group members respond to downward shifts in significant political boundaries by downward shifts in the focus of group identity, and the probability is that secession and partition will result in contracted group boundaries but not necessarily less ethnic diversity.

Third, there is the opposite option: expansion of political boundaries through "international regional integration" or federation. All else being equal, this should produce a strong pull toward amalgamation. Conceivably, a skillful multiplication of political boundaries at various levels could also multiply significant levels of ethnic identification so that no one level remains so salient as to create unmanageable conflict. This is essentially the notion of controlling conflict by apportioning it. I do not know whether Europe can save Belgium. But it does seem clear from the expansion and contraction of group boundaries with political boundaries that a fresh look at the impact of changing territorial boundaries is well warranted. This kind of proposal is very much—too much—out of vogue at the moment, because social science, and especially political science, continues to rebel against the excessive formalism of an earlier period. Nevertheless, the contextual character of ethnic identity suggests that the strong links between formal and informal processes can hardly be ignored.

5

DANIEL BELL

Ethnicity and Social Change

In the last decade, there has been a resurgence of ethnic identification as the basis for effective *political* action in widely divergent societies. Unlike the world-wide student movements of the 1960s, there does not seem to have been any coherent liaison between these diverse ethnic events, or a contagion of effects in these ethnic stirrings. Nor would there seem to be a common ideological current, as was probably the case in the student situation.[1] One would suppose, however, that there are some common *structural* sources which derive from common underlying trends in the different societies for the upsurge of ethnicity, even though each national instance produces its own idiosyncratic consequences.

The single most important fact about these varied movements, that they have taken *political* form, would indicate that certain basic

1. In the United States, the ethnic stirrings and the student movement took place almost simultaneously, but there was no organizational and ideological linkage between the two. The reason is that they had totally different foci. The student movement was diffuse, expressive, moralistic; its targets, the war and the authority structure in the university and the society. The ethnic movements were focused largely on status and political gains *within* the society and, to the extent they were aware of the students, they were hostile to the students as a middle-class movement, which they saw as attacking or undermining a structure from which they were able, by ethnic organization, to make gains. Yet, paradoxically, there was a common structural feature in that such ethnic gains could only come also when the traditional elite and authority structure of the United States—that of the white Anglo-Saxon Protestants—was being eroded; and the student movement contributed heavily to that erosion.

shifts in power and values are occurring in which *ethnic* (rather than some other form of group) *identification* has an effective (that is, instrumental and expressive) quality, and has become salient. In this chapter, I intend to relate ethnicity to major macro-social trends in the world today in order to see what may be illuminated thereby.

I begin with a schematic outline of major social trends which are reworking the structures of society; go on didactically to an inventory of the macro-social units in a society in order to identify the conditions under which one or another of these units becomes salient; and finally, consider the relation of ethnic groups to the other social units, and to these major social trends.

MAJOR SOCIAL TRENDS

The simple and truistic starting point is that a number of major social trends—convergent, overlapping, and divergent—are forcing the reworking of existing societal arrangements. These are the enlargement of political boundaries and arenas; the increase in the number of actors and claimants in a political arena; the challenges to the present-day distribution of place and privilege; and the questioning of the normative justifications and legitimations which have sanctified the status quo.

Is this *more* true today than at any previous time in the last one hundred and seventy-five years? "More" is an elusive word, and there is no metric to pin down the number and extent of the upheavals. I think it is more true because of a simple and fundamental structural change in the world community: new and larger networks and ties within and between societies have been woven by communication and transportation, shocks and upheavals are felt more readily and immediately, and the reactions and feedbacks come more quickly in response to social changes. This does not mean an increase in the *pace* of change; that term is too loose. The effect of "more" change is primarily an enlargement of the *scale* of an action or institution, and the foreshortening of response time. And change of scale becomes a change in institutional form; a change in response time becomes a change in intensity.[2]

2. As to the pace of change: within the lifetime of any single community, a hundred years ago the changes introduced by railroad, electricity, and telephone

The following, then is an inventory of what I would regard as major social changes in the western world, particularly in advanced industrial society, which create new problems and force new re-alignments.

The tendency toward more inclusive identities. This is, after all, one of the most persistent tendencies in the western world. Within each civilization, we have seen movements from tribe to city, from city to empire, or from region to nation and from nation to world. For small classes of persons—scribes, intellectuals, artists—the question of primary attachment has always been problematic as they moved from the geographical periphery to the cultural center, from the provincial clubs to the cosmopolitan salon. Deracination is an historical experience. What is different today, however, in the contrasting terms of "tradition" and "modernity," is the way large masses of persons find inherited ways and old creeds "outdated," and new modes and creeds of uncertain validity; and therefore the sense of uprootedness spreads throughout entire societies.

The extension of wider inclusive identities operates in all the realms. In the culture there is more and more syncretism, for with the greater mingling and jostling of peoples there is more stylistic borrowing and exchange; and this is probably the strongest pull in the breakup of older parochial beliefs. While not as pervasive, the institutional pulls for wider and more inclusive economic and political ties are strong: there are the multi-national corporations, economic regionalisms, and the great power penumbras with their satellite shadows. In Africa, there is the effort of nations to overcome tribal identifications; in Europe, there is the Common Market; in the Arab world, the efforts to strengthen political federation (Egypt, Libya, Syria) or some common cultural loyalty. And, on an

---

may have been as upsetting as those introduced a century later by aviation, transistors, and television. And for those who experienced, say, the Russian Revolution, fifty-five years ago, life has been more intense than any concentrated period in the lives of most peoples. The "new" factor today is not the fact of change (almost *all* peoples historically have experienced "shock" and upheaval, usually wars) but the multiplicity, simultaneity, and scale of change, and the crucial consequences for the changes in institutional form. For a further discussion of these points see *The Coming of Post-Industrial Society* (New York, Basic Books, 1973), chap. 3, and "Nature, Technology and Society," *The American Scholar,* 42.2 (Summer 1973), 385–404.

international basis, there is the United Nations, with its tenuous, but still important symbolic image of one world, one people.

The most important form of inclusiveness is political, for common sovereignty provides a common set of laws and common rules for the regulation of conflict. Historically, those tendencies toward wider, inclusive political ties have been strongest where there has been a powerful military force to impose an allegiance, or where there has been a "civil theology" to provide a locus for identification (for example, Rome, as a symbol; the "city of God" of Augustine; the national monarchs; "Americanism" as a civil religion; and so on).[3] Today there are strong tendencies toward wider economic and social unities, yet no real "civil theology" to bind them. In fact, it is where the "civil theology" has broken down, or where it cannot be created, that one finds the centrifugal forces of separatism gaining strength. In these instances one would expect the rise of parochial forces to provide psychological anchorages for individuals; and ethnicity is one of these.

The shift from market to political decision. A "pure" market economy is one where demands (purchases) are made by individuals acting independently of each other, and where the responses by the producers of goods and services are an aggregate of multiple, competitive supply decisions at relative prices. To the extent there is any commonality, it is primarily cultural: the tastes and life-styles of different social classes shape the pattern of demands and thus the kinds of goods that are produced. But this pattern is unorganized, and for that reason the market remains uncoordinated and atomized.

Yet the efforts of groups in the economy to exempt themselves from the hazards of competition lead to quasi-monopolistic behavior, principally in the commodity and labor markets: for example, administered prices by business firms; union shop, or restriction of

3. See Eric Voegelin, *The New Science of Politics* (Chicago, University of Chicago Press, 1952). The idea of a Civil Theology was formulated by the Stoic philosopher Varro in 47 B.C. and elaborated by Cicero. The function of the Civil Theology was to cement a sacramental bond between the citizenry and to create a common allegiance through a political myth. In the case of Rome, it was the auspices of Romulus and the rites of Numa that laid the foundations of the state. The *Leviathan* of Hobbes, if one follows Voegelin, was an effort to create a "public truth" by "establishing Christianity . . . as an English *Theologia civilis* in the Varronic sense." Ibid., pp. 81–83, 155.

entry into a trade, by labor. In these instances, key decisions become negotiated, privately or politically, by these groups. The nature of the negotiated decisions shapes the character of the *organizations* in the market.

More and more, however, both economic and non-economic decisions which previously had been left either to the market, or to privately negotiated bargains, now come under the purview of political entities (from the local communities to the federal government). These political decisions may either be government funding (of school expenditures, health, housing, research and development, and so on) or direct interventions to reshape environmental or social patterns (land use, airport location, mass transit or highways, busing, and so on), or the setting of standards for pollution, product safety, or the like. The essential point about the change from market or negotiated to political decisions is that in the latter instance everyone *knows* where the decision will be made, and whose ox will be gored. A market is dispersed, and the actors largely "invisible." In politics, decisions are made in a cockpit, and confrontation is direct. Inevitably, therefore, the spread of political decision-making forces the organization of persons into communal and interest groups, defensively to protect their places and privileges, or advantageously to gain place and privilege. The multiplication of groups increases community conflict; in self-protection, more and more persons are impelled to join one or another of the groups in order not to be excluded from the decisions.

What we have witnessed in the past thirty years—I take America as my chief example—is the "politicization" of the society in a way no one had entirely anticipated; not on single polarized issues, such as national economic class conflict, but on multiple community issues at all levels of society. In effect, there is probably *more* participation in political life today than in previous periods. And yet, in consequence of this, more and more groups act as veto powers and check each other's purposes. And when this takes place without effective political bargaining, it leads to frustration and delay in "getting things done," thus increasing the sense of helplessness or anger on the part of individuals who thought that their own participation would lead to the kind of action they wanted.

One of the major sources of the salience of ethnic groups in

American life in recent years, I would argue, is the rise of a "communal society," and without the importance of status and community issues alongside economic problems.

The re-definition of a major value—equality. Equality has been the central value of the American system and the legitimating agent—particularly when tied with the value of achievement—of the American polity—if not of all democratic societies. One only has to turn to the opening pages of Tocqueville's *Democracy in America* to realize the sustained power of this commitment.

The difficulty with this commitment has been its ambiguity. Tocqueville spoke of the "equality of conditions." What this seemed to mean was that no person should "lord it over others" or take on airs. (This persists even today in the easy informality and the quick "first name" basis between people who scarcely know each other.) When the idea was translated into policy terms, equality was invariably defined to mean "equality of opportunity," or open mobility based upon talent.

Yet in the recent effort to "include" the black community into the American polity, the conclusion was reached that "equality of opportunity," if defined formally, would work to the disadvantage of a group long culturally deprived; hence the Johnson administration, in its "affirmative action" programs, sought to provide compensating mechanisms to allow such a group to catch up, in order to have a "true" equality of opportunity. The dismaying fact for social policy, however, has been the argument that if education is the mechanism to gain equality, such a catch-up is not possible, since the schools, as the Coleman report indicated, are ineffective in these purposes; and that economic advancement between individuals may largely be a "lottery," since luck and personal qualities are more decisive than any others—the thrust of the recent argument by Christopher Jencks and associates. This empirical argument receives normative support in a powerful philosophical discussion by John Rawls (in his *Theory of Justice*), who claims that "inherited" advantage or even "natural" ability are as arbitrary, say, as height in determining privilege and that social policy as a matter of justice has to give priority to the disadvantaged.[4]

4. I discuss the Jencks findings and the Rawls argument in an essay, "Meritocracy and Equality" in *The Coming of Post-Industrial Society.*

The presumed failure of the idea of equality of opportunity has shifted the definition of that value to *equality of result;* and by fiat if necessary. The increasing thrust by disadvantaged groups, or their ideological mentors, has been for direct redistributive policies in order to equalize incomes, living conditions and the like; and on a group basis. In the shorthand of game theory, equality of opportunity is a non zero-sum game in which individuals can win in differential ways. But equality of result, or redistributive policies, essentially are zero-sum games, in which there are distinct losers and winners. And inevitably these conditions lead to more open political competition and conflict.

If one moves to western society, generally, we find a subtle but pervasive change, namely, that the revolution of rising expectations, which has been even more tangible in the advanced industrial societies than in the underdeveloped countries, has become a sustained demand for entitlements. To be a "citizen" has usually meant to share fully in the life of the society. In the earliest years, this meant the claim to liberty and the full protection of the law. In the late nineteenth and early twentieth centuries, this was defined as *political* rights, principally the full right to vote or hold office by all adult citizens, a status which was achieved only fifty years ago in most western societies. But the major claim in recent decades has been for *social* rights: the right to a job, insurance against unemployment and old age indigence, adequate health care, and a minimum, decent standard of living. And these are now demanded from the community as entitlements.

Distributive justice is one of the oldest and thorniest problems for political theory. What has been happening in recent years is that entitlements, equity, and equality have become confused with one another, and the source of rancorous political debate. Yet they are also the central value issues of the time.

The onset of a post-industrial society. In the western societies the emergence of a large and rapidly growing technical and professional stratum has placed a greater emphasis on skill as the basis of position and privilege, and education as the mode of access to these positions, than ever before. In turn, this has led to a growing emphasis on "credentials" and on "certification," as the barriers through which individuals must pass in order to get ahead.

There are many consequences for the stratification system in this reworking of the occupational order, but for our purposes the essential point is that, as the mechanisms for occupational advancement become increasingly specialized and formalized, the political route becomes almost the only major means available for individuals and groups without specific technical skills to "upgrade" themselves in society. For such persons, therefore, the political arena becomes more salient in the society as a means of gaining place and advantage. And this becomes one more reason why political decision making, rather than the market, becomes more central for the society.

The decline of authority. In a variety of institutions, cutting across the society, the old authority structures are being challenged and the bases of authority becoming eroded. To wit:

1. *In the status system of the society.* The fact that the acronym WASP is now used so freely, and has become a symbol of faint derision and mockery, indicates that the idea of "old family" and native descent may be losing its hold in the society. Does being a member of the D.A.R. count for much now? Perhaps in a few cities or towns, but not in the society as a whole. In fact, how many persons in the society would even recognize the initials D.A.R.? Does anyone defend the Establishment? Does the Establishment even defend itself? If one looks at the major institutions of the Establishment—the Council on Foreign Relations, the major foundations, Harvard University—one finds only a defensiveness about their position and a readiness, even, to abdicate any idea that they form an elite.

2. *In organizational life.* In few institutions does one see effective one-man authority. In most, there are committees and consultations, even at the top of many business corporations where there is often no longer a President, but the Office of the President, or a dual authority between a chairman of the executive committee and the president. The idea of chains of command or bureaucratization is being replaced by diverse kinds of task force or consultative groups. In organizational life, there are fewer "bosses."

3. *In professional life.* Here, the widespread populist attack on "elitism" has carried over into an attack on professionalism as such,

as the source of authority, and the demand, even, that in such technical and scientific areas as medicine, physicians should abdicate their authority in clinics and hospitals, or that in schools, teachers should abandon their professional "distance" from students and acknowledge an equality of roles based on a commonality of purpose.

4. *In cultural life.* The attack on authority goes hand in hand with broader currents in the culture: in the arts, the denial of standards of judgment, and the destruction of the idea of genre; in the value system, the denial of respect for age and experience, and the argument that since the society is changing so quickly the old do not know as much as the young. All this produces a sense of disorientation in the society and the feeling that traditional modes no longer hold. Sociologists have made a distinction between authority and power. Authority is a superior position which rests on a technical competence or traditional criteria (for example, age) and is recognized in the ready assent of others. Power is the issuance of command which is backed up, either implicitly or explicitly, by force. Where there is no authority, people resort to force. And this, too, is one of the sources of instability in the contemporary polity.

The shift in ideology. In a book published almost fifteen years ago, entitled *The End of Ideology,* I argued that in the west the older nineteenth-century ideologies were exhausted. The title perhaps was somewhat misleading, not because that thesis was wrong—I think it was not—but for the inference drawn by those who know a book only by its title, that *all* ideologies were finished. In the concluding essay to the book I specifically argued that among intellectuals there is always the hunger for ideology, and that the *new* ideologies of the last third of the twentieth century would be drawn from the third world.

In the middle and late sixties there was a flare-up of ideological hope particularly because of the student outbursts. In large measure, however, the content of the student ideologies in the west were drawn from "third world" ideas, rather than from the circumstances in the home country. This consisted, first, of the fanciful notion that "the students" would be a revolutionary force and second, an identification with Fanon, Debray, Che, and the adventuristic and romantic movements tied to third world liberation.

The youth movements, with the possible exception of West Germany, have largely subsided, as amazing in the rapidity of its burning out as in its eruptive flare-up; and probably for the same reason. The largest organized left-wing force in the western world today is the Communist labor movement. Yet in the countries where they are strongest, Italy and France, they have become movements without passion or driving ideology. And in the Soviet Union itself, one can say that as a serious force, ideology has ended; apart from the party functionaries (and even they may be the most cynical), few persons take seriously the Communist rhetoric and, as a practical fact, the Soviet Union is less and less of a socialist society, which makes it all the more difficult to square ideology with reality.

The chief ideological passion in the world today is anti-imperialism. This is aimed, in the first instance, at the United States, even though the United States has had few "colonies" (for example, Puerto Rico, the Philippines), and the majority of its foreign investments, particularly in recent years, has been in advanced industrial economies and not in the "backward" or "developing" nations. Yet, if imperialism is less an economic fact, it is clearly a political and symbolic reality and represents the perceived power hegemony, and feared cultural paramountcy, of the United States. To that extent, anti-imperialism becomes the common rhetorical cry for Arab feudal sheiks, African national leaders, and Latin American military dictators, as well as for left-wing revolutionaries.

For some individuals, anti-imperialism is equated with being socialist. The difficulty in carrying out that equation, however, is that there is little in common between the "Socialist" countries—the centralized statism of the Soviet Union, the Koranic socialism of Algeria or Libya, the patchwork statist economy of Cuba, the struggling collectives of Tanzania, the market socialism of Yugoslavia, and the commune collectivism of China—other than the word "Socialist." [5] What "socialism" means as a positive socioeconomic

5. Curiously enough, what *is* common to all these "socialist" regimes is a hostility to all cultural radicalism: to experimentalism in the arts, freer sexual mores, and the use of drugs. Yet it has been cultural radicalism, more often than not, that

program, or as ideology or doctrine, has become hard to define. And whether it can have a vivifying effect in the advanced industrial societies as a means of providing a political passion for people is even more difficult to tell. Yet it remains an important symbol, even in this negative sense, against capitalism.

The "external" proletariat. The international order today is, more than ever before, an interdependent world economy, with a core of advanced industrial societies in the "West," and a periphery of agrarian and newly industrializing societies in Latin America, Africa, and Asia. The interdependence derives from advanced technology and resources (agricultural, energy, and mineral), and no society can escape its net. Not even the Soviet Union, vast as it is, can build "socialism in a single country" and it, too, has to enter the international trading network. Whether China can develop an economic self-sufficiency remains to be seen.

There are three consequences to this new interdependent system:

1. The "division of labor" between the core and the periphery has tended to favor the advanced industrial societies so that the relative gap between "rich" and "poor" nations has become more obvious.

2. Nations with strategic resources can seek to use their economic strength for political advantage and technological gain: the Arabian gulf countries with oil; the Soviet Union with natural gas and minerals; the United States with food and technological items (for example, computers).

3. The rapid expansion of industry and the shifting technological bases of production act as a huge suction for vast migrations of unskilled and skilled labor: within countries from rural areas to cities; between countries from labor-surplus to labor-scarce economies.

For our purposes, there are two consequences to these sets of changes which are summed up in the phrase "the external proletariat."

has fueled the political passions of middle-class "rebels" in the western industrial societies.

First, within Europe there has been a huge migration of southern Europeans—Yugoslavs, Greeks and Italians—into Germany,
France, Switzerland, and northern Europe, resulting in the creation of large foreign minorities who are at the bottom rungs of
the society and are effectively excluded from participation in the
political life of these host countries. (Foreign workers comprise 10
percent of the working population in Germany, 9.7 percent in
France, 7 percent in Belgium, and 25 percent in Switzerland. In all
there are about 9 million "foreign workers" in Western Europe, and
the U.N. forecasts an additional 4 million by 1980.) While Common
Market policies tend to provide an equalization of benefits, and the
rapidly growing Mediterranean economy may reverse the migrations
in the next decades, the fact remains that in the advanced industrial
societies there has been an enormous change in the character of the
labor force with the new divisions being along national or ethnic lines.

Second, the international gap between core and periphery, rich
and poor, has created a mentality, if not the political fact, of a
"Third World"—a third world which has thought of itself as a
"proletariat" in relation to the advanced industrial societies as a
whole. Whether this "Third World" has the capacity for common
action remains to be seen. In 1965, Lin Piao, then Mao's designated
successor, in a striking speech virtually declared war on the advanced industrial nations in the name of the "external proletariat."
With the downfall of Lin, that theme is no longer heard from
Communist China. Yet from Bandung in 1956 to Algiers in 1973,
the efforts to organize the third world in some political bloc persist; and while the division between advanced industrial and developing or backward nations is nominally economic, the passions
behind the attack on economic exploitation often disguise color,
ethnic, and cultural interests as well as political and ideological purposes.

THE MACRO-SOCIAL UNITS OF SOCIETY

Though we live in an international economy, the social unit of
effective action is the political society, primarily the nation-state.
The nation is the unit of competition between states in the international order; the national society is the domestic arena for political

competition between groups to gain advantage and to claim or enforce rights and protections.[6]

While one is a citizen of the nation (a legal and political status), the sociological fact is that most persons have multiple social attachments which cross-cut one another, and these sociological designations can be emphasized or minimized depending upon the situation in which an individual finds himself. All this is summed up in the terms *identity* or *belonging*. Identity has psychological connotations, while belonging or group membership (in the Durkheimian sense) is sociological. I do not think one can readily assimilate psychological and sociological categories to each other, and there are distinct consequences in using either *identity* or *group membership* as one's organizing concept. Since my focus, here, is on political action, the term I shall use is *group membership,* though identity is essential for individual motivation.

Questions about multiple group memberships always raise the question: "With whom can I act, and for what?" In the past, this question was rarely problematic. The answer to "Where do I belong?" was a *given* fact, in which a primary attachment was stipulated by one's clan, religion, or race, depending on the historical context in which rival group memberships were defined. It is only in modern times, under conditions of rapid social change, of mobility and modernization, that one can *choose* one's identification or attachment in a self-conscious way. It is for this reason that the kinds of sociological units which are capable of being salient for psychological identification or group action become important; and it is useful, at this point, to review the major social categories in order to see how "ethnic" memberships fit in.

Nation. A nation is an effective unit of identification where there is a congruence between the nation and a single primordial group, since such congruence reduces any ambiguity as to who belongs or does not. But few nations today have this congruence. One might say that Yugoslavia is a nation, but individuals within the country

6. Capitalism is an international economic system, and Marx said that the "workers know no country"; yet what is striking is that the degree of international political cooperation between workers in advanced industrial societies today is probably less than at any time in the past hundred years.

identify themselves more readily as Serbians, Croatians, Slovenians, and so forth, designations which combine subnational with ethnic characteristics. Thus membership in a "larger" nation may be ambiguous, since it confuses political sovereignty with primary or secondary identifications. In assessing the nation as an affective political unit, that is, one capable of arousing a fierce emotional loyalty, one has to distinguish the component national identities from the larger political unit.

Religion. Religious differences, historically, have been one of the more potent and destructive forms of rivalry where "corporate" identifications have been possible: for example Christianity versus Islam in the Crusades; Catholic versus Protestant in the sixteenth and seventeenth centuries. Today, in most instances, these corporate identifications, particularly of "universal" religion, are cross-cut by national and other memberships which make the corporate attachment on a transnational basis more difficult. It is doubtful, for instance, whether French, Italian, and Spanish Catholics act as Catholics, rather than as Frenchmen or Italians or Spaniards. (In the Spanish Civil War, though, Franco did get some support by raising the banner of Catholicism versus leftist atheism.) Within the United States, one would question whether Irish, Polish, and Italian Catholics act primarily as Catholics (and if so, on what kinds of issues) rather than in their more parochial "ethnic" interests.

The fact that some religions are particularistic, rather than universal, does not necessarily make for close emotional identification. Jews, as a cultural group, do have a high degree of affective identification which cuts across national lines, but this derives more from a sense of peoplehood, from fate, than from religion. Shintoism, when fused with emperor worship, has been a potent reinforcement of national feeling in Japan, but the emphasis there was the nation, not religion. In Sweden and England, the existence of national churches, in which the heads of the churches are chosen by the heads of state, has not brought any effective reinforcement of religious feeling, though in England, to some extent, the church has served as an Establishment in the sense of being the formal arbiter of moral conduct.

Institutional religion, by and large, has lost its ability to be an overrriding group membership (though individuals may retain strong emotional identifications with the religion) and this is why the intensity of the religious conflict in Northern Ireland comes as such a surprise today. But even though the religious affiliation there is salient, it has to be understood against a national background in which the Catholics are in a minority in a land that was arbitrarily partitioned to provide a Protestant-dominated country, and that the Catholic Irish still regard the Ulstermen as "outside" settlers from England or Scotland, even though many of the Protestant families have lived there for several hundred years. Without the nationalist sentiment to fuel the conflict, it is questionable whether the religious division alone would have created that intensity of feeling.

Communal. Throughout the world today, the largest and most important category of group membership (particularly in its ability to rouse emotional feelings) is that broad set which we call "communal"—individuals who feel some consciousness of kind which is not contractual, and which involves some common links through primordial or cultural ties. Broadly speaking, there are four such ties: race; color; language; ethnicity.

Race, in terms of "blood," is a nineteenth-century concept (like nation and class, though it developed earlier than these two) and it is striking how central it was to so many writers—Carlyle, Froude, Kingsley, J. F. Green, Matthew Arnold, Stendhal, Madame de Stael, Taine, Renan, Saint Beuve, all of whom used the idea to designate "peoples" who had some common descent.[7] But the concept was brought into disrepute by writers such as Gobineau, Houston Stewart Chamberlain, Richard Wagner, and Treitschke, who made

---

7. In the eighteenth century, beginning with Linnaeus, the effort to define race was principally in physical anthropological terms, on the basis of color, skull shape, hair, and so on. Linnaeus divided the world into Americans, Europeans, Asians, and Africans on the basis, principally, of the continents. Others divided the human race into five groups and some went as far as to identify seventeen groups and twenty-nine races. In Europe, a conventional division was between blue-eyed tall Nordic, the darker short-headed Alpine, and the short, long-headed Mediterranean. While classification efforts still persist in physical anthropology, the idea of race as "common blood" became the predominant theme in the nineteenth century, and among the authors cited.

it the basis of a claim of Aryan superiority over other white races, and of the white as against all others. Race today is a discredited idea, but that very fact now gives it a powerful negative affect in the accusation of racism which can be hurled against groups or even entire societies, such as that white culture in America is "racist," or that major institutions are "racist," and so on. In that negative way, racism, again, has become a blanket term.

Color, which once played a minor and submerged role (and was even a negative identification, since in the United States or India, or other mixed societies, one usually married "up" to lighter color), today is used in a positive, binding role—in the concept of *negritude,* or that "black is beautiful." The great "scare" of the Aryan theorists in the early part of the twentieth century was that the next century would see a "color war" between peoples. Paradoxically, the theme of a color war, to the extent it is voiced, now comes from black extremists who seek to use the idea as a way of bringing a social group together, or to make scare demands on dominant groups and nations.

Language identification finds its strength where groups have distinct cultural identification through language, but find themselves commingled nationally and politically: for example, India where there are large linguistic groups such as the Bengalis, Gujeratis, Marathis, whose language is spoken by tens of millions; in Belgium, split between Flemish and Walloons; or where the linguistic identification serves to identify a submerged group, for example, Tamil in Sri Lanka, French in Canada, and so on.

Given these multiple overlapping components, the term *ethnicity* is clearly a confusing one. It may be either a *residual* category, designating some common group tie *not* identified distinctively by language, color, or religion but rather by common history and coherence through common symbols, for example, the WASPs as ethnics; or it may be a *generic* term which allows one to identify loosely *any minority* group within a dominant pattern, even though the particular unit of identification may be national origin (Irish, Italian, Pole in the United States), linguistic, racial, or religious. Some sociologists have sought to escape these confusions by talking of *primordial groups* as the sociological category for primary ties, reserving the particular designation of national, linguistic, or religious groups for the specific historical context. The term *primordial,* however, also includes clans and tribes, or even extended families, and thus has its own limitations. The term *ascriptive groups* has been proposed for those whose ties are "bound" or given in some way, as against achievement groups; but the term is embedded in an analytical sociology that is too austere to be used for sociographic purposes. Though there is an obvious difficulty in using the term *ethnic* in any consistent way, that common designation for a culturally defined "communal group" is too pervasive to escape, and by and large, it will have to serve.

Class. Class is an economically based group, defined in ideological or interest terms, in relation to the structure of production, or occupation, or the market. The conditions under which a class can become a highly effective symbolic and corporate unit depend on the context of conflict. Identification with a class (as with all other social units) competes with the wide array of other modes of attachment open to an individual. The strength of the class tie lies in the fact that it is derived from an interest; and this has been the effective basis of common action. Yet the very notion of class, with its overtones of social differentiation, also carries with it, for every class but the highest, a lowered social ranking and esteem and a sense of inferiority which, if reinforced by distinctions in language (accent), manners, and tastes, reduces the ability of a class identification to be an effective source of cohesion.

The embourgeoisement of the working class in advanced industrial societies, plus, in the earlier years of the twentieth century, a sense of strong national identification, has tended to diminish the power of corporate class consciousness. In the first half of the twentieth century it would not have been uncommon for a worker in England or Sweden to say, "I will rise *with* my class, not *out* of it." It is doubtful that one would hear such sentiments stated widely today. The reduction in class sentiment is one of the factors one associates with the rise of ethnic identification.

Sex. A half dozen years ago, one would not have listed gender as a major macro-social unit, yet in the United States and to a lesser extent in other western societies, identification on the basis of sex is relevant in the demarcation of effective acting units in the social arena. Just as with color, sexual identification (women's liberation) cuts across class or religion as an action unit in claiming group rights.

The intention of this broad classification should be apparent by now. There are few, if any, identifications of a broad social character that are exclusive as a mode of emotional attachment. There is such a multiplicity of interests and identities that inevitably they cross-cut each other in extraordinary fashions. In India, an original demarcation was religious between Hindus and Muslims; and after independence the country was partitioned primarily on that basis into India and Pakistan. Yet there was equally a cultural as well as geographical demarcation among the Pakistani between Bengalis and West Pakistanis (and the latter include among themselves a half dozen distinct linguistic and cultural groups) which finally led to a separatist revolt by the Bengalis that itself raised other questions. In eastern India, is the axis of demarcation to be cultural and linguistic (combining Dacca and Calcutta) in a common Bengali state, or do the Bengalis remain divided religiously between Muslim and Hindu, resulting in an independent Bangladesh and a Bengali state within India? In Israel and the Middle East, is it *class* or *national feeling* (and what is Jordan?) or *revolutionary* ideology that is the overriding identification? At one time, left-wing Zionists hoped to unite Jewish workers and Arab workers in one class front against the "bourgeoisie." But that effort failed. And though there is a Jewish Communist party in Israel, it finds itself constantly torn apart by the national issue.

Identity—and group definition—is not only immediately "spatial," that is, the relation with one's immediate neighbors, but involves levels of inclusiveness as well.[8] In Spain, one can think of oneself as a Basque or Catalan, or Castillian or Andalusian; yet outside Spain, one is a Spaniard as against a Frenchman or Italian, and, in a third level, as a European as against the American. One may be an Argentinian, or a Chilean, or a Brazilian, but one is also

8. I owe this point to Immanuel Wallerstein from his intervention at the Academy discussion in October 1972.

a Latin American as against a North American. And in the larger modalities, the entire American and European worlds may be thought of as Occidental, as against Oriental.

The question of what one is, is not only a matter of one's own choice, but the label of others as well, a situation summed up metaphorically, in the linguistic distinction of the subject "I" and the object "me": "who am I," and "who is the me, as regarded by what others." At particular times—*but usually in relation to an adversary, which gives it its political character*—one specific identification becomes primary and overriding and prompts one to join a particular group; or, one is forced into a group by the action of others. But there is no general rule to state which identification it might be. In particular societies, and in different regions, there are different polarizing issues, rooted in the dominance structures of these societies, and only the historical nature of these structures and the issues at hand define the specific divisions and confrontations in those societies.[9]

9. Since the intention of this section is to indicate the range of diverse identities available, it might be useful to move below the macro-social level and list as well the multiplicity of subordinate identities that also act in cross-cutting form. Because the general argument has already been made, I will content myself with a simple listing of some of these units in order to illustrate the range of interests and identities which unites and divides peoples.

Intermediate Social Units
1. Political parties
2. Functional groups
   a. Major economic interests: business, farm, labor
   b. Segmented economic interest: for example, professional associations
   c. Economic communal groups: for example, the poor, the aged, the disabled
3. Armies
4. Voluntary associations (for example, consumer, civic)
5. Age-graded groups (for example, youth, students)
6. Ethos communal groups (for example, the "community" of science)
7. Symbolic and expressive identifications
   a. Regional (for example, Texans)
   b. Socially "deviant" (for example, drug cultures, homosexual)

The lines between "macro" and "intermediate" units, necessarily, are not hard and fast. In general, the "macro" unit would signify an attachment at a level above the organizational. Thus, membership in a political party or trade union while important for particular purposes is not, usually, the overriding criterion of one's identity or group membership. In recent times, youth, like sex, has become a

THE ROLE OF THE ETHNIC GROUP

Most societies in the world today are "plural societies." By plural societies, I simply mean the existence of segmented sociological groups which can establish effective cultural and political cohesion within the society and make cultural, economic, or political claims on the society, on the basis of that group identity.[10] Sometimes these cohesions are direct and primordial; sometimes these cohesions are created out of adversary conflicts.

In most countries, and this has been true historically, the plural society was a product of conquest in which various minority groups were subjugated by force and incorporated into a society. In North America, however, the plural society was created largely out of the free mingling of peoples through immigration, and with impressed black slaves brought by traders.[11]

------

primary identification and for certain purposes one might want to include youth among the macro-social units.

Micro-Social Units
1. Families
2. Clans
3. Friendship circles
4. Neighborhood groups

10. The range and extent of such plurality are striking. The largest countries in the world, India, the Soviet Union, the United States, and China, are plural societies, as are most countries in Asia, Africa, and Latin America. In fact, the relatively homogeneous society is the rare exception in the world—Japan (though it has a despised caste, the Eta), the Scandinavian countries, France (though with a strong Breton separatist movement), Italy (if we include Sicily as culturally "Italian" and if we minimize regional particularism)—and even where there have been strong and established national political institutions, as in Great Britain, we find distinctive nationalist movements such as the Scottish and the Welsh, and the predictions that within a decade there may be a new federal structure to British political life, rather than the present-day control from Westminster. For a review of the problems of plural societies, see the issue of *International Social Science Journal*, "Dimensions of the Racial Situation," 23.4 (1971), especially the review article by Leo Kuper, "Political Change in Plural Societies," 594–607.

11. As Pierre L. van den Berghe has written: "The plural societies of Asia, Africa and Spanish America more recently studied by sociologists and anthropologists have, in fact, been far more typical of conquest states than the frontier immigrant and/or slave plantation societies which underpinned much of the previous ethnic relations literature. In the more classical case of the conquest state, the in-

Until fairly recently, there was little overt competition between these plural groups. In colonial countries or empires, an open system of overt domination kept most of the indigenous peoples subjected. In multigroup societies such as the United States, the oldest settler segment exercised customary social and economic dominance. But with the destruction of imperialist rule in former colonial countries, and the erosion of the older authority structures in the industrial west, competition between the plural groups today has become the norm.

Except where minorities (or majorities even) are openly repressed (for example, South Africa, Angola), competition between plural groups takes place largely in the political arena. The reason is simple. Status competition is diffuse and lacks a specific site. Economic competition is dispersed between interests and occupations. But political competition is direct and tangible, the rewards are specified through legislation or by the direct allocation of jobs and privileges. The very nature of interest-group rivalry, where the plural groups are evidently distinct, makes it certain that the political arena becomes the most salient in the competition for the chief values of the society.

There is a second general reason why the political arena has become so salient. This is the "shrinkage" of the economic order in

---

digenous population is subordinated and exploited but neither exterminated nor enslaved; the dominant group remains a minority and is not supplemented by massive and continuous immigration after the conquest; cultural and social pluralism of the various ethnic groups is fairly stable and long-lasting; and much of the immigration which takes place subsequent to the conquest is likely to take the form of an interstitial pariah merchant class, ethnically distinct from both the indigenes and the politically dominant minority. This is the pattern characteristic of most empires, including most of the colonial territories of the European powers in Asia and Africa. The United States, Canada, Australia, Argentina, Uruguay, Chile, Brazil and the West Indies are the exceptions, made possible by the low pre-conquest population density, low level of indigenous military and productive technology, and sensitivity of the natives to imported epidemic diseases." "Ethnicity: The African Experience," *International Social Science Journal*, 23.4 (1971), 508. To these patterns, one would have to add the Russian empire which represented a combination of conquest and amalgamation and which, in the Soviet form, despite the formal equality of the multiple peoples, still sees a Great Russian domination both politically (in that Russians occupy the key political positions in most of the constituent Republics) and culturally.

advanced industrial societies. For two centuries, as Emile Durk-heim pointed out seventy years ago, "Economic life has taken on an expansion it never knew before. From being a secondary function, despised and left to inferior classes, it passed on to one of first rank. We see the military, governmental and religious functions falling back more and more in face of it." [12] In effect, the economic order "swelled up" as if to encompass, almost, the entire life of society and the "horizontal" divisions of the economic order, that of capitalist and worker, became the central socio-political division of the society as well. But now, as I have pointed out earlier, the economic order in almost all advanced industrial societies has become increasingly subordinated to the political system: first, because of the need to manage the economic system; and second, because the rise of noneconomic values (environment, ecology, health, culture, freer personal styles—elements subsumed under that phrase "the quality of life") has led to the demand for the control of economic production.

The third major reason for the centrality of the political order is that the major processes of modernization—the transformation of societies—in Africa, Asia, the Soviet Union, and to some extent, Latin America, are being carried out "from the top," by elites, and through the force and coercion available only through the political system. Marx may have felt that social change is initiated in society in the economic substructure, but the most striking fact of the industrialization of the Soviet Union and the transformation of peasant agriculture into communes in China is that these are "directed" efforts, carried out by political means.

But politics is more than just the arena of interests or of social transformations. Politics is also the arena of passions, where emotions can be readily mobilized behind one's own flag, and against another group. The "risks" of such inflamed political competition is that issues may not be negotiable (as they are when tied to interests alone), but become "causes" that invite violent conflict and even civil war.

12. Emile Durkheim, *Professional Ethics and Civic Morals* (Glencoe, The Free Press, 1958), pp. 10–11.

In the western world, up to the seventeenth and the eighteenth centuries, such passions were expressed largely in religious terms, even where, as in the religious rhetoric of the English civil war, they masked a political content. Today the clashes are in overt political terms, though behind some of the political rhetoric lurk the passions of secular religions, the national, class, or ethnic embodiments of ideological politics.

In the nineteenth century, particularly in Europe, the most potent ideology was nationalism. Nationalism joins culture and politics in a common purpose. It brings together the high-born and the low and gives those, even of the meanest circumstance, a pride in being able to feel at one with the highest classes in the country, and in a common culture and history. Nationalism has the appeal of unifying a country behind a common loyalty, and focusing emotional aggression against an outside neighbor. For this obvious reason, where there has been a strong, aggressive nationalism, class and ethnic rivalries have been subdued or muted. As World War I and other wars have shown, country rather than class had the overriding appeal, even among workers.

It is questionable whether in the western world today that kind of inclusive nationalism any longer has such a compelling power. It may be that nationalism has an emotional power within Yugoslavia, or in eastern Europe, or in Northern Ireland, but these are almost entirely instances of national groups subordinated to a larger political entity whose cultural and social dominance is resented. There is much less emotional nationalism in the state of Eire itself, than in Northern Ireland. The nationalism of Ukrainians and Uzbeks within the Soviet-dominated world is a weapon for independence; under conditions of independence, would the passions remain?

If one takes the western powers, those along the Atlantic littoral, is there much emotional patriotism in Great Britain, France, Western Germany, Italy, or the United States? For one crucial fact, nationalism was an ideology fashioned by intellectuals who created the consciousness of a common culture out of the myths, folklore, songs, and literature of a people. Nationalism, to that extent, was a product of romanticism, with its emphasis on history and nature, against the rationalism of modern life. But that kind of romanticism is no longer attached to the mystical notion of an "organic" nation, and the intellectuals have decamped from patriotism.[13]

The second fact is that almost all these western societies are "fatigued." Nations and peoples, where circumstances are favorable, often display "historical energies" which drive them forward to seek a place on the stage of history. These are the upsurges which reflect a military or economic vitality of a people. The historic drive of the western powers took place in the century between 1850 and 1950, largely in industrialization and imperialism, and took pride in technological achievement and empire. Yet those forces now seem spent, frayed by internal problems or exhausted in internecine wars; and few of those countries display that sense of "national will," which is what unites historical destiny with national purpose. Nationalism in these countries is at a low ebb.

And that creates a problem for them. The historical lesson is that societies undergoing rapid social change, or nation building, or territorial or political expansion, can escape or postpone internal political difficulties—the fear of established groups for the loss of privilege, the demand of disadvantaged groups for the reallocation of privilege—by mobilizing the society against some "external" force, or for some common ideological purpose. Yet both ends are spent.

In the American hemisphere, the external force, initially, was "nature," and the energies of the society were channeled into the opening and developing of a large new continent. Later, the source of internal cohesion became some ideologically defined outside enemy. In the United States, in the 1950s, there was a large degree of social unity because the society was mobilized during the Korean war and after, against the threat of communism. When that ideological threat, which had been defined in monolithic terms, began to dissipate (though great power rivalry remained), the internal social divisions in the society that had been held in bound erupted. A large number of structural changes had been taking place in the society—the creation of a national society and a communal so-

13. That romanticism, of course, is now channeled into the idea of "liberation" and the renewed mystique of "revolution."

ciety—and the claims of disadvantaged social groups, such as the blacks and the poor.[14] Those now, inevitably, came to the fore, and they, too, were expressed in political terms.

The crucial question for all politics is what are the social bases of cohesion and cleavage—the objective basis for cohesion (interests), and the subjective basis for a common symbolism and shared consciousness (emotional tie); what determines the composition and character of corporate groups? Analytically speaking, there are two kinds of social movements: symbolic and expressive movements whose ties are primarily affective; and instrumental groups whose actions are bound by a set of common, usually material, interests.

Social units that are entirely symbolic-expressive are of two sorts: they may be simply fraternal, such as veterans' organizations reliving old glories, and thus become attenuated; or, if they are oriented to action, their life may be transient, since the need to heighten and mobilize feelings—in order to keep their zeal alive— drives them to extremes (for example, the Weathermen in student politics). Where social units are entirely instrumental, it becomes difficult to extend their range beyond the limited interest which impelled the organization, so, lacking any emotional basis for cohesion, either new interests have to be found, or the attachments and purposes of the organization become diminished. In short, the problem for symbolic-expressive groups is that while they can be mobilized quickly in periods of stress and peak experience, without a sustained, continuing interest which is real, and which has tangible payoffs for the members, the movements burn themselves out. The problem for instrumental organizations is the need to readapt themselves to new purposes when the old goals have become realized.

Those social units are most highly effective, clearly, which can combine symbolic and instrumental purposes. In the political history of our times, it is clear that "class" and "ethnicity" have been the two such dominant modes of coherent group feeling and ac-

14. For a detailed discussion of the underlying structural changes in American society and the emergence of new social groups and constituencies, see my essay, "Unstable America," *Encounter* 34 (June 1970), 11–26.

tion, and we can raise the general question, under what conditions has one or the other become most salient for action, or under what conditions might the two be fused?

Class, in industrial society in the last two hundred or so years, has justly been defined in terms of property relations, and class issues as the conflicts between those who have to sell their labor power and those who buy it. Working class politics, in that period of time, has been oriented either to the complete change of the system, or a sharing of power within it.

The fundamental fact is that few working class movements in the advanced industrial societies in recent years have had a revolutionary purpose. Even those which, rhetorically, still seek such a change, such as the Communist-dominated labor movements in France and Italy, no longer act that way in practice. Their chief effort is to have an effective voice over the control of working conditions. Since the end of World War II, industrial conflict in most countries has been institutionalized. This does not mean, necessarily, that all militancy vanished, nor that some of the economic conflicts may not spill over into politics, as in Italy, where parliamentary impasses threaten to polarize the society, or England, where the successive governments, Labor and Tory, have sought to restrict the activities of the unions. But it does mean two things: that some rough and ready rules of the game have tended to limit the conflict, and to force some negotiated solutions; and that these conflicts, as Ralf Dahrendorf has put it, had become "institutionally isolated" so that there was little carry-over from the job to other areas of life; the occupational milieu lost its ability to mold the personality and behavior of the worker; and the industrial issues were no longer the overriding issues that polarize a society.[15]

15. What modern society does, writes Dahrendorf, is to separate industrial conflict from political conflict. Or, as Anthony Giddens writes, in emendation of this idea, " 'conflict consciousness' is in a certain sense inherent in the outlook of the worker in capitalist society; 'revolutionary consciousness' is not." See Ralf Dahrendorf, *Class and Class Conflict in Industrial Society* (Stanford, Stanford University Press, 1959), pp. 271–277; and Anthony Giddens, *The Class Structure of the Advanced Societies* (London, Hutchinson University Library, 1973), pp. 201–202.

What is striking in Giddens' effort to reformulate a theory of class in advanced industrial societies is the total absence of any discussion of ethnicity or ethnic divisions within the class structures. Truly, a one-eyed vision of modern society.

The second fact is that structural changes in the society have tended to reduce the role of property and introduce a new criterion, that of technical skill, as the basis of class position. In more immediate terms, the changeover in most western societies from a goods producing to a service economy expands the proportion of white-collar jobs and emphasizes education as the mode of access to the expanding technical and professional vocations. The working class, as a proportion of the labor force, is shrinking, and the new service occupations and professional positions rarely carry the history or traditions of the older working class forms of activity. Thus, there is not a single but a double-based economic class system, of property and skill, in the society.[16]

One important consequence of the institutional change is that "class" no longer seemed to carry any strong affective tie. To put it most baldly, what had once been an ideology had now become almost largely an interest. The labor movements in western industrial society have always been a cleft stick. On the one end, they have been part of a "social movement" which seeks to transform society; on the other, a "trade union" seeking a place within it. As a social movement, labor sought to mobilize affect as a means of maintaining a permanent hostility to an employer class, husbanding its zeal until the "final conflict." As a trade union, it has had to live on a day-to-day relation with particular employers and even, at times, adopt their point of view and interest, in order to save their jobs against competitive employers and other unions. The institu-

16. Whether the structural changes—the emergence of knowledge or skill as the basis of class—will bring a coherent class identity on the part of the new technical classes is an open question. The knowledge elites have long had a specific ethos, defined usually as "professionalism." And this conception of their role in the past has militated against a traditional class identification. Yet even though these groups are defined by a common ethos, in the post-industrial society, as I have argued, it is likely that the *situs,* or locale of work, such as a business corporation, the university, the government, or the military, may be more important than the *stratum* as the source for political organization and political claims for the elite constituencies so that politics, more likely than not, would be on corporative rather than class lines. Among the "semi-skilled intellectuals," like teachers, one finds an increasing readiness to accept trade unionism and forego the traditional guild and professional identification and this may represent a new kind of class organization. But it is doubtful whether this "educated labor," in the United States, at least, would become an active ideological force.

tionalization of bargaining, necessarily, has meant a lowering of ideological sights. (One interesting indicator is the decline of "labor songs" as a means of inspiring emotions; the only such songs in recent years have been those of the black civil rights movement.) The "social movement" aspect of labor, with all the attendant aspects that the ideology sought to stimulate—fraternal organizations, cooperatives, theater and cultural groups—is no longer a "way of life" for its members. The union has focused on the job, and little more.

The further fact, in the United States at least, is that this "interest" often has been converted into a quasi-monopoly job position—either by the direct exclusion of blacks from certain occupations (a situation largely true in the building trades until recently), the operation of a "merit" system as in teaching, which tends to restrict the opportunities of latecomer blacks for rapid advancement, or even the normal "seniority" system in most union agreements, which acts to keep blacks and other minorities in the lower paying positions. For these reasons, one finds blacks often hostile to trade unions and, even though the overwhelming majority of them are workers, we find them in the unions emphasizing the "ethnic" as against their "class" identities. For the blacks, particularly, and more so for the radical blacks, the question whether they organize in "race" or "class" terms is a crucial one. Given the fact that their advancement has come largely through political pressure, and the ability to make gains by mobilizing votes, the emphasis, overwhelmingly, has been in race or nationalist terms.

In a plural society, class cuts across ethnic lines. Sometimes class becomes congruent with ethnicity, where there is a bipolar situation in which one ethnic group is economically predominant and another ethnic group economically exploited. More often than not, in the advanced countries at least, ethnicity cuts across class lines and members of the different ethnic groups are both in the economic majority and economic minority. Where class issues become attenuated, and communal questions come to the fore, understandably, the ethnic tie becomes more salient.

The conversion of the working class into an "institutional interest," with an elaborate bureaucratic structure of its own, is a process that has taken place primarily within the last twenty-five years. During that time the economic locus of conflict diminished. And where interests became institutionalized and instrumental, the adversary conflicts which tend to polarize emotions also diminished; for this reason the saliency of an identity as a worker tended to attenuate. At the same time, within this period, the political arena became more central. Where this has taken place on the local and community level, as has been evident in this period, interest-group unionism has become less important and other group memberships have come to the fore. For this double reason, ethnicity has become more salient in the last decade.[17]

Ethnicity has become more salient because it can combine an interest with an affective tie. Ethnicity provides a tangible set of common identifications—in language, food, music, names—when other social roles become more abstract and impersonal. In the competition for the values of the society to be realized politically, ethnicity can become a means of claiming place or advantage.

Ethnic groups—be they religious, linguistic, racial, or communal—are, it should be pointed out, *pre-industrial* units that, with the rise of industry, became cross-cut by economic and class interests. In trying to account for the upsurge of ethnicity today, one can see this ethnicity as the emergent expression of primordial feelings, long suppressed but now reawakened, or as a "strategic site," chosen by disadvantaged persons as a new mode of seeking political redress in the society.

Two historical factors are relevant here. One, which I have pointed to, is the loss of social dominance of the old social elites, a situation which derives from the breakup of the "family capitalism," which joined family directly to economic power in the western world.[18] Within the family system there has been an erosion of

17. Involvement beyond the borders of the country—the Jews with Israel, the blacks with Africa, the "new left" with national liberation movements—has been a conspicuous feature of the last decade, an "internationalism," again which contrasts with the small degree of internationalism of the trade-union movements in working-class issues.

18. For a discussion of this question see my essay, "The Break-up of Family Capitalism," in my *The End of Ideology* (Glencoe, The Free Press, 1960).

the social authority, of the major "family" names in high society, particularly of the WASPs. One finds less of "society" and more of "celebrity," less emphasis on large social estates and great houses, and more on movement and travel. If there is a "social hierarchy" in the United States, it tends to hide itself, rather than flaunt its position as in the Gilded Age.

The second historical fact is the breakup of imperialism, which I discussed previously from the point of view of its significance for ideological developments. Imperialism has been looked at largely in economic and political terms, but clearly it had a cultural component which emphasized the superiority of the older nations and which had extraordinary psychological effects on the personalities of those who lived under imperialist rule. The resurgence of ethnicity, in that respect, is part of the broader historical upsurge against imperialism, reflected now, on the cultural side. Since no group can now claim explicit superiority, each group can emphasize its own language, religion, and culture as of intrinsic value and can assert a pride in the aggressive declaration of one's own ethnicity. Ethnicity becomes a badge that one can wear more openly and show as a mode of personal self-assertion.

These two facts, social and cultural, merge with the changed context of economic advancement and political organization. In industrial societies, access to economic and professional position becomes defined increasingly by technical criteria. In the modernizing world, as well, achievement becomes linked with technical competence, which involves higher education, specialized skills, and professional achievement. The one route largely open is the political one. One can move ahead by mobilizing a following, become elected to office or get a job by supporting a victorious candidate; or one can make demands for quotas or some other means of enforcing an allocation of position on some criterion other than the technical and professional.

In this context, claims are made on the basis of ascriptive or group identity rather than individual achievement, and this is reinforced by the nature of the political process which emphasizes some group coherence as a means of being effective in that arena. *What takes place, then, is the wedding of status issues to political demands through the ethnic groups.* In the recent historical situation, ethnic groups, being both expressive and instrumental, become sources of political strength.

In sum, there would be three reasons for the upsurge of the salience of ethnic identification:

1. In the greater mingling of peoples, with the expansion of more inclusive, yet attenuated, identities, in the simultaneous development of a culture that is more syncretistic and a social structure that is more bureaucratic, the desire for some particular or primordial anchorage becomes intensified. People want to belong to "smaller" units, and find in ethnicity an easy attachment.

2. The breakup of the traditional authority structures and the previous affective social units—historically, nation and class—in turn make the ethnic attachment more salient.

3. The politicization of the decisions that affect the communal lives of persons makes the need for group organization more necessary, and ethnic grouping becomes a ready means of demanding group rights or providing defense against other groups.

What I think is clear is that ethnicity, in this context, is best understood *not* as a primordial phenomenon in which deeply held identities have to reemerge, but as a strategic choice by individuals who, in other circumstances, would choose other group memberships as a means of gaining some power and privilege. In short, it is the *salience* not the *persona* which has to be the axial line for explanation. And because salience may be the decisive variable, the attachment to ethnicity may flush or fade very quickly depending on political and economic circumstances.

The paradox is that with more syncretism and intermingling, formal ethnic attachments may weaken, as evidenced by the high degree of intermarriage between groups, yet, if one wants to, one can now identify oneself more readily, and without lessened esteem, in ethnic terms, and make claims on that basis of that identity. The simple point, then, is that ethnicity has become fully legitimate—and sometimes necessary—as an identity, and this carries over, in a political situation, into a group attachment.[19]

19. This chapter has dealt generally with broad sociological trends, but has drawn the implications largely for advanced industrial societies with especial ref-

A CODA

As a postscript I would like to note three qualifications.

First, the focus of this chapter is ethnicity and the attempt to account for its upsurge and salience at the present time, in terms of structural determinants and precipitating situations. Ethnicity is one response, in many instances of hitherto disadvantaged groups, to the breakup of older, and historically fused social and cultural, political and economic dominance structures, and represents an effort by these groups to use a cultural mode for economic and political advancement. Yet this should not be taken to mean that eth-

---

erence to the United States. I have less competence as to other areas, yet would venture these observations.

In developing nations, where rapid and sustained economic developing is under way, class may be the more salient sociological unit because such development, requiring heavy capital accumulation, creates large economic disproportions in the population. In Latin America, where economic development is tied with the ideological history of imperialism, class would still seem to be more salient, particularly in the more Europeanized societies such as Argentina, Chile and Brazil.

In Africa, however, where almost all political boundaries have been artificially drawn, the existence of plural tribal groups has tended to emphasize ethnicity more than any other factor. One means has been the wholesale expulsion of non-African groups that had dominated some of the mercantile and professional sectors such as the Arabs in Zanzibar or the Indians from Uganda, and to restriction of the number of whites in the country. But even then, the existence of multi-tribal groups becomes an inescapable fact and while sociologists, a decade before, had expected, simplistically, that the modernizing situation would produce an emphasis on individual achievement and universalism, the politicization of these societies has led, in fact, to a reinforcement of tribalism. As Pierre van den Berghe has superbly summarized the situation: "A polity of universalism based on merit is resented by the 'backward' groups as a cloak to maintain the head start of the 'advanced' groups . . . Given this restricted opportunity structure, and the existence of ethnic cleavages, it can be expected that competition within the privileged classes would be along ethnic lines. In the scramble for salaried positions in the civil service, the army, the schools and Universities, the State corporations, and the private bureaucracies, the easiest way to eliminate the majority of one's competitors is by making an ethnic claim to the job and by mobilizing political support on an ethnic basis. Once the practice of ethnic conflict is established it becomes an almost inescapable vicious circle. Everyone expects everybody else to be a 'tribalist,' and thus finds it easy to justify his own ethnic particularism on defensive or pre-emptive grounds, or ostensibly to re-establish the balance destroyed by the 'tribalism' of others." "Ethnicity: The African Experience," *International Social Science Journal,* p. 515.

nicity is the central concept to analyze social change in the world today. The forces of nation and class are latent and other circumstances could readily bring them to the fore.

Second, ethnicity is an aspect of the fusion of the status order with the political order, as class is a dimension of the relationship of the economic order to the political order. Status politics, however, usually become salient during periods of prosperity, when men have advanced economically and are concerned with a sense of possessions and place in the society. Economic issues, however, become more relevant during periods of retrenchment, when the cost burdens of the society, either depression or inflation, are levied differentially on social groups. The fact that economic growth in western societies has been slowed drastically because of the changed costs of energy and raw materials, and that the industrial world is in for a period of both scarcity and inflation, may make economic class issues central again to the political concerns of the society.[20]

The sociological fact that, throughout the western world, the industrial working class is shrinking, relative to other classes, and one can say that, "historically" it is moving off the stage of world history as have farmers (though not farming!) in advanced industrial society, ignores the question of time. Social systems and social groups, as I argued in my book on post-industrial society, take a long time to "expire." (World War I did not so much sound the death knell of capitalism as the final eclipse, in the political realm, of the feudal order—in the overthrow of the monarchies in Germany, Austria–Hungary, and Russia—three hundred years after the rise of the bourgeoisie.) The most important fact about the working-class parties and trade unions is that they are still the best organized groups in the society, and in a society which is becoming increasingly

20. For a discussion of the distinction of status politics and class politics, see the essays by Hofstadter, Lipset, and Bell, in Daniel Bell, ed., *The Radical Right* (New York, Doubleday-Anchor, 1962). I have dealt with the questions of growth and inflation in an essay, "The Next Twenty-Five Years," a paper for the CIBA Foundation conference on The Future of Foundations (June 1974), to be published by Elsevier in 1975. The crucial point, one should note, about any inflation, and the rise in taxes, is the unsettling effects on the middle classes and the reactions of the middle classes which may result in the breakup of existing party systems.

amorphous, with the multiplication of structures and constituencies, that very fact of organization gives the trade unions (like the military in underdeveloped societies) an enormous importance, particularly in a period of crisis. To that extent, therefore, one would have to say that while ethnicity has become more salient than before, saliency is not predominance, and that for many political issues, functional interest groups and classes may be more important than the ethnic and communal groups in the society.

Third, I would like to sound a note of normative caution on the role of ethnicity in politics. The upsurge of ethnicity is a cultural gain in that it allows individuals whose identities have been submerged, or whose status has been denigrated, to assert a sense of pride in what they regard as their own. In equal measure, it is a means for disadvantaged groups to claim a set of rights and privileges which the existing power structures have denied them. Yet if one looks down the dark ravines of history, one sees that men in social groups need some other group to hate.[21] The strength of a primordial attachment is that emotional cohesion derives not only from some inner "consciousness of kind," but from some external definition of an adversary as well. Where there are *Gemeinde,* there are also *Fremde.* And such divisions, when translated into politics, become, like a civil war, *politique à l'outrance.* It was once hoped that the politics of ideology might be replaced by the politics of civility, in which men would learn to live in negotiated peace. To replace the politics of ideology with the politics of ethnicity might only be the continuation of war by other means. And those are the drawbacks of ethnicity as well.

21. As Sigmund Freud has remarked: *"Homo homini lupus.* Who, in the face of all his experience of life and of history, will have the courage to dispute this assertion? . . . It is always possible to bind together a considerable number of people in love, so long as there are other people left over to receive the manifestations of their aggressiveness." *Civilization and Its Discontents* (London, Hogarth Press, 1961), XXI, 111, 114.

THE OLD WORLD AND THE NEW

6

WILLIAM PETERSEN

On the Subnations of Western Europe

In Europe, *nation* is ordinarily understood literally, as a community based on common descent. Many American scholars, on the contrary, seem reluctant to use the very terms of genetic differentiation: they are likely to interpret *nation* as meaning "state," to eschew *race* altogether and substitute the presumably less sullied "ethnic group" (from the Greek rather than the Latin for the same concept). It may be significant that one can speak of "la race française," "die französische Rasse," "het Franse ras," and even, in Britain, "the French race," but in modern American English the phrase would be seen as an affectation. And few European intellectuals seem able to understand that the notion of "un-American activities" stems from the concept of nation as an obviously heterogeneous population that derives its unity from a shared political faith.

On the other hand, it is difficult for any American, reared in a convictional nation, to understand sympathetically the constraints imposed by the European concept. Why should the French or Swiss democracies make naturalization so difficult; why should the small colored minority of Britain become so explosive a public issue? As the American observer is likely to notice, the myth of

Note: Some of the background material for this paper was collected under a travel-research grant from the Ford Foundation in 1971. I am happy to acknowledge this assistance. Valuable comments on an earlier draft were given me by Professors Hans E. Keller of Ohio State University, Aristide R. Zolberg of the University of Chicago, and Lucien Huyse of the Catholic University of Leuven.

common descent from a putative ancestor has generally survived the palpable genetic variation that exists in even the smaller nations of Western Europe. One common mode of resolving the contradiction is to delineate an ethnic structure of "ideal" or constructed types: "the" Swede is tall and fair, "the" Frenchman short and dark. Apparently such a quasi-empirical classification can persist (though with some strain, after the Nazis) so long as the actual internal differentiation has not become too great. With the rise of Scots and Welsh nationalisms, the distinction between "English" and "British" is now more pointed, and it is doubtful whether the small minorities from the West Indies or India and Pakistan will soon acquire a full English identity, no matter what their passport status.

When circumstances induce Europeans to shift from the genetic concept of nation, they do not usually take over the American (and, in spite of the differences, also the Soviet) concept of an entity united by political faith. They speak rather of a *cultural* heritage, and perhaps the most frequent symbol of a supposed common descent is a common language. Europe does contain such isolated ethnic pockets as, for example, the Basques, who deviate markedly from their neighbors in both blood groups and language. More generally, the rough association between the two kinds of heritage is far less than most persons assume, and scholars have long tried to break the bond in the popular mind between race and language. For Max Müller, as a prime example, "An ethnologist who speaks of Aryan race, Aryan blood, Aryan eyes and hair, is as great a sinner as a linguist who speaks of a dolichocephalic dictionary or a brachycephalic grammar." Americans need but look around at their English-speaking fellow Americans to know that at least in their country language and ethnicity are disjunctive. And certainly Europeans are also well aware that, until President Wilson's principle of self-determination was partly realized in the treaties following the First World War, neither ethnicity nor language was an important organizing principle on the continent. In a stimulating but half-forgotten essay, Max Weber noted the generally slight political salience of a shared language in nineteenth-century

Europe.[1] The ethnic Germans of the east then had no interest, in his view, in joining a greater Reich; and "Until a short time ago most Poles in Upper Silesia . . . were loyal if passive 'Prussians,' but they were not 'Germans.' " In Western Europe, on the other hand, "The term nationality does not seem to be quite fitting" for such multilingual states as Belgium and Switzerland. Tocqueville also saw Switzerland as a non-nation, which, "properly speaking, has never had a federal government." [2] In his opinion, such diverse cantons as Uri and Vaud comprised a union that "exists only on the map," as would become evident "if an attempt were made by a central authority to prescribe the same laws to the whole country."

However many scholars like Max Müller have tried to separate genetic from linguistic classifications, in a practical sense the common man who persists in confusing the two is half-right, for the effect on current behavior of a belief in either type of heritage is likely to be the same. Indeed, whatever characteristic it is that marks the separation of "ethnic" groups has usually made little difference in their intensity of feeling, their typical demands, or even their symbols of communal adherence. Recent disputes in Western Europe have been based on differences in both race (England or France) and language (Belgium or Norway), but also in religion (Netherlands or Northern Ireland), nationality (Switzerland), and region (Germany). Most of the analyses that transcend case studies, however, generalize in terms of only one of these patterns, and even the supposedly generic terms are not much broader. To reject these designations is not mere pedantry, for each of them has taken on meanings that are the more insidious for being half-hidden.

One of the more common terms, *minority group,* is ordinarily linked to an alleged censurable subordination; thus, entities not associated with a "social problem" (such as, in the United States, New

1. Max Weber, *Economy and Society: An Outline of Interpretive Sociology* (New York, Bedminster Press, 1968), I, 385 ff.

2. Alexis de Tocqueville, *Democracy in America* (New York, Vintage, 1959), I, 176.

Englanders or Lutherans) are not ordinarily included under the rubric. On the other hand, if the egalitarian norm is contravened, then the relative size of the group is deemed to be unimportant; as Louis Wirth put it, "The people whom we regard as a minority may actually, from a numerical standpoint, be a majority." [3] This extension is not only semantically inelegant but conceptually impermissible, for Wirth thus glossed over the fundamental distinction between democratic and nondemocratic societies. Only in the former does one find what Tocqueville called "the tyranny of the majority." [4] In most of history, as well as in most of the non-Western world today, the overwhelming social division has been between a small ruling elite and a vast ruled mass, with the latter not significantly differentiated by the possession or the lack of civil rights. Any delineation of a "minority," moreover, can be both ambiguous and therefore arbitrary. In the British Isles the Irish are a widely dispersed minority; in all of Ireland the Protestants are a minority; in the Six Counties the Catholics are a minority.[5] Simply by drawing the appropriate boundary and stressing the self-serving portion of Europe's inordinately complex history, any sector can represent itself as victimized. For example, some spokesmen for Dutch Catholicism have until recently demanded "emancipation," [6] though the Catholic plurality—about 40 percent of the total population—has for most of this century, at least, constituted the largest and most powerful cultural-political sector of the Netherlands.

Some analysts have preferred the term *interest group,* which substitutes for the persecution of Wirth's "minority" a competition among many minorities.[7] For most of the ethnic patterns in the United States or Western Europe, this is a far less distortive concept, but it also focuses the analysis on power relations. Again, in

3. Louis Wirth, "The Problem of Minority Groups," in Ralph Linton, ed., *The Science of Man in the World Crisis* (New York, Columbia University Press, 1945).

4. Tocqueville, *Democracy in America,* I, 269 ff.

5. Cf. Robert E. Kennedy, Jr., *The Irish: Emigration, Marriage, and Fertility* (Berkeley, University of California Press, 1973).

6. W. Goddijn, *Katholieke minderheid en Protestantse dominant* (Assen, Van Gorcum, 1957).

7. For example, Nathan Glazer and Daniel P. Moynihan, *Beyond the Melting Pot* (Cambridge, Harvard University Press and MIT Press, 1963).

most contexts New Englanders and Lutherans are hardly "interest groups," yet they illustrate important parts of a complete ethnic classification. Moreover, the term passes over the frequent dissensus between the ideologues who speak in the name of interest groups and the individuals that they supposedly represent. This disjunction, which Olson argued in general terms,[8] is likely to apply doubly to ethnic relations. In Belgium, for example, the most notable victories that the Flemish movement has recently achieved displaced the French language from areas and institutions now designated as Flemish. However, many of the Flemings who moved to the bilingual area around Brussels eventually represent themselves simply as francophones, for the language that they used at first only in business and public affairs eventually became a symbol of their new position. Many individuals, in short, are caught between a pride in the new status they have been realizing as one of a rapidly advancing Flemish subnation and a reluctance to pay the personal cost involved in this rearrangement of social groups.

Ethnic group would be unobjectionable except that it is used precisely to designate a variety of entities: some would include a religious denomination under the rubric, others not; some would identify a race as an ethnic group, while for others the latter is a smaller subdivision of races; and so on. *Community* is etymologically excellent, for it suggests the commonality that all these terms connote; but the association with a particular geographical location has become too strong to challenge successfully. *Basic group identity*, introduced by Isaacs, is essentially psychological, and one needs still a social correlative.[9]

What is lacking is a term similar in meaning to the European concept of *nation* but applicable to a smaller population—that is, a people, a folk, held together by some or all of such more or less immutable characteristics as common descent, territory, history, language, religion, way of life, or other attributes that members of a group have from birth onward. In earlier writings, I have pro-

8. Mancur J. Olson, *The Logic of Collective Action: Public Goods and the Theory of Groups* (New York, Schocken, 1968).

9. Harold R. Isaacs, "Group Identity and Political Change: Nationalism Revisited," *Survey*, no. 69 (1968), 76–98.

posed the term *subnation* for these smaller units.[10] The concept is purposefully vague both in the specific characteristics that define the group and, thus, in its precise boundaries. Such recurrent difficulties must be resolved by anyone using ethnic statistics, but at a conceptual level it is preferable to define the genus without concern about how one species in it is differentiated from another.

Subnation is set against the other principal classificatory system of any society—namely, *social class*. It is true that if a Marxian class consciousness develops or particularly if in the country under discussion one can speak realistically of a "culture of poverty," the two structures, cultural and social, might overlap. In general, however, the differentiation is empirically well based and no less useful than Ralph Linton's apt division of an individual's statuses between "ascribed" and "achieved." To measure the movement of a person up the social ladder, or of a nation toward full economic development, analysts use changes in occupation, education, income, and rural-urban-metropolitan residence—all as indices of social class. And to mark off the relatively unchanging groups in the same societies, analysts use race, origin, language, citizenship, religion, region (in the sense of a cultural rather than a political subdivision), and so on—all as indices of a second genus, the subnation.

TRENDS IN EUROPEAN NATIONALISM

Nationalism, one of the strongest ideational forces of modern times, was a European invention. As it spread through the rest of the world, social and political analysts repeatedly prophesied an imminent demise on its continent of birth. In fact, there has been a kind of cyclical rise and fall in nationalist cohesion. The romanticism of the early nineteenth century—the historical novels of Walter Scott and his imitators, the accumulation of ballads and Märchen, the quest in language or folklore of the cultural roots of one's own ancestors, the gradual accretion, in a word, of modern nationalist sentiment—can reasonably be interpreted as a reaction against the rationalistic, sometimes arid cosmopolitanism of the

10. For example, William Petersen, *Japanese Americans* (New York, Random House, 1971), chap. 10.

Enlightenment. In spite of the subsequent vigorous and seemingly bellicose competition among European powers, they constructed an elaborate international system (comprising the balance of power, the gold standard, and similar institutions) efficient enough to bring about what Karl Polanyi termed the hundred years' peace.[11] From 1815 to 1914, apart from the "more or less colonial event" of the Crimean War, the major European nations fought one another during only eighteen months, as contrasted with sixty to seventy years in each of the two preceding centuries. According to the programs of pre-1914 Socialists, this relative absence of war was to be made absolute: the worker knew no fatherland, and class conflict would also become a mere memory of an obsolete past.

European nationalism reached a new peak in the subsequent generation. Its most frenetic expressions, however, reflected less a folk ebullience than a relatively weak cohesion of states that had achieved formal unity as recently as the late nineteenth century. It was not mere coincidence that Fascist movements were generally unsuccessful; that in Spain, for example, the Falangist party had to share its control with the army, the church, and the upper bourgeoisie; but that in Italy and Germany, where divisive regional loyalties persist to this day, the Fascists were able to take full power. After the carnage of two world wars and the nauseating excesses particularly of German nationalism, the continent again sought routes to a West European cooperation, a mood that initially was reinforced by the serious threat of Soviet aggression. Europe may be, as in the title of Carl Friedrich's survey of recent internationalist sentiment and institutions, "an emergent nation?," [12] though the phrase (even with the question mark) hardly represents the West European consensus. Since the book was written the Six have become the Nine, and other integrative trends have continued even after the Soviet-Western détente. But the economic crisis, devastating in Italy and serious everywhere, hampered the earlier sometimes easygoing cooperation. In 1974 the British Labour

11. Karl Polanyi, *The Great Transformation* (New York, Rinehart, 1944).
12. Carl J. Friedrich, *Europe: An Emergent Nation?* (New York, Harper & Row, 1969).

party won an election based in part on a promise to submit the terms of Britain's membership in the Common Market to a referendum, and the possibility of extended renegotiation or even of withdrawal reverberated through the international bureaucracy.

In the recurrent shifts between a greater and a lesser unity among European nations, those trying to set a new style commonly jumped over the immediately prior generation to earlier models. There is no necessary political implication, however, in this temporal ordering: the humanists are not dubbed "reactionary" because they sought new stimulation from Greek and Latin writers. Nor is it generally appropriate to classify nationalist movements per se as either "reactionary" or "progressive." In their usual stereotype, Scottish and Welsh nationalisms, for instance, comprise a quaint hodgepodge of amateurish antiquarianism and ultraconservative politics, which hostile commentators have exemplified with hilarious, if highly selective, tidbits. In fact, these nationalists have not only competed with Socialists but have competed on the basis of similar appeals: demands for a better economic return to relatively impoverished areas and for a more satisfactory communal life. "The Scottish National Party has flourished most in the middle-class suburbia, and notably in the New Towns," partly because the new middle classes are "ready to adopt new ideas and new values" [13] but also partly, one would suppose, because these agglomerations of freshly constructed houses need a social bond. The restlessness, the anomie, that frequently seem to be fostered by the complexities of modern society can sometimes be countered by a renewed relation to a simpler past, even a partly mythical past. This quest for community, as Robert Nisbet called it,[14] has no necessary political coloration, and indeed defies a classification based on "right" and "left" pointers from another century. In the Swiss Jura, a leader of the nationalist movement was completely comfortable with his mélange of seventeenth-century local heroes and

13. H. J. Hanham, *Scottish Nationalism* (Cambridge, Harvard University Press, 1969), p. 24.

14. Robert A. Nisbet, *The Quest for Community: A Study in the Ethics of Order and Freedom* (New York, Oxford University Press, 1953).

Lenin, and with his program of achieving a new arcadia through ultramodern terrorist means.

Correlative with the developing European federalism that Friedrich analyzed [15] there has been a beginning disintegration of the separate nations. In some respects, it would seem, the countries of Europe are both too small and too large—too small to afford the maximum efficiency in economic production and distribution, but in many instances too large to give their heterogeneous populations a full and "natural" sense of identity. The continent's traditional elements are being attacked, as it were, at both ends, by a partial transfer of nations' prerogatives to both international and subnational units. "Ethnicism is becoming one of the incontestable expressions of federalism," for "only a federal society provides the conditions in which a complete freedom can blossom for all ethnic groups, large or small, compact or dispersed." [16]

Whether by genetic stock, language-dialect, or any other characteristic that subnations use to mark their separation from all others, the potential number of self-conscious ethnic units in Europe is staggering.[17] Moreover, since nationalist aspirations are bounded by no inherent limit, a yielding to the first demands is as likely to excite the appetite as to satiate it. The farcical trend in the United Nations, which has been overrun by delegates from postcolonial states too small to exert a genuine force in any other arena, suggests the possibilities, happily not yet realized, in Europe. However, the successes of two minute groups, the Romansh and the Frisians, may be indicative.

Romansh (also called Rhaeto-Romance or Ladin) is spoken by tiny populations, mostly in the Swiss province of Grisons but also in portions of the South Tyrol and of Friuli, the neighboring area of Italy. In Grisons it is divided into four official and six school dialects, and the total number speaking all of these constitutes less

15. Friedrich, *Europe: An Emergent Nation?*

16. Guy Heraud, *L'Europe des ethnies* (Paris, Presses d'Europe, 1963), preface by Alexandre Marc, p. 19.

17. Cf. John Geipel, *The Europeans: The People—Today and Yesterday—Their Origins and Interrelations* (New York, Pegasus, 1970).

than 1 percent of the Swiss population.[18] Even so, in 1938 Romansh was recognized as the fourth national language of the Confederation—according to one interpretation, as an expression of the Swiss nationalism resurgent after the First World War.[19] This gesture did not halt the decline of the language, for migrants continued to leave the isolated valleys and they (or, at latest, their children) forgot the language and spoke German or French. The main consequence of the policy for them, or for the Romansh minority as a whole, has been to aggravate their cultural isolation and to make it considerably more difficult for peasants' sons to advance themselves. The nationalist spokesmen are inclined to view such upward mobility as disastrous; for them, the survival of the group is a cause to which the welfare of the individuals in it must be sacrificed.

Another example is the Dutch policy toward Frisian, an ancient Germanic language surviving among some inhabitants of the Dutch province of Friesland, an area of Germany close to the Dutch border, and the German or Danish islands off Schleswig-Holstein. According to a recent survey, most Dutch Frisians can speak the language but more than 30 percent cannot read it and 69 percent cannot write it; moreover, the differences by age and rural-urban residence suggest a continuing decline.[20] Whatever encouragement The Hague has given the self-conscious nationalists who would like to reverse the trend and establish Frisian as the first language of Friesland has stimulated further demands. As in Grisons with Romansh, local school administrators could begin classes in Frisian and shift to Dutch from the fourth year onward; and the movement's principal demand—that, as a means of teaching all children "their" language, this pattern be made compulsory throughout the province—has now become law. Any periodical that manages to get at least 250 subscribers can thereafter shift some of its costs to the central

18. Erich Gruner and Beat Junker, *Bürger, Staat und Politik in der Schweiz* (Basel, Lehrmittelverlag, 1968), pp. 9–10.

19. Franck Jotterand, "La politique culturelle," in Erich Gruner, ed., *Die Schweiz seit 1945: Beiträge zur Zeitgeschichte* (Bern, Francke, 1971), pp. 281–282.

20. L. Pietersen, *De Friesen en hun taal* (Drachten, Lavermen N.V., 1969).

government, which now subsidizes at least four Frisian publications and may soon be paying for several more. There is a developing sentiment that the province must have its own tax-supported university, to supplement the regional museum and archival society. Obviously these concessions to what had been seen as one regional dialect have reverberated to other portions of this small country. Groningen, the province adjacent to Friesland, is building a regional literature, and in eastern Overijsel and Gelderland a small group is propounding a regional ideology.

In these two cases the central governments of Switzerland and the Netherlands seem to have been guided, within the spirit of their democratic institutions, mainly by what one could call the preposterous demands of self-appointed spokesmen for minuscule groups. As a somewhat better guide to such policy, one might suggest an optimum size of a subnation, which should be small enough to foster a genuine social identity and yet large enough to furnish its members with more than a parochial culture. It is true that the term, as in the parallel concepts of the optimum population of a country or a city, cannot be defined precisely, yet one can with some assurance denote either end of a size continuum to be beyond the optimum range.

The Romansh and the Frisians, it is also true, represented in themselves no conceivable threat to the nations that gave them special rights, for they are not only small but also without any link to foreign powers. Many of the ethnic minorities in Europe, on the contrary, speak the language of a neighboring state and thus, irrespective of other characteristics, are often regarded as potential fifth-columnists. Hitler's appeals for support from ethnic "brothers" in Eastern Europe got little response, for example, from the Sudeten Germans, most of whom were Social Democrats, but the Czechoslovak state sharpened its control of the area and in all probability facilitated the Nazi infiltration of the German-speaking minority. The smaller enclaves of ethnic Slavs in Western Europe were the object of a similar attention during Stalin's *Drang nach Westen*. Until diplomats and journalists had their curiosity piqued by the many Soviet references to "the Wends," certainly few of them had ever heard of this remnant, several tens of thousands living along the upper reaches of the Spree who speak a variety of Slavic dialects collectively known as "Sorbian."

More generally, many of Europe's problem areas—Alsace and Brittany, Upper Silesia and Schleswig, and so on—are at the frontier of contiguous states. The myth of a core national type has been reinforced by the fact that the most obvious deviations are located at the periphery. Many European nations have no natural frontiers, and those that exist are often inhabited by the same peoples on both sides. Among mountain ranges, for example, the Pyrenees divide Basques from Basques and Catalans from Catalans, and even so obvious a barrier as Brenner has German Tyrolese to the south as well as to the north.[21] The experiment after the First World War of liquidating alien enclaves through mass population transfers usually, however unexpectedly, heightened nationalist feelings: the dispossessed minorities, typically given good reason to hate their prior host country, transferred this sentiment with their few remaining possessions. Indeed, any policy based on a willful simplification of Western Europe's fascinating complexity is likely to boomerang, for with the revival of nationalist sentiment any new affronts stimulate it and thus exacerbate old disputes.

The most recent changes in West Europe's ethnic structure are too varied to summarize easily, particularly since any new pattern can be satisfactorily analyzed only against the specific historical background. The rest of this paper, thus, comprises two sections on the more significant trends in Switzerland and Belgium. The present institutions of these countries reflect the accretion of their common history: the confrontation of Roman legions and Germanic peoples, of the Catholic and Protestant churches, of urban and rural ways of life. By a world standard, both are small; their populations in mid-1973 were estimated, respectively, to be 6.5 and 9.8 million. Both are relatively prosperous; their respective gross national products per capita in 1970, converted to U.S. dollars, were 3,320 and 2,720. Yet underlying these common elements is a remarkable diversity not only between the two nations themselves

21. Cf. Alfred Cobban, *The Nation State and National Self-Determination* (New York, Crowell, 1969), p. 296.

but among the subnations within them, and this heterogeneity is in some ways becoming still greater.

SWITZERLAND

The nucleus of the Swiss federation was a union that the "forest cantons"—Uri, Schwyz, and Unterwalden—formed in 1291 to defend themselves against the Hapsburgs. Over the following centuries these three were joined by surrounding cantons, all of which were careful to retain their local authority. For a brief moment a fully centralized government was imposed in Napoleon's Helvetic Republic, which did not last, however, even as long as the emperor himself. In the post-Napoleonic settlement, every one of the cantons sent a separate delegate to the Congress of Vienna, and the Allied representatives struggled to untangle their competing claims. The settlement that was finally reached (though still opposed by four of the then nineteen cantons) established less a nation than an arena for ideological dispute. When several urban cantons sought to extend the central government's power so as to include the rights to tax church property, establish secular schools, and guarantee freedom of worship, seven Catholic cantons responded by setting up a so-called *Sonderbund* ("special union"), a half-secession that in their view renewed their medieval federation and the protection of their ancient liberties. In 1847 this confrontation between Catholics and Liberals, between the country's rural nucleus and urban radicals, climaxed in a three-week civil war in which the Catholic forces were decisively defeated.

Fortunately it was not the radicals but moderate Liberals who fashioned a new constitution, which with amendments remains the country's basic law. According to various accounts, the model used in accommodating national unity to disparate local rights and traditions was the U.S. Constitution,[22] but the result approximates rather the earlier and far looser Articles of Confederation. Indeed, the 1848 constitution established one Swiss citizenship in a nation with one foreign policy, one national economy with a single customs union, and the right of any Swiss to settle in any canton. Apart

22. For example, Hans Kohn, *Nationalism and Liberty: The Swiss Example* (London, Allen and Unwin, 1956), p. 111.

from a number of anti-Catholic provisions (in particular, the prohibition of new monasteries and the banning of the Jesuit order), the
constitution relegated to the cantons the governance of church–
state relations. It recognized the three main languages—German,
French, and Italian—as official throughout the country and the
three language groups as equal; but the schools, the instruments of
cultural continuity, stayed under the cantons' jurisdiction. The
general allocation of power is suggested by Article I of the constitution: "The peoples of the twenty-two sovereign cantons of Switzerland form together the Swiss Confederation." Most of the
prerogatives of statehood, in short, were reserved to the cantons.
"If it is the function of a national state to guarantee the political
means by which a people united through its common characteristics and environment can further its particular needs and interests, this can be carried out nowhere better than in the Swiss cantons." [23]

The Swiss Confederation reestablished in the 1848 constitution
was remarkably successful. As we have seen, scholars as perceptive
as Tocqueville and Max Weber wondered whether so heterogeneous a population could ever constitute a viable nation. Yet it developed, though without coal, iron, oil, or colonies, a truly startling
prosperity; and, from its unmitigated diversity there arose a national culture of the highest quality. From 1901 to 1960, the
number of Nobel laureates per million inhabitants was 2.62 for
Switzerland, which ranked first in the world and almost twice as
high as Denmark, which ranked second.[24] Achievements of this
order foster an overall national pride that inhibits internal divisions. Yet Switzerland constitutes an anomaly, a miracle of intergroup harmony, which depends on a complex and sometimes
precarious institutional balance of still hostile forces. The wisdom
of the nineteenth-century statesmen was reinforced by a number of

23. Hermann Weilenmann, *Pax Helvetica, oder die Demokratie der kleinen Gruppen*
(Zurich, Eugen Rentsch, 1951), p. 288.

24. Denis de Rougemont, "Swiss Federalism," in Théo Chopard, ed., *Switzerland, Present and Future: A Small Country Re-examines Itself* (Bern, New Helvetic
Society, 1963).

fortuitous circumstances, which in sum have made Swiss nationhood possible.

The three language communities, each speaking a tongue common with a contiguous foreign country, inevitably share these alien
cultures in some respects; yet the fissiparous effect has been less
than one might have anticipated. According to Hans Kohn, in the
middle of the nineteenth century "many German-speaking Swiss
felt a dual loyalty: the Swiss canton was their political fatherland,
the still ill-defined Germany their cultural homeland." Strangely,
this adherence to the larger entity was reinforced by German radicals who found refuge in Switzerland after having fought, and lost,
against German autocracy. As late as 1902 a professor at Bern University, one Ferdinand Vetter, marked the opening of a Germanic
museum in Nuremberg with the assertion, "We are happy to celebrate this German institution among Germans, because we German
Swiss are spiritually Germans and hope to remain so." This view,
however representative it may have been, was dissipated by the
First World War; and even before that the cantons' fierce independence, which impeded their assimilation to Swiss unity, also
blocked any even quasi-political adherence to Germany. The poet
and novelist Gottfried Keller, of far greater importance than any
professor, offered a concept of Switzerland significantly similar to
the American idea of nationality: "a community not determined
primarily by biological factors but representing the idea of personal liberty." [25] With the rise of Prussia and particularly after the
Nazis took power, the cultural bond with Germany was negated by
growing political alienation. There was even a movement in the
1930s to drop the German language and substitute "Allemanic"; it
came to nothing principally because the various dialects of Swiss
German are both too different and too precious to their users to be
easily consolidated.

How and why do the francophone Swiss differentiate themselves
from the French, Rougemont asked, and his reply is an apt statement of one side of a similarly ambivalent relation.

25. Kohn, *Nationalism and Liberty*, pp. 89, 94, 127.

Culture in our cantons is not linked with the state and has never been used as a means of power by the state. Culture in our country exists within small natural or historical compartments, which have never been unified or standardized by a central power . . . Protestantism is predominant in French-speaking Switzerland . . . We are not only neighbors of the Germanic world, but we are in an osmotic relationship with it.[26]

On the other hand, there has been a mood in France to bolster its hegemony with cultural dependencies, to take the place of lost colonies and waning political influence. President de Gaulle himself ended a speech in Montreal with the slogan "Vive le Québec libre!" and there are movements to "liberate" French-speaking minorities from non-French "oppressors" in Canada, Belgium, Italy, and Switzerland—though in the last case not in the principal francophone area.

Apart from the factors listed by Rougemont, a French-speaking population is more likely to accept cultural (or even political) guidance from Paris if it lacks self-confidence. One index of the relation of language to provincial cultures is the work of professional linguists, who it so happens differ fundamentally between French Switzerland and Walloon Belgium. In both areas, as one would expect, the study of local dialects has been a dominant concern, but the significance of this topic has not been the same. Ferdinand de Saussure, a native of Geneva and professor at its university, founded a school in linguistics important enough to transcend national boundaries but strongest among his own students. In Belgium, on the contrary, one of the main interests has been in "preserving 'le bon usage'; as peripheral users of French they are more than conscious of regional differences in their language, and locked as they are in an ethno-linguistic struggle with their Flemish co-citizens, they fear to lose grip of linguistic standards." [27] The contrast is not limited to philologists. Rougemont reflects a typical stance when he writes of the French and the Swiss francophones simply that "we speak more or less the same language." In Belgium

---

26. Rougemont, "Swiss Federalism."
27. Rebecca Posner, "Thirty Years On," supplement to Iorgu Iordan and John Orr, *An Introduction to Romance Linguistics: Its Schools and Scholars* (Berkeley, University of California Press, 1970), p. 419.

a book titled *Chasse aux Belgicismes,* published by an "Office du Bon Langage," became something of a bestseller.[28] The Belgicisms to be "hunted down" include especially the regional accent and also those elements, particularly if they derived from the Dutch, of vocabulary and idiom that distinguish the Walloon dialects from cultured Parisian.

The generalizations about French-speaking Swiss do not pertain, however, to the inhabitants of the Jura, whose demand for a canton of their own has become the country's most explosive ethnic issue. The rationale for the demand, at least in the publications of the militants, goes back to the Thirty Years' War. The main separatist organization sent a memorandum to each of the signatory states at the Congress of Vienna, which had granted jurisdiction of the area to Bern canton rather than its earlier ruler, an autocratic Prince-Bishop of the Principality of Basel. The present cycle of conflict began with some routine politicking in 1947; three years later an overwhelming majority of the canton's electorate revised its constitution to specify French as the sole official language of the six francophone districts and to guarantee the Jura two seats on the canton's executive council. It was even decreed that the new Jurasian flag be flown next to the Bernese one. Neither these concessions nor subsequent ones satisfied the rebels. The issue, as always, is less simple than a one-to-one confrontation.

In the Bernese constitution the Jura is viewed as a single entity under the designation "the Jurasian people," but in fact the Jura is divided into three parts: North Jura, which according to the 1959 vote is inclined to be separatist; South Jura, inclined to be antiseparatist; and the district of Laufon, whose population speaks German. One must take this division into account if one wants to try to propose a durable solution to the Jurasian problem.[29]

The situation exemplifies a general proposition: when subnations differ by not one but several overlapping characteristics, the combined divisive force is of course greater than from any one of

28. Joseph Hanse et al., *Chasse aux Belgicismes* (Brussels, Fondation Charles Plisnier, 1971).
29. Max Petitpierre et al., *Premier rapport de la Commission confédérée de bons offices pour le Jura du 13 Mai 1969* (Bern, 1969).

them. Most of the population of Bern canton are German-speaking Protestants, and Jurasians who either speak German or adhere to Protestantism have generally been content with the status quo. It is among the Catholic francophones that the separatist movement has developed.[30] Its principal organization, the Rassemblement Jurassien, derived its name from de Gaulle's "Rassemblement du Peuple Français," and its journal, *Le Jura Libre,* reflects the same ideology. Two terrorists from more extremist organizations escaped abroad and were granted political asylum by France and Spain, respectively. On the other side there are several overlapping antiseparatist organizations (Union des Patriotes Jurassiens, Groupement Interpartis pour l'Unité Cantonale, Jeunesses Civiques du Jura Bernois, Groupement des Jeunes Ajoulots), which together represent a substantial opposition to the proposed new canton and especially to the arson and bombings used to achieve it. The Rassemblement Jurassien does not support terrorism, but its notion of democracy is also cut to its own program; by its view, all German-speaking inhabitants of the Jura should be denied a vote, and all French-speaking "Jurasians," including even those who have emigrated permanently, should be given it. The vote (by more than six to one) in favor of a compromise that the federal government and Bern canton had jointly proposed, thus, was rejected by the separatists because these "jurassiens de l'extérieur" had not been polled. In the summer of 1974 another vote was taken, overwhelmingly in favor of the formation of a twenty-third canton in the francophone Catholic area but opposed to it or ambivalent in the others. At the time of writing, the issue is more or less resolved, with the separation of the Jura assured but with its precise boundaries yet to be determined.

The support of the Jura's status quo among French-speaking Protestants illustrates a structural feature of much broader significance. During the nineteenth century, as nationality gradually replaced religion as the dominant ideology of Switzerland's subnations, it so happened that sizable proportions of both Catholics and Protestants were included among both the German and the

30. Kurt B. Mayer, "The Jura Problem: Ethnic Conflict in Switzerland," *Social Research* 35 (1968), 707–741.

French-Italian sectors. Whatever antipathy arose either between religious or between language groups, then, was mitigated by the fact that the adversaries in one context could be the allies in another. Moreover, the proportions of the several subnations remained more or less the same for over a century. Nothing is so likely to exacerbate interethnic antagonism as what the French Canadians call "la revanche des berceaux"—the vengeance of the cradles: with a differential growth rate every settlement is tentative, in force only till the day—eagerly awaited or fearfully dreaded— when the minority and the majority change places. By a fortunate happenstance, the greater natural increase of the German Swiss was offset by their higher net emigration.[31] Nor did movement within the country disturb its structural balance, for since the language of the schools is set locally, children typically adopt the language of the canton into which their parents had moved. In short, the divisive force along any one dimension is less if it cuts across a division by another characteristic.

The balance that was reached by these more or less fortuitous circumstances seems now to be endangered, and not merely by the mainly local contretemps in the Jura. The principal threat to the traditional equilibrium has come from the very large influx of foreign laborers, who are more numerous relative to the native population than in any other European country. In mid-1970 there were about 660,000 aliens with work permits plus about 160,000 permanent alien residents. In a country with a total population of only 6.5 million, the issue of what is called *Überfremdung* (hyperforeignization) was perhaps inevitable. One horn of the country's dilemma is that the rapid postwar development of the economy was built on a broad base of imported labor, which cannot now be replaced entirely by natives. In the summer of 1971 the government officially reported a total of only 51 unemployed in the whole country; retail shops and other small establishments were restricting their activities or closing down completely for lack of workers. On the other hand, many Swiss see in the large bloc of foreigners a danger to the society, partly because many come from areas quite

31. Kurt B. Mayer, *The Population of Switzerland* (New York, Columbia University Press, 1952), chap. 8.

distinct from Swiss culture (southern Italy, Spain, and other Mediterranean countries), partly because the legal impediments to naturalization are so great that they are unassimilable almost by definition. Naturalization is difficult even for a Swiss-born child of alien parents, and one cannot apply for even the right of permanent residence until after ten years of renewed temporary visas. In this thoroughly middle-class society, where the embourgeoisement of workers and of Socialists in particular has been all but total, the foreign laborers have introduced a new type of proletariat. Thus, the remarkable industrial peace—a full generation without a single strike or lockout—has been broken (for example, by Spanish workers constructing the new ILO building in Geneva).

A very sharp confrontation between the two halves of this dilemma was a vote in June 1970 to amend the constitution so as to limit the alien residents to 10 percent both of the whole country and of each canton (except Geneva) separately. The move was sponsored by Senator James Schwarzenbach and opposed by other political parties and by labor, business, and church leaders. Even so, it was defeated by only 96,874 votes out of 1,212,302 cast, and by that small margin mainly because some months before the plebiscite the government had taken new steps to restrict the inflow of foreign workers. The consequence of the new system is somewhat paradoxical: fewer foreign workers are admitted, but those that do immigrate stay longer on the average and come closer to a full participation in Swiss society. In demographic fact, though not in citizenship, several hundred thousand "temporary" immigrants are already affecting the country's culture. According to the 1960 census, moreover, 41.7 percent of Swiss citizens were aged 40 and over, but only 13.1 percent of the aliens with temporary permits. The trend during the following decade certainly did not greatly change this imbalance in the age structure in either direction. Nor has the opposition to *Überfremdung* lessened. Late in 1972 Dr. Schwarzenbach's former party, the Nationale Aktion für Volk und Heimat (the National Movement for People and Home), began to collect signatures for a yet more drastic proposal. Under its terms about two out of every five of the 540,000 non-Swiss residents would have been expelled by the year 1978. The referendum was put to a vote a full two years later, in the fall of 1974, when it was defeated by about two to one. Almost half of the electorate were willing to damage the economy to halt the inflow of foreigners, and a third courted economic disaster in order to reduce their number. One can suppose that the issue is not dead.

Cutting the number of aliens is less pertinent than the effect of the foreigners' presence on the relations between the religious and language groups of the Swiss themselves. In 1960, 79.7 percent of the aliens, but only 41.9 percent of Swiss citizens, gave their religion as Catholic. By the same census, the respective percentages of Swiss citizens and aliens speaking the country's main languages were as follows: German, 74.4 and 27.5; French, 20.2 and 7.8; and Italian, 4.1 and 54.1. Italian, which once was more or less restricted to the single canton of Ticino, has become an important second language especially in the cities of German Switzerland, where most of the immigrants work. But if they are allowed to stay, they and particularly their children will adapt to the language of the area. Thus, the large immigration of Italians, which has reduced German speakers to the lowest proportion in Swiss history, may in the long run have the contrary effect, greatly reinforcing the German ascendancy over French.[32]

In sum, Switzerland's famous ethnic harmony is too well established in thoroughly rooted institutions to be broken altogether, but several trends have been troublesome. The most notorious episode, the demand of French-speaking Catholics in the Jura for an autonomous canton of their own, is less important than the disparity between the economic need for foreign workers and the unwillingness of many Swiss citizens to have them assimilated into the population. In spite of the fact that more foreigners are permitted to come in than restrictionists would prefer, the lack of low-skill workers has squeezed the economy.

It is more difficult to gauge the effects of constitutional revisions on cantonal patriotism. At Expo 1964, the sixth of the national fairs held every quarter-century, the usual commercial emphasis

---

32. Kurt B. Mayer, "Postwar Immigration and Switzerland's Demographic and Social Structure," in William Petersen, ed., *Readings in Population* (New York, Macmillan, 1972).

gave way to a grand attempt at national self-appraisal. True, the avant-garde and experimental exhibits were not popular, so that the fair incurred a deficit estimated at 10–12 million francs, but the mood persisted. In 1971 a constitutional amendment finally gave women the vote on federal issues (only three cantons and two half-cantons still lacked local female suffrage). No significant change took place in the composition of the Parliament, but with the first nationwide referendum in which women could vote the federal government acquired new powers to combat air and water pollution—perhaps an issue on which the two sexes differ. In the past several decades the power of the federal government has been extended also with respect to the protection of the family, the national economy, atomic energy, national roads, the movie industry, oil pipelines, university scholarships, the protection of nature, and regional zoning.[33] The miscellany is made up of matters that clearly transgress cantonal boundaries (a continuation, as it were, of the customs union established in the 1848 constitution) but also issues that have only recently become important. If most of the problems of modernity are to be assigned to the federal government, the functions of the cantons will gradually shrink. It would seem, thus, that the heightened hostility between language and possibly even religious groups has been countered by an increased central authority. The equilibrium is delicately balanced, as it always has been.

BELGIUM

After Charlemagne died in the year 814, his vast domain was divided into three parts, one in modern France, one in modern Germany, and the third, called Lotharingia, lying athwart the Romance-Teutonic language boundary. Partly just because of its population's heterogeneity, Lotharingia soon dissolved into its component parts. These were reassembled, however, by the Counts of Flanders; and after they were joined by marriage with the House of Burgundy, the area developed into one of the showpieces of medieval culture. The seventeen provinces of the "Burgundian Cir-

33. Jean-François Aubert, "Histoire constitutionnelle," in Erich Gruner, ed., *Die Schweiz seit 1945*.

cle" (present Belgium, Netherlands, and part of France) were brought into the Holy Roman Empire, another vast structure that again disintegrated under Philip II of Spain. Under the treaties ending the Thirty Years' War, two new republics were recognized as independent of the Empire: the Swiss Confederation and the United Netherlands. Control over the southern half of the Low Countries, however, merely passed from the Spanish to the Austrian Hapsburgs. In the next century France's revolutionary government annexed the area *in toto,* and Napoleon tried to complete its assimilation by forcibly introducing the French language throughout the Flemish provinces. In the post-Napoleonic settlement, a buffer state comprising present Belgium and the Netherlands was set up under Willem I of the House of Orange. Much that Willem did was well intentioned and even wise, but he was also opinionated and stubborn enough eventually to alienate most of his Belgian subjects. A revolt in 1830 developed into a desultory war of independence, and the modern state thus came into being.

What particular strains of this complicated background constitute the authentic history of Belgium is a question, obviously, to which the current nationalist movements give different answers. The country's name comes from Belgae, an ancient people about whom Caesar wrote briefly. The first time it was used with its present meaning, rather than to designate either the area populated by that tribe or the whole of the Low Countries, was in 1790, when assembled deputies declared a short-lived republican federation: the United States of Belgium. The country's limits conform to no natural or cultural boundaries. The Dutch are on both sides of the Scheldt estuary to the north, and Dutch Limburg projects like a giant pendant into territory physically and culturally indistinguishable from it. The plains of Flanders stretch with no visible divider into France, and on the eastern border the one or two percent of the population who speak German point up the lack of any distinct separation also on that side. If the boundary had been drawn along the language frontier, half of Belgium would have been included with France; if it had been drawn by religion, the southern, solidly Catholic third of the Netherlands would have been Belgian. "Belgium is the most contrived country in Western Europe . . . Belgium's frontiers—like those of some colonial territories—were imposed, not by force of the country's own arms but by the great powers." [34]

The cultural-social-political division between the language sectors, which in retrospect is now viewed as a basic theme during Belgium's entire existence, has become both sharper and more pervasive in the decades since 1945. During the wartime occupation, the German administration had tried, with some success, to exacerbate regional hostilities by favoring the "Aryan" Flemish, but it accepted deference as well from the Rexists, a pro-Nazi, predominantly French-speaking group. In truth, neither in Flanders nor in Wallonia were there many who either collaborated with the occupying force or actively opposed it, but in subsequent recriminations much was sometimes made of the pro-Nazi activities of small minorities. Moreover, some of the most important political struggles after the war, in particular over whether King Leopold III should return to the throne and whether schools should be secularized, reinforced the overall division. That "the relation between the two language communities," as the issue is termed in official writings, continued to deteriorate in the 1960s also reflected the frustrations that the whole nation was suffering. The surplus of coal on hand in 1959 was estimated at 7 million tons; some mines were closed, and miners worked part-time. The Congo, which attained its independence in 1960, quickly degenerated into chaos, leaving Belgium with neither its prior financial stake nor even the moral satisfaction of having relinquished it to a responsible successor state. The government's austerity measures were answered with widespread strikes in 1961, followed by one of physicians in 1963 that gained notoriety throughout the world.

Even without such political aggravations of ethnic divisions, it is not likely that the Flemish would long have remained satisfied with their inferior status. Walloon industry, based in part on obsolescent factories and mines either soon to be depleted or becoming marginal to the European market, has been in relative decline, while in Flanders, at least comparatively, commerce and industry

---

34. Frank E. Huggett, *Modern Belgium* (London, Pall Mall, 1969), pp. 1–2.

have boomed. Flemings are no longer only peasants or industrial workers; increasing numbers have become owners or managers of large business firms or high-level civil servants. Always a majority of the population, the Flemish have been growing at a slightly faster rate than the Walloons: the Flemings' considerably higher fertility had been largely canceled, as in Switzerland, by their greater emigration and their acculturation to the Walloon sector in the Brussels area.[35] Nevertheless the Flemish increased at a faster rate than the Walloons, and in the most recent period this has continued because the mortality in Flanders is lower than in Wallonia. With demographic and economic ascendancy, the Flemish have resented the superiority accorded to the French language and the implicit political power that Walloons acquired thereby, seemingly as their natural right.

Paradoxically, as the two languages became more and more an issue of public policy, data on their use became ever harder to assemble and analyze.[36] The last census to include a query on language was in 1947, and some charged that that question was unfairly worded. For the two main regions it is now usually presumed that the legal definition represents reality—that is, that the north is Dutch-speaking and the south French-speaking. But none of the several alternative sources of language data for the nineteen bilingual townships of the Brussels agglomeration are satisfactory. In a number of situations each person ostensibly selects either language freely, but actually the choice may be distorted by extraneous factors. For example, the identity card that everyone is required to have can be in either language, but since it used to be that most officials in the Brussels area were Walloons, a Fleming was likely to be given a "carte d'identité" unless he made a point of demanding an "identikeitskart." Similarly, civil marriage ceremonies can be per-

35. R. Cliquet, "On the Differential Population Development of the Flemings and the Walloons and Its Influence on the Flemish-Walloon Relations," *Homo* 11 (1960), 67–88; Frans Van Mechelen, "De demografische 'taalgrens' in België," *Mens en Maatschappij* 38 (1963), 444–457; Jean Morsa, "Fécondité, nuptialité et composition par âge," *Bevolking en Gezin* 5 (1965), 83–112.

36. Paul M. G. Lévy, *La querelle du recensement* (Brussels, Institut Belge de Science Politique, 1960); Lévy, "La mort du recensement linguistique," *Revue Nouvelle* 18 (1962), 145–154.

formed in either language at the couple's option, but many of the burgomasters have been so deficient in Dutch that the Flemish, who in the Brussels area are typically bilingual, select the less inconvenient medium for an occasion they want to go smoothly. In the Belgian army officers must be competent in both languages, but soldiers may choose a unit using one or the other. Many of the Flemish draftees, however, used to serve their term in a Walloon unit in order to perfect their school French. Two sociologists, finally, recently surveyed the Brussels population and issued their findings in a mimeographed report, since become "très chaud," as it is called in intentional franglais.[37] To the extent that I could judge, it was a competent job, and any bias of the two authors, both of Flemish origin, was presumably not pro-Walloon. But since only 17.7 percent of their sample reported their *current* language to be Dutch (or far less than almost everyone had guessed from estimates about the number of in-migrants whose *original* language was Flemish), the survey was attacked by Flemish nationalists in Parliament and the press. The two authors, who have since shifted to market research, do not want even to discuss their earlier work. That no figures are accepted as valid by both sides helps, of course, to lower the tone of the debate.

The gathering of language statistics, in sum, encompasses an inescapable dilemma. Among upper-class Flemings of the nineteenth century, it was routine to speak Dutch to the servants and French among themselves. With the democratization of Belgian society, this association between language and social status did not disappear but, on the contrary, spread through the other classes. Since French is still the dominant medium of communication in the Brussels area and internationally, for ambitious Flemish (or, alternatively, their children) the acquisition of a facile and accentless French is a means of upward mobility. Those who either are truly bilingual or would like to consider themselves to be such once acquired prestige by reporting themselves as "francophones." Thus, if Walloon officials sometimes used their bureaucratic power to

37. P. Kluft and F. Van der Vorst, "Enquête à Bruxelles: Le problème linguistique et politique" (Brussels, Institut de Sociologie, Université Libre de Bruxelles, n.d.).

improve the record from their point of view, some of the Flemish, threatened with the loss of an important route up, were quite willing to cooperate in this half-falsification. The statistics, in short, could be accurate if they were not used, but since they have become a part of many political decisions,[38] some citizens respond less in terms of objective fact than as a means of casting a vote.

The antagonism between the language communities is aggravated by the fact that both look to neighboring countries for cultural guidance. In other countries nationalist movements generally seek roots in the speech and customs of the common people, using folklore as a step to folk history, trying to redefine a dialect as another national language, and so on. In contrast, Walloon nationalists take Paris as their model, and Flemish take The Hague. This cultural subservience may have political implications, which those on the other side often exaggerate.

The concept of Groot-Nederland, "Greater Netherlands," though still denigrated on both sides of the Belgian-Dutch border, represents an important element of cultural (if not yet political) reality and will not disappear. The best presentation has been in the works of Pieter Geyl, perhaps the most eminent Dutch historian of the past generation, who took as his main target the life work of his no less eminent Belgian predecessor, Henri Pirenne. Tracing the history of a fictive "Belgium" back through centuries, Pirenne had accomplished this reconstruction with such consummate attention to detail as to make a plausible case for the existence of a Belgian patriotism antedating Belgium. For Geyl, the true historical division was along the language boundary, virtually unchanged for a millennium and a half; the southern sector of Dutch speakers was cut off by historical accidents, from the fact that the invasion in the

---

38. A law was proposed to set a speed limit of 90 kilometers on ordinary two-lane roads between towns, retaining the prior absence of any limitation only on the major four-lane highways with limited access and other safety features. But as one Walloon member of Parliament pointed out, most of these better roads are in Flanders, whose inhabitants would thus enjoy the right to drive faster than French-speaking motorists. Some of the older roads of Wallonia were therefore exempted from the speed limit, in order to extend the privilege over an equal distance in both sections of the country even though this would presumably mean a higher death toll among Walloon drivers and their families.

sixteenth century was stopped at the Rhine and the Meuse to the cooperation of the great powers in fashioning a composite Belgium in 1830 in order to insulate the resurgent revolution in France. Even one who admires Pirenne's craftsmanship might well find Geyl's thesis markedly more plausible. Its presumed consequences for the Low Countries of the present day are propagated in such journals as *Streven* ("Striving"), edited by several Dutch-speaking Jesuits on both sides of the border, and *Neerlandia,* published in Ghent, the site of a Flemish university.

The most important effort to develop cultural unity pertains to the language itself, which is no longer called *Vlaams* (that is, Flemish) but *Nederlands* or sometimes *Zuid-Nederlands* (Southern Dutch). Radio and television programs in the two countries take pains to use a uniform pronunciation, and books published in the Netherlands reportedly find a third of their market in Flanders. Several binational commissions have labored to reform the spelling on both sides of the border. A number of books have been published in Flanders offering an exposition of "Algemeen Beschaafd Nederlands" (General Cultured Dutch) in place of the several regional dialects, and there is an association of schoolteachers, the Vereniging voor Beschaafde Omgangstaal, with the same purpose. The words and expressions that are most to be avoided, according to these precepts, are of course those that derive from the French. One of the remaining differences between the typical idioms, thus, is that the Dutch spoken in the Netherlands is full of French words and phrases. Some of the older acquisitions are half-hidden (for example, *krant,* "newspaper," from the French *courant,* as contrasted with *dagblad,* more common in Flanders), but many new ones are brought in as well, for in the Netherlands French represents not a competing subnation but a symbol of chic cosmopolitanism.

There are Walloon counterparts, as we have suggested, to every one of these efforts. A nonprofit organization founded in 1966, the Centre d'Action Culturelle de la Communauté d'Expression Française, publishes a review of the Belgian and foreign press on matters of interest to francophones everywhere. In the summer of 1970 representatives of French-speaking minorities met in Geneva to lay out a joint program of action; delegates attended from the Swiss Jura, the Vallée d'Aosta in Italy, and Wallonia. Some of these international manifestations of francophone unity go beyond mere cultural exchanges and verge on political alliances against the non-French sectors of European populations.

In Belgium (contrary to the crosscutting equilibrium that we noted in Switzerland), differences in language have been partly reinforced by those in religion. In a country that is nominally completely Catholic, one needs data (which apparently do not exist) on what proportions attend mass, perform their Easter duties, and so on in order to judge the actual influence of the church. In the past the association of language with social class meant that the upper levels of the hierarchy were French-oriented and only some of the local priests in Flanders favored the Flemish movement. It was opposed by the hierarchy generally, especially in secondary education. Nevertheless there has been a contrast between solidly Catholic Flanders, where at least the lower clergy have been sympathetic to nationalist demands, and predominantly Socialist Wallonia, where Catholicism is weaker and likely to be anticlerical. In the past decade or so, however, the Flemish movement has become noticeably more secular. At its 1968 convention, the Davidsfonds, the largest of the Flemish cultural-welfare organizations, changed its slogan from "Godsdienst, Taal, Vaderland" (religion, language, fatherland) to "Godsdienst, Taal, Volk," thus in effect changing the object of its formal allegiance from Belgium to Flanders. Two years later a sizable minority tried—this time unsuccessfully—to cut the tie to the church, a proposal that would have left only the link to the language community.

Of the several issues that have divided nationalists from the church hierarchy, the most important concerned the future of the Catholic University of Louvain. Because Louvain (Flemish: Leuven) is in Flanders, the nationalist students demanded that this be entirely a Dutch-speaking institution, and their rioting spread to Antwerp and other Flemish cities. For a while the episcopate resisted the pressure and supported the bilingual status quo. The academic council of Louvain-French, feeling itself under siege, petitioned the national government to impose a solution, but the prime minister understandably replied that an institution governed by the Catholic church was outside its jurisdiction. Even so, the government fell in 1968, with the mounting crisis at Louvain as the proximate cause. The following year funds were provided for the transfer of the French section some miles south to Wallonia, at a campus now being constructed. (At the same time the Dutch section of the Free University of Brussels was made entirely autonomous.) Louvain's valuable library holdings were divided in half, books with an even catalogue number to one section, those with an odd one to the other; but this was only the basis for protracted negotiations that continued until all the once joint property was apportioned. The university, one of the oldest and most distinguished in Europe, will undoubtedly survive its bifurcation, but presumably not without significant losses in academic standards. The acrimony pervading the negotiations diverted scholars from more productive activities, and the money spent on building and operating new facilities at Ottignies will reduce budgets for other functions.

The national election of 1968 marked, in retrospect, a turning point of postwar politics. From 1920, when universal suffrage was established, to the mid-1960s (excepting only 1936), the party system had been very stable, and all parties were given important though a different support in each region.[39] The prior coalition between Socialists and Social Catholics, however, had been suffering from nationalist threats: André Renard acquired a considerable following in the trade unions and Socialist party around a Walloon program, and the Catholic-Flemish quarrels we have noted obviously weakened the Social Catholic party. From 1961 to 1968, thus, the number of seats held by the Social Catholics fell from 96 to 69, that of the Socialists from 84 to 59.[40] In earlier local elections, similar losses had resulted in gains by the Liberals and Communists, but in 1968 the victors were nationalist parties on both sides: the Volksunie went from 12 seats to 20, the Front Démocra-

39. Aristide R. Zolberg, "The Making of Flemings and Walloons: Belgium, 1830–1914." Unpublished manuscript, 1973.

40. Cf. Lucien Huyse, *Passiviteit, pacificatie en verzuiling in de Belgische politiek: Een sociologische studie* (Antwerp, Standaard Wetenschappelijke Uitgeverij, 1970).

tique des Francophones from 3 to 5, and the Rassemblement Wallon from 2 to 7. From 1971 to 1974, however, both nationalist factions lost votes, the Volksunie about 51,000 and the Rassemblement Wallon and the Front Démocratique des Francophones together about 110,000.[41] This reversal may have reflected increased concern about more general issues, in particular the inflation and the weak economy. More fundamentally, it reflected the facts that the regional structure demanded originally by Flemish nationalists had been incorporated into the programs of both the Social Catholic and the Socialist parties and that, indeed, outside the Brussels area it had been largely realized.

Under the 1932 law that made Dutch official in the north and French in the south, with the two languages competing in the Brussels metropolitan area, the decennial census was supposed to determine whether any villages along the frontier should be shifted. But thereafter, only one census—in 1947—included a question on language; and both that and every other count were controversial. No matter what the results, they were not accepted by the losing side. In 1963, after some 85,000 persons were shifted from Flemish to Walloon territory and about 20,000 in the opposite direction, the main boundary between the language areas was fixed. A commission established to resolve the remaining differences labored for a year to bring forth two tiny offspring: uniform bilingual identity cards and a Dutch translation of the constitution of 1831. The dispute dominated politics for the rest of the decade, and under a compromise adopted in 1971 full cultural autonomy in the two principal regions was realized. The new system supposedly eliminated linguistic competition in most of the nation; all primary instruction, for example, is only in the language of the area, so that (as in Switzerland) new arrivals or their children will presumably acculturate to this permanent medium. Even more than before, then, the Brussels agglomeration became the dominant arena, for the Flemish nationalists are determined to establish their language as truly coordinate in the nation's capital—working, however,

41. Vincent Goffart, "Comment les Belges ont voté le 10 mars 1974," *Revue Nouvelle* 59 (1974), 405–419.

against the "denationalization" of many of the Flemish in-migrants and the dominance of French (or even English) in the growing number of West European organizations established there.

The most interesting general feature of the language dispute in Belgium is that it contradicts the conventional wisdom about what determines ethnic identity. Subnations, we have been told, are a manifestation of backwardness: they look to the past, thrive on folklore and folk history, maintain themselves best in a village-based culture. In this case (as in many others throughout the world), the very movement of more Flemish into upper levels of a fully urban society, with an accompanying partial secularization of some important institutions, seemingly resulted in a sharp rise of subnational sentiment. Walloon nationalism can be reasonably interpreted as mainly defensive: parity for Dutch means a relative decline of French.

In sum, two of the most civilized countries of the West, Belgium and Switzerland, with full democratic rights bred in the marrow, manifested an increase in what we call "parochial" feelings as parishes and their nonreligious counterparts were more fully absorbed into the greater society. Obviously, our general theory of ethnic relations is badly in need of repair, and Western Europe can offer many new insights.

7

ANDREW M. GREELEY

AND WILLIAM C. MCCREADY

The Transmission of Cultural Heritages: The Case of the Irish and Italians

There is a plethora of theorizing, or at least speculation, about the persistence of ethnicity in American society, with a good deal of it highly moralistic (ethnicity is either a "good" thing or "bad" thing, depending on your viewpoint), but a paucity of hard (by which a social scientist usually means medium soft) data to prove or disprove such speculations. As in most other controversial matters, people with strong opinions—even social scientists with strong opinions—need scarcely be bothered by evidence.

We propose in this chapter to ask one question and to provide for the question a limited and imperfect answer, as part of the hewing of one building block for the construction of, if not a grand theory of American ethnicity, at least a better understanding of that phenomenon in our society.

The question is: do the cultural heritages of the Old World persist among children and grandchildren of the immigrants from the various European countries? We shall choose two ethnic groups— the Irish Catholics and the Italians—about whose country of origin there exists a substantial anthropological and sociological literature. From this literature we will derive a considerable number of hypotheses about their respective differences from the Anglo-Saxon American norm and from one another. To the extent that these hypotheses are sustained by the available evidence, we will be able to assert that there is a persistence of diversity of cultural heritage within the United States, predictable on the basis of the culture of the countries of origin. We will also have, incidentally, established the fact of ethnic cultural diversity in the United States, a fact which many social scientists are not yet prepared to concede.

It is necessary before we begin to provide some kind of a description of an American ethnic group, though we must note that we make no claim that this description has any validity beyond the borders of the United States. An ethnic group is a large collectivity, based on presumed common origin, which is, at least on occasion, part of a self-definition of a person, and which also acts as a bearer of cultural traits.

In this chapter we are concerned with the second element of the definition. A respondent may think of himself as Irish or Italian only when our survey interviewer asks him what his nationality background is. We assume that such a response indicates the possible presence of predispositions to attitudes, values, norms, and behaviors, which are part of the baggage the immigrant groups brought from their country of origin and passed on largely through an implicit socialization process, through their children and then to their grandchildren. Our main concern is not with the explicit awareness of ethnic heritage (whether there is a difference between those Irish who are frequently conscious of being Irish and those Irish who are not), nor with the decline of ethnic attitudes and behaviors through the generations. We are merely concerned with the facts of the existence of ethnic diversity and the predictability of some aspects of this diversity from knowledge of the culture of the land of origin.[1]

Not all differences among ethnic groups are to be attributed to the cultural heritages whence they came. These groups arrived in America at different times in that nation's development; they settled in different regions of the country, and they have experienced different histories since their arrival. Thus, time of arrival, place of settlement, and history may also account for some of the dif-

---

1. In fact, there is some evidence available that would suggest that consciousness of ethnicity does increase, but only very slightly, the levels of ethnically linked behavior, and there is also evidence that these levels do not decline very rapidly across generations. But in order to keep this chapter within reasonable limits, we will defer to another occasion an extended treatment of these questions.

ferences that are to be observed among ethnic groups. We will limit ourselves to the differences that can be predicted from cultural patterns which existed in the country of origin, simply because these differences are much easier to sort out in the absence of elaborate social histories of the various immigrant groups.[2]

There are four principal weaknesses in the strategy we are pursuing:

1. The anthropological literature upon which we are relying was written after most of the immigrants left Italy and Ireland and came to the United States. There is a sufficient amount of historical information available to persuade us that southern Italy and western Ireland, as they are described in our literature, are similar enough to those regions 50 to 100 years ago, but there obviously have been some changes in Connaught and the Mezzogiorno between the time the immigrants left and the arrival of Arensberg and Kimball in the one, and Edward Banfield in the other.

2. There may well be deficiencies in the literature on Ireland and Italy, of which we as American social scientists are not aware. The literature on Italy is more extensive and, as far as we know, has not been subject to critical disagreement. The literature on Ireland is more limited and has been the subject of some enthusiastic critical disagreement on the part of Irish scholars.

3. Some of the hypotheses to be derived from reading the literature on Italy and Ireland are of much greater value than other hypotheses because they are based on observations that are at the core of the description of the two societies. Thus, our hypothesis suggesting that Italian Americans would be more fatalistic than Anglo-Saxons is indeed substantiated. This validation is of considerably more importance than the failure of other hypotheses because the theme of fatalism in the Mezzogiorno is of capital impor-

2. Many researchers seem surprised by the phenomenon of a correlation between ethnic background and attitudes and behavior in the absence of a strong explicit ethnic consciousness. However, it should be noted that the cultural patterns of the old country existed before the ethnic groups came into being. The ethnic group as a self-conscious collectivity is the result of the American experience, but Irish behavior with regard to drink, Italian behavior with regard to sex, and the values of both groups about family life existed before immigration to the United States.

tance in all the writings on that area. Similarly, given both historical anthropological evidence on drinking behavior in Ireland, the difference between the American Irish and others in drinking behavior outweighs many "non-differences" based on less important observations about Irish peasant culture.

4. Finally, in our comparison of the Italians with the Irish, we had to make certain decisions on the basis of descriptions that were scarcely written to facilitate such comparisons. For example, we predicted that the Irish would score higher on a measure of trust than the Italians because there seemed to be somewhat more emphasis on the importance of religion as generating at least ultimate trust in the Irish literature than in the Italian literature. Similarly, we predicted that the Italians would score higher than the Irish on measures of fatalism, because the theme of fatalism seemed to us to be more obvious in the Italian literature than in the Irish. While these decisions then were not completely arbitrary, they cannot be justified as possessing the precision that would be desirable in the best of all possible worlds (the world in which, incidentally, neither the Italians nor the Irish seem to live).

The literature on southern Italy (see, for example, Banfield, Cronin, Ianni, and Parsons) describes a society in which the social *structure* is close to a state of collapse, while the *culture* postulates an extended family value system. The extreme poverty of daily life precludes the effective operation of the extended family and indeed dictates that individuals have as little to do with an extended family as possible, lest they be caught in the ancient web of obligation, which they now no longer honor.[3]

While Banfield's "amoral familism" may have a value connotation that is unfortunate, the reality to which he attaches that label is recorded by all other observers. Little, if any, trust persists beyond the nuclear family. It is difficult enough to honor the obligations to one's spouse and children without running the risk of entanglement in any other sort of relationship. Hence, the society is permeated by distrust and suspicion. Anxiety and fear are at a very

3. Cronin's study of Italian immigrants in Australia shows that when it becomes economically possible to sustain the values and norms of the extended family system, the extended family reemerges.

high level. Men and women are caught in the grip of a fatalism which tells them that none of their efforts really matter very much. The principal proof of a man's quality as a father is his ability to protect the chastity of the female members of his family. An unfaithful wife or promiscuous daughter becomes an absolutely intolerable social disgrace and the virgin symbol of the Italian version of Catholicism is central to the southern Italian belief system, both because it emphasizes the importance of biological integrity and because it stresses the automatic and fatalistic elements of life. Relationships between man and woman tend to be formal and tense. The behavior of girls is rigidly controlled, while the behavior of boys is less closely supervised. Young men learn early the need to prove their maleness by being superior to women, which means protecting the chastity of one's own family and threatening the chastity of other families—insofar as one can get away with it and not get caught.

The peasant society of Ireland (Arensberg, Kimball, Humphreys, Messenger and Jackson) is not so grim and disorganized as that of Italy. While both societies have known poverty and oppression, one compares the literature on the two countries and concludes that the social structure of western Ireland was much less traumatized than that of the Mezzogiorno. Both the demands and the support of the extended family are much more evident. The nuclear family displays a higher level of trust and indeed a capacity for political organization of rather a sophisticated variety (dating at least from Daniel Connell's Catholic Association of the early nineteenth century). In the west of Ireland there is a great concern about the transmission of family property, and indeed marriage contracts concerning the exchange of property in dowries are of the highest importance. The rearing of children and the planning of marriage, the assumption of the roles of wife and husband, retirement from active direction of one's family farm, all are decisively affected by the property contract at the time of marriage. Such concern would seem to indicate a more prosperous and better organized culture than that described in Sicily and in southern Italy.

On the other hand, there seems to be even more sexual repression in Ireland than in Italy and hence a very high level of frustration, repression, and suppressed anger, which find outlets in prodigious feats of alcohol consumption. Precisely because the west of Ireland is apparently less disorganized than the south of Italy, there are external means of social control in the former that do not exist in the latter, particularly the highly skilled ridicule of extended family and local community and the harsh, punitive and omnipresent moralism of Irish Catholicism.[4]

While the Irish country family is, with some exceptions, almost as patriarchal as that of Italy, studies of country families migrating to Dublin indicate that matriarchy emerges rather quickly in the large cities—much more quickly than in southern Italian cities such as Naples. While mothers "spoil" their sons by waiting on them themselves and constraining their daughters to wait on them, the Irish male seems to have less freedom and independence than does the Italian male, if only because it is for all practical purposes impossible for him to marry without parental approval. The family structure in Ireland looks somewhat less rigid than that of Italy, but it is still rigid enough. While Connaught may not be as harsh and repressive a place as the Mezzogiorno, there is still substantial evidence in the available literature that the life of the peasants in the west of Ireland is filled with anxiety, insecurity, repression, and powerful conformity-oriented norms. Both Italy and Ireland then are presented in the literature as peasant societies with all the narrowness and conservatism characteristic of peasant societies and the special problems that come with poverty, oppression, and less than enlightened religious world views.

We now turn to a number of hypotheses about Italian and Irish Americans derived from this literature. The seven accompanying tables are arranged in such a way that in each table a comparison is made between the Irish and the Anglo-Saxons, the Italians and the Anglo-Saxons, and the Irish and Italians. In the first column the direction of the hypothesis is indicated, the second and third columns provide the scores of the two groups. The next column indicates whether the hypothesis is sustained and in the first four tables the level of statistical significance is indicated in the final

4. For a brilliant, historical account of the development of contemporary Irish Catholicism see Emmett Larkin's "Devotional Revolution in Ireland, 1850–1875," *The American Historical Review* 77.3 (June 1972), 625–652.

column. (In Table 5 the size of the samples makes even the smallest differences "significant.")

PERSONALITY SCALES

In Table 1, the three groups are compared on seven personality variables, which are described in the appendix, derived from a survey of a national sample of American males.[5]

Table 1. Personality Variables

Variable	Hypothesis	Score		Confirmed	Significance
Irish and Anglo-Saxon					
		Irish	*Anglo-Saxon*		
Trust	Anglo	2.50	0.24	No	(.01)[a]
Fatalism	Irish	1.97	−1.34	Yes	.01
Authoritarianism	Irish	−1.24	−1.01	No	(.05)[a]
Anxiety	Irish	−2.10	−0.01	No	(.05)[a]
Conformity	Irish	1.00	0.01	No	
Moralistic	Irish	2.24	1.45	No	
Independence for children	Anglo	2.03	0.40	No	
Italian and Anglo-Saxon					
		Italian	*Anglo-Saxon*		
Trust	Anglo	0.05	0.24	No	
Fatalism	Italian	0.54	−1.34	Yes	.01
Authoritarianism	Italian	1.52	−0.01	No	
Anxiety	Italian	1.10	−0.01	No	
Conformity	Italian	−1.30	0.01	No	
Moralistic	Italian	1.40	1.45	No	
Independence for children	Anglo	−2.30	0.40	Yes	.01
Irish and Italian					
		Irish	*Italian*		
Trust	Irish	2.50	0.50	Yes	.05
Fatalism	Italian	1.97	0.54	No	
Authoritarianism	Italian	−1.24	1.52	Yes	.01
Anxiety	Italian	−2.10	1.10	Yes	.01
Conformity	Irish	1.00	−1.30	Yes	.01
Moralistic	Irish	2.24	1.40	Yes	.05
Independence for children	Irish	2.03	−2.30	Yes	.05

[a] Differences are significant in the opposite direction to the one hypothesized.

5. For a complete description of the sampling procedure see Melvin L. Kohn, *Class and Conformity* (Homewood, Ill., Dorsey Press, 1969), pp. 236–238.

The following hypotheses were generated on the basis of the literature we examined. 1. The rigid family structures, value systems, and religious norms of both Italy and Ireland should make both the Irish and the Italians less "trusting," more "fatalistic," more "authoritarian," more "anxious," more "conformist," more "moralistic," and less concerned about "independence for children" than Anglo-Saxon Americans—who represent the statistical "norm" of American society. However harsh and rigid American Protestantism may be in some of its manifestations, it certainly does not seem to compare with the situation as described in either southern Italy or the west of Ireland.

2. The Irish will be higher than the Italians on "trust," but also on "conformity" and "moralism." The Italians will score higher on "fatalism," "authoritarianism," and "anxiety," and the Irish are probably somewhat more likely than the Italians to stress "independence for children."

Our hypotheses have only a limited amount of success as far as the comparisons between the two Catholic immigrant groups and the Anglo-Saxons are concerned. Both the Irish and the Italians are significantly higher than the Anglo-Saxons in "fatalism," thus confirming in the United States one of the principal themes of the literature on the two countries, but significant differences between Italians and Anglo-Saxons exist only on one other scale. As predicted, the Anglo-Saxons are more likely to emphasize the independence for children than Italians.

But only the fatalism hypothesis is validated for differences between the American Irish and their Anglo-Saxon fellow citizens. Indeed, in four cases ("trust," "authoritarianism," "anxiety," and "independence for children"), the differences between the Irish and the Anglo-Saxons are in the opposite of the hypothesized direction and in three of these, the differences are significant. The Irish are, despite our hypothesis, significantly less "anxious" and "authoritarian," and more "trusting." Another difference, slightly less than significant, indicates the Irish are more likely than the Anglo-Saxons to value "independence for children." [6]

6. Ought one to be concerned about the possibility that the Irish may be more "cute" (to use their word) in answering questions than other respondents? May it

On the other hand, on all but one of the scales, the differences between the Irish and the Italians are significant in the direction hypothesized. The Italians turn out to be less fatalistic than the Irish, but in every other respect, the predicted differences do, in fact, exist. One way to summarize Table 1 would be to say that with the exception of fatalism, the Italians and the Anglo-Saxons are relatively similar to one another, while the Irish are significantly different from both, with the difference between the Irish and the Italians being in the direction predicted by our hypothesis, and the differences between the Irish and the Anglo-Saxons being in the *opposite* directions from those predicted by our hypothesis. Knowledge of the culture of land of origin, then, is of some help in understanding the differences between the two ethnic groups, but of rather little help in understanding their differences from the Anglo-Saxons—at least with regard to our personality scales.

But two questions remain after an examination of Table 1:

Why are the Irish different in the opposite direction from that which we had predicted? Perhaps there are aspects of the Irish personality that are more complex than the field workers in the west of Ireland were able to report.

Why are the Irish—a group that came to the United States before the Italians—more likely to be significantly different from Anglo-Saxons on personality measures than are the Italians? Perhaps Irish Catholicism provides a much stronger structural and cultural focus around which the Irish can rally and sustain their values and world view than does the Italian version of Catholicism.

POLITICAL PARTICIPATION

We now turn to differences among the three ethnic groups on political participation measures developed by our colleagues Norman Nie and Sidney Verba.[7] The following hypotheses were de-

be possible that among the cultural traits that have survived the immigration is the facility at blarney, which has been defined as the capacity never to mean what one says and never to say what one means? Anyone who has attempted to get a straight answer when wandering through the west of Ireland must be at least alive to this possibility.

7. Sidney Verba and Norman Nie, *Participation in America* (New York, Harper & Row, 1972).

rived. Given the high level of political activity and sophistication reported by historians and contemporary political scientists in Ireland (for example, see the work of Chubb), one would predict that the Irish would be more likely to engage in voting and political campaigning than Anglo-Saxons, though less likely to engage in the organization-joining "civic activity"-type of political behavior (which Verba and Nie report to be a "Protestant" mode of participation). Given a lack of a viable political culture in southern Italy and Sicily, one would expect that both the Irish and the Anglo-Saxons would score higher on political participation than the Italians. This expectation would be reinforced by the fact that the Irish learned their politics as part of an Anglo-Saxon system and that after 1875 most of the Irish immigrants spoke English as their first language.[8]

Table 2 indicates that in six of the nine cases hypotheses are sustained at a significance level of .01. The Irish indeed are more likely to vote and to campaign than the Anglo-Saxons, but despite

Table 2. Political Participation

Variable	Hypothesis	Score		Confirmed	Significance
Irish and Anglo-Saxon					
		Irish	*Anglo-Saxon*		
Voting	Irish	30.6	06.2	Yes	.01
Campaigning	Irish	42.4	06.8	Yes	.01
Civic activity	Anglo	22.3	13.7	No	
Italian and Anglo-Saxon					
		Italian	*Anglo-Saxon*		
Voting	Anglo	17.6	06.2	No	
Campaigning	Anglo	−15.4	06.8	Yes	.01
Civic activity	Anglo	−32.5	13.7	Yes	.01
Irish and Italian					
		Irish	*Italian*		
Voting	Irish	30.6	17.6	No	
Campaigning	Irish	42.4	−15.4	Yes	.01
Civic activity	Irish	22.3	−32.5	Yes	.01

8. Larkin points out that many of the "famine" Irish probably did not speak English as their first language and some of them may not have spoken it at all, since the principal famine migration was from the west of Ireland which, in the middle of the last century, was a primarily Irish-speaking region.

our prediction and despite the expectations of the work of Verba and Nie they are also more likely to engage in civic activities than the Anglo-Saxons. Similarly, both the Irish and the Anglo-Saxons are significantly more likely to campaign and engage in civic activity than are the Italians. The Irish are also more likely to vote than the Italians, but the difference here is not significant. The Italians, on the other hand, are somewhat more likely to vote than the Anglo-Saxons, but once again the difference is not significant.

Our predictions, then, turn out to be much more successful when we are dealing with participation behavior than when we are dealing with personality variables, a phenomenon which has some consolation in it because political participation is, as social science measures go, something much "harder" than responses to social psychological personality scales.

There are a number of important questions, of course, about these differences in political participation. We have addressed ourselves to some of these questions elsewhere and we return to them in the conclusion here.[9]

MORAL ISSUES

The next issue to be raised is whether knowledge of the culture of the country of origin can enable us to predict attitudes toward sexuality and drinking behavior in the three groups that we are studying.[10] It can be hypothesized on the basis of the literature that the Irish will be more likely to drink than the Anglo-Saxons and would be also more likely to have serious drinking problems. It also could be hypothesized that the Irish would be more restrictive than the Anglo-Saxons in their attitudes toward both male and female sexual behavior.

Although little is said about drunkenness in southern Italy in the literature, one might conclude that the very fact that it is not mentioned would indicate that it is a problem that does not plague that otherwise problem-burdened region. Hence, the Italians, we expect, will have lower scores on the alcohol question than do the

9. A. M. Greeley, "Political Attitudes among American White Ethnics," *Public Opinion Quarterly* (Summer 1972), 213–220.

10. These data are from the NORC study of 1961 college graduates.

Anglo-Saxons. We would also expect that because of the sexual double standard, the Italians will score lower on restrictiveness toward male sexual behavior, but higher in restrictiveness toward female sexual behavior.

Finally, we hypothesize a greater alcohol problem for the Irish than for the Italians, more sexual restrictiveness for the Italians with regard to female sexuality, but more restrictiveness for the Irish with regard to male sexuality.

Our hypotheses about the differences between the Irish and Anglo-Saxons on alcohol and sexuality are simply not supported in any way, but three of the four hypotheses about the differences between the Italians and the Anglo-Saxons are supported (Table 3). Our only mistake was to assume that Italian sexual restrictiveness would be limited to female sexual behavior. In fact, the Italians are also sexually restrictive for males. The Italians are also significantly less likely to have alcohol problems than the Irish and are more

Table 3. Moral Issues

Variable	Hypothesis	Score		Confirmed	Significance
Irish and Anglo-Saxon					
		Irish	*Anglo-Saxon*		
Drink	Irish	1.63	1.64	No	
Drunk	Irish	4.17	4.05	No	
Male sex [a]	Anglo	3.53	3.71	No	
Female sex	Anglo	3.87	3.93	No	
Italian and Anglo-Saxon					
		Italian	*Anglo-Saxon*		
Drink	Anglo	0.43	1.64	Yes	.01
Drunk	Anglo	1.69	4.05	Yes	.01
Male sex	Anglo	4.06	3.71	No	(.01) [b]
Female sex	Italian	4.14	3.93	Yes	.01
Irish and Italian					
		Irish	*Italian*		
Drink	Irish	1.63	1.43	Yes	.01
Drunk	Irish	4.17	1.69	Yes	.01
Male sex	Irish	3.53	4.06	No	.01 [b]
Female sex	Italian	3.87	4.14	No	

[a] The score measures restrictiveness in attitudes toward male sexual behavior.
[b] Differences are significant in the opposite direction to the one hypothesized.

likely to be sexually restrictive than the Irish in the case of male sexual behavior.

Table 3 then presents a picture that is exactly the opposite of Table 1. On the personality scales the Irish were significantly different from the Italians and the Anglo-Saxons, who were quite similar to one another (save on fatalism). One would have concluded from Table 1 that the Italians had "assimilated" and the Irish had not. However, in Table 3 the Irish and the Anglo-Saxons are the ones that are similar and both are different, in most cases, significantly so, from Italians. One concludes with what must surely sound like a truism; the processes of differentiation and acculturation among the American ethnic groups are far more complicated than we might have expected.

RESPECT FOR THE DEMOCRATIC PROCESS

Only one scale is presented in Table 4, a measurement of the respondent's respect for certain elements in the democratic process. Ireland became a political democracy long after most of the immigrants had left, and while the Irish were a politically involved people, their involvement was not such as to incline them to respect the niceties of democratic process (one need only look at the present situation in Ulster to see why). Similarly political democracy was never effectively established in Sicily or the Mezzogiorno and the processes of the democratic government seemed to mean

Table 4. Respect for Democratic Processes

Hypothesis	Score		Confirmed	Significance
Irish and Anglo-Saxon				
	Irish	*Anglo-Saxon*		
Anglo	.60	.05	No	(.01) [a]
Italian and Anglo-Saxon				
	Italian	*Anglo-Saxon*		
Anglo	.05	−.16	Yes	.01
Irish and Italian				
	Irish	*Italian*		
Irish	.60	−.16	Yes	.01

[a] Differences are significant in the opposite direction to the one hypothesized.

relatively little in such an impoverished society. Furthermore, the
levels of trust and openness reported in the anthropological literature on both countries would lead one to expect less concern for
civil liberties among those affected by such cultures than among
Anglo-Saxon Americans. Finally, the allegedly authoritarian pro-
clivities of Roman Catholicism might also ill equip Italians and
Irish to respect the democratic processes. Hence one would predict
that the Anglo-Saxons would be higher on the democratic process
scale than either the Irish or the Italians and that the Irish would
probably be higher than the Italians.

Table 4 indicates two of these expectations are supported. Both
the Irish and the Anglo-Saxons have higher scores on the democratic process scale than do the Italians. However the expectation
of a higher score for the Anglo-Saxons than for the Irish is dramati-
ically disproven. The Irish are significantly and indeed overwhelmingly higher on a democratic process scale than are the
Anglo-Saxons. Mr. Greeley has pointed out elsewhere [11] that the
American Irish are more "liberal" than much of the mythology
about them would have led one to believe. It may well be that a
thousand-year revolutionary tradition does generate a respect for
political democracy, which survives even embourgeoisement.

FAMILY STRUCTURE ATTITUDES AMONG
COLLEGE WOMEN STUDENTS

Our final set of hypotheses has to do with attitudes toward family
structure measured in the middle 1960s among a representative
sample of 1961 college alumnae. It should be noted that there are
both advantages and disadvantages in looking at this subpopula-
tion. An advantage is that age and educational level are held constant; a disadvantage is that given the fact that the Italians are still
less likely to go to college than the Irish, the Italian respondents
may be far less typical of their generation than are the Irish respondents.

The following hypotheses are generated for the differences between the Irish and the Anglo-Saxons: The Irish would be more

11. Greeley, "Political Attitudes among American White Ethnics."

likely than the Anglo-Saxons to think that the principal career of a wife is to support her husband's pursuit of his career. The Anglo-Saxons would be more likely than the Irish to value independence for their daughters. The Irish would be more likely than the Anglo-Saxons to stress security. Similarly the Irish would be more opposed to working mothers, more likely to maintain contact with parents and in-laws, more likely to report tense relationships with parents and less likely to report good health.

Exactly the same differences would be predicted between the Anglo-Saxons and the Italians, and in a comparison between the Irish and Italians, one would expect the Irish to value independence for daughters somewhat more than the Italians, to record more overt tension with parents than the Italians and perhaps to assert more frequently that they enjoy good health.

Of the ten possible comparisons in the first panel of Table 5, the important differences (of six percentage points or more) are in the expected direction six times. Irish women respondents are indeed

Table 5. Attitudes toward Family Structure of College Alumnae

Variable	Hypothesis	Percent		Con-firmed	Percent Difference
Irish and Anglo-Saxon					
		Anglo-Saxon	*Irish*		
Woman primarily helps husband	Irish	32	41	Yes	9
Daughter's independence important	Anglo	49	33	Yes	16
Security important	Irish	53	48	No	
Working mother frequently harmful to children	Irish	31	45	Yes	14
Principal role wife/mother only	Irish	42	58	Yes	16
Keep up relationships with parents and in-laws	Irish	45	34	No	(−11) [a]
Family contacts important	Irish	45	33	No	(−12) [a]
Relationship with mother was tense	Irish	20	21	No	
Relationship with father was tense	Irish	47	61	Yes	14
Health very good	Anglo	27	26	No	
N =		(838)	(163)		

Table 5. Attitudes toward Family Structure of College Alumnae (*Continued*)

Variable	Hypothesis	Percent		Con-firmed	Percent Difference
Italian and Anglo-Saxon					
		Anglo-Saxon	Italian		
Woman primarily helps husband	Italian	32	20	No	(−12) [a]
Daughter's independence important	Anglo	49	63	No	(−14) [a]
Security important	Italian	53	33	No	(−20) [a]
Working mother frequently harmful to children	Italian	31	20	No	(−11) [a]
Principal role wife/mother only	Italian	42	48	No	
Keep up relationships with parents and in-laws	Italian	45	52	Yes	7
Family contacts important	Italian	45	54	Yes	9
Relationship with mother was tense	Italian	20	18	No	
Relationship with father was tense	Italian	47	33	No	(14) [a]
Health very good	Anglo	27	16	Yes	9
N =		(838)	(54)		
Irish and Italian					
		Irish	Italian		
Woman primarily helps husband	Italian	41	26	No	(−15) [a]
Daughter's independence important	Irish	33	63	No	(−30) [a]
Security important	Italian	48	33	No	(−15) [a]
Working mother frequently harmful to children	Italian	45	20	No	(−25) [a]
Principal role wife/mother only	Italian	58	48	No	(−10) [a]
Keep up relationships with parents and in-laws	Italian	34	54	Yes	20
Family contacts important	Italian	33	52	Yes	11
Relationship with mother was tense	Irish	21	18	No	
Relationship with father was tense	Irish	61	33	Yes	28
Health very good	Irish	26	16	Yes	10
N =		(163)	(54)		

[a] Differences are important (more than 6 percent) in opposite of predicted direction.

more likely to view the woman's role as a helpmate, to place less emphasis on independence of daughters, to think working mothers could have a bad impact on their children, to see a woman's role primarily that as wife and mother, and to report tense relationships with their fathers. On the other hand, the differences between the Irish and Anglo-Saxons on valuing frequent contacts with family run in a direction opposite to that which we expected. We were less successful in predicting differences between young Anglo-Saxon and young Italian women. Italians are, as predicted, more likely to discuss family relationships and less likely to report good health. They are more in sympathy with independence for children and working mothers and less likely to see their role as a traditionally feminine one. They are also less likely to report tension in their relationships with their fathers. It is quite clear from the second panel of Table 5 that the young Italian-American women in this sample do not fit in any way the stereotype of the southern Italian female.

They are also, as we note in the third panel of Table 5, substantially different from their Irish Catholic age peers in the opposite direction to that predicted on attitudes toward the role of women. However, four differences in the expected direction do exist between the Irish and the Italians. The latter are more likely to stress family relationships while the former are both more likely to claim good health and more likely to report tension between themselves and their fathers. The very high level of tension, incidentally, reported between Irish daughters and their fathers is a subject to which we hope to return on another occasion.

Table 5 presents yet a new pattern of diversity among the three ethnic groups. The Italian college-educated women are even more likely than Anglo-Saxon women to have broken from the traditional view of women's role, while the Irish in this case are substantially less "progressive." On the other hand, young Irish women are less likely to value traditional family ties than are Anglo-Saxons and the Anglo-Saxons, in turn, are less likely to value them than young Italian women. The Italians, then, are more traditional on family ties, the Irish more traditional on the role of women.

SUMMARY OF PREDICTIONS AND
TESTS OF HYPOTHESES

On the whole, our efforts to predict differences in attitudes and behavior among the three American ethnic groups has been moderately successful. Of 75 hypotheses, we have been right at a statistically significant level 34 times (assuming that for our college alumni a six percentage point difference is one worth writing about).

On the other hand, in 18 cases (mostly dealing with either Irish personality or Italian and Irish family structure) there were statistically significant (or numerically important) differences in the direction *opposite* to the one predicted. With the exception of "fatalism" the Italians were basically similar to the Anglo-Saxons in personality, but different in the predicted direction from the Irish. The Irish, on the other hand, were different from the Anglo-Saxons, but in the opposite of the predicted direction. We were most successful in predicting political participation, with the Irish the most politically active and the Italians the least active, though both groups were significantly different from the Anglo-Saxon mean. The Irish were rather like the Anglo-Saxons in their sexual attitudes and their drinking behavior, but the Italians were both less likely to drink and more likely to be sexually restrictive than either of the other groups, as the literature on the country of origin would have led us to believe. The Irish, unexpectedly, were more likely to respect the democratic processes than the Anglo-Saxons, while the latter, expectedly, were more likely to respect such processes than the Italians. Finally, the Irish, as predicted, took more conservative views on the role of women than the Anglo-Saxons, but were less "conservative" on family ties, while the Italians were less "conservative" on the role of women and more "conservative" on family ties.

Or to put the matter somewhat differently, on some 52 of the 75 comparisons made among the three ethnic groups in our tables, "significant" differences are to be found. If one knows something of the culture of the countries of origin, one can correctly predict the direction of the difference about two thirds of the time. This is a degree of predictability that is at least somewhat superior to flipping a coin (in which case we would be correct half the time). How successful our enterprise has been depends on what the assumptions were with which we started. If one begins by believing that there are no important differences among Anglo-Saxon Americans, Irish Americans and Italian Americans, then our enterprise will produce a shocking surprise. If on the other hand one begins with the conviction that ours is a diverse society in which differences among the three groups in question are to be expected on almost every variable, then the enterprise has been a disappointment. The truth seems to lie somewhere in between. The three groups are in many ways similar and in many ways different.

If one begins the exploration with the assumption that virtually all differences that do in fact exist among the three ethnic groups being considered can be explained in terms of the cultural heritages whence they, or more likely their parents or grandparents came, then our search has been something less than a complete success. The majority of differences are in fact of the sort that could be predicted by a study of the literature of the two countries of origin, but a substantial minority of the differences are exactly opposite to the predictions such a literature would lead us to make. On the other hand, if one assumes (and many commentators on American life seem to have made this assumption) that the European heritages of the American ethnic groups are irrelevant to an understanding of the present attitudes and behavior of such groups, one can find very little consolation in the tests reported in this paper. The European heritage may not be all important, but it is still important, and indeed, if one may hazard the statement, probably more important than most of us would have thought.

THE RELATIONSHIP BETWEEN SOCIAL CLASS, GENERATIONAL, AND ETHNIC DIFFERENCES

Some final questions need to be asked. "Are the differences among American groups diminishing as social class differences diminish and as the number of years the family has been in the

United States increases?" [12] Tables 6 and 7 provide data with which to fashion a response to this question. In Table 6 we present the zero-order correlations between ethnicity and political participations for each of the three comparisons and then the standardized correlation with region and educational level held constant. If an increase in education is leading to a decline in the differences in political behavior, the standardized coefficient should be smaller than the zero-order coefficient. However, the data in Table 6 make

Table 6. Zero-Order and Standardized Coefficients between Ethnicity and Political Participation

Variable	Zero Order	Standardized for Region and Education
Irish and Anglo-Saxon		
Campaigning	.10 [a]	.11
Civic participation	.03	.04
Italian and Anglo-Saxon		
Campaigning	−.07 [b]	−.06
Civic participation	−.11	−.11
Irish and Italian		
Campaigning	.27 [a]	.28
Civic participation	.28	.31

[a] Positive correlation with Irish.

[b] Positive correlation with Anglo-Saxon.

it perfectly clear that even taking into account the regional and educational differences among the three ethnic groups, the differences in political participation remained unchanged.

In Table 7 we ask whether generation in the country (foreign born is the first generation, native born with foreign parents is the second generation, native born with native parents is the third generation) has any effect on political participation. The assimilationist theory would lead us to believe that the longer the immigrant family is in the country, the more likely it is to participate in political activity. The high level of Irish political participation and the low level of Italian political participation then would be seen as a function of the time the two immigrant groups have been

12. G. Lenski, *The Religious Factor* (New York, Doubleday, 1961). See this book for the initial formulation of these questions.

Table 7. Correlations between Generation and Political Behavior [a]

Variable	Irish	Italian	Jewish
Campaigning	.04	.04	.30
Civic participation	.04	.08	.34

[a] A positive correlation indicates that the longer a respondent's family has been in the United States, the more likely he is to participate.

in the United States. However, as Table 7 makes clear, there are only very small correlations between generation and political participation for the Italians and the Irish. However, so far as the relationship between generation and active political participation is concerned, the assimilationist model may be relevant for Jewish Americans.

The differences between Irish and Italian Americans in political participation, in other words, has very little to do with generation or with social class, and while the assimilationist model may be tested with many other variables, one can say with some confidence that as far as the relatively "hard" variable of political participation is concerned, the differences among the Irish, the Italians and the Anglo-Saxons show no signs of going away.

CONCLUDING REMARKS

This chapter began with a very simple question. "Does a knowledge of the cultural heritage of an immigrant group help us understand its present behavior?" On the basis of the evidence presented, we think it can be safely said that it would be very difficult to understand the present behavior of American immigrant groups without knowing something of the cultural heritage from which they came. The heritage may not explain everything, but it is clear that much cannot be explained without investigating the cultural background of the country of origin. The critical question becomes not one of choosing between the culture of origin, on the one hand, and the immigration and post-immigration experiences on the other, but of asking rather how the interaction between the Old World culture and the New World experience shaped the phenomenon of American ethnic group cultures. Why in the immigrant experience were some parts of the Old World culture ignored, others rejected, others perhaps vigorously reinforced and maintained with little conscious effort and still others vigorously and tenaciously reinforced? To put the matter more concretely, why do young women of Italian background who graduated from college in the early 1960s tend to cling to an Old World view of the importance of maintaining ties with parents and in-laws, while vigorously asserting the modern view of the role of women, while the Irish Catholic counterparts endorse exactly the opposite values? Something strange, fascinating, and as social science concerns go, quite possibly important has happened in the socialization experiences of those girls and their parents and their grandparents since their families left behind the sun-drenched hills of Sicily or Calabria and the soggy peat bogs of Clare, Kerry, or Mayo.

APPENDIX

Scales Used in This Study

1. *Personality Scales*
   The seven personality measures used represented a number of the factors that emerged from a battery of 57 items. We present below the items which had a factor loading of over .200 for each scale.

   Conforming
   According to your general impression, how often do your ideas and opinions about important matters differ from those of your relatives?
   How often do your ideas and opinions differ from those of your friends?
   How about from those of other people with your religious background?
   How about from those of most people in the country?
   How often do you feel that you can't tell what other people are likely to do, at times when it matters?

   Anxious
   I feel useless at times.
   At times I think I am no good at all.

On the whole I think I am quite a happy person.

How often do you feel that there isn't much purpose in being alive?

How often do you find that you can't get rid of some thought or idea that keeps running through your head?

How frequently do you find yourself anxious or worrying about something?

How often do you find yourself counting unimportant things, such as the number of cars passing by?

How often do you find that you are really enjoying yourself?

How often do you feel bored with everything?

How often do you feel powerless to get what you want out of life?

How often do you feel so restless that you cannot sit still?

How often do you feel that the world just isn't very understandable?

How often do you feel downcast and dejected?

How often do you feel that you are about to go to pieces?

How often do you feel guilty for having done something wrong?

How often do you feel uneasy about something without knowing why?

Authoritarian

Young people should not be allowed to read books that confuse them.

In this complicated world the only way to know what to do is to rely on leaders and experts.

People who question the old and accepted ways of doing things usually just end up causing trouble.

There are two kinds of people in the world, the weak and the strong.

Prison is too good for sex criminals; they should be publicly whipped or worse.

The most important thing to teach children is absolute obedience to their parents.

No decent man can respect a woman who has had sex relations before marriage.

Moralism

When you get right down to it, no one cares much what happens to you.

If something works, it doesn't matter whether it's right or wrong.

It's all right to get around the law as long as you don't actually break it.

Once I've made up my mind I seldom change it.

You should obey your superiors whether or not you think they are right.

It's all right to do anything you want if you stay out of trouble.

It generally works out best to keep doing things the way they have been done before.

Do you believe that it's all right to do whatever the law allows, or are there some things that are wrong even if they are legal?

Fatalism

To what extent would you say you are to blame for the problems you have—mostly, partly, hardly at all?

Do you feel that most of the things that happen to you are the results of your own decisions or things over which you have no control?

When things go wrong for you, how often would you say it's your own fault?

How often do you feel that you are really enjoying yourself?

How often do you feel bored with everything?

How often do you feel guilty for having done something wrong?

Trust

It's all right to get around the law so long as you don't actually break it.

Human nature is really cooperative.

You should be able to obey your superiors whether or not you think they are right.

If you don't watch out, people will take advantage of you.

Do you think most people can be trusted?

How often do you feel that you can't tell what other people are likely to do, at times when it matters?

Independence for Children
(Positive loadings)
   Considerate of others
   Interested in how and why things happen
   Responsible
   Self-control
   Good sense and sound judgment
(Negative loadings)
   Good manners
   Neat and clean
   Good student
   Obey his parents

2. *Political Participation Variables*

The *voting* variable was composed of four items: voting in the last two presidential elections, last congressional election, frequency of voting in local elections.

The *campaigning* scale was composed of four items: attending political meetings, contributing money to a campaign, working for a candidate, trying to persuade others to vote for a candidate.

The *communal* (or *civic*) scale was composed of items indicating membership in civic organizations and working for community "improvement."

The *particularized contact* scale was composed of two items indicating direct approach to public officials either in person or through mail.

3. *Moral Items*

The items in the *drink* scale were:

I neglect my regular meals when I am drinking.

Liquor has less effect on me than it used to.

I awaken next day not being able to remember some of the things I had done while I was drinking.

I don't nurse my drinks; I toss them down pretty fast.

I stay intoxicated for several days at a time.

Once I start drinking it is difficult for me to stop before I become completely intoxicated.

Without realizing what I am doing, I end up drinking more than I had planned to.

The items in the *drunk* scale were:

Has an employer ever fired you or threatened to fire you if you did not cut down or quit drinking?

Has your spouse ever left you or threatened to leave you if you didn't do something about your drinking?

Has your spouse ever complained that you spend too much money on alcoholic beverages?

Have you ever been picked up or arrested by the police for intoxication or other charges involving alcoholic beverages?

Has your physician ever told you that drinking was injuring your health?

The *permissiveness for men* items were:

I believe that kissing is acceptable for the male before marriage when he is engaged to be married.

I believe that kissing is acceptable for the male before marriage when he is in love.

I believe that kissing is acceptable for the male before marriage when he feels strong affection for his partner.

I believe that kissing is acceptable for the male before marriage even if he does not feel particularly affectionate toward his partner.

I believe that petting is acceptable for the male before marriage when he is engaged to be married.

I believe that petting is acceptable for the male before marriage when he is in love.

I believe that petting is acceptable for the male before marriage when he feels strong affection for his partner.

I believe that petting is acceptable for the male before marriage even if he does not feel particularly affectionate toward his partner.

I believe that full sexual relations are acceptable for the male before marriage when he is engaged to be married.

I believe that full sexual relations are acceptable for the male before marriage when he is in love.

I believe that full sexual relations are acceptable for the male before marriage when he feels strong affection for his partner.

I believe that full sexual relations are acceptable for the male before marriage even if he does not feel particularly affectionate toward his partner.

(The women items were the same with "female" substituted for "male.")

4. *Democratic Processes*

The items in the *democratic process* scale were:

If the government makes a decision that most people think is a good one, do you think other people should be allowed to criticize it—always, sometimes, or never?

Do you think people should be allowed to circulate petitions to ask the government to act on some issue, always, sometimes, or never?

Do you think people should be allowed to vote even if they are not well informed about the issues—always, sometimes, or never?

BIBLIOGRAPHIC REFERENCES

Ireland

Arensberg, C., and Kimball, S. T. *Family and Community in Ireland.* Cambridge, Harvard University Press, 1948.

Jackson, Kenneth H. *The Oldest Irish Tradition: A Window on the Iron Age.* Cambridge, Cambridge University Press, 1964.

Humphreys, Alexander. *The New Dubliners*. New York, Fordham University Press, 1966.

Larkin, Emmet. "Devotional Revolution in Ireland, 1850–1875," *The American Historical Review*, 77.3 (June 1972), 625–652.

MacLysaght, Edward. *Irish Life in the Seventeenth Century*. County Cork, Cork University Press, 1950.

Messenger, J. C. "Sex and Repression in an Irish Folk Community," in D. S. Marshall and Robert Suggs, eds., *Human Sexual Behavior*. New York, Basic Books, 1970.

Messenger, John C. *Inis Beag, Isle of Ireland*. New York, Holt, Rinehart and Winston, 1969.

Stein, Rita. *Disturbed Youth and Ethnic Family Patterns*. Albany, New York State University Press, 1972.

Italy

Banfield, Edward. *The Moral Basis of a Backward Society*. New York, The Free Press, 1958.

Chapman, G. C. *Milocca: A Sicilian Village*. Cambridge, Schenckman, 1971.

Cronin, Constance. "The Sicilians." Unpub. diss. University of Chicago, 1971.

Handlin, O. *The Uprooted*. Boston, Little, Brown, 1951.

Ianni, Francis J., with E. R. Ianni. *A Family Business*. New York, Russell Sage, 1972.

Parsons, Ann. *Belief, Magic and Anomie*. New York, The Free Press, 1970.

Stein, Rita. *Disturbed Youth and Ethnic Family Patterns*. Albany, SUNY Press, 1971.

Tomasi, Lydio. *The Italian-American Family*. New York, Center for Migration Studies, 1972.

8

MARTIN KILSON

Blacks and Neo-Ethnicity in American Political Life

In the past decade only a few American cultural groups have escaped the influence of neo-ethnicity. Irish, Italians, Jews, Negroes, Poles and even Protestants—especially working-class and lower middle-class Protestants—have been affected. *By neo-ethnicity I mean either the revitalization of weak ethnic collectivities (for example, Negro Americans) or the rehabilitation of dwindling ethnic cohesiveness (for example, Irish Catholics, Jews, Italians).*

Negro Americans initiated the current flurry of neo-ethnicity in American political life. They did so, ironically, in a period when, for the white majority, the traditional pattern of ethnicity was attenuating. Compared with two generations ago, all major white ethnic groups are experiencing significant attentuation of their ethnic cohesiveness. More Jews marry gentiles, more Protestants marry Catholics, more Irish marry Italians, and more whites marry Orientals and Negroes than at any period in modern American history. Religion, a central attribute in the hold of ethnic constraints upon individual choice, has likewise weakened.

For Afro-Americans, the formal attributes of their distinctive cultural patterns, such as religion, have also been in decline. But

Note: I am indebted to the Ford Foundation, and especially its president, McGeorge Bundy, for financial assistance which helped support the research on which this paper rests. Nathan Glazer and Arthur Maass, as well as my wife, Marion Dusser de Barenne Kilson, read the paper in manuscript and provided me with invaluable comments.

the salient factor in Negro behavior is rather the historical refusal by white supremacist American society to accord Negroes a quality of ethnic characterization comparable to that accorded white ethnic groups. The new black ethnicity is, then, initially an effort to redress this inferior ethnic characterization. What is more—and what lends a special force to black neo-ethnicity—Negroes themselves share the belief that in some basic way, they do not possess a full measure of ethnic attributes.[1] This gives black neo-ethnicity, as an ethnocentric revitalization movement, a complex conflict dynamic, both within the Afro-American subsystem and between blacks and whites.

Among blacks there is a variable view of the inferior ethnic characterization. *Il y a nègre et nègre:* some blacks have a qualified self-doubt about their ethnicity and are thus capable of informing the movement of black ethnocentric revitalization with more than identity-fulfilling purposes or goals—especially with power-mustering goals. Other blacks (the vast majority) infected with self-doubt seek through the movement of ethnocentric revitalization thoroughgoing identity-re-formation, catharsis, and therapeutic benefits. This situation shapes the major cleavages that have characterized neo-ethnicity in American political life in the past decade. Among blacks it has produced a moderate–militant cleavage which, in turn, has had a significant impact upon the political characteristics of white neo-ethnicity.

The militants in the black ethnocentric movement tend to influence those aspects of the movement that are readily perceived by the white majority—particularly its anti-white attributes. The militants determine, therefore, the nature of the black–white polarization that has accompanied the rise of black neo-ethnicity. The formation of a white neo-ethnicity thus acquires a rationale for militancy (largely anti-Negro) that might otherwise be harder to develop. Throughout the 1950s and early 1960s the traditional fervor of white anti-Negro attitudes had attenuated somewhat, even though a restrained form of black assertion had appeared under

1. For the classic study of the Negro's negative or inferior characterization of black ethnicity, see Kenneth B. Clark, *Prejudice and Your Child* (Boston, Beacon Press, 1955).

Dr. Martin Luther King's leadership from the late 1950s to the middle 1960s.[2] But from 1966 onward with the rise of a full-fledged anti-white movement of black ethnocentric revitalization, militant and violent, the formation of a militant white neo-ethnicity, anti-Negro in outlook, became possible.

The moderate section of the black movement—comprising some established bourgeois blacks, along with the entrepreneurial and political sectors of the newcomers to the black elites—could not prevail over the militants in the years following the murder of Dr. King by a white assassin. Or rather there was a significant lead-time before the moderate section could redefine the behavior of the revitalization movement along political (universalistic) rather than purely ethnocentric (particularistic) lines. This redefinition asserted its presence in 1970 and is currently ascendant.

Paradoxically, at the point where the black ethnocentric movement is in transition to a political rather than mainly particularistic movement, white neo-ethnicity is acquiring its own particularistic (ritualistic anti-black) attributes. Equally ironic, whereas the federal government under the Kennedy–Johnson administrations aided the transformation of black neo-ethnicity from a ritualistically anti-white movement to a political movement (or put another way, aided the ascendance of the moderates over the militants in the black movement), the federal government under Richard Nixon has played a different role with regard to white neo-ethnicity, sharpening its particularistic attributes vis-à-vis blacks. Indeed, no small part of the neo-conservative political realignment which has provided support for the Republican administrations since 1968 was produced in this fashion.[3]

NATIONAL POLITICS AND BLACK ETHNICITY

Richard Nixon's election in 1968 prepared the way for a fundamental redefinition of the relationship of national institutions—especially the federal government—to the movement of

2. See Paul B. Sheatsley, "White Attitudes toward the Negro," *Daedalus* 95 (Winter 1966), 217–232.

3. Cf. Gary Jacobson, "Race by Any Other Name," *Social Policy* (July–August 1973), 36–41.

black ethnocentric revitalization. Under the Kennedy–Johnson administrations the federal government was sympathetic to the political goals of the movement as defined by its moderate sector. The appointment of Dr. Robert Weaver, a Negro, to President Johnson's cabinet, the appointment by Lyndon Johnson of Thurgood Marshall, a Negro, to the Supreme Court, the Economic Opportunity Act of 1964, the Civil Rights Act of 1964, and the Voting Rights Act of 1965 all added up to an unprecedented alignment of national political processes with the needs—symbolic as well as substantive—of Afro-Americans.

Within two years of the 1968 election, the Nixon administration began a fundamental redefinition of the relationship between the federal government and Negroes. The War on Poverty was treated as a carry-over from the Kennedy–Johnson era, not as a policy of intrinsic value.[4] It was killed outright after the 1972 election. The Nixon administration formulated policies which attacked violence and riots as such, regardless of their social causes and their roots in the racist patterns of black–white relationships. It launched, in fact, a veritable anti-crime crusade. However, one unintended result of this was a modification of white Americans' perceptions of the blacks' political goals in cultural terms. Thus in the eyes of millions of whites—perhaps a majority—such goals of black militants as cessation of police brutality, community control of police, prison reform, expanded welfare coverage, government responsibility for reducing Negro unemployment, and so on, were no longer to be treated as legitimate political issues deserving action by political decision makers. Instead, these goals became in some sense intrinsically *Negro goals*, hence un-American. Through them millions of Negroes sought to continue a life of crime, avoid apprehension by officers of the law, freeload on welfare agencies, and evade honest labor—or, in Nixon's term, shirk responsibility to the "work ethic."

Thus through a process that might be called *ethnicization* of racial perceptions the Nixon administration has helped attach to Afro-

4. An exception to this was President Nixon's abortive program for a guaranteed income, conceived by a liberal presidential adviser, Daniel P. Moynihan. See Daniel P. Moynihan, *The Politics of a Guaranteed Income* (New York, Basic Books, 1973).

Americans a variant of an ethnic label—albeit negative in character. But this did not significantly modify white perceptions for few
whites accord Negroes those positive societal and cultural attributes
associated with the term "ethnic groups"—*attributes that attract historical celebration in time, ancestry, and heritage.* It will require the
growing political influence of the movement of black ethnocentric
renascence, aided by Democratic administrations, before whites
grudgingly accord blacks the cultural regard given an "ethnic
group."

LEGITIMATION OF ETHNICITY

The power-mustering dimension of ethnicity appears to endow it
with legitimacy in American life. Social group legitimation in
American society—especially for non-WASP social groups—is incomplete until the ethnic dimensions have realized, through whatever mechanisms, their power-creating capability. Negroes, American Indians, and Spanish-speaking groups are the last sizable
ethnic groups to undergo this transition to legitimacy.

What has deprived Afro-Americans of this essential attribute of
viable social status in American life has been the authoritarian restrictions upon political participation.[5] For as Robert Merton has
taught us, effective political participation—especially through city
political machines, that special form of political organization—provides American social groups both manifest and latent
functions. The latent functions of political machines are, in fact, of
more salience to the long-run institutionalization of ethnic groups
than the manifest functions such as political information and vot-

---

5. The dynamics of anti-Negro authoritarianism in American politics, both outside and within the South, has yet to receive adequate attention from social scientists. Parties and police systems have been the main instruments of this authoritarianism. Some material on the role of police systems is found in Gunnar Myrdal,
An American Dilemma (New York, Harper, 1944), and especially in William A.
Westley, *Violence and the Police: A Sociological Study of Law, Custom, and Morality*
(Cambridge, MIT Press, 1970), which has excellent data on the Gary, Indiana,
police system's anti-Negro behavior in the 1930s and 1940s. The classic study of
the constraints of the lily-white party system of the South on Negro participation,
though far from adequate, is V. O. Key, *Southern Politics in State and Nation* (New
York, Knopf, 1949).

ing.[6] The Irish, Jews, Poles, Italians, and others realized both the substantive and symbolic means of legitimation by using political machines to politicize ethnicity. No small part of the political strategies of these social groups in American cities in the era 1870s to 1940s was directed to this purpose.[7]

The weak opposition from the Protestant majority is fundamental to the legitimation of ethnicity. It allows social groups whom Protestants perceive as highly alien to gain some attributes of power through what might be called ethnic renovation. Why the relatively weak Protestant opposition? First, for much of the Protestant leadership—especially on the East Coast—the greater time-depth and thus, if you will, the deeper social heritage of Protestants enables them to entertain fewer status anxieties. But this hardly applies to the vast majority of Protestants. The sub-ethnic diversity of the Protestant group—on the surface unimportant but actually profound (for example, fundamentalist Christian versus cosmopolitan Christian, Southern WASPs versus Northern, and so on)—restricts the Protestant capacity for a unified political response. This, among other things, explains the failure of the major national effort by Protestants to curb the legitimation of ethnicity by alien social groups—the Prohibition movement in the 1920s.[8]

But when the alien social groups push too hard and fast in legitimating ethnicity through political machines—as they did most notably with the nomination of an Irish Catholic presidential candidate for the Democratic party in 1928—the Protestant majority surmounts its sub-ethnic divisions. In 1928 it squashed the bid by the "alien" social groups for the full complement, substantively and symbolically, of national power. Ironically, the failure of Alfred Smith's candidacy was of long-run significance to political stability. In the depression of the 1930s the alien social groups were to prove of major importance in the victory of a reformist Democratic

6. See Robert K. Merton, *Social Theory and Social Structure* (Glencoe, The Free Press, 1949).

7. Cf. Harold Zink, *City Bosses in the United States* (Durham, Duke University Press, 1930). Cf. Oscar Handlin, *The Uprooted* (Boston, Little, Brown, 1951).

8. Cf. David Burner, *The Politics of Provincialism: The Democratic Party in Transition, 1918–1932* (New York, Knopf, 1968), pp. 95–96, passim.

administration, joined of course by important segments of Protestant voters who shared with the Irish, Poles, Jews, Italians, and so on, a common lot of economic and social dislocation. Had the Smith candidacy succeeded in 1928 and been followed by the depression, it is doubtful that the Protestant majority—despite the depression—would have supported a reformist regime in 1932.[9] The anxieties generated by a Smith victory, I suggest, would have been seen by the Protestant majority as a premature power outcome of the politicization of ethnicity by non-Protestant groups. *In a word, a premature power consolidation of ethnicity provokes a normalcy response—a backlash, if you will—by the majority social groups.*

The Nixon victories in 1968 and 1972 are not dissimilar in function to the Hoover victory in 1928. The relatively successful politicization of black ethnicity through the aid of the federal (not the local) components of American politics in the Kennedy–Johnson era was perceived by the majority white social groups as a premature consolidation of ethnicity. It is ironic that among the majority white social groups are formerly stigmatized ethnic groups like Irish, Poles, Italians, and Jews; but this does not affect their perception. In fact, this perception is intensified because Negroes are the most stigmatized or alien of American ethnic groups. The ultra-stigmatization of blacks, moreover, reduces the chance of either empathy or plain objectivity in whites' perception of their plight. Thus a Harris Poll in December 1972 shows only 40 percent of whites agreeing that Negroes are discriminated against in terms of "getting full equality," and even a smaller proportion (38 percent) consider Negroes discriminated against in the "way treated as human beings." (See Table 9.)

The 1968 and 1972 presidential elections were shaped in no small way by this situation. Nixon strategists conceived the 1972 campaign partly as a subtle attack not only upon the premature power consolidation of black ethnicity but on its legitimacy. In the minds of millions of whites, Nixon identified black ethnicity with a life of crime, welfare freeloading, and evasion of the "work ethic." This was not without influence upon the outcome of the elections;

9. Cf. Ibid., chaps. 8–9.

voters of formerly stigmatized ethnic groups like Jews, Irish, Italians, and Poles voted one of few times in two generations between 40–60 percent Republican. For blacks, then, the route to a greater power consolidation of their ethnicity will, like other transformations they face in American life, be significantly more difficult than the comparable experience of white social groups.[10]

BLACK ETHNIC LEGITIMATION: CONCEPTUAL NOTE

Unlike the ethnicity of white social groups, black ethnicity lacked until recently the quality of authenticity—that is, a true and viable heritage, unquestionable in its capacity to shape and sustain a cohesive identity or awareness. Anti-African attitudes, widespread among most Afro-Americans until recently, were fundamental to this situation.[11] Thus black ethnicity has the status in American society of a curiously dependent cultural cluster: it borrows from white society much, though by no means all, of its culture-justifying ingredients.[12] Indeed, Ralph Ellison suggests persuasively that, owing to close black-white cultural interdependence, this might remain the crux of the Afro-American's plight.[13] And perhaps too of other blacks in the diaspora.[14]

In order to gain greater viability, black ethnicity becomes curiously wedded to politics, more intricately dependent upon poli-

10. For a somewhat different perspective, cf. Nathan Glazer, "Blacks and Ethnic Groups: The Difference, and the Political Difference It Makes," in Nathan Huggins, Martin Kilson, and Daniel Fox, eds., *Key Issues in the Afro-American Experience* (New York, Harcourt Brace Jovanovich, 1971).

11. An excellent study of this issue is Harold Isaacs, *The New World of Negro Americans* (New York, Day, 1963).

12. My conception of this is influenced by Richard Wright, *Native Son* (New York, Harper, 1940). See also Allison Davis and John Dollard, *Children of Bondage: The Personality Development of Negro Youth in the Urban South* (Washington, D.C., American Council on Education, 1940), and E. Franklin Frazier (with Harry Stack Sullivan), *Negro Youth at the Crossways: Their Personality Development in the Middle States* (Washington, D.C., American Council on Education, 1940).

13. Ralph Ellison, *Shadow and Act* (New York, Random House, 1964). See also Ralph Ellison, "What America Would Be Like without Blacks," *Time* (April 6, 1970), 54–55; E. Franklin Frazier, *The Negro in the United States* (New York, Macmillan, 1948).

14. Cf. Orlando Patterson, "Toward a Future That Has No Past: Reflections on the Fate of Blacks in the Americas," *The Public Interest* (Spring 1972).

tics than the earlier ethnic legitimation of white social groups. At
the elite level of Negro society, middle-class blacks—seeking legitimation in the new era of black ethnocentric revitalization—have
little but politics to offer. Other leadership attributes important to
such revitalization are in short supply among middle-class Negroes,
for in the pre-revitalization period they were, after all, highly dependent upon white society for their orientation and lifestyles.[15]
Politics affords them, as it were, a corrective for past limitations.
Thus the black bourgeoisie adopts the anti-white activism and the
ideology of white cultural denigration which have characterized the
black revitalization movement since the late 1960s because they
serve as effective political tools in unifying blacks. Had the Negro
elites refused to play a leading role in the ideology of white cultural
denigration their legitimacy as a leadership class would have been
seriously weakened.

BLACK ETHNIC LEGITIMATION: THE DYNAMICS

Politics have been central to the new dynamics of black ethnocentric revitalization. At one level this process entails the sharp polarization of black-white perceptions and relationships: to be more
positively or viably black, ethnically speaking, requires both anti-
white activism and the denigration of white society and values.
Thus since the 1960s a majority of American Negroes have been
willing to participate in a wide range of anti-white activities. The
young and middle class have been more militant than others. For
example, in 1969 only 25 percent of low-income Negroes in the
North were willing to "take part in a sit-in," whereas some 53 percent of middle-class Negroes were willing to do so; only 28 percent
of low-income Negroes would "march in a demonstration," while
62 percent of middle-income Negroes would; and while only 16
percent of low-income Negroes would risk "going to jail," 43 percent of middle-income Negroes would. (See Table 1.)

15. For an intellectually incisive but exaggerated and empirically dubious characterization of this situation, see E. Franklin Frazier, *Black Bourgeoisie* (Glencoe,
The Free Press, 1957). A first-rate sociological analysis of the black bourgeoisie
remains to be done. For a critique of the approach initiated by Frazier, see Martin
Kilson, "Militant Rhetoric and the Bourgeoisie," *The New York Times Book Review*,
sec. 7, pt. 2 (February 21, 1971), 2, 28–29.

Table 1. Negro Attitudes toward Militancy, by Age and Income, 1963, 1966, 1969 (by percent)

Total Sample	1963	1966	1969
Take part in a sit-in	49	52	40
March in a demonstration	51	54	44
Picket a store	46	49	41
Stop buying at a store	62	69	57
Go to jail	47	45	33

North	Total	Under 30	30–49	50 and Older	Low Income	Low Middle	Middle Income
Take part in a sit-in	43	57	47	27	25	45	53
March in a demonstration	49	63	51	36	28	51	62
Picket a store	43	59	47	25	29	46	55
Stop buying at a store	56	67	56	44	44	57	66
Go to jail	32	45	35	19	16	31	43

Source: Peter Goldman (and Gallup Poll), Report from Black America (New York, Simon and Schuster, 1970), p. 242.

The greater participation of middle-class Negroes in anti-white activism cannot be overemphasized: for ethnocentric revitalization requires, wherever it occurs, the strong support of the leadership strata. The local-level leadership—heads of communal associations and networks—are particularly prominent among those middle-class blacks who proffer strong support of anti-white militancy, favoring it more than do the cosmopolitan or established middle-class leadership.[16] The local-level leadership is especially essential to the process of sharpening the communal nexus and the we–they identity axis of movements of ethnocentric revitalization.[17]

The denigration of white culture and values is, of course, the logical corollary of a strong preference for anti-white political ac-

16. Cf. William McCord, et al., Lifestyles in the Black Ghetto (New York, Norton, 1969).

17. See, for example, Alex Gottfried, Boss Cermak of Chicago: A Study of Political Leadership (Seattle, University of Washington Press, 1962); Lloyd Wendt and Herman Kogan, Lords of the Levee: The Story of Bathhouse John and Hinky Dink (Indianapolis, Dodd-Mead, 1943); Humbert S. Nelli, The Italians in Chicago, 1880–1930 (New York, Oxford University Press, 1970); and Zink, City Bosses in the United States.

tivism. Support for the latter implies sympathy for the former. Here, too, middle-class Negroes display stronger preferences than low-income Negroes. For example, in 1969 some 54 percent of all Negroes believed that "Negroes have a special spirit or soul that most white people have not experienced," but only 38 percent of low-income Northern blacks (33 percent Southern) believed this, compared with 67 percent of middle-income Northern blacks (56 percent Southern). (See Table 2.) In regard to new group nomenclature, 19 percent of all Negroes favored the term "black" in 1969 (nearly two thirds in 1972) but only 17 percent of low-income Northern Negroes (6 percent Southern) favored this nomenclature, compared with 34 percent of middle-income Northern Negroes (17 percent Southern). And in regard to the wearing of the "Afro" hair style, 45 percent of all Negroes favored this style in 1969, but 58 percent of middle-income Northern Negroes did (50 percent Southern) compared with 42 percent low-income Northern Negroes (26 percent Southern).[18] Finally, with regard to the politi-

Table 2. In your opinion, do most Negroes have a special spirit or soul that most white people have not experienced? (by percent)

Total Sample	1963	1966	1969			
Yes	x	x	54			
No	x	x	22			
Not sure	x	x	24			

North	Total	Under 30	30–49	50 and Older	Low Income	Low Middle	Middle Income
Yes	60	79	62	39	38	62	67
No	20	8	19	32	27	25	13
Not sure	20	13	19	29	35	14	20
South							
Yes	48	59	50	39	33	49	56
No	24	22	25	24	22	27	26
Not sure	29	20	25	37	45	24	18

Source: Goldman, *Report from Black America,* p. 263.

18. Peter Goldman (with Gallup Poll), *Report from Black America* (New York, Simon and Schuster, 1970), pp. 262–263.

Table 3. Do you favor the idea of black power, or not? (by percent)

Total Sample		1963		1966		1969		
Favor		x		25		42		
Don't favor		x		37		31		
Not sure		x		38		27		

North	Total	Under 30	30–49	50 and Older	Low Income	Low Middle	Middle Income
Favor	50	68	47	38	31	46	59
Don't favor	28	16	30	40	39	27	27
Not sure	22	16	24	22	30	27	14
South							
Favor	34	49	42	17	19	30	52
Don't favor	34	21	31	45	52	33	24
Not sure	32	30	27	38	29	37	24

Source: Goldman, *Report from Black America*, p. 264.

cal ideas associated with black ethnocentric revitalization, some 42 percent of all Negroes favored "Black Power" in 1969 (a two-fold increase over 1966), but only 31 percent of low-income Northern Negroes did (19 percent Southern) compared with nearly two thirds of middle-income Northern Negroes (52 percent Southern). (See Table 3.)

The middle-class role in black ethnocentric revitalization is, however, ridden with paradox. It owes as much to psychological as to political factors. Ethnocentric revitalization movements—of which modern nationalist movements are a variant—always entail a perplexing admixture of psychological-cultural (particularistic) and political (universalistic) processes.[19] For the black movement, the particularistic must derive strength through politics; the weakness of black ethnicity in American society means it cannot of itself generate the means of greater ethnic viability. This dependence of the particularistic upon politics, however, is not fully satisfying, because blacks would like to believe that their ethnocentric revitaliza-

19. Cf. Talcott Parsons, *Structure and Process in Modern Societies* (Glencoe, The Free Press, 1960), pp. 126–128.

tion is fully realizable without the modifications or concessions that politics perforce require. But this is not the case.

In themselves particularistic forces sustain only ritualistic tendencies, which are high in cathartic effect but productive only of a ethnocentric *cul-de-sac*—the equivalent of Karl Marx's opiate of the masses. The political (universalistic) forces must be utilized, which means that they must be borrowed or adapted from the adversary society or group. The resultant dilemma is exceedingly troublesome for the leadership of movements of ethnocentric revitalization. But the leadership of successful movements of ethnocentric revitalization—which the current black movement clearly is—do what they must: modify the particularistic through politics while proclaiming belief in the particularistic—a proclamation which their identity, legitimacy, and control require.[20]

One example of the paradoxes in the movement of black ethnocentric revitalization—a movement whose psychological-cultural processes are posed as antithetical to white America—is the fact that the federal government is overwhelmingly responsible, directly and indirectly, for the extraordinary occupational mobility of middle-class Negroes in the past decade—precisely those blacks who now supply leadership to the revitalization movement. This mobility, which began in the early 1960s under the Kennedy–Johnson administrations, has suffered less than one might have expected under the Nixon administration. The mobility of middle-class Negroes is one of the few areas of compromise between the neo-conservative Republican administration and blacks, owing partly to Nixon's reelection organization's willingness to bid for middle-class Negro voters. Another factor is also involved in this crucial compromise between the Republican administration and middle-class Negroes. For the sake of maximizing federal government benefits, many middle-class Negroes who were identified with

20. This problem has plagued the black revitalization movement from the start and has begun to attenuate only since 1971. See Martin Kilson, "Black Power: Anatomy of a Paradox," *Harvard Journal of Negro Affairs*, 2.1 (1968). Negro college students have tended to insist on the particularistic dimensions of the black revitalization movement more than one would have expected. See Martin Kilson, "Black Student Militants," *Encounter* (September and October 1971), and Martin Kilson, "Blacks at Harvard," *The Harvard Bulletin* (April and June 1973).

the black revitalization forces modified their anti-white activism. Those elements involved in black capitalism have shrewdly translated ethnocentric revitalization into free-enterprise terms which are acceptable to a Republican administration.[21] This strategy has also been successful for white-collar workers, as can be seen in the following report from a recent Civil Service Commission survey of white-collar jobs held by Negroes in the federal government:

The number of blacks in federal jobs ranked GS-9 and above—the top half of the government's jobs—has risen 28% since May 1970, the new Civil Service Commission survey shows. As of last November blacks held 29,796 or 4.7% of the jobs in the GS grades 9 to 18 range. Much of the gain reflects workers hired in the 1960s who are "progressing nicely up the ladder," a spokesman says. Negroes hold 15.3% of all federal jobs, the figures show. Other minorities fill another 4.7% of the positions. Of 5,712 jobs at the highest GS grades 16 to 18, blacks hold 145 or 2.5%; Spanish-surnamed hold 33, American Indians 12, and Orientals 23. The gains in minority hiring come at a time when federal employment is falling; full-time federal jobs decreased by 31,703 in the year ended November 30th.[22]

The strategy that produced these results emerged from a highly divided movement of black ethnocentric revitalization. In the formative period of this movement, two elements within the black middle classes coalesced to ensure that the movement's outcome would include substantive or material, as well as symbolic and identity-oriented, benefits. This coalition, the moderates in the revitalization movement, comprises the following: (1) the innovative sector of the established black bourgeoisie, that is, those capable of seizing

21. Sophisticated leadership of this strategy has been provided for four years by the black business journal *Black Enterprise*. It is published by a highly able Negro businessman, Earl G. Graves, and controlled by a Board of Advisors under the chairmanship of Henry Parks, head of the Parks Sausage Corporation—probably the largest Negro manufacturing firm—and made up of leading business and political figures like William Hudgins, Vice Chairman of the Freedom National Bank in Harlem, Shirley Chisholm, Congresswoman from Brooklyn, Senator Edward Brooke, and Julian Bond, member of Georgia House of Representatives. For an example of this style of politicizing the black revitalization movement, see *Black Enterprise* (August 1970 and May 1971), especially the sections entitled, suggestively, "Making It."

22. *The Wall Street Journal,* July 17, 1973, p. 1.

new opportunities; (2) the entrepreneurial and lawyer–politician newcomers to the black bourgeoisie. These two sectors of the bourgeoisie coalesce either in action or policy, differentiating their positions in the ethnocentric revitalization movement from those who might be termed the militants—mainly deviant intellectuals (usually first-generation college-educated like Imamu Baraka), para-professionals (social workers, schoolteachers, and so on), and self-educated leaders or what I describe elsewhere as para-intellectuals.[23] This distinction between coalescence in action and in policy is important: interest groups who *coalesce in action* do so, of course, visibly; but *coalescence in policy* is often implicit or muted—through discreet political cues emitted by the leaders or articulate persons in the coalescing interest groups. Coalescence in policy is highly suitable to situations where established and *parvenu* sections of the elites become allies; it allows both sections discretion (which is important to their control or authority over their own support structure) but does not jeopardize the pursuit of their objective interests. Such discretion is especially important as a political option for the new black capitalists and lawyer–politicians. Fledgling in authority and legitimacy, they are vulnerable on the left-flank, and susceptible to anomic thrusts by the Negro masses, which of course is what the black ghetto riots of the late 1960s were.

The success of this strategy for maximizing the substantive goals of the black ethnocentric revitalization depends upon the moderate leadership's ability to manipulate the symbolic or ritual dimensions of the movement. Charismatic leadership and the unique legitimacy attached to it by Negroes are especially significant in this regard. Successful symbolic and ideological manipulation by the moderates (exemplified in the use of militant speech and wearing the Afro hairstyle) shelters the basically establishment goals they seek—namely, to bring the black bourgeoisie and blacks generally more firmly into the American power structure. Such manipulation also reduces the division between the moderates and militants: it enables the militants to view the moderates' establishment goals as something other than a threat to the particularistic attributes of black ethnocentric revitalization.

23. See Martin Kilson, "The New Black Intellectuals," *Dissent* (July–August 1969).

It is an extraordinary feature of this movement that the moderates' strategy has been thus far relatively successful.[24] The success of this strategy has also been functional to the movement. *No such movement can approximate its particularistic or identity-focused goals without the aid of the substantive benefits derived from politics and power.* Without such benefits, the particularistic dimensions of movements of ethnocentric revitalization *turn in on themselves:* they become ritualistically self-indulgent, messianic, and millenarian.[25] The movement of black ethnocentric revitalization faced such an outcome throughout its formative and middle period (say, 1966–1970). Had the revitalization militants (the deviant intellectuals, social workers, teachers, and para-intellectuals) vanquished the alliance of the old bourgeoisie and the middle-class newcomers in this period, the outcome would have been markedly different from what it is. So too would the current conflict dynamic between blacks and whites.

CONFLICT, CLEAVAGES, AND THE POLITICS OF BLACK ETHNICITY

The conflict surrounding movements of ethnocentric revitalization is highly contentious and not infrequently bloody. This is especially true of movements whose *culture indigène* is ideologically diffuse or poorly differentiated from an adversary (often the dominant) culture. The Afro-American subculture is of this variety: so much of what it means to be *black* in America is intricately linked to white society, and the formation of black ideas, values, and institutions occurs in complex dialectical interaction with this society.[26]

24. See the data in Ben J. Wattenberg and Richard M. Scammon, "Black Progress and Liberal Rhetoric," *Commentary* (April 1973).

25. Black revitalization movements, including nationalist movements, have been plagued with this problem throughout the world, always bordering on millenarian disorientation. For a West Indian variant, see the novel by Orlando Patterson, *Children of Sisyphus* (London, New Authors Ltd., 1964). Aspects of this problem in African nationalist movements are considered in Martin Kilson, *Political Change in a West African State* (Cambridge, Harvard University Press, 1966).

26. Cf. Frazier, *The Negro in the United States*. There is, of course, little consensus on the characterization of the *culture indigène* of black Americans. The debate begins with Melville J. Herskovitz, *The Myth of the Negro Past* (New York, Harper, 1941) and progresses through E. Franklin Frazier, Ralph Ellison, and more recent

The primary cleavage within the movement of black ethnocentric revitalization has evolved against this background of ambivalence between black and white in American life. This cleavage exists, in the first instance, between the established or old black bourgeoisie and the bourgeois newcomers. Relatively well socialized into American politics and acculturated to middle-class lifestyles for two generations, the established black bourgeoisie was initially marginal to black ethnocentric revitalization, and not infrequently opposed to it.[27] Only with the effective politicization of black ethnocentric revitalization by the bourgeois newcomers—the new Negro middle class of the 1950s and early 1960s—did a section of the old black bourgeoisie discover the movement of ethnocentric revitalization. Dr. Martin Luther King, Jr., member of an established bourgeois Negro family, led this discovery, organizing it through the Southern Christian Leadership Conference (SCLC).

The SCLC pioneered a variant of black ethnocentric revitalization, casting it within a framework of restrained black-white conflict, buffered by a nonviolent ideology. While Dr. King lived, his unique legitimacy—largely charismatic—imposed a ceiling upon effective competition for leadership of the revitalization movement from the bourgeois newcomers.[28] A measure of this situation can be seen from two Harris polls of Negro opinion toward their political leaders in 1963 and 1966. In both polls 88 percent of Negroes gave Dr. King an "approving" vote, while only 15 percent gave an "approving" vote in 1963 to Elijah Muhammad, leader of the Black Muslims, and 12 percent in 1966.[29] Furthermore, until his death in

---

contributions by Nathan I. Huggins and Houston Baker. The latter contributions are found in Huggins, Kilson, and Fox, eds., *Key Issues in the Afro-American Experience.*

27. See Harold F. Gosnell, *Negro Politicians: The Rise of Negro Politics in Chicago* (Chicago, University of Chicago Press, 1935). See also Martin Kilson, "Political Change in the Negro Ghetto, 1900–1940s," in Huggins, Kilson, and Fox, eds., *Key Issues in the Afro-American Experience,* pp. 167–192.

28. On the appeal of the charismatic figure—the virtuoso individual performer—among Negroes, see Charles Keil, *Urban Blues* (Chicago, University of Chicago Press, 1966). The best analysis of King's strategy is August Meier, "On the Role of Martin Luther King," *New Politics* (Winter 1965).

29. William Brink and Louis Harris, *Black and White: A Study of U.S. Racial Studies Today* (New York, Simon and Schuster, 1967), p. 54.

1968 Dr. King's SCLC ranked high in the "excellent" rating column of the Harris polls, with a 30 point lead over the Black Muslims in 1963 and 1966, and a 22 point lead over the Student Non-Violent Coordinating Committee (SNCC) in 1963 and an 11 point lead in 1966. (See Tables 4–6.) Moreover, the SCLC's strongest support came from the middle class, the majority of which in the 1960s was *parvenu.*

Table 4. Negro Ranking of Southern Christian Leadership Conference 1963, 1966 (by percent)

							Non-South			
	Total all inter- views		Total non- South		Low income		Lower middle income		Middle and upper income	
Rank	1966	1963	1966	1963	1966	1963	1966	1963	1966	1963
Excellent	34	32	36	40	28	31	30	40	41	42
Pretty good	21	24	24	25	25	25	24	25	23	21
Only fair	5	9	7	6	9	6	7	5	7	9
Poor	1	2	2	2	3	–	–	2	3	2
Not sure	39	33	31	27	35	38	39	28	26	26

Source: William Brink and Louis Harris, *Black and White: A Study of U.S. Racial Attitudes Today* (New York, Simon and Schuster, 1970), p. 250.

Table 5. Negro Ranking of Student Non-violent Coordinating Committee 1963, 1966 (by percent)

							Non-South			
	Total all inter- views		Total non- South		Low income		Lower middle income		Middle and upper income	
Rank	1966	1963	1966	1963	1966	1963	1966	1963	1966	1963
Excellent	23	10	25	13	28	8	26	14	25	7
Pretty good	21	8	26	9	25	13	24	9	29	5
Only fair	10	3	9	2	9	–	7	2	9	2
Poor	4	1	6	1	–	–	3	1	6	2
Not sure	42	78	34	75	38	81	40	74	31	84

Source: Brink and Harris, *Black and White,* p. 250.

Table 6. Negro Ranking of Black Muslims 1963, 1966 (by percent)

	Total all inter- views		Total non- South		Low income		Non-South Lower middle income		Middle and upper income	
Rank	1966	1963	1966	1963	1966	1963	1966	1963	1966	1963
Excellent	4	4	4	5	3	8	3	5	2	5
Pretty good	5	7	6	8	3	13	8	7	6	14
Only fair	6	6	7	8	3	6	11	7	6	14
Poor	43	38	52	43	57	25	47	43	60	49
Not sure	42	45	31	36	34	50	31	38	26	18

Source: Brink and Harris, *Black and White,* p. 254.

But less than two years before Dr. King's death at the hands of a white assassin, the SCLC's nonviolent method of black ethnocentric revitalization began to lose ground to a more racially strident approach. The SNCC leadership—especially Stokely Carmichael—initiated the strategy of "Black Power" in 1965, giving it a powerful advantage. It increased its "excellent" rating from 10 to 20 percent and reduced its comparative position with the SCLC from 22 points below SCLC in 1963 to 11 points below it in 1966. Among middle-class blacks, the SNCC's "excellent" rating increased nearly four-fold: from 7 percent in 1963 to 25 percent in 1966. The significance of this can be judged by the fact that from 1966 onward the movement of black ethnocentric revitalization entered a new phase; it shed the restraint on racial conflict that characterized Dr. King's leadership of the movement, with any middle-class Negroes acquiring an explicit interest in sharp fission with white society and culture, manipulating this fission as a primary instrument of massive popular mobilization of Negroes, often in violent ways.

Thus by the time of Dr. King's death in 1968 a new militant phase of black ethnocentric revitalization was well underway, possessing two salient political features: one, both the old and new black bourgeoisie had been extensively politicized and radicalized—at least with regard to racial assertion; two, a political nexus between the middle classes and the black working and lower classes was created and began to display basic political institutionalization

Table 7. Do you agree or disagree that Negroes can get what they want only by banding together as black people against the whites, because the whites will never help Negroes? (by percent)

Total Sample	1963	1966	1969
Agree	x	25	27
Disagree	x	64	59
Not sure	x	11	14

North	Total	Under 30	30–49	50 and Older	Low Income	Low Middle	Middle Income
Agree	30	45	26	25	22	34	32
Disagree	54	43	57	61	47	56	53
Not sure	16	13	17	14	32	10	15

Source: Goldman, *Report from Black America,* p. 260.

through the rise of numerous elected middle-class Negro politicians. In short, by the end of the 1960s and early 1970s, a militant ethnocentric revitalization of Negroes had produced a political transformation of the Afro-American subsystem.

Yet as Table 7 shows, in 1969 some 59 percent of Negroes polled disagreed with the statement that "Negroes can get what they want only by banding together *as black people* against the whites, because the whites will never help Negroes." This outlook prevailed, moreover, despite the fact that in 1966 and 1969 only 27 and 20 percent of Negroes respectively felt that whites wished a "better break" for blacks, while as many as 38 and 43 percent respectively felt that whites wished "to keep blacks down." [30] Why this ambivalence?

The key to this ambivalence is that black ethnocentric revitalization *occurs within a framework not of rigid socio-political constraints upon Negroes but of steady modification of the social parameters dividing blacks and whites in American society.* The proportion of Negroes who were poor or lower class declined from 48 percent in 1959 to about 30 percent in 1971; and the number of blacks in white-collar and craftsmen-cum-skilled occupations increased 76 percent during the past decade, from 2.9 million in 1960 to 5.1 million in 1970, compared with a 24 percent increase for whites. These occupational

30. Goldman, *Report from Black America,* p. 250.

shifts are associated with significant educational change: median
school years completed for Negroes aged 25–29 increased from 7
years in 1940 to 12 years in 1970; furthermore, 10 percent of
Negroes aged 18–24 were enrolled in college in 1965 (26 percent
whites) and 18 percent in 1971 (27 percent whites), reducing the
black–white differential to only 9 percent. Also blacks are now 6
percent of the college population.[31]

There is, moreover, considerable ambivalence among blacks
about how far anti-white activism—the precondition of black ethnocentric revitalization—should be carried. This ambivalence is a
stablizing factor in two respects: it sustains the coalition of the established black bourgeoisie and the new middle class; and, it con-
strains black–white polarization, allowing room for consensus and
fusion. Yet blacks perceive a causal relationship between the social
advances noted above and the movement of ethnocentric revitalization: the latter seems to produce the former. The intensification of
anti-white activism and white cultural denigration seems, therefore,
from one point of view, a productive tactic for black social advancement.

In the mature phase of black ethnocentric revitalization (1969)
more Negroes considered white churches "more harmful" than
helpful to black advancement than in 1966—20 and 16 percent respectively. Some 25 percent considered white businesses "more
harmful" in 1969, compared with 19 percent in 1966, with 35 percent of middle-class Negroes in the North expressing this view and
only 14 percent of lower-income blacks. Furthermore, some 16
percent felt Jews "more harmful" in 1969, compared with 5 percent in 1966—with 24 percent middle-class Negroes in the North
and only 4 percent low-income expressing this view. Finally, 20
percent considered labor unions "more harmful" in 1969 compared with 13 percent in 1966—with 40 percent middle-class and
18 percent low-income Negroes in the North holding this view.[32] *In
short, though partly reducing the racial-conflict element in the movement of*

31. These data are from Wattenberg and Scammon, "Black Progress and Liberal Rhetoric," pp. 37–39.
32. Goldman, *Report from Black America,* pp. 254–255.

black ethnocentric revitalization and facilitating cleavage stabilization within the movement, the social gains of Negroes also pull in the opposite direction.

Politically this entails, in one respect, a form of false consciousness: blacks' perception of the relationship of ethnicity to power is distorted.[33] For example, the trade union movement, though very slow to admit Negro workers, actually had by 1970 a black membership of 12 percent—a proportion equal to the percentage of Negroes in the population. On the one hand, this false consciousness is functional to the extent that it generates a measure of antiwhite activism which is essential to black ethnocentric revitalization. On the other hand, it is dysfunctional in that it distorts perception by Negroes of real advances, causing blacks to persist in hostile stances toward white groups and institutions who today are less guilty of resistance to blacks than they were in the past.

This situation poses enormous tactical problems for Negro leadership today, especially the newly elected black politicians—the inevitable heirs to the leadership of the black renascence movement insofar as this movement can realize substantive benefits for blacks only through the established political processes. The growth of the new black politician class, based upon established or newly fashioned political machines rather than upon civil rights organizations and the clientage ties with liberal whites of the older Negro leadership, has been extraordinary. In the early 1960s there were around 600 elected Negro politicians in the United States; today (1974) there are 3,500. The enormous increase of Negroes in medium-size and big cities (some 20 such cities now have 20–50 percent Negro population) is at the basis of the new black politician class. There are now 58 congressional districts with 25 percent or more Negro voters, and 20 of these are outside the South. Furthermore, in the 1972 presidential election there were 52 congressional districts in which the Negro population of voting age was at least twice the

33. Cf. Kenneth B. Clark and Jeannette Hopkins, *A Relevant War against Poverty* (New York, Harper & Row, 1970), p. x. Clark observes that "Separatism . . . is now desired and fought for by a growing number of young black militants out of . . . false perceptions."

successful white candidate's margin of victory.[34] Other factors associated with the new black politician class are shown in Table 8.

It now remains for the new black politician class, the beneficiary of the movement of black ethnocentric revitalization, to translate the emergent power-mustering capacity of Negroes into public policies that will raise the standards of the Negro social system to levels comparable to those of white America. There are numerous obstacles in face of such a transformation, but none is as perplexing as the role of racial perceptions in black–white relationships.[35] It is a major paradox of the movement of black ethnocentric revital-

Table 8. Political Attributes of Negro Population in Selected Cities

City	Total Population [a]	Percent Negro	Negro Percent VAP [b]	Negro Percent City Council Seats [c]	Negro Percent Police Force [d]
Baltimore	905,759	46.4	43.7	26.3	13
Detroit	1,511,482	43.7	39.4	33.3	12
Cincinnati	452,524	27.6	24.4	37.5	4.9
Cleveland	750,903	38.3	36.6	36.6	7.7
Buffalo	462,768	20.4	17.8	20	2
New York	7,867,760	21.2	19	5.4	7.5
Newark	382,417	54.2	48.6	33.3	15
Camden	102,551	39.1	34	28.6	–
Jersey City	260,545	21	17.4	11.1	5.4
Kansas City, Mo.	507,087	22.1	18.8	33.3	7.5
St. Louis	622,236	40.9	35.9	20.6	14
Philadelphia	1,948,609	33.6	31.1	17.6	18.6
Pittsburgh	520,117	20.2	18.4	22.2	6.4
Oakland	361,561	34.5	29.4	12.5	7
Chicago	3,366,957	32.7	28.2	28	16.5
Wilmington	80,386	43.6	36.7	41.7	11.5

Source: Reports of Joint Center for Political Studies, Washington, D.C.
[a] Total population figures from 1970 census.
[b] VAP denotes "Voting Age Population." Figures for 1970.
[c] City council seats figures for 1972.
[d] Black police figures for 1970.

34. These data are from Joint Center for Political Studies, *Focus* (March 1973), tables I–II, pp. 4–5.

35. For a case study of the politics of this dilemma, see Martin Kilson, *Political Dilemmas of the Black Mayor: Carl Stokes in Cleveland,* Washington, D.C., Joint Center for Political Studies, forthcoming.

ization in the 1970s that at the point where the influence of anti-white activism is beginning to attenuate, or at least becoming susceptible to political control by the black politician class, a politicized white neo-ethnicity is evolving.

Moreover, this convergence-in-time of politicized black and white neo-ethnicity has conservative national political implications. The reasons for this are several. First, the thrust of a politicized black ethnicity is basically at the left of the political spectrum; and during its formative phase, before it was harnessed by the new black politician class, it was even anarchistic, as evidenced by the riots of the late 1960s.[36] The neo-ethnicity of urban whites, on the other hand, is basically conservative. This is partly because the resort to neo-ethnicity reflects a desire of many urban whites to regain a firmer self-orientation in an era of sharp societal shifts, as exemplified by the spread of neo-ethnicity among Jews. At the same time that enormous upward social mobility has placed 80 percent of Jews firmly in the middle classes—a proportion without equal among American ethnic groups—many Jews exhibit a strong need for the identity-sustaining benefits of neo-ethnicity. It seems that, for Jews at least, a cost of upward mobility has been a growth in ethnic decomposition. For example, intermarriage of Jews (especially males) with gentiles is at an all-time high, and the Jewish separation and divorce rate is high. For example, a sample retake of census for Boston by the Harvard–MIT Joint Center for Urban Studies found that there were more Jewish female heads of households than Negro. In this situation, neo-ethnicity has conservative implications; it is being cultivated by numerous established Jewish organizations such as rabbinical associations, the American Jewish Committee, the American Jewish Congress, some of which have turned their backs on their liberal principles, opposing for example a popular television program about a Jewish and Irish couple ("Bernie Loves Bridget"), thereby causing its termination. When this pattern of Jewish neo-ethnicity is combined with that of other white ethnic groups at the level of national politics—as it was dur-

36. This is treated in Martin Kilson, "Black Politics: A New Power," in Irving Howe and Michael Harrington, eds., *The Seventies: Problems and Proposals* (New York, Harper & Row, 1972).

ing the 1972 presidential campaign of Richard Nixon—the result is a veritable neo-conservative political realignment. In this situation, black neo-ethnicity assumes a new significance.

NEO-ETHNICITY AND THE NEO-CONSERVATIVE REALIGNMENT

Neo-ethnicity among urban whites is in large part a response to the relative political success of an emergent black ethnicity. It is concentrated in marginal-income, working-class, lower middle-class, and even some middle-class city whites, who retain some vestiges of ethnic lifestyles, values, and perceptions.[37] The marginal-income city whites are especially central to neo-ethnicity, insofar as they provide the sharpest core support for a fundamental attribute of white neo-ethnicity—anti-Negro orientation. They deny more strongly than other whites the prevalence of deprivations among Negroes (for example, only 46 percent of marginal-income whites believe "Negro housing worse than whites," compared with 65 percent of all whites), and they are more likely to accept the most prejudiced views of blacks as human beings (for example, 61 percent believe "Negroes smell different," compared with 52 percent of all whites). Neo-ethnicity among marginal-income city whites is also related to the high degree of alienation they seem to display. Their rate of alienation might even be higher than that of the Negro population. For example, national data for 1966 show that 68 percent of low-income whites felt that "rich get richer, poor get poorer," compared with 49 percent of Negroes sharing this outlook and 48 percent of the total population; also 40 percent of low-income whites felt that "nobody understands problems I have," compared with 30 percent of Negroes and 17 percent of the total public.[38]

Furthermore, there is some evidence that alienation is high also for skilled working-class and lower middle class white city dwellers. Thus a study of Wallace supporters in 1968 in Gary, Indiana,

37. Cf. Nathan Glazer and Daniel P. Moynihan, *Beyond the Melting Pot* (Cambridge, Harvard University Press, and MIT Press, 1963). See also Mark R. Levy and Michael S. Kramer, *The Ethnic Factor* (New York, Simon and Schuster, 1972).
38. Brink and Harris, *Black and White*, p. 135.

found that highly skilled white workers in the $7,500 to $10,000 income range had a distrustful or alienated outlook and "are in an extreme state of relative deprivation." This situation seems to facilitate a turn to neo-ethnicity (on the part of such white city dwellers) and its subsequent politicization. As Thomas Pettigrew, a highly perceptive social psychologist, has put it: "The bitter irony for our nation is that the same powerful social psychological mechanism— relative deprivation—is leading to racial strife on both sides of the color line. Black Americans typically regard themselves as victims of injustice when they compare their still largely low status with that of other Americans. Yet the white Wallace voters in Gary shared much the same feeling. They understandably deduced from all the publicity about civil rights gains of the past decade that Negroes, in contrast with themselves, were in fact 'making it big.' Yet the hard truth is that most blacks are not 'making it'—indeed do not as a group approach the position of the threatened Wallacites." [39]

Moreover, a white political leadership willing to articulate this position has been central to the politicization of neo-ethnicity among white city dwellers. Although some form of ethnicity has always been present in city politics, what I call neo-ethnicity is unique because of the *traditionalistic aura* associated with it in an era of sharp societal shifts. Numerous studies of modernization around the world have demonstrated the political importance of traditionalism in periods of rapid social change.[40] Modern man is, after all, particularly vulnerable in matters of identity, and periods of rapid change intensify the problem. Americans, after 25 years of extraordinary societal shifts, yearn for connections with the past— the moorings of identity. For both blacks and whites neo-ethnicity has become the medium of such retrieval of the traditional sources of identity, and thus a greater sense of personal worth. Paradox-

39. Thomas F. Pettigrew, "Ethnicity in American Life: A Social-Psychological Perspective," in Otto Feinstein, ed., *Ethnic Groups in the City* (Lexington, Mass., D. C. Heath, 1971), p. 35.
40. Cf. Lloyd I. Rudolph and Susanne Rudolph, *The Modernity of Tradition* (Chicago, University of Chicago Press, 1967); Martin Kilson, *Political Change in a West African State.*

ically, *the new black ethnicity is reformist in thrust, while the new white ethnicity is conservative. But both, alas, are militant: for as an instrument of political mobilization ethnicity is curiously metapolitical—something more than politics.* Herein lies the danger of neo-ethnicity in American political life—a danger still poorly appreciated by some liberal social scientists.[41]

Some of the best data illustrative of the modalites of neo-ethnicity in city politics are found in the study by the Harvard political scientist William Schneider of the political attitudes of 600 Jewish voters in New York's 1973 Democratic mayoralty primary. The hard-core Jewish supporters of Mario Biaggi, a New York State assemblyman who has emerged as a leading spokesman for white neo-ethnicity in city politics, were typically older, poorer, and less educated than the typical Jewish voter. For example, 53 percent were in the 30–60 years age group, 17 percent had incomes below $10,000 and 40 percent never attended college. Biaggi supporters also displayed a militant approach to neo-ethnicity, including an anti-Negro orientation. Thus some 62 percent of Biaggi's Jewish supporters believed the city government is doing too much for blacks and minorities; 84 percent supported the militant demonstrations against low-income public housing in the middle-class Forest Hills district; and 90 percent supported the boycotts by Catholic and Jewish parents and pupils of schools slated for integration in the Canarsie school district.[42]

41. I draw attention to this danger in my chapter "Political Change in the Negro Ghetto, 1900–1940s," in Huggins, Kilson, Fox, eds., *Key Issues in the Afro-American Experience,* p. 192. Noting that some social scientists attempt to deify ethnicity in American life, I observe that "Surely, in the form of white racism toward blacks since the end of Reconstruction, ethnicity can be evaluated as nothing other than a deadly force: an albatross, or worse, around the neck of American society. Today ethnicity, in the hands of a new set of Negro leaders—bent like their Irish, Polish, Jewish, Italian historical counterparts on the ethnic redress of differentials between subordinate and superordinate groups—might well lead to profound political crisis at many levels of the American political system." On the deification of ethnicity in American politics, see Andrew N. Greeley, "Turning Off 'The People': The War and White Ethnic Groups," *New Republic* (June 27, 1970), pp. 14–16. See also Michael Novak, *The Rise of the Unmeltable Ethnics* (New York, Macmillan, 1972).

42. These data are reported in Richard Reeves, "Splitting the Jewish Vote," *New York* (June 18, 1973), pp. 57–63.

But the anti-Negro ideology in the political appeal of white neo-ethnicity enables it to cut across social class and generation lines, mobilizing support outside its core group of supporters. Thus another 54 percent of Biaggi's Jewish supporters had between $10,000 and $20,000 income and 35 percent were under 30 years of age. Furthermore, the strength of the ideological element in the appeal of white neo-ethnicity is underlined by the fact that although 65 percent of the Jews in Schneider's survey were characterized as "liberal" [43] more than half (52 percent) of the "liberals" supported the demonstrations against public housing in Forest Hills and 51 percent of these backed the Canarsie school boycotts.

The conservatism of Jewish voters in New York's 1973 Democratic mayoral primary election contrasted strikingly with Jewish ideological and political preferences of a decade ago. The Gallup survey done for Lloyd Free and Hadley Cantril in 1964 found that 83 percent of American Jews polled (largely resident in New York State) had an "ideological-liberal" preference and 90 percent an "operational-liberal" preference (that is, they did not believe the federal government had too much power).[44] Both Catholics and Protestants ranked significantly below Jews in these preferences: 65 percent of Catholics favored an ideological-liberal and 77 percent an operational-liberal view; 42 percent of Protestants favored the former and 60 percent the latter. Thus if the Schneider survey during the 1973 New York City mayoral primary indicates a trend that can be projected for Jews and other whites, neo-conservatism is rising sharply.

CONCLUSION: FISSION AND FUSION

The ultimate paradox surrounding neo-ethnicity in American political life today might well be that as white neo-ethnicity evolves into a multifaceted neo-conservatism—carefully orchestrated at the national level by the

43. The "liberals" in the survey were those who replied "not enough" or "just about right" to the question "Is the city government doing too much for minority groups?" Forty-two percent responded "not enough," and 22 percent said "just about right." Reeves, "Splitting the Jewish Vote," p. 63.

44. Lloyd A. Free and Hadley Cantril, *The Political Beliefs of Americans* (New Brunswick, N.J., Rutgers University Press, 1968), pp. 148–149.

Republican party—the politics of black ethnicity is de-emphasizing militancy and anti-white orientation. The web of contradictions within which black ethnicity functions suggests this scenario.

The proportion of blacks preferring housing in racially mixed neighborhoods increased from 64 percent in 1963 to 74 percent in 1970, the years of the maturation of neo-ethnicity among Negroes. A similar pattern prevailed for another basic area in black-white interaction—the job milieu. Negro preference for a racially mixed job milieu increased from 76 to 82 percent between 1963 and 1969, and the middle-class preference (86 percent) is somewhat stronger than the total black preference.

What these data suggest is that despite nearly a decade of marked black-white polarization related to the ideological movement of black ethnocentric revitalization, this process is not perfectly continuous at the institutional level—or, rather, a significant proportion of Negroes do not wish it to be.[45] Data for 1969 through late 1972 illustrate this conclusion, as shown in Table 9, revealing a sharp decline in Negro perception of discrimination in all major spheres of black-white interaction. For example, in 1969 some 83 percent of Negroes felt discriminated against in housing compared with 66 percent in late 1972. It would seem that as the movement of black ethnocentric revitalization realizes social benefits for blacks, the pluralist pressures of American society function as a counterweight to long-run Negro antagonism toward whites. This tendency toward fusion has been observed in other historic areas of conflict in American society, as Robert Dahl has demonstrated in regard to both ethnic and class conflict in New Haven (late nineteenth to middle twentieth century) involving working-class Catholics (Irish) and patrician WASPs.[46]

Yet the sharpening of ethnic perceptions in black-white relations is on the increase and is likely to remain so. In addition to the powerful forces of relative deprivation among working-class and lower middle-class white city dwellers and the politicization of neo-eth-

45. Cf. Martin Kilson, "Dynamics of Nationalism and Political Militancy Among Negro Americans," in Ernest Q. Campbell, ed., *Racial Tensions and National Identity* (Nashville, Vanderbilt University Press, 1972), pp. 111–112.

46. See Robert A. Dahl, *Who Governs? Democracy and Power in an American City* (New Haven, Yale University Press, 1961), esp. chaps. 5–6.

Table 9. Let me ask you about some specific areas of life in America. For each, tell me if you think blacks are discriminated against in that area or not (by percent)

Discriminated against in	Late 1972	1969
Getting decent housing		
Nationwide	52	50
Whites	51	46
Blacks	66	83
Getting full equality		
Nationwide	44	47
Whites	40	43
Blacks	72	83
Getting white-collar jobs		
Nationwide	41	42
Whites	40	44
Blacks	68	82
Getting skilled labor jobs		
Nationwide	42	40
Whites	40	35
Blacks	66	83
Way treated as human beings		
Nationwide	41	39
Whites	38	35
Blacks	64	77
Getting into hotels, motels		
Nationwide	33	38
Whites	31	35
Blacks	44	68
Getting quality education in public schools		
Nationwide	32	28
Whites	29	23
Blacks	53	72
Getting into labor unions		
Nationwide	30	26
Whites	28	22
Blacks	47	64
Way treated by police		
Nationwide	29	25
Whites	25	19
Blacks	66	76
Wages paid		
Nationwide	26	27
Whites	22	22
Blacks	61	78
Getting manual labor jobs		
Nationwide	23	22
Whites	20	18
Blacks	35	51

Source: The Harris Survey (December 1972).

nicity within this context, it is the Republican party's strategy for a neo-conservative majority that sustains neo-ethnicity in political life.[47] Ideologically, the Nixon administration was neo-racist insofar as it manipulated negative symbols associated with white perceptions of blacks. Politically, it was willing to go as far as violating the doctrine of separation of church and state in order to cultivate support among Catholics and Jews, whose leadership seeks government funds for fledgling religious schools. Many liberal intellectuals, exhibiting a strong perference for normalcy after 25 years of extensive societal shifts, are quick to flirt with this neo-conservatism, lending it intellectual respectability.[48] It is, then, ironic that as the black ethnic input into the politics of neo-ethnicity attenuates, other forces emerge to sustain it. Politics is, no doubt, known for its bitter ironies. But the politics of race and ethnicity in America is particularly stubborn in this regard. *Plus ça change, plus c'est la même chose.*

47. Cf. Kevin P. Phillips, *The Emerging Republican Majority* (New Rochelle, Arlington House, 1969).

48. See, for example, Seymour Martin Lipset's defense of public funds for parochial schools in S. M. Lipset, *Group Life in America: A Task Force Report of the American Jewish Committee* (New York, 1972), pp. 79–81. This and other neo-conservative implications of the report are debated in the appendix by other intellectuals who participated in the Task Force, including myself. Ibid., pp. 102–111. See also Novak, *Rise of the Unmeltable Ethnics.*

9

JOHN PORTER

Ethnic Pluralism in Canadian Perspective

Canada, like the United States and many other societies around the world, has been experiencing a revival of ethnicity. The reasons for this world phenomenon are many and complex. In part it can be traced to the post-World War II decolonization which was so often bitterly fought over, as in Algeria, for example, where a heightened consciousness of racial and ethnic differences, beyond the visibility of color, was a part of the demand for independence and self-determination. In eastern Europe, socialist societies were allegedly suppressing the national cultures that lay within their borders, a situation which émigrés sought to counteract by enlisting their fellow countrymen and sometimes the descendants of previous generations in a national movement in exile. The escalation of the Vietnam war was interpreted in many parts of the world as the United States taking over from the retreating European powers the role of white domination through force in the affairs of the world.

In the United States a highly visible deprived minority was not sharing in the affluence that the society was supposed to have produced. In Canada, similarly, the French had been denied much of the opportunity and had carried a good deal of the cost in less education and lower paid jobs—lower, that is, than some immigrant groups that were coming in near the bottom—of Canada's take-off as an industrial society. The demand by some intellectuals in French Canada that something be done about this inequality led to the establishment in 1963 of the Royal Commission on Bilingualism and Biculturalism.

Canada was caught up in a global movement and although all the examples of the world-wide revival of ethnicity can best be understood within their own local and historical contexts, they have, through modern communications and common intellectual leadership, become mutually supportive. Fanon becomes widely read in Quebec and Wounded Knee takes on symbolic significance far beyond South Dakota.

One feature of this ethnic revival common to the two modern societies of North America is, then, the depressed status of a large minority group, but there are three important respects in which the Canadian situation differs from that in the United States. In Canada the deprived ethnic group that is large enough to have a political impact is white and hence ethnicity does not have the wide visibility that it has across the border. However, there is the barrier of language which can operate as effectively as color differences to reduce friendly interaction between groups. If people from two groups cannot communicate, as is the case in Canada where the French and English have been effectively out of communication with each other, then the language division is as real as that of color.

The long-standing hostility of so many of the English in Canada to learning French is analogous to the hostility toward blackness that has marked black-white relations. In both cases the psychological elements are deep-layered, all the more so because Anglophones in Canada, like whites in the United States, are the dominant majority in both numbers and power. Occasionally the psychological tensions of color may be invoked by referring to the French as "les nègres blancs d'Amérique." [1]

Such symbolism, however dramatic, is scarcely appropriate because of the second major difference between these two plural societies of North America. That difference is that some French Canadians have enjoyed high status and power in collaboration with English-speaking Canadians and foreign investors, largely

1. The title of a widely read book by Pierre Vallières, Éditions Parti Pris, Montréal, 1968. Reprinted as *White Niggers of America* (Toronto, McClelland and Stewart, 1971).

United States corporations. Canada has had three French prime ministers and two French governors-general as titular head of state. Moreover, in Quebec the French have power. There has never been an English *premier ministre* of Quebec. This seeming contradiction between being a large deprived minority within Canada and having representatives in the structure of power can be explained in terms of the class structure of French Canada which until recently has been premodern, with a narrow band of classically educated elites and members of the learned professions at the top, and a mass of poorly educated at the bottom who increasingly left a rural way of life for the industrialized cities. It was an American and an "adopted" Canadian, E. C. Hughes, who first drew attention to this phenomenon in his *French Canada in Transition,* or as its French title says, *Rencontre de deux mondes.* [2]

By and large the French elites of church and state have been prepared to collaborate in the federal state, although in doing so they have exacted a price which has given a particular shape to Canadian federalism and has generally served the interests of the class from which they came rather than the interests of Quebec society as a whole. The strongest of the intellectual critics will argue that the French elites of Quebec have aided its colonization by English-speaking Canadians and Americans.[3] Whether or not one agrees with such strictures there is little to be said against the notion, whatever the behavior of their elites, that French Canadians within the global context of Canadian society, until recently, were an "ethnic class" of deprived status.[4]

The third and perhaps the most important difference between

2. Les éditions du boréal express, Montreal, 1972. The original is *French Canada in Transition* (Chicago, University of Chicago Press, 1943).

3. See, for example, Sheilagh Hodgins Milner and Henry Milner, *The Decolonization of Quebec* (Toronto, McClelland and Stewart, 1973).

4. The idea of French Canadians as an ethnic class was first discussed by Jacques Dofny and Marcel Rioux in a 1962 paper reprinted in Marcel Rioux and Yves Martin, *French-Canadian Society* (Toronto, McClelland and Stewart, 1964), as "Social Class in French Canada." There has been criticism, particularly from Marxist writers, of the "dubious metaphor" of an ethnic class. See Stanley B. Ryerson, "Quebec: Concepts of Class and Nation," in Gary Teeple, ed., *Capitalism and the National Question in Canada* (Toronto, University of Toronto Press, 1972). In the same volume see also Gilles Bourque and Nicole Laurin-Frenette, "Social Class and National Ideologies in Quebec."

Canada and the United States in the sphere of ethnicity is that French Canadians, concentrated as they are in Quebec where about 80 percent of them live, have territory or a homeland which was conquered, a historical and immensely symbolic fact which makes some sense and gives an impetus to a separatist movement for an eventual French-speaking state of Quebec as the visionary solution to the deprived status that the French as an ethnic class have experienced. It should be remembered also that the French are a large minority within Canadian society, comprising about three tenths of the population, a demographic fact that makes such a solution as the "equal partnership" recommendations by the Royal Commission on Bilingualism and Biculturalism a possible resolution of the current tensions. But the same demographic fact of numbers combined with the concentration in a "homeland" makes the separatist solution also possible.

FRENCH-ENGLISH RELATIONS: AN ASSESSMENT

The wide-ranging examination from 1963 to 1968 of French-English relations by the Bilingualism Commission took place over the same period as official and unofficial inquiries were being made in the United States on the condition of non-white minorities and of increasing violence in interethnic relations. Even though in Canada violence has been minimal, the Royal Commission found the future of the society itself in question and suggested that with or without violence, Canada had a far greater problem in the solution of its interethnic tensions than had any other modern society.

In a preliminary report in 1965 the commission had said, "Canada, without being conscious of the fact, is passing through the greatest crisis in its history." [5] This view was reiterated in the first of several volumes of its *Report*. Canada was facing a national crisis, a time when, the commission said, "Decisions must be taken and developments must occur leading either to its break-up, or a new set of conditions for its future existence." [6] For all the violence in

5. *A Preliminary Report of the Royal Commission on Bilingualism and Biculturalism* (Ottawa, Queen's Printer, 1965), p. 13.

6. *Report of the Royal Commission on Bilingualism and Biculturalism*, Book I, *The Official Languages* (Ottawa, Queen's Printer, 1967), p. xvii.

the United States, or to take another modern society, for all the suppression in South Africa, it is doubtful that similar commissions would come to such gloomy conclusions about the future of their societies.

It is not my intention exhaustively to review here the relations between the English and the French in Canada. They have involved varying degrees of hostility and cooperation since the English conquest of 1759 and have been the major preoccupation of Canadian history, politics, and sociological investigation for over two hundred years. With my rather optimistic observations about French-English relations since the Royal Commission's report and a brief discussion of Canada's non-English, non-French groups I intend rather to serve the more general purpose of critically examining the revival of ethnicity in modern societies.

In response to the recommendations of the Royal Commission for "equal partnership" and "institutional bilingualism," the federal government embarked on a series of policies to improve the position of the French and the French language in those agencies and institutions within its jurisdiction.[7] Bilingualism within the federal public service improved. The French became better represented than formerly within the higher levels of the bureaucracy. Ottawa began slowly taking on the aspect of a bilingual national capital.[8] Much money was spent on language training and grants were made to provincial governments to improve their provision of second language education. The federal government saw itself as constitutionally responsible for safeguarding the two official languages even though language, because it is the principal means of cultural expression, would normally be considered a provincial responsibility.

Since the Royal Commission's somber accounts it is becoming increasingly likely that an adaptive and flexible federal system can

7. The main instrument was the Official Languages Act of 1969, *Statutes of Canada,* 17–18 Elizabeth II, Chapter II.

8. One of the provisions of the Official Languages Act of 1969 was the appointment of a Commissioner of Official Languages whose task was to ensure compliance with the spirit and intent of the act. On the whole his annual reports (Information Canada, Ottawa) have tended to be critical of the rate of progress toward the objectives of the act.

come about. Perhaps this is possible because on the matter of political and constitutional solutions concerning the French and Quebec within confederation, the Royal Commission literally gave up the ghost and failed to complete its job. The evolving Canadian federalism of the last few years is not without its problems for nation building, but neither is it confined to a rigid blueprint.

According to some Anglo-Canadians the concessions made to Quebec particularly in social welfare legislation appear to come close to providing a special status for that province. Somewhat the reverse has happened, however. As an outcome of ingenious diplomacy on the part of federal and provincial bureaucrats and politicians, all the other provinces are becoming more like Quebec, the final and ironic outcome of the insistence of the French that Quebec was not a province *comme les autres.* The lessening of federal power particularly in a wide range of social policy can be seen as a loss of the ability to establish national goals and as a process of decentralization.

Much of the change can be attributed to French political leaders and an intellectually strengthened provincial bureaucracy in Quebec who were determined to do something about the deprived status of the French. They were more conscious of the need for social and educational reforms than were earlier elites. Thus, as in the past, the French have continued to exercise great power in the shaping of Canadian federalism. Other provincial political leaders and bureaucrats are enjoying the enhanced power that Quebec has won for the provinces as the federal government has become enfeebled in a wide range of important economic and social issues. The alternative of a special status for Quebec within the federal system is scarcely considered any more outside the context of complete separation. Special status is anathema to the present federal leadership under Mr. Pierre Trudeau, as indeed is separation.

The October 1973 provincial election in Quebec was an important test of the type of federalism that has been developing. The results indicate that a majority of those in Quebec favor *le fédéralisme rentable* combined with *la souveraineté culturelle,* slogans of the Liberal party which won 54 percent of the popular vote and 102 of the 110 seats in the National Assembly. However, in the same election the separatist *Parti Québécois* increased its proportion of the popular vote from 24 percent in 1970 to 30 percent in 1973.[9] Since the other parties running were all federalist—that is, wanting to work within confederation—the 30 percent for the *Parti Québécois* can be taken as a good measure of those who would like to create a separate French state. As yet no extensive analysis has appeared, but it is taken as self-evident that the separatist supporters were almost all French and heavily representative of the young. The less sanguine might, therefore, still consider the future of Canada in question. There are also some doubts about the legitimacy of an electoral system which gives a party 30 percent of the votes, but only 9 percent of the seats.

Whatever directions "diplomatic" or "executive" federalism [10] and constitutional bargaining may take over the next decade, the future of French-English relations really lies within the provinces, particularly in Quebec where 19 percent of the population is non-French-speaking, in New Brunswick where 34 percent of the population speak French, and in Ontario where though overall only 6 percent are French-speaking, in some parts of northern Ontario almost half the population is French-speaking and in some counties in the St. Lawrence–Ottawa River triangle the proportion that is French-speaking is over 80 percent. The absolute number of French-speaking people in Ontario is much greater than in any other province outside Quebec.[11]

9. *La Presse,* Montréal, October 30, 1973.

10. "Diplomatic" and "executive" federalism are terms to describe the ways in which provincial and federal cabinet ministers and committees of federal and provincial bureaucrats bargain on a wide range of issues, like urban problems and higher education, and work out the responsibilities of the two levels of government. The federal Parliament and provincial legislatures become almost ratifiers, an unusual role for them in the traditional parliamentary system. See R. Simeon, *Federal-Provincial Diplomacy* (Toronto, University of Toronto Press, 1972), and Donald V. Smiley, *Canada in Question* (Toronto, McGraw-Hill, 1972).

11. Proportions based on mother tongue. There are bilinguals in both French- and English-speaking groups. The 19 percent includes immigrants in Quebec whose mother tongue would be neither English nor French. *Census of Canada, 1971,* vol. I, pt. 3, Statistics Canada, Ottawa, 1973. If "ethnic origin," the definition of which is dealt with later in this chapter, is used the proportions are non-French in Quebec, 21 percent; French in Ontario, 9.5 percent; and French in New Bruns-

Areas in which provincial government policies will be crucial for the improvement in French-English relations are education, language training, the provision of governmental services in French and English where both groups live in sizable numbers, and extending French as the language of work in Quebec.

It is not possible here to provide a province by province balance sheet on French-English relations. We might instead look at the country's two major and neighboring provinces, Quebec and Ontario. It is in the development within these provinces that the future of Canada may well be settled.

In Quebec it is clear that English-speaking parents (and French for that matter) will always be able to have their children educated in English. Quebec will never become unilingual in education. No party seeks to remove this right from the English minority. However, one of the most seriously discussed issues in the 1973 provincial election was the existing legislation permitting immigrant parents to educate their children in either English or French. Immigrant parents, such as Italian and Portuguese, have shown a strong preference for having their children go to English-speaking schools because of the greater opportunities that an education in English provides in North America. The French on the other hand, highly sensitive to their own falling fertility rates and substantially unable to recruit immigrants from the French-speaking world, foresee a gradual decreasing use of French in the province. In the last election all political parties recognized this threat, and the reelected Liberal government promised to review the legislation.

Among the most striking of the documentations of the Royal Commission on Bilingualism and Biculturalism was the use of the French language in the industries of Quebec, large segments of which are owned by American or Anglo-Canadian corporations. The pattern was familiar; French blue-collar workers, bilingual foremen, and a large over-representation of unilingual Anglophones in managerial and higher occupational levels of the private

---

wick, 39 percent. *Census of Canada, 1971,* Advance Bulletin, *Population by Ethnic Group* (Ottawa, Statistics Canada, 1973).

sector. French who did achieve these levels because of their professional education in fields such as law, accounting, and public relations were most often required to work in English. The upper levels of the work world were essentially English-speaking, imposing a requirement of written and oral bilingualism on the French, but not on the English Canadians or Americans. This condition was strongly resented by the younger French as they were being turned out in increasing numbers from a reformed educational system where their upward mobility in their home province might be blocked because their English was not adequate, and their own language was downgraded or never used by a "foreign" management.

The Royal Commission recommended that in private industry in Quebec the objective should be French as the language of work at all levels and that the Quebec government should set up a task force to discover means of achieving such an end.[12] The Quebec government did set up a special commission under the chairmanship of Jean-Denis Gendron. After four years of examining the problem the Gendron Commission recommended that French become the provincial *official language* and French and English be provincial *national languages*.[13] There is widespread recognition on the part of the government and political parties that French cannot be made the language of work at all levels by lightning legislation.

By the end of 1973 there was still no official government policy on language of work. There was, however, a set of basic guidelines pressing firms in the direction of bilingualism. French should be the language in internal oral communication and all oral and written communication with customers, suppliers, and government agencies. Many firms have responded positively to this pressure and have set up French instruction programs for managerial personnel at all levels. The situation is complex, not only because of the ingrained habits of the past, but also because Quebec appeals to foreign investment and does not want to scare it away. That is why

12. *Report of the Royal Commission on Bilingualism and Biculturalism,* book III, *The Work World* (Ottawa, Queen's Printer, 1969), p. 559.

13. *Report of the Commission of Inquiry on the Position of the French Language and on Language Rights in Quebec* (Montreal, l'Éditeur officiel du Québec, 1972).

the tone of the language at work problem exemplified by the Gendron Commission is moderate, encouraging gradual change. Not all French nationalists are moderate however. This is particularly true of Montreal where the proportion of French speakers (66 percent) is lower than in the rest of the province and the demographic forces of anglicization are most strong.[14]

With the democratization of education and an increased emphasis on science and technology in curricula, the prospects for the improvement in the occupational opportunities for the French are very good. Upward mobility and participation in an increasingly transnational and post-industrial world will, however, lead to a further erosion of traditional culture begun with the earlier industrialization of Quebec which transformed the rural *habitant* into an urban proletarian. The French face the dilemma of modernization or of maintaining a traditional culture. But there need not be a loss of language. If bilingualism can increase, and that requires a great effort on the part of the English, this distinctive dualism of Canada will remain, if not across the entire country at least in Quebec, where French and English have lived long together. The undesirable relationship of elite collaboration and low occupational status for the majority of the French is becoming gradually transformed, not rapidly enough for some, but at least in the direction of a more equal partnership.

Ontario, the province which is the very heart of Anglo-Canadian traditions, pride, privilege, and power, has taken very positive steps, particularly in education, to improve the position of its large French-speaking minority in response to the Royal Commission's report, and to some militancy on the part of Franco-Ontarians. Until new legislation took effect in 1969, children from French-speaking families suffered a variety of handicaps in obtaining instruction in their own language. Educational attainment levels were low except for those whose families could afford to pay fees for private Catholic French-speaking schools. The legislation of 1969 transferred these fee-paying schools to the system of provincially supported local boards of education. The legislation also provided that when ten or more French-speaking parents submitted a writ-

14. For a series of interesting papers on contemporary Quebec see Dale C. Thomson, ed., *Quebec Society and Politics* (Toronto, McClelland and Stewart, 1973).

ten request to have French instruction for their children, local school boards were to provide it. Thus schools are English-speaking, bilingual, and French-speaking. The process of introducing bilingual schools has led to community conflicts but most of them have been successfully mediated.

Educational opportunity for Ontario's French in their own language is a major change. On the other hand extensive new programs to teach French to English-speaking students have been much less successful. French instruction is not compulsory. In 1972 the proportion of Ontario secondary school English students that were taking courses in French was only 37 percent.[15] It would seem, therefore, that much of the strong resistance to learning French on the part of English-speaking Canadians continues.

The teaching of French in Anglophone Canada has been described as a continuing catastrophe. If that is so the future of a bilingual Canada remains very much in question. What will probably happen is that enough bilingual Anglophones will be found to work with bilingual Francophones within federal institutions, and there will be a gradual movement toward more French spoken at work throughout Quebec. In the rest of the country bilingualism will decline the greater the distance from Quebec and Ottawa. An increase in bilingualism can make a workable system which might result in positive and beneficial French-English relations in Canada.

The future of French-English relations will also depend, of course, on factors outside provincial control, particularly economic conditions, for which the federal government has a major responsibility, and also on the visibility and vitality of ethnicity, nationalism, and tribalism in the world at large, which, as I pointed out at the beginning, was an important element in moving French-Canadian nationalism in a more active and even militant direction.

CANADA'S OTHER ETHNIC GROUPS: A VIEW FROM THE CENSUS

Interethnic relations in Canada are not confined to the French and English. Canada has always drawn and continues to draw its

---

15. Norman Webster, "French Language Education: For Anglophone Bigots the Going Is Tough," *Globe and Mail,* Toronto, December 1, 1973.

population from diverse sources. Some indication of this diversity can be seen from the following table. The first point to be noted is the decreasing proportion of those of British origin since the beginning of the present century. The second is the relatively stable proportion represented by the French. The drop to 28.7 percent in 1971 reflects the fact that the lowest fertility rates in Canada are now in Quebec, making for one of the most interesting reversals of reproductive behavior to be found, a fact which many French Canadians view with alarm.[16]

Ethnic Origin of the Canadian Population 1901–1971 [a]

Origin	1901	1921	1941	1961	1971
British	57.0	55.4	49.7	43.8	44.6
French	30.7	27.9	30.3	30.4	28.7
German	5.8	3.4	4.0	5.8	6.1
Italian	0.2	0.8	1.0	2.5	3.4
Dutch	0.6	1.3	1.9	2.4	1.9
Polish	0.1	0.6	1.5	1.8	1.4
Scandinavian	0.6	1.9	2.1	2.1	1.8
Ukrainian	0.1	1.2	2.7	2.6	2.2
Indian and Eskimo	2.4	1.3	1.1	1.2	1.3
Other	2.5	6.2	5.7	7.4	8.6
Total	100.0	100.0	100.0	100.0	100.0

Source: Report of the Royal Commission on Bilingualism and Biculturalism, book IV, 248

[a] Newfoundland was excluded from the Canadian census until 1951.

The table also indicates that no other ethnic group comes close in size to the British or the French although in total they come to somewhere between one quarter and one third of the population of Canada. The ethnic categories shown in the table are those of the 1971 census. The 1961 census used twenty-eight categories, many of which are contained under "Other" in the table. These included in 1961, for example, Icelandic, Lithuanian, Roumanian, and Japanese, each with 0.2 percent of the population.[17] Thus the

16. *Vital Statistics* (Ottawa, Statistics Canada, 1973).

17. *Report of the Royal Commission on Bilingualism and Biculturalism,* book IV, *The Cultural Contribution of the Other Ethnic Groups* (Ottawa, Queen's Printer, 1970), p. 32.

non-British, non-French component of the Canadian population is extremely diverse.

At this point it is important to note that all the distributions of ethnic origins shown in the table are artifacts of the census itself and result from the questions from which the data are derived. Ethnic "origin" has been asked for in a variety of ways in different censuses, and the instructions to census enumerators have also varied, adding a further artifactual element to the distributions.

In 1961 the question was "To what ethnic or cultural group did you or your ancestor (on the male side) belong on coming to this continent?" Two important facts are clear from the census treatment of ethnicity. One is that one's ethnic origin was to be patrilineally traced, and second, except for native Indians and Eskimo, there was no recognition in any census tabulations of Canadian or American ethnic origin. Thus for census purposes both those born in Canada and immigrants had to have a non-North American ethnicity. For the first time, in the 1951 census if all the techniques in their manuals failed them enumerators were allowed to write in "Canadian" or "American" if the person absolutely insisted. The same was also permitted in 1961. In that year according to an administrative report on the census only 118,185 persons reported their origin as "Canadian," 15,786 as "American," and 70,163 as "Unknown." These numbers combined make up slightly more than 1 percent of the population, about the same as in 1951.[18] These insistent and uncertain people were lost in the residual "Other" category in all census tabulations.

In 1971 the ethnic question was asked in the same way, but for the first time the census was self-enumerated. Neither Canadian nor American was among the response categories provided. The only possibility was "Other-Specify." The 1971 census form also included a question on citizenship, the main purpose of which was to enable those persons who wished to identify themselves as Canadian to do so, since Canadian was not a valid answer to questions on language or ethnicity. The conscientious self-enumerator, who

18. *Census of Canada, 1961*, Bull. 7.1–6. There is a brief history of the ethnic origin question in Warren E. Kalbach, *The Impact of Immigration on Canada's Population* (Ottawa, Statistics Canada, 1970), pp. 3–9.

would like to feel above all that he was Canadian, might have been satisfied by being able to say, two questions before he came to the ethnicity one, that he was a Canadian citizen.[19] His instruction booklet was clear on what the census officials wanted for the ethnic question. It read, "Ethnic or cultural group refers to descent (through the father's side) and should not be confused with citizenship. Canadians belong to many ethnic or cultural groups." [20] The patrilineal emphasis which has existed throughout becomes sociologically absurd where there have been exogamous marriages, because of the important role the mother plays in the socialization of children, and in language learning.

Why the ethnic origin concept took the form it has—that is, non-North American and exclusively patrilineal—is rather obscure, but it can probably be traced to the basic duality of Canadian society. Censuses before the confederation of 1867 classified the population as "French origin," "not of French origin," and "Indian." The successive censuses after confederation have not been consistent. The earlier ones defined origin according to the birthplace of the individual or of his paternal ancestor before coming to North America. Two major wars in the twentieth century have broken up international boundaries, making it rather absurd to relate ethnic origin to political entities, and there has been a gradual evolution toward a cultural and linguistic definition of ethnic group. Discussions of the 1931 census placed a great emphasis on "racial" differences and their importance to Canada because of the extensive European migration to Canada after the opening up of the West in the 1890s. There was a suggestion in the official comments on the 1931 census that, as the "races" fused, there would no longer be any need to differentiate between them, indicating some orientation at that time to a "melting pot" concept. Because of the discrediting of the concept of race during and after the Second World War a 1941 census monograph on ethnic origins was not published until 1965! [21]

19. *The 1971 Census of Population and Housing: Development of Subject Matter Content* (Ottawa, Statistics Canada, 1969), p. 13.
20. Instructions accompanying 1971 census self-enumeration forms (Ottawa, Statistics Canada, 1971).
21. Kalbach, *The Impact of Immigration,* p. v.

A trenchant critique of Canadian origin statistics was made by Norman Ryder in 1955.[22] He suggested that if the origin question were to have any sociological or cultural meaning it should be asked in terms of language. If the important socio-political question of assimilation to either French or English was to be reasonably answered, the question should be about the language first learned by the individual and by his parents. Two generations of English or French as mother tongue would give some indication of assimilation.

The 1971 census asked not only a mother tongue question but also one on the language most often spoken at home. The assimilation to English has been very marked. While the English-speaking ethnic origin constituted 45 percent of the population, English as the language most often spoken in the home was 65 percent. While the non-English, non-French ethnicities made up 28 percent of the population, only about 12 percent had the same mother tongue as their ethnic origin, and only about 6 percent spoke their ethnic origin language most often in the home. Thus if ethnicity and culture are based on language a considerable process of assimilation has gone on. The French ethnic origin showed a minor language loss, with 28 percent of the population reporting French ethnic origin and 25 percent as speaking French in the home.[23]

Despite the historical variations, the focus on patrilineal descent, nonrecognition of Canadian or American origin, and other inadequacies in the census statistics, it has proved impossible to eliminate the question or change its form, as indeed the federal government sought to do for the 1961 census, when John Diefenbaker was prime minister and spoke out strongly against hyphenated Canadians. The French were insistent on its retention because it provides them with some measure of their survival and their claims for co-charter group status within Canada, a status which can scarcely be denied. Organizations of the other ethnic groups have also demanded its retention because it gave grounds to their claim that

22. N. B. Ryder, "The Interpretation of Origin Statistics," *The Canadian Journal of Economics and Political Science,* 21.4 (1955), 466—479.

23. *Census of Canada, 1971, Population by Language Most Often Spoken in the Home and by Official Language* (Ottawa, Statistics Canada, 1973).

Canada is a cultural mosaic rather than the so-called American melting pot.

A comparison of the history of the censuses in Canada and the United States would tell in a fascinating way how the two countries have attempted to treat ethnicity in the course of nation building. Melting pot and mosaic are almost stereotypical terms to describe the divergent ways in which these two new nations have tried to deal with ethnicity, but they do reflect the two opposed orientations, clearly to be seen in the policies and instructions surrounding the two censuses from the last century.[24] We know now that the lives of ethnic groups are not responsive to the intentions of the policy makers and the bureaucratic organizations that take the censuses. Melting pot and mosaic are not such extreme opposites as the terms would imply because in the United States, ethnicity, in the sense of awareness of European national origins of ancestors, is still very much alive while in Canada many reject European ancestry and identify with the country where they were born.

THE ORGANIZATION OF ETHNIC GROUPS

If the Canadian census gives an artifactual quality to the ethnic structure of Canadian society a different impression is gained from ethnic organizations which are very much alive, ably led and responding predictably to the widespread ethnic revival. With the demands in Quebec for a reconstruction of Canadian society, the other ethnic organizations also made demands to be heard and, when the Royal Commission on Bilingualism and Biculturalism was established, the government of Canada felt compelled to include in the commission's terms of reference "The contribution made by the other ethnic groups to the cultural enrichment of Canada and the measures that should be taken to safeguard that contribution." Two of the ten commissioners were members of these other ethnic groups and an entire volume of the commission's *Report* was devoted to the matter of the other ethnic groups.

24. Some comparison between the two censuses has been made by Joel Smith, "Melting Pot—Mosaic: Consideration for a Prognosis," in *Minorities North and South,* Proceedings of the Third Inter-Collegiate Conference on Canadian-American Relations, Michigan State University, 1968.

Government policy makers, as do politicians who seek their electoral support, like to view these diverse non-British, non-French ethnicities as a "third element" despite the fact that, as I have said, they were listed in the 1961 census as 28 ethnicities ranging from 5.6 percent of the population to 0.2 percent.

Despite this fragmentation, the so-called third element has its own spokesmen such as Senator Paul Yuzyk who, in a paper presented to the Canadian Association of Slavists in 1965 entitled "Canada: A Multi-Cultural Nation," said, "The third element ethnic groups now numbering approximately five million persons, are co-builders of the West and other parts of Canada, along with the British and French Canadians and are just as permanent a part of the Canadian scene. . . . As co-founders they should be co-partners who would be guaranteed the right to perpetuate their mother tongues and cultures." [25] He called for the government, and government agencies such as the Canadian Broadcasting Corporation, actively to promote all other cultures. This was not only a right belonging to these groups, but the policy had other merits as well. He quoted approvingly an American sociologist, Charles Hobart, working in Canada as saying, "Multiculturalism beats the melting pot idea all to Hell." At about the same time, at a Toronto conference on "national unity" a spokesman for other ethnic groups talked about the disunity that would result from emphasizing the English and the French elements in Canada to the neglect of the others and suggested that there should be an "estates-general" to explore ways of preserving non-English and non-French cultures in Canada.[26] Views such as these were typical of many forcefully articulated before the Royal Commission on Bilingualism and Biculturalism.

Ethnic group leaders were given much encouragement by the last volume [27] of the commission's *Report* which was devoted to the other ethnic groups, and since then there has been a great deal of promotion of the idea of "multiculturalism." Although one gets the

25. *Canadian Slavonic Papers*, 7 (Toronto, University of Toronto Press, 1965).
26. *Globe and Mail*, Toronto, December 16, 1968.
27. *Report of the Royal Commission on Bilingualism and Biculturalism*, book IV, *The Cultural Contribution of the Other Ethnic Groups* (Ottawa, Queen's Printer, 1969).

impression that most of the commissioners would have preferred to have confined their attention to French-English relations the spokesmen on the commission for the other ethnic groups were firm, leading in one case to a strong dissenting opinion to the commission's views in the first volume of the *Report* that English and French should be the only two official languages.[28]

MULTICULTURALISM WITHIN A BILINGUAL FRAMEWORK

In October 1971 Mr. Trudeau, the prime minister, announced in the House of Commons a new policy which he called "multiculturalism within a bilingual framework" and which he considered "the most suitable means of assuring the cultural freedom of Canadians." [29] The government had already taken a number of steps mentioned earlier, such as the Official Languages Act of 1969, to make French and English equal as official languages within the federal jurisdiction, to promote the teaching of both the official languages, and to introduce bilingualism into the Public Service.

Canada was becoming caught up in the ethnic revival. The government was attempting to maintain a difficult balance between the hostility of many in Quebec to any formal recognition of the other groups and the electoral support that would be forthcoming from a program to promote multiculturalism. French critics of the new policy argued that it was an about-turn from the earlier position, on the basis of which the commission had been set up, that is, that Canada should be a truly bilingual and bicultural society based on the central ideas of two founding peoples, two societies, and two dominant cultures. Some argued that it was impossible to talk of multiculturalism without multilingualism because culture could not be detached from language. If that were true then the official bilingualism that was developing at the federal level, and in some provinces, would be endangered by demands that other languages be recognized. Moreover, multiculturalism in some provinces would be more likely to promote a bilingualism in the form Anglo-

28. *Report*, book I, *The Official Languages*, pp. 155–169.
29. "Statement by the Prime Minister, House of Commons, October 8, 1971," Office of the Prime Minister, Ottawa.

Ukrainian or Franco-Italian rather than English-French bilingualism which had basic sociological and historical links and which was so important for the future of Canada as a viable society.[30] Indeed, it has always been assumed that immigrants to Canada would assimilate to either the French or the English communities. If that was no longer to be so, French Canadians would interpret it as a threat to their own survival. As I mentioned earlier, lowering French fertility rates and English-speaking school attendance by immigrant children gave substance to these French fears.

The multicultural pronouncement has many critics also among English-speaking Canadians, particularly those who see the only hope for Canada to lie in a policy of biculturalism and bilingualism based on the two collectivities which they represent,[31] and seems to contradict the view of the commission which had written, "To the degree that the demands of certain ethnic groups make awareness of the fundamental duality of the country more difficult, to that extent they aggravate the state of crisis in Canada. Above all, they provide new arguments for the partisans of a 'One Canda.' "[32]

The Canadian government took quite the opposite view to the common sense one that strong ethnic loyalties, because they are little nationalisms, would be divisive. Mr. Trudeau, in fact, argued that multiculturalism would be integrative. He said Canada would become "a special place, and a stronger place as well. Each of the many fibres contributes its own qualities and Canada gains strength from the combination. We become less like others; we become less susceptible to cultural, social or political envelopment by others." [33]

All major political leaders outside of Quebec support some policy of multiculturalism. Robert Stanfield, the federal leader of the Opposition, referring to the government's program as "grudging ac-

---

30. Guy Rocher, "Les Ambiguités d'un Canada bilingue et multiculturel," paper presented to the 1972 Annual Meeting of the Canadian Association of Sociology and Anthropology, mimeo, Département de Sociologie, Université de Montréal.

31. See editorial in *Journal of Canadian Studies* (November 1971).

32. *A Preliminary Report of the Royal Commission on Bilingualism and Biculturalism* (Ottawa, Queen's Printer, 1965), p. 128.

33. "Notes for Remarks by the Prime Minister to the Ukrainian-Canadian Congress, Winnipeg, Manitoba, October 9, 1971," Office of the Prime Minister, Ottawa.

ceptance," went on to say, "If we really believe that Canadian pluralism should be encouraged, and not merely tolerated, government should work together with the various ethnic groups to help them survive, not simply as folklore, but as a living contributing element of the Canadian cultural mosaic." [34]

On the subject some achieve new heights of rhetoric. Mr. John Yaremko, the Ontario Provincial Secretary and Minister of Citizenship, in announcing a 1972 multicultural conference *Heritage Ontario* said:

No other part of the globe, no other country, can claim a more culturally diversified society than we have here in this Province . . . But does everyone really grasp that Ontario has more Canadians of German origin than Bonn, more of Italian origin than Florence, that Toronto has more Canadians of Greek origin than Sparta, that we have in our midst, fifty-four ethno-cultural groups, speaking a total of seventy-two languages? . . . Just as a hundred years ago the Canadian identity was moulded in the crucible of nationalism, it is now being tempered by the dynamics of multiculturalism.

Mr. Yaremko also touched upon another cause of the current revival of ethnicity and that is the large non-British component of postwar immigration. He then went on to make the common mistake of seeing this component, made up of people from such a variety of countries, as in some way being homogeneous:

There are generally speaking four demographic groups among us—Indians, Anglo and Franco-Ontarian, and members of the third element . . . One effect of the post-war boom in third element immigration has been to bolster ethno-cultural groups, some of which have been here through four generations. The Government has welcomed and encouraged this immigration. We have recognized and helped foster all our constituent cultural communities. Is it then any wonder that these communities have heightened expectations in many areas? [35]

In the bolstering of ethno-cultural groups, as Mr. Yaremko puts it, the postwar immigrants have played an important leadership role because of their long association with nationalist political

---

34. *Globe and Mail*, Toronto, May 1, 1972.

35. Press release of minister's address, Office of the Provincial Secretary, Toronto, March 20, 1972.

struggles in their European homelands. They have continued their activities, often ideological as well as national, aimed at keeping alive in Canada the culture they believe is being obliterated abroad. This leadership has managed in some cases to shift the focus of activity of their national organizations from the problem of integration within Canadian society to the problem of cultural survival either in Europe or in Canada as a locus for cultures in exile.

The official Canadian government policy of "multiculturalism within a bilingual framework" has as its goal the encouraging of non-British, non-French ethnic cultures. A multicultural program, established in the Citizenship Branch of the Department of the Secretary of State, was to study such aspects of multiculturalism as broadcasting in third languages, the role of the ethnic press, and language training in third languages. The most important part of the program, though, was the giving of grants to ethnic organizations to help them preserve their culture. Initially the program was modest. One and one half million dollars were allocated for grants in the first year, but by 1973 the budget had increased to 10 million dollars, and a cabinet minister was appointed whose exclusive responsibility was multiculturalism.

The grants are given to viable ethnic organizations for specific projects. For example, among the 400 grants that were given in the first year of the program was $1,500 to the Canadian Arab Associational in Montreal to teach Arab folklore and dancing, and $5,000 to the Mennonite community in Waterloo to celebrate the Amish quincentennial.[36]

The "Guidelines for Submissions for Grants under the Multicultural Programme" emphasize the "multicultural" goal of the program in the Canadian context.[37] The criteria considered for granting funds to a specific project include whether it is "designed to share a cultural heritage with other Canadians," whether it will "promote an awareness of Canada's cultural diversity," and whether it will "assist immigrants to become full participants in Canadian society."

36. *Globe and Mail,* Toronto, October 15, 1973.
37. Citizenship Branch, Department of the Secretary of State, Ottawa (undated).

A problem is that many ethnic organizations are more interested in promoting their cultures within their own ethnic communities than in sharing cultures with other Canadians. Because of that, the program could become a multi-unicultural one. In October 1973 the federal government sponsored the first national conference on multiculturalism in Ottawa to which 400 delegates went from across the country. In his speech to delegates Dr. Stanley Haidasz, the minister responsible for multiculturalism, said,[38] "Those who think multiculturalism is a cynical form of tokenism or a sop to keep some ethno-cultural groups happy" should know that multiculturalism is a permanent government policy.

Non-English, non-French ethnicity, then, continues to be a salient feature of Canadian social structure. Whether it will eventually be integrative or divisive, in that the emphasis on Canada's multiethnicity will intensify French nationalism, must be left to time. For those who view the ethnic revival as something good because it represents something deep and primordial and genuinely human, Canada must appear as an attractive place to live. However, it is my intention to raise some serious doubts about this revival of ethnicity, not only for Canada, but for other advanced societies and perhaps developing ones as well.

SOME QUESTIONS ABOUT THE REVIVAL OF ETHNICITY

In some respects the revival is regressive. Because it emphasizes descent group identification and endogamy, important principles of ethnic group survival, it runs the risk of believed-in biological differences becoming the basis of invidious judgments about groups of people, a matter to which we will return later. Moreover, where ethnicity is salient there is often an association between ethnic differences and social class and inequality. That is why much of the discussion of the relations between ethnic groups concerns equality, equality of legal rights, political rights, and in the more recent period, social rights such as education, jobs, good health, and equality of opportunity. Class inequality becomes obscured

38. *Globe and Mail,* Toronto, October 17, 1973.

and more difficult to analyze where there is ethnic heterogeneity in the social structure. This may reflect some inadequacy in the sociological theories of class, almost all of which assume ethnic homogeneity.

Some scholars contest the view that when ethnic differentiation is an important organizing principle of social life it must also result in ethnic groups forming a hierarchy of inequality, creating what has come to be called ethnic stratification. One writer, Donald L. Noel, raises that question in developing a theory of the origins of ethnic stratifications and answers it in this way.[39] "Distinct ethnic groups can interact and form a stable pattern of relations without super-subordination." The "classical example" he gives is of the Tungus and Cossacks of northwestern Siberia from an anthropological study of 1938. This at least suggests that ethnic differentiation without some hierarchical features is rare. Certainly the degree and strength of hierarchy depend upon many factors, and there have been many studies of the conditions under which super- and subordination exist in plural or multiethnic societies.[40]

My own view is that ethnic saliency or differentiation in social structure always creates a high risk of ethnic stratification. To understand the interplay between ethnic inequalities and class inequalities it is important to look at how ethnic differentiation in a society comes about. Multiethnic societies are created through conquest or migration. Where there is conquest, the conquerors take over the high status activities—even if these are confined to

39. Donald L. Noel, "A Theory of Ethnic Stratification," Social Problems, 16 (Fall 1968), 157–172.

40. See, for example, Tamotou Shibutani and Kian M. Kwan, Ethnic Stratification: A Comparative Approach (New York, Macmillan, 1965); Stanley Lieberson, "A Societal Theory of Race and Ethnic Relations," American Sociological Review, 36 (December 26, 1971), 902–910; Burton Benedict, "Stratification in Plural Societies," American Anthropologist, 64 (1962), 1235–1246; John Rex, Race Relations in Sociological Theory (New York, Schocken Books, 1970); R. A. Schermerhorn, Comparative Ethnic Relations; A Framework for Theory and Research (New York, Random House, 1970); M. G. Smith, Stratification in Granada (Berkeley, University of California Press, 1965). For two earlier statements see J. S. Furnival, Colonial Policy and Practice (Cambridge, Cambridge University Press, 1948), and Everett C. Hughes, "Queries Concerning Industry and Society Growing Out of Study of Ethnic Relations in Industry," American Sociological Review, 14.2 (April 1949), 211–220.

exercising power as dominant minorities—and relegate the conquered populations to inferior statuses.

Migration of peoples from one part of the world to another has been much more important than conquest in the creation of multiethnic societies, at least in the modern historical period, but it too creates relationships of subordination of some groups to others. There was, first of all, unfree migration by which slaves have been transported for plantation economies, for cotton and cane. There was also the constrained migration of indentured labor, which was a common practice of the European powers in their colonial empires, and many of their former colonies, which are now developing countries, have the roots of their ethnic diversity in these processes. European powers also often forced together various tribal groups of great cultural differences into administrative units convenient for their own purposes. Now that most of the colonies have achieved independence from their European creators many of them are subject to severe strains. These conflicts are between ethnic groups and most of them are about which one should rule, who should have privilege and who should have the good jobs. One has only to mention the Congo, Nigeria, Pakistan to remember the violence with which these disputes are settled.

New nations developed mainly by Europeans in sparsely populated regions such as the United States, Canada, Australia, and South Africa first forced the aboriginal groups to the base of the stratification structure. Ethnic differentiation then arose through immigration which was free, or relatively free, if the economic and political factors in some of the countries of origin which prompted it are considered. It was only relatively free also because the receiving societies were dominated by people who got there first and from their position of early "entrance status" determined the conditions under which other groups might enter.

Migration is an economic process, the movement of labor with capital. The host society regulates the movement with varying degrees of rigidity by making invidious judgments about the appropriateness of people of particular origins for particular jobs. This selective process, by which people were sorted out according to the qualities or aptitudes that were thought to suit them for different economic activities, was intensified in the twentieth century as the North American societies became more industrialized. Even the *laissez-passer* system by which Europeans came into the United States, or leapfrogged through Canada, was abandoned, and the legal restrictions which were ultimately imposed in both Canada and the United States were racist in that they had as their objective the maintenance of the existing ethnic composition, based on the dominance of British and Northern European groups.

Along with this mixing up of the peoples of the world through empire and economic expansion went an ideology of racism, masquerading as a pseudo-science of race differences, which attempted to demonstrate that some groups were inherently superior to others and that it was more than a coincidence that those who were ranked highest controlled the economic processes of the society.[41]

More recently we have seen the further differentiation of stratification systems as a result of new ethnic migrations, in the United States Puerto Ricans, in England immigrants from the colored Commonwealth, in France Algerians. Throughout western Europe Italian, Spanish, and Portuguese laborers have entered the social structure, generally as unskilled labor and sometimes, unless protected by common market agreements, with few legal rights.[42]

In Canada this historical relationship between migration and economic or class position has been reinforced by the heavy immigration since 1945, despite recent changes in immigration regulations designed to reduce the preferential position of the British and others most like them.[43] Immigrants from Britain and the United States continue to be heavily over-represented in the higher professional, managerial, and white-collar occupational levels, while those from Portugal and Greece are taking over from Italians

41. See, for example, Madison Grant, *The Passing of the Great Race* (New York, Scribners, 1921).

42. Hans van Houte and Willy Melgert, *Foreigners in Our Community* (London, Research Services Ltd., 1972). See also "Immigrant Laborers in Western Europe," *New York Times,* September 21, 1973, and "Europe's Hired Poor," *New York Times Magazine,* December 9, 1973.

43. John Porter, *The Vertical Mosaic* (Toronto, University of Toronto Press, 1965), chap. 3; and Bernard R. Blishen, "Class and Opportunity in Canada," *Canadian Review of Sociology and Anthropology,* 7 (May 1970), 110–127.

at the lower levels of the immigrant labor force. Caribbean and Asian countries are now appearing as a new source of immigrants to Canada and will, because of early controls on immigration of Chinese and Japanese, and the previously small black population, make color a newly visible element in the structure of ethnic stratification.

All multiethnic societies have to deal with the problems of legal, political, and social rights which stem from the inequality between their component ethnic groups. They vary so widely with respect to basic features of economic development and political culture that it is questionable whether it is very instructive to pursue an understanding of interethnic relations, or the management of them, through comparative analysis. However, the temptation to construct another typology, even though others already exist, is difficult to avoid.[44]

Consider four sets of dichotomies. There are old and new nations; there are developed and underdeveloped ones; there are those built up through migration or "pasted" together in the process of decolonization; there are those in which the ethnic units have territory and those in which they are dispersed. How societies deal with problems of ethnic inequality will depend to a great extent on where they fall within this set of dichotomies.

Much of the recent sociological discussion of interethnic relations concerns the stability of multiethnic societies which are on the road to development and whose basic institutions and culture are premodern. The stability and development of the Third World is without doubt a desirable objective, but any solutions to its ethnic problems are not likely to be very helpful in the discussion of employment quotas in the United States or policies of multiculturalism for Canada. The ethnic identity of a Hutu or an Ibo must surely be of such profoundly different psychological quality and social consequence from that, say, of an Italian American or a Ukrainian Canadian that the subjective states involved are scarcely of the same order. It is questionable whether both can be considered "primordial."

44. See the typologies in R. A. Schermerhorn, *Comparative Ethnic Relations*, and Stanley Lieberson, "A Societal Theory of Race and Ethnic Relations."

A premodern tribal culture, in which a people consider it legitimate to dominate by brutal means rivals whom some act of history has placed in a common political state, is a vastly different situation from a society with legally safeguarded rights and freedoms and a history of liberty. Thus minority rights have very different meanings in different multiethnic societies, but because modern communications contribute to the world phenomenon of ethnic revival, these differences are overlooked. Ethnicity may be genuinely primordial and essential to individual survival in a former African colony made into an artificial political unit, but in a society on the threshold of post-industrialism it could, with its great emphasis on the particularistic, be considered atavistic if it were to become a salient organizing principle of social life.

Comparison is, however, useful between societies which can be located in similar positions with respect to the previously mentioned dichotomies. Canada and the United States, for example, are both new nations built up through migration and have "democratic" political cultures. Generally this political culture has been liberal in the sense which Parsons has recently used in tracing the secularization that followed the democratic revolutions with their slogans of liberty, equality, and fraternity.[45] Among these liberal values was the notion that the ethnic stratification which resulted from immigration was temporary and would not harden into a permanent class system.

Most liberal social scientists viewing this phenomenon of ethnic stratification assumed that over time processes which they called absorption, assimilation, and acculturation would eliminate this relationship between national or ethnic origin and economic condition and they advocated policies that would lead to such a result. Moreover, educational institutions, more so in the United States than in Canada, were geared to provide some equality of opportunity for all young people. The emphasis was on individual achievement and in the context of a new nation with universalistic standards of judgment it meant forgetting ancestry and attempting to establish a society of equality where ethnic origin did not matter.

45. Talcott Parsons, *The System of Modern Societies* (Englewood Cliffs, N.J., Prentice-Hall, 1971), chap. 5.

Some fears were expressed, of course, that these liberal assimilationist values would require a large measure of Anglo-conformity on the part of "non-Anglo" groups. In a large measure these fears were probably justified, but it could also be said that what was being advocated was conformity to the values of societies leading in the modernizing process.

If universalistic standards and achievement values were important for the mobility offered by the occupational structure of a modernizing society, then liberal assimilationist policies served to provide opportunity for those of all ethnic origins. The revival of ethnicity and the consequent labeling could mean an emphasis on the contrary values of particularism and ascriptive criteria which would be less conducive than imperfectly applied universalistic standards to equality of opportunity and mobility in the two major North American societies.

Mobility means movement up more than the occupational system. It also means movement into higher levels of political and economic power structures. Hence, as ethnicity has operated in the past as a selective device to sort and sift people within the occupational structure it has also served as a form of class control of the major power structures by charter ethnic groups who remain overrepresented in the elite structures.

Thus the United States and Canada, both societies within the western liberal tradition with ethnicity as a salient feature, seem to be faced with a dilemma; on the one hand if they value and emphasize ethnicity, mobility and opportunity are endangered, on the other hand if they emphasize mobility and opportunity, it will be at the cost of submerging cultural identity.

The dilemma is stated in the hypothesis of Frank Vallee, in his study of French Canadian communities outside of Quebec, communities which are like ethnic groups anywhere else in Canada in that they are spatially dispersed and without territory. His hypothesis is as follows:

The more a minority group turns in upon itself and concentrates on making its position strong, the more it costs its members in terms of their chances to make their way as individuals in the larger system . . . Among ethnic minority groups which strive to maintain language and other dis-

tinctions, motivation to aspire to high-ranking social and economic positions in the larger system will be weak, unless, of course, it is characteristic
of the ethnic groups to put a special stress on educational and vocational
achievement.[46]

The last observation applies especially to Jews, but generally Vallee argues that any collectivity has limited resources and energies
and cannot spend them on maintaining ethnic specific institutions
and at the same time prepare its members for achievement in the
larger society of which it is a part. The choice is no doubt a cruel
one, particularly so because it cuts across the generations, introducing a contradiction between the parents' rights and choices with
those their children might prefer. Nonetheless, the present drift
seems to be against the liberal assimilationist views, now pejora-
tively referred to as being overly rational, secular, and universalistic.[47]

For some, the revival of ethnicity has come about precisely because of the failure of universalistic and achievement values to take
hold, and thus create a society of equality of opportunity and condition. Ethnic stratification has been a feature of both the United
States and Canada. Consequently there has been a shift to achieving equality through a system of organized minorities demanding
rights and making claims *qua* minorities, and away from human
rights legislation, fair employment practices legislation and the like,
which were a product of the liberal value system and which were to
provide individuals—not groups or collectivities—with rights, en-
forceable in the courts, against discrimination.

It is no doubt understandable that because of the failure of these
instruments, fashioned as they were for the individual, minorities have had to organize to obtain some measure of distributive
justice when deprivation remained concentrated within particular
groups. The increasing demands of deprived groups and the ac-
cumulating evidence of their deprivation have brought certain pol-

46. Frank G. Vallee and Norman Shulman, "The Viability of French Groupings
Outside Quebec," in Mason Wade, ed., *Regionalism in the Canadian Community*
(Toronto, University of Toronto Press, 1969), p. 95.
47. See Andrew Greeley, "The Rediscovery of Diversity," *The Antioch Review* 31
(Fall 1971), 349; and "The New Ethnicity and Blue Collars," *Dissent* (Winter 1972).

icy responses by dominant majorities as represented by governments and other power groups. These policy responses have
produced a new terminology; affirmative action, positive discrimination, preferential hiring and benign quotas. The new instruments, focused as they are on groups, and providing what
might be called group rights, for example, to proportional representation within all institutional hierarchies, constitute a radical
departure from a society organized on the principles of individual
achievement and universalistic judgments, even if these were often
honored as much in the breach as in the observance, to one organized on group claims to representation on the basis of particular,
rather than universal, qualities.

It is interesting in this respect that the Universal Declaration of
Human Rights, which encouraged a good deal of the postwar
human rights legislation, nowhere mentions group rights, but
speaks entirely in terms of the rights of individual human beings.
It is not possible, in Canada at least, to find the concept of group
rights embodied in jurisprudence except perhaps for the so-called
aboriginal rights and treaty rights of native Indians.

When the evidence is very clear that discrimination and deprivation bear so heavily on ethnic minorities, it seems logical to correct
the condition through positive discrimination in which institutions,
corporations, universities, and the like, are required to maintain
quotas throughout their hierarchical structures to make them representative with respect to minorities. These processes have gone
much further in the United States than in Canada, where they are
largely confined to federal government attempts to improve the
position of the French in the federal public service, and of native
people—the most wretchedly deprived of all—in areas where the
federal government awards contracts. However, in response to recommendations of the Royal Commission on the Status of Women
(1970) similar policies of positive discrimination for this deprived
"minority" are beginning to appear.[48]

Positive discrimination brings a new problem in disturbing existing relationships between ethnic and other minorities within oc-

48. *Report of the Royal Commission on the Status of Women in Canada* (Information
Canada, 1970).

cupational structures that have been accepted and institutionalized in the course of their historical development. In Canada, an English-speaking person reacts against appointments and promotions which favor the French, as an eastern European "ethnic" in the United States would to positive discrimination in favor of non-whites, or a man against such discrimination in favor of a woman. Whatever its benefits, and however much its purposes can be understood, positive discrimination brings these institutionalized differences in power and privilege between the majority and minorities well into view and gives a new saliency to minority and perhaps pseudo-minority group membership, and intensifies hostility and rivalry. The individual, in order to make his claims, will have to determine to which group he belongs, and one can visualize a somewhat complex pass-book arrangement. Membership could cross-cut in several ways, making it necessary to calculate the maximum advantage for preferential employment and career program. The possibilities are endless, since societies can be viewed as intersecting sets of minorities and majorities, defined by an infinite number of criteria, all of different relevance at different times.

The organization of society on the basis of rights or claims that derive from group membership is sharply opposed to the concept of a society based on citizenship, which has been such an important aspect in the development of modern societies. The individual makes claims as a citizen, a status common to all members. T. H. Marshall has traced [49] the development of citizenship rights and the manner in which they have served the process of class abatement, and Parsons has recently drawn on Marshall's ideas about citizenship as central to the development of the system of modern societies. They are essential also to the development of modern egalitarianism. First civil rights provided equality before the law, then political rights allowed participation in government, eventually social rights brought about education, health, and decent living standards and some measure of equality of condition. As Parsons has said: "The emergence of 'full' modernity thus weakened the ascriptive framework of monarchy, aristocracy, established

49. T. H. Marshall, *Class, Citizenship and Social Development* (Garden City, N.Y., Anchor, 1965).

churches and an economy circumscribed by kinship and localism to the point at which it no longer exercised decisive influence." [50]

Citizenship rights are essentially universalistic whereas group rights are essentially particularistic. One of the reasons why many developing societies cannot be compared with modern societies is that they have not yet embodied some, or indeed any, of these citizenship rights in either their value systems or their social organization. They remain essentially premodern, emphasizing tribalism and localism and resolving their ethnic conflicts, sometimes even to the point of genocide, with the particularistic focus. In modern western nations that have established democratic procedures and, albeit inadequately, but nonetheless perceptively, have developed the social rights of citizenship, ethnic conflict is about equality of condition and full participation in a modernizing opportunity structure as well as the political community. To resort to the group basis of settling claims, if necessary, is regrettable.

I now return to the matter to which I referred earlier, that ethnic groups, because they are biological descent groups, are a regressive means of safeguarding and transmitting culture, a responsibility which many would assign to them. No doubt cultural survival can be most efficiently achieved through the biological descent group because when coupled with another principle firmly embedded in our values—that parents have the inalienable right through cultural transmission to make their children the vehicles of their values—recruits are always available. The use of the family for ethnocultural transmission requires that groups impress upon their members the value of marrying within their own group. If they do not they will lose the primordial link with tribe or nation and the exclusive ethnic claims on culture will be eroded. Endogamy is a process of exclusion. There was a time when lowering rates of endogamy could be taken as an index of lessening prejudice in a more liberal and open society. In the current return to ethnicity it seems a different judgment, that such lowering rates can be interpreted as a loss of ethnic communal strength, is being made. The metal of endogamy is more attractive because it is unmeltable.

50. Talcott Parsons, *The System of Modern Societies* (Englewood Cliffs, N.J., Prentice-Hall, 1971), pp. 81, 86.

When descent groups are the principal carriers of culture there are dangers of new forms of racism. If "races" have been evaluated as inferior and superior, so can cultures be. Racism and "culturism" stem from the fact that both are linked to the maintenance of descent group solidarity and endogamy. After all, if ethnicity is so important, if cultures are so different, then it is easy to extend the argument that those of different ethnic groups and cultures must also be different with respect to qualities which are thought important in different parts of the work world and for entrance to elite status. It may not take very long before that view becomes extended even further, to include the notion that qualitative cultural differences are inborn. When that point is reached we have come full circle and we begin to realize that those theories of race and ethnic differences which we thought destroyed or at least highly discredited by World War II have reappeared in a new guise with culture replacing race.

Along with the arguments supportive of the revival of ethnicity can be found also the view that cultures have a right to live and individuals and societies have an obligation to see that they survive, although surely history is as much the graveyard of cultures as it is of aristocracies. The desirability and responsibility of preserving culture through historical, archeological, and anthropological study, because we want to know how people lived at different times and places, is beyond question. Often, in discussions of the survival of culture, one gets the impression that the reference is to cultural artifacts such as dance, folklore, cuisine, music, crafts, and the like. Cultural artifacts always will survive, because people enjoy them, and that is good because they add variety. However, they do not require descent group identification to survive. Artifacts are unlike values, some of which when embedded in particular cultures are particularly inappropriate for modernity, for example, the low evaluation of education for girls.

If there are dangers of biological descent groups preserving cultures through living them, there are available associational ways of conserving culture. Some people find the culture of ancient Egypt fascinating and rewarding to study. But if the culture of ancient Egypt is of value the various groups that preserve it— archaeologists who get money to investigate it and amateur Egyptologists who make it a hobby—must recruit new members to carry on their interests. One way would be to require as a condition of membership that members marry within the Egyptology group, and, given the traditional role of the family as the unit of cultural transmission, ensure the survival of the culture of ancient Egypt through the generations. Alternatively, they can do as they always have done and that is to recruit members by persuading others that studying and keeping alive this particular culture is a good thing.

The obligation to conserve culture is different from the obligation to live it. In Canada, for example, it is at times suggested that the Eskimos should be left alone to live their traditional hunting and nomadic culture rather than be encouraged to modernism even though, for the individuals involved, life is more often than not nasty and brutish and seldom long, at least until modern government health services are delivered to even the most remote areas. Yet few would argue that medical attempts to control tuberculosis should be abandoned in favor of the more primitive harshness.

Not all cultures have equal claims on our moral support. Some cultures treat human beings in profoundly inhumane ways. As Conor Cruise O'Brien has said in a recent discussion of the rights of minorities in developing countries:

> The culture of a group may include systematic violations of basic human rights. When we are told to respect the cultures of groups we are being told to respect things which may include for example the Hindu caste system, the treatment of women in Islam and a number of other cultures, female circumcision in certain cultures, ostracism of twins, for example in others, and so on.[51]

So strongly are cultural rights advocated that people in modern nations, particularly those that make claims to being democracies, are reluctant to persuade developing countries to be either democratic or modern. Perhaps considering their histories of imperialism and aggression they do not speak with much moral authority. But our claim to the judgment of cultures is not put forward because we have created a perfect society, but because in the course

51. In *The Times*, London, reprinted as "In Secession a Case for the Individual," in the *Globe and Mail*, Toronto, January 27, 1973.

of social evolution some principles of social life have emerged which are more morally supportable than others.

So far my emphasis has been on the costs of ethnic saliency in modern societies. Are there no benefits? One strong argument for ethnic pluralism, widely accepted to support the idea of multiculturalism in Canada, is that it creates diversity. A society with a number of different ethnic cultures in which the members of relatively exclusive groups behave alike, it is said, will be heterogeneous rather than uniform. Yet it could be that such diversity is more enjoyed by the beholder—whatever Olympus he might be viewing it from—than any of the actors within their enclaves. Moreover, modern societies are the most differentiated of all. Diversity is almost a defining attribute for them, but their diversity is one of choice rather than of descent. Indeed, the call to ethnic loyalty stems largely from the fear of the descent group that members will desert it for the diversity of an associational rather than a communal type.

A strong case can be made for the role of ethnic group affiliation in solving problems of personal identity in the modern world of bureaucracy and technology. There is no doubt that ethnic groupings can play this role, but, as I have argued, at the possible cost of perpetuating ethnic stratification. Identities and psychic shelters can be found in other forms of association and interest groups which are not based on descent, for it is this aspect of the ethnic group which is the source of irrational invidious comparison.

The psychic shelter function of ethnic affiliation has been and continues to be important in Canada and no doubt in other modern societies as well, in two special contexts. One is that of recently arrived immigrants, of which Canada continues to have large numbers in its population. The other is the positive function which ethnic affiliation has for the raising of the self-concept of members of low status groups.

For the immigrant the transition to a new social environment can be fraught with psychic hazards, particularly if he comes from the Azores or the Abruzzi to metropolitan Toronto. The question from the point of view of general social goals is whether the useful staging camp role of the ethnic community becomes permanent, or whether some dispersion into the wider society of the various groups increases his chances of achievement and mobility in the receiving society.

Commitment to the receiving society on the part of immigrants may not be as strong now as it was sixty or seventy years ago. Immigrants come in modern jet aircraft, settle into enclaves in the receiving metropolis, and charter aircraft to take them home for visits. What the jet aircraft does between Milano and Toronto, fast special trains do from Torino to Amsterdam. So the link with the society of origin is not as completely broken as it was in the time of the long steerage passage across the Atlantic, and with this shrinking of distance the social status of migrating labor will be ever more ambiguous in the societies to which it moves to work. The social status of permanent stranger is something new for modern societies. But where the status of citizenship can be acquired, as in the United States and Canada, social mobility and achievement almost imply a commitment to the values of modernism and a movement away from the ethnic community with each succeeding generation.

There remains the positive function that ethnic identification can play in raising the self-concept of members of low status groups. The enhancement of self-concept can serve contrary ends. One is to compensate for low status without doing anything about it, very much as evangelical religions do for lower classes in ethnically homogeneous societies or low status ethnic groups in ethnically heterogeneous societies. The other is to provide a firm base from which to achieve, although many cultures do not emphasize individual achievement, nor do they provide the appropriate skills for it. From the point of view of the Indians, does promoting their own culture help them toward equality in the postindustrial society?

If strong ethnic identification is to enhance the self-concept of an individual and thus provide a firm base from which to achieve, it is important to emphasize language rather than culture. Identification with and the use of their own language, particularly in school, may be important in providing opportunity for very low status groups. For example, the use of an immigrant language, say, Italian or Portuguese and certainly the language of native peoples in Canada, may help a child in overcoming learning impediments that arise from using one language at school and another at home. He acquires some self-confidence when his language is not despised. But such use of language is quite different from the goal of having ethnic communities become a permanent compensation for low status, or as psychic shelters in the urban-industrial world. We would hope for a society in which the compensatory role of the ethnic community is not necessary.

I have tried to argue what, particularly in my own country, is an unpopular view, and that is that the saliency of ethnic differences is a retreat from the liberal notions of the unity of mankind. But I would be naive indeed—an inappropriate state for a professional sociologist—if I were not aware of the political realities in those modern societies where deprived minorities seek to redistribute social resources to redress grievances. Political realities are not principles although they are often confused with them, and hence, the question is whether interethnic conflicts can be solved in ways which are both ethically acceptable and sociologically possible.

It is my view that in Canada, in the emerging postindustrial phase, with its one culture of science and technology and its extensive transnational network, bilingualism can survive. But that phase can scarcely be bicultural, much less multicultural. If bilingualism is to be a part of Canada's future, we will require more exogamous marriages to offset falling fertility rates in Quebec. We will also require vastly improved language learning programs. Under such circumstances, there would be no need to rely only on group exclusiveness and endogamy for Canada's two languages to survive.

What of cultures? Cultures are tradition bound. Anthropologists view culture as established ways of doing things, or of viewing the world, or as designs for living and survival passed from generation to generation, and, while for societies more simply organized than those of today, the role that cultures played and for many continue to play was important, they are less and less relevant for the postindustrial society because they emphasize yesterday rather than tomorrow. Can cultures of the past serve societies facing the coming of postindustrialism? The one recurring theme in many of the analyses of the next twenty-five years is the rapidity of change, of the shock of the future. One can almost speak of the end of culture, as some have written of the end of ideology. Many of the historic cultures are irrelevant to our futures. Opportunity will go to those individuals who are future oriented in an increasingly universalistic culture. Those oriented to the past are likely to lose out.

One would like to think, too, that in the United States the morally desirable and sociologically possible would take the direction of solving problems of non-white deprivation and all inequalities through the liberal emphasis on individual rather than group rights. In the short run in both Canada and the United States it may not be possible, but we should be aware of the danger of institutionalizing short-run policies: if we do we may well be turning back on the principles which have been evolving in our histories and which the revival of ethnicity contradicts.

10

ORLANDO PATTERSON

Context and Choice in Ethnic Allegiance: A Theoretical Framework and Caribbean Case Study

THEORETICAL FORMULATION

The objectives of this chapter are to argue that ethnicity can only be understood in terms of a dynamic and contextual view of group allegiances; that what is critical about an ethnic group is not the particular set of symbolic objects which distinguishes it, but the social uses of these objects; and that ethnic loyalties reflect, and are maintained by, the underlying socioeconomic interests of group members.

In pursuing these objectives, we assume the following: that human beings have a variety of group allegiances; that these allegiances may coincide or overlap or conflict with each other; and that human beings seek to maximize their economic and social status and minimize their survival risks in the societies in which they live.

One type of group allegiance is characterized by the quality referred to as ethnicity. The use of this term in the sociological literature is unsatisfactory, indeed, often confused.[1] The term may be defined in two ways: one static and descriptive, the other dynamic and analytic. Most definitions of the term have been descriptive and static in an attempt to isolate a set of characteristics or traits by

1. The situation is quite similar to what Blalock calls the "healthy confusion" existing in the closely related and overlapping field in minority group relations. See H. M. Blalock, Jr., *Toward a Theory of Minority-Group Relations* (Santa Barbara, Capricorn Books, 1967), p. 2.

which the term may be delineated. Herein lies much of the confusion. Such definitions emphasize culture and tradition as the critical elements, and in so doing, are so descriptive that they become analytically useless, and often so inclusive that they are not even worthwhile as heuristic devices. Cultural attributes are of no intrinsic interest from a dynamic structural perspective. From the latter viewpoint, what is important about the American Jews is not the fact that they worship on Saturdays, or that they have certain unique rituals or patterns of socialization, but the functions of these rituals for the group—the ways in which they are used to maintain group cohesiveness, sustain and enhance identity, and to establish social networks and communicative patterns that are important for the group's optimization of its socioeconomic position in the society. A theory of ethnic cultural elements and symbols is an absurdity, because these symbols are purely arbitrary and unique to each case.

Second, it is extremely important to note that the context of a given ethnic experience is one of the most critical factors in defining it. Once we understand this, we can begin to clear up a persistent error which is often found in the descriptive literature. This is the view that what is most critical about ethnic identity is the fact that it is involuntary and cannot be changed. This fallacy has an ancient heritage: the biblical refrain "Can the Ethiopian change his skin or the leopard his spots?" is one of the earliest recorded versions of it. It is often stated that a distinguishing feature of these groups is the fact that individuals are born into such groups and have no choice in the matter. One does not choose to be Jewish or black or Chinese, it is claimed; rather, the condition is chosen for one by fate.[2]

If one emphasizes—as one should, if one wants to be analytic—not the symbolic and cultural objects but the structural significance of these objects, then one immediately recognizes the irrelevance of such assertions. From a structural and contextual viewpoint, there is an important sense in which the significance of a given ethnic at-

2. The most articulate modern proponent of this view is Harold R. Isaacs. See his chapter, "Basic Group Identity," in this volume. See also M. Gordon, *Assimilation in American Life* (Oxford, Oxford University Press, 1964), p. 29.

tribute can change and, as such, one can be said to have some choice in the matter, since one can choose the sociological and psychological significance of the given trait. And the way in which this is done is simply by changing one's social context or seizing the opportunity offered by a change, over time, in one's social context.

I will illustrate the point with an individual case study. Take the case of a black Jamaican who is a citizen of Jamaica and a permanent resident of the United States. He lives and works for a total of eight months in the United States and four months in Jamaica. He travels between both countries twice a year. In Jamaica, which is 95 percent black, he belongs to the demographically dominant majority and is a member of the elite. In the United States he is a member of an ethnic group—the blacks, although he holds a position of some status in that society. Clearly, in one social context—Jamaica—the individual in question is not a member of any ethnic group; on the contrary, he is an elite member of the dominant group and his primary allegiance is to the nation. In the other context, however, he is consciously a member of an ethnic group. He regards himself as a member of this group, and he is so regarded by non-members of this group in America. Thus, while he does not change the color of his skin, there is a real and meaningful sense in which the individual changes his ethnic identity four times each year. He does so by changing his social context.[3]

Other examples may be noted. The many Puerto Ricans who migrate back and forth between Puerto Rico and New York are cases in point. In Puerto Rico a black person might belong to the black ethnic group of that society, whereas in New York he belongs to the Puerto Rican ethnic group. Furthermore, there are cases of highly Americanized black Puerto Ricans who consciously choose and manipulate different ethnic identities to serve their own best interests. In certain contexts (for example, running for local office or applying for a job in which Affirmative Action has created a black bias) he will emphasize his blackness. In other contexts (for example, personal relations with whites) he may choose to mute the impact of his dark skin by emphasizing his Latin background, espe-

3. These remarks are based on the author's participant observations of West Indians in New York and the Caribbean.

cially his Spanish accent.[4] Or take the case of the Sephardic Jews of Jamaica who travel to England or the United States. In the new social setting, some of these individuals choose to maintain their Jewish allegiance, identifying with the Jews of the new host society; others choose to identify with the Jamaican ethnic group in the new society; and still others abandon ethnicity, marry Gentile women and blend into the host society. Similar range of choices are made by members of the Sephardic Jewish community from Curaçao living in Holland.[5] Finally, it should be noted that changes in the context of ethnic identification can take place by movement from one society to another in a given time period, or it can take place over given periods of time within a single society.

With these preliminary observations in mind, we may define ethnicity as follows: that condition wherein certain members of a society, in a given social context, choose to emphasize as their most meaningful basis of primary, extrafamilial identity certain assumed cultural, national, or somatic traits.

The groups formed in this way vary, of course, in size, duration, intensity of involvement, variety and number of shared traits, and in complexity of structure. Clearly there are numerous ways of classifying such groups, and while the exercise might have some descriptive value, it can be, and often is, theoretically pointless.[6] It is best to concentrate on the analytic qualities such groups have in common: namely, the fact that they are the structural expressions of primary, extrafamilial identity.

They resemble the family in the intensity of involvement of members and in the tendency to equate and rationalize relationships with other members in consanguineal terms—"kith and kin" is a term often used to describe members of one's ethnic group. But they are certainly not kinship groups, in spite of the

4. This manipulation of multiple ethnic identities was brought to the author's attention by several of his Puerto Rican students at Harvard. See Sam Betances, "The Prejudice of Having No Prejudice," unpublished paper, 1971.

5. See Frances P. Karner, *The Sephardics of Curaçao: A Study of Socio-Cultural Patterns in Flux* (Assen, The Netherlands, Van Gorcum, 1969), esp. pp. 64, 66–67.

6. See, for example, the papers of N. Shaler, E. Freeman, W. Petrie, and A. Toynbee, in E. T. Thompson and E. C. Hughes, eds., *Race: Individual and Collective Behavior* (Glencoe, The Free Press, 1958), pt. 3.

ideological fiction among members to the contrary; nor are such groups necessarily endogamous.

The members of an ethnic group may be restricted to a single nation, or the group may cut across several national boundaries. Occasionally, the ethnic group may coincide with the nation.[7] It is important to keep in mind, however, the fact that ethnic allegiance and national allegiance are not necessarily the same thing. The idea of the national *Volk,* the view that a nation is or should be a community of people sharing a common history and "blood," is a peculiar product of modern political thought.[8]

The fact that ethnicity is a chosen form of identification cannot be overemphasized. An ethnic group only exists where members consider themselves to belong to such a group; a conscious sense of belonging is critical. It implies, on the one hand, that where all other criteria are met except this sense of belonging, the ethnic condition is not met—even where other members of the society may regard a given group of individuals as constituting an ethnic group. And it implies, on the other hand, that where, in objective sociological terms, the assumed bases of group allegiance do not exist, should members subjectively assume the existence of such "mythical" bases, the salient condition of ethnicity is met.

Before moving on to a statement of our hypotheses, a few other definitions and distinctions must be made. First, we must distinguish between an ethnic group and a cultural group. A cultural group is simply any group of people who consciously or unconsciously share an identifiable complex of meanings, symbols, values, and norms. Such a group differs from an ethnic group in the following respects: first, there need not be any conscious awareness of belonging to a group on the part of the members of such groups, and, indeed, it is usually the case that no such conscious

7. I agree with E. K. Francis, who, while not identifying the concept "nation" with "ethnic group," allows for the possibility of the two being the same. Thus the French and the Irish in France and Ireland respectively are said to be ethnic groups. See E. K. Francis, "The Nature of the Ethnic Group," *American Journal of Sociology,* 3 (March 1947), 393–400.

8. For a discussion of the relationship between ethnicity and nation building see C. H. Enloe, *Ethnic Conflict and Political Development* (Boston, Little, Brown and Co., 1973).

group identity exists. Second, a cultural group is an objectively verifiable social phenomenon. The meaning, symbols, values, and norms, in short, the tradition, which they share, can be anthropologically observed, regardless of the ideological statements, or expressed opinions, of members about their tradition of their relationship with it. Third, a cultural group, or segments of it, may become an ethnic group but only when the conditions of ethnicity are met. The fact that a segment of a cultural group becomes an ethnic group does not mean that all members of the cultural group thereby become an ethnic group.

Another term to be distinguished is "class." We define class as an economic group determined by the relation of its members to the mode of production of a society. The term can be used in two senses, a distinction which goes back to Marx: in the abstract sense, namely, as an arbitrary abstraction from reality based on certain objective criteria established by the analyst; and, in the concrete sense of an objectively real group, existing independently of any arbitrarily defined instrumental criteria of definition.[9] I tend to agree with Ralf Dahrendorf that it is possible to live with both these conceptions of class, using one or the other as one's intellectual needs demand.[10] In line with my objectives, I shall be operating on the principle that classes are concrete, objectively observable groups. We also assume that class groups act in their own best interests, even if they may not do so consciously. Our definition of classes, then, is that they are economic groups determined by the productive forces of the society which, consciously or unconsciously, behave in such a way as to optimize their economic interests and position in the society. From what we have already said about ethnic groups, it should not be necessary to belabor the obvious differences between such groups and class groups.

I propose to argue that there are three basic principles determin-

9. The distinction is discussed at length in L. Gross, "The Use of Class Concepts in Sociological Research," *American Journal of Sociology* 54 (March 1949), 402–421.

10. R. Dahrendorf, *Class and Class Conflict in an Industrial Society* (London, Routledge and Kegan Paul, 1959), p. 151. We are, however, in complete disagreement with Dahrendorf's idiosyncratic operationalization of the term. See, for example, p. 204.

ing the relative choice of allegiances, including ethnic allegiances. These are: the principle of reconciliation (or least conflict) of interest; the principle of optimization of interests; and the principle of the primacy of class interests.[11]

The first principle proposes that individuals with several allegiances will, whenever possible, seek to reconcile the varying interests implied in their separate allegiances. Thus an individual will, ideally, want his class, cultural, ethnic, and status interests to harmonize with each other and, wherever possible (although the principle of reconciliation does not require it), to complement each other. The principle of reconciliation should not be confused with that of equalization of interests. I am not arguing that individuals seek to equalize or identify their varying interests, or even that they actively seek to have one complement the other. The East Boston Italian construction worker thinks in class terms on his job and in trade negotiations, and he thinks in ethnic terms in community affairs. He does not expect trade union negotiations on his behalf to have any necessary direct impact on his community, but he does expect, however, that his class activity will not actively conflict with his community activity. This is why the principle of reconciliation is perhaps best described as the principle of least conflict.

The principle of optimization posits that, in all those instances where interests cannot be reconciled, that is, where there is inevitable conflict of interest implied in the individual's varying allegiances, there will be a tendency to choose that set of allegiances which maximizes material and social gains in the society at large, and minimizes survival risks. This may be a roundabout way of saying that individuals tend to act in their own best interests. We state it as a basic principle because, while it may appear obvious to

11. Note that these hypotheses are stated in the individualistic terms often associated with the sociology of George C. Homans. All hypothetical statements regarding ethnicity must be microsociological, since the critical problem is to explain the individual's relation to the group, not the group itself. A concern with the ethnic group shifts the theoretical emphasis from ethnicity to the macrosociological level of intergroup relations. See G. C. Homans, "Bringing Men Back In," in Herman Turk and Richard L. Simpson, eds., *Institutions and Social Exchange* (Indianapolis and New York, The Bobbs Merrill Co., 1971), pp. 102–116, and H. M. Blalock, *Toward a Theory of Minority-Group Relations*, pp. 21–34.

some, it is by no means obvious to all sociologists, and it seems least obvious to precisely that group of social scientists who work in the area of ethnicity.[12] A truism becomes worthy of the status of a principle, or law of action, when it ceases to be, or is no longer regarded as, a truism.

Students of ethnicity tend to emphasize the non-rational implications of ethnic behavior as one of its critical attributes; Harold Isaacs, for example, thinks that the quintessence of ethnicity is the primordiality and near primeval intensity of involvement with, and allegiance to, one's ethnic group.[13] As such, it becomes highly possible that where there is a clash between ethnic and other interests, the individual will act against his other interests in favor of the integrity of his ethnic allegiance. It is one of my major contentions that such a view is false; I do not think that primordiality and intensity of involvement is a distinguishing feature of ethnicity. This is not to say that such involvement does not sometimes characterize ethnic allegiance; it often does. But it is not peculiar to ethnic allegiance, and, indeed, is not required by it.

I think, instead, that individuals will be most intensely involved with those allegiances, or that allegiance, which is in their own best social and economic interests. Where ethnic allegiance is in individuals' own best interests, intense feelings will be attached to it. This is true, for example, of a persecuted ethnic group faced with a genocidal or otherwise hostile majority. But it is also true of those individuals whose survival and best interests are threatened on a class basis or a religious basis. In such cases people are quite prepared to abandon their ethnic allegiance in favor of their class allegiance, and attach to the latter the same kind of "primordial" intensity which is exclusively associated, in the vulgar sociological imagination, with ethnic allegiance.

This brings us to our third principle. Where a plurality of allegiances involves a conflict between class interests and other inter-

12. Thus, the individual who, in pursuing his own best interests, chooses to abandon his ethnic allegiance is dubbed a "marginal man," a social "deviant" by students of ethnicity ranging from Park to Gordon. See M. Gordon, *Assimilation*, pp. 54–59.

13. H. Isaacs, "Basic Group Identity."

ests, individuals *in the long run* will choose class allegiance over all other allegiances, including ethnic allegiance. I say "in the long run," because this takes account of those special situations in which individuals face severe survival risks on bases other than class. As I indicated above, individuals whose very existence is threatened by a hostile majority, on, say, purely ethnic terms, will, in such crisis situations, temporarily suspend all other allegiances in favor of the one in which they are being threatened. Such situations, however, are by their very nature short term; no group of people can continue to live in a society which constantly threatens their existence. Either the majority group withdraws the threat, or the threatened group withdraws from the society, or the dominant group exercises its threat and destroys the group, or finally, if this is a possibility, individuals may abolish the basis of their allegiance to the group which offends the hostile majority, in this way solving the problem by destroying the group in order to ensure the survival of the members of the group.

In the short run, then, we readily concede that survival threats may create situations in which other allegiances may take primacy over class interests, but in the long run—and it is only in the long run that sociological generalizations are viable—there is definitely a tendency for class membership, and its implied interests, to assert primacy over all other allegiances.

CASE STUDY

I shall demonstrate the feasibility of the above hypotheses with a comparative case study of two Chinese communities in the Caribbean: the Chinese of Jamaica and Guyana. Before examining the data on the Chinese, however, it is necessary to discuss the social contexts of these communities, namely Afro-Caribbean societies.

Context: Afro-Caribbean Societies. The societies of the Caribbean area fall into two main groups: the Latin and the Afro-Caribbean.[14] The Latin area, which will not concern us, is distinguished

14. For a useful introductory overview, see S. W. Mintz, "The Caribbean as a Socio-Cultural Area," *Journal of World History,* 9.4 (1966), 912–937. See also, D. Lowenthal, "The Range and Variation of Caribbean Societies," *Annals of the New York Academy of Sciences,* 83, art. 5 (1960), 786–795.

by the overwhelming presence of the New World version of Iberian culture, by its greater cultural homogeneity, by its larger size and by differing political experiences and structures. The Afro-Caribbean societies are characterized by the overwhelming presence of people of African descent, by a common colonial experience, by the prolonged historical experience of slavery on a large scale, by their relatively small size, and their continued economic dependence on the former European colonizing powers.

The societies we will be mainly concerned with—Jamaica and Guyana—like all Afro-Caribbean societies, have a similar pattern of sociocultural evolution or development. There was, first, an early phase of discovery and European settlement. The early phase, which lasted from the beginning of the sixteenth century to the latter part of the seventeenth century, saw attempts at establishing white settlement colonies. The attempt was only partly successful on the part of the Spaniards. When the Spanish were displaced by the North Europeans, the attempt was repeated for a brief period of about forty years, but finally failed, as the North Europeans shifted to large-scale, plantation agriculture, concentrating on a single crop—sugar.

This shift in economic base ushered in the second phase of development of Afro-Caribbean societies. The sugar plantations, which became all-important by the turn of the eighteenth century, made the Afro-Caribbean societies the richest areas of the world.[15] They also set the basic social structure and tone of these societies. African slaves were brought in on a large scale, resulting in the early demographic dominance of black people. Ruling them was a small minority of white planters, many of whom were later in the century to become absentee landlords, their estates being managed by attorneys and overseers with little commitment to the societies they managed.[16]

15. For an excellent analysis of this period, see R. Sheridan, *The Development of the Plantations* (Barbados, Caribbean Universities Press, 1970).

16. On the growth of the slave population in the Caribbean, see O. Patterson, *The Sociology of Slavery* (Rutherford, N.J., Fairleigh Dickinson University Press, 1969), and E. Goveia, *Slave Society in the British Leeward Islands* (New Haven, Yale University Press, 1965), esp. ch. 2.

Between masters and slaves a third group soon emerged—the coloreds—or people of mixed ancestry. This group formed a useful racial and sociocultural buffer between the whites and blacks.[17] By the end of the eighteenth century a substantial number of them were freedmen, and, in Jamaica, these freedmen were sufficiently influential to win full civil liberties, along with the small Sephardic Jewish minority, from the white ruling class a little before the emancipation.[18]

While the pattern was similar, Guyana lagged behind in the development of its plantation-based economy, partly because of the enormous geographical difficulties which its low-lying coastal terrain presented, partly because of its peculiar political situation of being a Dutch-controlled territory with a majority of British settlers, and partly because of the lateness of the critical decision to shift from the river bank areas to the coastal strip.[19] Its period of economic expansion really moved into full swing after the British occupation in 1803, at a time when Jamaica's was already on the decline.[20]

The collapse of the slave-based economy, with the complete emancipation of the slaves in 1838 by the British, paved the way for the third phase in the development of Afro-Caribbean societies. This phase was marked by rapid economic decline on the national and international levels, reflected in the general neglect of the area by the former colonial powers, and a withdrawal of substantial segments of the former planter classes.[21] During the last two thirds of

17. E. Goveia, ibid., pp. 215–229.

18. On their fight for civil rights up to 1830, see S. D. Dunker's unpublished M.A. thesis, "The Free Coloureds and Their Fight for Civil Rights in Jamaica, 1800–1830," London University, 1960. A more substantial work which not only carries the analysis through to 1865, but explores, in part, their fascinating relationship with the Sephardic Jewish community during and after slavery is M. C. Campbell, "Edward Jordan and the Free Coloureds, Jamaica 1800–1865," unpublished Ph.D. thesis, University of London, 1970.

19. R. T. Smith, *British Guiana* (London, Oxford University Press, 1962), ch. 2–3.

20. P. Newman, *British Guiana: Problems of Cohesion in an Immigrant Society* (London, Oxford University Press, 1964), ch. 2.

21. On the decline of the plantation system and post-emancipation economic developments, see L. Ragatz, *The Fall of the Planter Class in the British Caribbean,*

the nineteenth century what may be called the segmentary Creole phase of Afro-Caribbean societies was to evolve from the precarious foundations which were laid during the period of slavery.[22]

The term creolization refers to the process whereby a group of people develop a way of life peculiar to the new locality in which they find themselves, as distinct from the cultures of their homelands.[23] We propose to make a distinction between two types of creolization: what I shall call "segmentary creolization" and "synthetic creolization." The meaning of these terms will be made clear in the ensuing discussion.

Segmentary creolization refers to that process of development in which each group, in the new setting, creates its own peculiar version of a local culture. In Afro-Caribbean societies, two main types of segmentary Creole cultures evolved. One involved the development of a peculiarly West Indian brand of the dominant metropolitan culture of the European ruling class. This resulted in what

---

1763–1833 (New York, Octagon, 1963). See also D. Hall, *Free Jamaica, 1838–1865* (New Haven, Yale University Press, 1959).

22. On the development of the two segmentary Creole cultures, see P. Curtin, *Two Jamaicas* (Cambridge, Harvard University Press, 1955), pp. 23–60. My own work, *The Sociology of Slavery,* discusses the foundations of these segmentary creoles in the slave society. More recently, E. Brathwaite's *The Development of Creole Society in Jamaica, 1770–1820* (Oxford, Clarendon Press, 1971), while not in basic disagreement with my own interpretation of the data, suggests that the process of creolization was far more developed during the period of slavery than either Curtin or myself would allow.

23. The term has acquired this special technical meaning among Caribbeanists and linguists concerned with the study of creole languages. It is not to be confused with the rather vague usage found in Louisiana where it refers to whites of French ancestry. On attempts to sharpen the meaning of the term, see: M. G. Smith, *The Plural Society in the British West Indies* (Berkeley, University of California Press, 1965), pp. 5–9, 307–308, who, however, restricts the use of the term to Euro-West Indian segmentary creoles only; S. Mintz, "Comments on the Socio-historical Background to Pidginization and Creolization," in D. Hymes, ed., *Pidginization and Creolization of Languages* (Cambridge, Cambridge University Press, 1970). See also: André Nègre, "Origines et signification du mot 'créole,' " *Bulletin de la Société d'Histoire de la Guadaloupe,* nos. 5–6 (1966); D. Lowenthal, *West Indian Societies* (Oxford, Oxford University Press, 1972), pp. 32–33; and P. Singer and E. Araneta, "Hinduization and Creolization in Guyana," *Social and Economic Studies,* 16.3 (September 1967), 221–236, who emphasize the psychological aspects of the creole process, but their analysis is rather idiosyncratic.

may be called Euro-West Indian segmentary Creole cultures. In form it is almost wholly European; that is, the institutional structures are direct borrowings from their European counterparts. They are also largely European in content, but with substantial variations in emphasis, and in interpretation, in certain areas. It also involved new developments to meet the specific needs of the colonial area, such as in the spheres of architecture and dietary patterns. The most important difference, however, is in the area of style. Thus, for example, there is no obvious difference in the form and content of the game cricket as played in England and in the West Indies, but there are numerous differences in the style, interpretation, and symbolic value of the game.[24]

Another important difference between Euro-West Indian Creole culture and its metropolitan counterpart is the high value placed on color—the "white bias" to use Henriques' phrase [25]—in all these societies. Such a value is, of course, the peculiar product of a racially segmented society in which the ruling class of one race dominates a colonized group of a different race.

This white bias, however, did not prevent the adoption of Euro-West Indian culture by the mixed-race freedmen, later to become the middle class in the post-emancipation society. In spite of the negative racial self-image it engendered, the new middle class vied with each other in their attempt to emulate all things European.[26] They compensated to some extent for the negative racial self-image implied in the acculturation by turning it against those lower in the shade hierarchy, and by lightening their own group by marrying "up," that is, by choosing spouses lighter than themselves.

The second type of segmentary creolization involved the development of a peculiarly West Indian peasant culture, forged partly out of the torn shreds and remnants of surviving African culture and out of a creative response to the exigencies of small-scale tropical peasant agriculture. This second type of segmentary creoliza-

24. On this see O. Patterson, "The Cricket Ritual in the West Indies," *New Society*, no. 352 (June 1969), pp. 988–989.

25. F. Henriques, *Family and Color in Jamaica* (London, Macgibbon and Kee, 1968), pp. 52, 57–59.

26. M. Campbell, "Edward Jordan and the Free Coloureds," pp. 35–42.

tion we may describe as Afro-West Indian segmentary creolization. The ex-slaves of the Caribbean varied in their responses to the challenge of emancipation, depending mainly on the availability of land after emancipation. In Jamaica, the largest of the Commonwealth Caribbean islands, it was possible to retreat to the mountain backlands and to buy up abandoned estates, both areas forming the nuclei of the peasant communities which were to form the economic and social context of black peasant life in the country for the next century.[27] In Guyana, while land was plentiful, it was difficult to bring into cultivation, so that the attempt to form a largely self-contained peasantry was only partly successful and a substantial number of blacks continued to depend on the estates as the major source of their livelihood.[28]

In all these areas the new ex-slaves forged an Afro-West Indian Creole culture distinctive in social organization, language, religion, attitude, and values. It should be noted, however, that these were first and foremost peasant cultures, and like all peasant cultures, open to the influence of the urban high culture, in this case the Euro-West Indian segmentary Creole of the ruling class.

While the brown-skinned middle class tried their best to imitate the Euro-West Indian culture of the ruling planter group, it was not entirely possible for them to do so, mainly because they lacked the educational and economic resources to sustain such a life style. Partly by default, then, they were obliged to create their own cultural patterns. What they finally developed was the second type of Creole culture: "synthetic Creole." The major difference between synthetic and segmentary creolization is that, whereas in the latter process each group develops its own local culture, with synthetic creolization the group attempts to forge a local culture which combines elements from all the available cultural resources. In the early period, this synthetic Creole was really nothing more than a kind of poor man's Euro-West Indian Creole culture. But with the growing influence of the middle classes, and with their increased

27. H. Paget, "The Free Village System in Jamaica," *Caribbean Quarterly*, 1.4 (1954), 7–19.

28. R. Farley, "The Rise of the Peasantry in British Guiana," *Social and Economic Studies*, 2.4 (1954), 76–103.

tendency to think in national terms rather than the earlier pathetic attempts simply to imitate the Europeans, the culture they evolved became more self-consciously synthetic. When the new middle class finally assumed complete control of the political systems of the area, they attempted to give an official seal to their culture, as reflected in the national motto in many of these Caribbean societies—"Out of many one people." [29]

Synthetic Creole draws heavily on Euro-West Indian culture for its instrumental components and on Afro-West Indian segmentary Creole for its expressive institutions and symbols. The political, economic, educational, and legal institutions of synthetic Creole are, essentially, slightly modified versions of Euro-West Indian segmentary Creole; whereas its language, theater, music, dance, art, and literature are actively drawn from Afro-West Indian segmentary Creole sources.[30] Later, I shall discuss the sociopolitical functions of synthetic Creole.

To summarize, Caribbean societies are, today, best seen as neocolonial systems with enormous class cleavages and other crosscutting cleavages based on race, color, ethnicity, and even urban-rural differences. Middle and upper class roles are increasingly occupied by an upwardly mobile brown and black population whose culture is synthetic Creole. At the same time, the economies are not expanding at the rate sufficient to allow for significant group mobility among the mass of the black lower classes. We have a situation, then, in which the elite view the system as highly fluid, since most of them are upwardly mobile themselves, but the mass of the population views it as static and undemocratic, since the few who have moved up from their ranks are really insignificant demographically.

This is clearly a volatile situation. Add the facts that expanding educational facilities have succeeded more in increasing expecta-

29. For a very sensitive discussion of this development by a West Indian intellectual who is actively involved with creating such a synthesis, see R. Nettleford, "The Melody of Europe, The Rhythm of Africa," in his *Mirror, Mirror: Identity, Race and Protest in Jamaica* (Kingston, Collins and Sangster, 1970), pp. 173–211.

30. R. Nettleford, "The Melody of Europe," and D. Lowenthal, *West Indian Societies*, pp. 250–292.

tions than in providing the opportunities to satisfy these expectations; that urbanization has brought in its train a well-known set of
problems; and that the rise of black racial consciousness has led to
an interpretation of the color-class hierarchy, not as a residue of
the old colonial system, but as an active consequence of ongoing
racist and imperialist policies, one begins to understand why, in
recent years, this part of the world is no longer the sleepy, tropical
paradise of travel agents' brochures, but has begun to show increasing signs of impending social and political upheaval.[31]

If or when such an upheaval takes place, the groups which stand
to lose most and are most fearful of their interests are the members
of the various ethnic and racial minorities, especially those who
now occupy high status positions out of all proportion to their
numbers.

Most prominent among these groups are the Sephardic Jews
who came to the West Indies during the seventeenth century from
northern Brazil after the Portuguese reclaimed that area from the
Dutch.[32] Unlike their counterparts in Curaçao, the Jamaican Jews
have slowly given up their ethnic identification in favor of middle
and upper class allegiance and a growing identification with the
white and light-skinned community at large. Today they are found
in all aspects of the country's life, including its economy, its political system (the recently elected minister of National Security and
Justice comes from a prominent Jewish family), in the professions,
and in the arts and recreational institutions. It is only a matter of
time now before the group becomes completely absorbed into the
creole elite.[33]

31. On the recent army mutiny and riots in Trinidad, see I. Oxaal, *Race and
Revolutionary Consciousness* (Cambridge, Schenkman Publishing Co., Inc., 1970).
See also, on Jamaica, N. Girvan, "October Counter-Revolution in Jamaica," *New
World Quarterly* (High Season, 1968), 59–68.

32. G. Merrill, "The Role of the Sephardic Jews in the British Caribbean Area
During the Seventeenth Century," *Caribbean Studies*, 4.3 (1964), 32–49.

33. B. Schlesinger, "The Jews of Jamaica: A Historical View," *Caribbean Quarterly*, 13.1 (1967), 46–53. On the history of the Jews in Jamaica see: S. J. and E.
Hurwitz, "The New World Sets an Example for the Old," *American Jewish Historical
Quarterly*, 55:37–56; M. Campbell, "Edward Jordan and the Free Coloureds," ch.
5–7, passim. For a less critical view of the policy of the Jews in post-emancipation
Jamaica, see S. J. and E. Hurwitz, "A Beacon for Judaism," *American Jewish Historical Quarterly*, 56:3–76.

Table 1. Some Basic Statistics on Guyana and Jamaica

Country	Area (km)	Population	Political Status	Per Capita Income	Ethnic Composition (by percent)	
Jamaica	11,425	1,800,000	Independent Member of British Commonwealth	$408(US)1967	Blacks (including mixed)	95.0
					Indians	2.0
					Jews and other Whites	1.8
					Chinese	1.2
Guyana	210,000	714,000	Independent Republic of British Commonwealth	$200(US)1964	Blacks	34.0
					Indians	50.0
					Amerindians	4.0
					Portuguese	.9
					Chinese	.6
					Mixed and others	10.5

Source: David Lowenthal, *West Indian Societies* (Oxford, Oxford University Press, 1972), pp. 78–79.

The descendants of the nineteenth-century indentured East Indians now constitute over a third of the population of Trinidad, and almost a half of the population of Guyana. Descendants of the Chinese and Portuguese migrants (the latter coming from Madeira in the mid-nineteenth century), small in numbers but great in influence and occupational status, now add to the ethnic complexity of Guyana. Indian indentured labor on a large scale was also a failure in Jamaica,[34] although it was less unsuccessful than the attempts to use Chinese laborers. The descendants of these two immigrant groups make up small but highly visible—and in the case of the Chinese, highly successful—ethnic groups in the islands.

Table 1 summarizes data on the ethnic composition of Jamaica and Guyana.

THE CHINESE OF JAMAICA AND GUYANA

The Jamaican Chinese. Over a quarter of a century before the abolition of slavery in 1838, the possibility was raised of introducing Chinese indentured labor into the West Indies, and a small group did arrive in Trinidad as early as 1806.[35] It was not until the middle of the nineteenth century, however, when the labor problem really became severe, that the Chinese began to arrive in the Caribbean in significant numbers.

The first set of migrants arrived in Guyana, Trinidad, and Jamaica between 1853 and 1854.[36] This first scheme proved a disaster. There were enormous adjustment problems; the planters found the Chinese unruly laborers; and the physical condition of the migrants deteriorated rapidly. Most of this first batch ended

34. G. W. Roberts, *The Population of Jamaica* (Cambridge, Cambridge University Press, 1957), pp. 111–132.

35. The ensuing discussion of the Chinese in Jamaica is based primarily on two unpublished and two published works on the group. These are: R. A. Silin, "A Survey of Selected Aspects of the Chinese in Jamaica," unpublished honors thesis, Anthropology Department, Harvard University, 1962; P. Morrow, "Chinese Adaptation in Two Jamaican Cities," unpublished honors thesis, Anthropology Department, Harvard University, 1972; A. W. Lind, "Adjustment Patterns Among the Jamaican Chinese," *Social and Economic Studies,* 7.2 (1958), 144–164; L. Broom, "The Social Differentiation of Jamaica," *American Sociological Review,* 19 (April 1954), 121–125.

36. R. A. Silin, "A Survey of Selected Aspects of the Chinese in Jamaica," p. 7.

their days in hospitals and alms houses, and died as paupers, vagrants, and beggars, and the entire group vanished with the death of the first generation.[37] The disappointment of the planters, together with the hostility of the native population, dampened all attempts at further immigration on a substantial scale for the next thirty years.[38]

The labor shortage created by massive out-migration of the Jamaican working class to Panama in the early 1880s revived interest in Chinese immigration, and in 1884 a total of 696 indentured servants arrived from Hong Kong.[39] It was the last group to come directly from China under the indenture system. This second attempt at employing the Chinese as agricultural laborers was also a complete failure. By 1891 the vast majority of the Chinese were out of agriculture and in small trading activities.

Beginning in the 1890s, all new migrants were brought in by existing Chinese to augment their numbers, and to work in their growing commercial enterprises. The 1911 census shows a total population of 2,111 persons but a sex ratio of 540 males for every 100 women.

In 1919, following further tensions aroused by the growing Chinese presence and their increasing domination of the grocery trade, the first restrictive immigration laws were passed. The restrictions were mild, almost absurd, however, and by 1921 the population had increased to 3,696.[40] By this time the Chinese had begun to expand out to the countryside once again where they set up isolated retail shops. There were 52.8 percent now living outside Kingston. The high ratio of Chinese males to females also accounted for another development during the early period of the century: the growth of the colored Chinese (that is, half-black, half-Chinese) population. These were the children of the male Chinese shopkeepers and their black concubines and housekeepers.

The government stopped issuing passports to Chinese migrants in 1931, and in 1940 all Chinese, with the exception of diplomats,

37. A. Lind, "Adjustment Patterns Among the Jamaican Chinese," p. 148.
38. Ibid., p. 149.
39. Ibid.
40. Silin, "A Survey of Selected Aspects of the Chinese in Jamaica," p. 12.

tourists, and students, were barred from entering the island. By this time, however, the Chinese population, though still relatively small, had become a demographically viable unit. By 1943 there were 12,394 persons of Chinese extraction on the island, of whom 6,879 were "pure Chinese," and 5,515 were colored Chinese. (See Tables 2 and 3.)

The early period of settlement, 1854–1900, was marked by the inevitable tension involved in adjusting to and settling down in a new society. The major problem facing the Chinese during this

Table 2. Characteristics of the Jamaican Chinese Population, 1871–1960

Year	Total Population	Males	Females	Sex Ratio M/100 F	Percent Urban	Percent Total Population
1871	141	131	10	1310	82.2	0.0
1881	99	n.a.	n.a.	n.a.	88.9	0.0
1891	481	373	108	345	63.2	0.1
1911	2111	1783	328	543	45.0	0.3
1921	3696	n.a.	n.a.	n.a.	41.8	0.4
1943	12,394	6922	5472	126	50.3	1.0
1960	21,812	11,265	10,547	106	50.6	1.2

Sources: A. Lind, "Adjustment Patterns among the Jamaican Chinese," *Social and Economic Studies,* 7 (1958), 144–164; G. Roberts, *The Population of Jamaica* (Cambridge University Press, 1957); *Census of Jamaica,* 1960 (Kingston, Government Printing Office).

period was their continued survival, not so much as a group, nor as culture carriers, but as individuals. This point cannot be too strongly emphàsized. If our objective is to show how the Chinese developed as a group after coming to Jamaica, it would clearly be tautological to speak of them as if they were already a group on coming to the island. The Chinese who came to the Caribbean did have some rudimentary bases of group affiliation: these were their shared experience of crossing the ocean, and the experience of being physically and culturally different in an alien land. These shared traits offered the opportunity for group allegiance, but there is no compelling nor "primordial" reason why they had to accept this opportunity. They could choose not to. In Jamaica, they did, and in Guyana they did not.

Table 3. Characteristics of "Pure" and Colored Chinese Population Jamaica, 1943, 1960

	"Pure" Chinese				Colored Chinese				All	
Year	Males	Females	Sex Ratio M/100 F	Total	Males	Females	Sex Ratio M/100 F	Total	Total	Percent China Born
1943	4338	2541	171	6879	2584	2931	89	5515	12,394	22.8
1960	5693	4574	124	10,267	4631	5041	91	9672	21,812	9.5

Sources: Census of Jamaica, 1943 (Kingston, Government Printing Office); Census of Jamaica, 1960 (Kingston, Government Printing Office).

Why did this set of individuals with Chinese features and culture who came to Jamaica in the nineteenth century choose to use their shared social and cultural traits as the bases for establishing an ethnic group? Because it was in their best socioeconomic interest to do so. The post-emancipation society to which they came had one glaring gap in its economy—there was almost no retail trade system. This was not required in the plantation-slave economy where each plantation was a self-contained world in which master and slave provided for their own mutual needs through the domestic production and direct importation of goods and staples. Now, with emancipation, a more complex economy had evolved. There was a huge peasantry alongside the surviving plantation system; there was also a growing urban center, especially in Kingston, which had to be supplied.[41] Both the rural and the urban areas of Jamaica were increasingly in need of a retail system when the Chinese arrived, the needs of the urban areas more pressing than the rural. The Chinese immigrants quickly sized up the situation and set about seizing the opportunity.

But why, we may ask, was this possible? How could a struggling band of aliens take over, in so short a period of time, such a key sector of the host country's economy? The answer, quite simply, is this: they had no competition. Why was there no competition? The answer is twofold: those native members of the society who had skills and resources to develop the retail trade—the colored and the white middle and upper classes—were not interested in doing so.

Nor were the Jews interested in doing it. The status factor alone would have been critical for them, since it was precisely at this time that they had begun to move into the upper echelons of white society, from which they had been excluded for most of the period of slavery. But, like the British, they had better, and more lucrative, things to do. Those who might have been interested—the black lower classes—lacked the resources to do so.

The natural choice, then, should have been the new middle class of coloreds, for whom emancipation offered enormous opportu-

41. D. Hall, *Free Jamaica, 1838–1865* (New Haven, Yale University Press, 1959), chs. 5 and 7.

nities. But for this group, the status factor was all important. The dominating, all-pervasive quality of their lives was their desperate, and often pathetic, attempts to identify with the white ruling class. More than any other group, they despised the blacks with that self-destroying contempt characteristic of half-breed groups. Being physically closer to the blacks than to the British and Jewish groups they were so eager to emulate, it was much more vital for them to create even greater social distance between themselves and the black masses. A white man serving a black ex-slave was unthinkable to everyone. A colored gentleman serving an ex-slave was quite thinkable to the whites, and to the blacks; but to the coloreds, that such things were thinkable was a source of humiliation, outrage, and utter disgust, and its realization was to be avoided at all costs.

For these reasons, then, the Chinese found themselves with a remarkable opportunity. Add to this the fact that they were an immigrant group and that, like all such groups, it was easier to forego the social activities that full membership in a society demands, activities that require capital and time, and the success of the Chinese can be explained without in any way having to resort to questionable notions about the latter's greater initiative or resourcefulness.

At first, the Chinese responded to the opportunity on an individual basis. There was a rapid shift to the urban areas by the scattered Chinese population. It was in Kingston that they found their common interests and began to develop as a group. Soon the Chee Kung Tong Association was formed (a branch of the Hing Min Association). Later in 1891, the Chinese Benevolent Society was organized, mainly to perform charitable work among the aged and the poor.

Toward the end of the nineteenth century, having secured a strong hold on the retail trade in Kingston, the Chinese traders began to move back to the rural areas to take advantage of the retail opportunities developing among the peasantry. The Chinese, only 0.4 percent of the total population, had all but conquered the entire retail trade on the island. Only after securing an economic base did they begin to consolidate as an ethnic group. Prior to this, it is wrong to see them as an ethnic group; their efforts were largely on an individualistic basis. Each family had kept to itself.

There was only a vague sense of community brought about by the common experience of being strangers in a strange land and out of certain common necessities. Even on this minimal level, however, collective activity seems to have come with some difficulty. Indeed, early attempts at ethnic consolidation during the first decades of the twentieth century were marred by bitter feuds and disputes among the more prominent Chinese; so much so that the Chinese Benevolent Society collapsed in 1916 although its services were desperately needed, given the extremely high dependency ratio of the population.

One other thing of note is that race was never the most critical basis of whatever group activity that took place during this or the ensuing period, and for a simple reason: if the Chinese had tried to maintain their racial purity, they would have suffered the same fate as the earlier group—extinction with the first generation. For there was a desperate shortage among them, right through this and a good part of the next period, of women. To survive, the Chinese turned to the native population and took black women as concubines to mother their children. They rarely married these women, but it is unlikely that this was an expression of racial contempt, since black men did not marry them during their child-bearing age either.[42] And, further, the institution of concubinage, which the Chinese found among the native population, was by no means alien to their Oriental experience. A nice situation of cultural congruence presented itself, and the Chinese took advantage of it. Out of these unions an interesting pattern emerged. It was to persist through the second half of the century. There is no evidence that they ever considered this a problem, or that they had any strong feelings of primordial loss. What this meant, however, was that "pure Chinese" had to have a cultural rather than a racial meaning. This is exactly what the Chinese did. The sons born to them by their black concubines, and later by the racially mixed women, were later made over into the Chinese cultural mold. At first this was done by the fathers themselves, but as the Chinese

---

42. "In fact," Henriques writes, "black women frequently express their liking for Chinese as their 'Sweet Man,' and for the care they lavish on their concubines." Henriques, *Family and Color,* p. 98.

gained in prosperity, they sent their half-breed sons back to Hong Kong and China to be acculturated by their kinsmen.

The homeland kinsmen, however, did their job of enculturation well. Having left Jamaica at the tender age of five or six, the children returned to the island in early manhood totally Chinese, many of them even monolingually so. Later, the tendency was for these grownup male children to make a second and last journey to China to procure a wife, whom they would bring back to Jamaica with them.

What we have called the phase of ethnic consolidation, 1900–1940, began about the turn of the century, especially after the First World War. By then the Chinese had not only established themselves in Kingston but had fanned out to almost all the major and minor urban centers on the island. Only now, with complete economic security, did they turn in earnest to the task of forging a group identity.

The development of this identity was both caused and motivated by economic interests. Having taken over the retail sector of the economy, the Chinese began to move into the wholesale business after 1900 and had a firm hold on this area by 1920. The period between 1920 and 1940 also saw two levels of development of the Chinese wholesale business. In the major urban center of Kingston, concentrated around the Chinese quarter, were the primary wholesalers who bought directly from the import agents. These primary wholesalers supplied secondary Chinese wholesalers who had, by now, spread out over the countryside. Secondary wholesalers combined wholesale selling to local businesses with their own retail outlets.

Economic prosperity made ethnic consolidation possible in several ways. First, it meant that there was enough surplus wealth to support charitable causes among themselves. Thus in 1921, after being defunct for five years, the Chinese Benevolent Society was revived, and from that time served the community continuously for the next half-century. Second, prosperity allowed for the development of a Chinese press—*The Chinese Public News,* published in Chinese, began about this time. The press became an important instrument of community formation, not only in keeping the scattered community informed of news abroad but of other members in Jamaica. Economic prosperity also allowed for the development of another important institution which was to increase the cohesiveness of the group—the formation of the Chinese public school in 1924. Finally, economic prosperity permitted Chinese fathers to send even more of their sons on the expensive journey of enculturation to China and Hong Kong and, at the same time, to import more women, as well as other men, into the society. In this way the cultural distinctiveness of the group was enhanced, and its demographic position improved. Thus, the phase of ethnic consolidation was accompanied by the third stage in the racial composition of the Chinese population. In the earliest period, the group was pure Chinese but overwhelmingly male. During the first phase of adjustment there was a strong infusion of Negro "blood" into the group, creating a need to emphasize cultural factors rather than racial ones in group identification. This is now followed by a stage in which there is a re-infusion of Chinese genes through two sources: pure Chinese women from China, and the Chinese colored women who, while rejected as candidates for full enculturation, were preferred as mates, when they grew up, to produce more sons.

Even so, the emphasis remained on the cultural criterion for the group's definition. There were still not enough "pure" or colored Chinese women to meet the biological and social needs of the male Chinese community. Indeed, at no time in their history in the island could Chinese men expect to find mates wholly from among purely Chinese women. The technique of defining pure Chinese in largely social and cultural terms, then, became entrenched among the Jamaican Chinese, so that today one hardly ever hears the distinction "Chinese colored." Whether or not a person is Chinese depends on whether he or she chooses to define him- or herself as Chinese (always, of course, with the constraint that the individual must have some vague resemblance to Chinese), and whether they are accepted by the Chinese community as Chinese.

Economic factors not only made possible and encouraged the growth of Chinese ethnicity, but the consolidation was stimulated because it was good for business. What, after all, is retail and wholesale trading but a network of people among whom there is a flow of goods and credit in one direction, and a flow of profit in the other? Now that they were spread out over the country, it was to their economic advantage to consolidate into an ethnic group with excellent intragroup communications. Thus, the structure of the social network became one with the structure of the trading network. This is most tellingly reflected in the fact that the strongest community organizations were also trade associations, for example, the Wholesalers Association, the Chinese Retailers Association, and the Bakeries Association.

However much they may have tried to preserve the old culture, the fact remains that the Chinese were living in a host society to which they had to make some adjustments. They were totally dependent on this society for their livelihood. They were at its political mercy. They also depended on it for biological support. Though they were to remain, by and large, culturally exclusive and were to enrich their own cultural background through their prosperity during this period, one can detect the seeds of the segmentary Sino-Creole which was to develop later on. Dietary patterns had to change, if ever so slightly; some form of English had to be learned; adaptations had to be made to the black women (who had a highly developed sense of their own independence). Again, as the Chinese community grew larger, there was the problem of educating the young. Clearly, the technique of sending their children to China to be educated could not go on forever; it was prohibitively expensive. As the years separating the first generation grew in numbers, it was becoming increasingly awkward. Prosperity and expanding business also brought problems in educating the young. During the early period when businesses were on a small scale, being culturally Chinese and completely illiterate in the language of the host culture was no disadvantage. A larger business enterprise requires social skills in the host society.

Perhaps the area in which the Chinese, during this period of ethnic consolidation, made the greatest adjustment to the host society was in religion. Chinese religion did not appear to survive long among the Chinese in Jamaica, or for that matter, among the Chinese in other parts of the Caribbean. Instead, the Chinese during the early part of the present century began to convert to Roman

Catholicism.[43] As I will point out in comparing the Jamaican with the Guyanese Chinese, the choice of the Roman Catholic church, which was a small minority religion in Jamaica, was significant in that, while it involved a cultural compromise, it maintained the social exclusiveness of the group, an exclusiveness which the Roman Catholic church was quite willing to respect.

As the Chinese community grew larger and became more prosperous, and as a second and third generation emerged, basic problems began to develop with regard to the cultural exclusiveness of the group. They centered on the growing unwillingness of the younger generation to be deprived of a Western education and in this way suffer a disadvantage vis-à-vis their fellow Jamaicans. Furthermore, even within the Chinese community, the need for more Westernization was felt. This led to what can be referred to as the segmentary creolization period, which developed in 1940 to 1945.

Once again, then, the Chinese found that they had to make a fundamental choice critical to their own economic self-interest. It was a choice between continued ethnic solidarity on the basis of cultural exclusiveness or continued prosperity. A division soon emerged in the community centering on this issue, but exacerbated by other, more fortuitous developments. On the ethnically conservative side were the older generation of Chinese, as well as the remaining China-born (many, though not all, of whom were also of the older age group), and on the other side were the younger generation of Chinese, mainly Jamaican born, who opted for a more progressive, less exclusive approach to the host society.

What troubled the younger generation of Chinese Jamaicans in the early 1940s, however, was the fact that the colonial society in which they lived was in the first stages of fundamental change in the direction of independence. These early changes were brought about by the dissatisfaction of the mass of people, especially on the sugar plantations, with their lot, a dissatisfaction which was being articulated by the brown middle classes, who were beginning, for the first time, to assert their claim to national leadership. In pushing for independence and national leadership, the emerging mid-

43. F. X. Delany, S.J., *A History of the Catholic Church in Jamaica* (New York, Jesuit Missions Press, 1930), p. 271.

dle class began to forge a national solidarity around the theme of an explicitly stated national culture that incorporated all elements of the society. This is the official version of the synthetic Creole I described above.[44]

It was in this attempt to legitimize the synthetic Creole that the Chinese, for the first time, began to attract serious attention. They were resented, not because they were despised, or because there was any desire to keep them out, but, on the contrary, because it was felt that they were remaining aloof from the national effort and did not wish to be included. Many people felt indignation at the refusal of the Chinese to accept the invitation to join in the movement toward nationhood, and to share in the emerging synthetic Creole culture.[45] What is certain is that the younger generation took the statement seriously and their hands were strengthened by it.

One other development further weakened the position of the older generation—this was the Communist revolution in China and their final takeover of the Mainland. Immigration from China to Jamaica had been stopped completely by the 1940s; now, the possibility of returning to China, or of sustained contact, was removed. Besides, the Communist ideology of the new government in Mainland China created a real crisis of allegiance for many of the older group of culturally conservative Chinese.

To maintain their cultural exclusiveness, the conservative members of the Chinese communities had to support a government and an ideology (on the Mainland) which was totally inconsistent with their position and implicit economic philosophy in Jamaica. In rejecting this contradiction, the older generation of Chinese moved to reconcile their economic interests with their cultural orientation. The move also marked a grudging acceptance of the fact that Jamaica would remain their homeland.

These developments among the older generation were accom-

44. On the decolonization process and the role of the middle class in Jamaica, see T. Monroe, *The Politics of Constitutional Decolonization* (Kingston, Institute of Social and Economic Research, 1972), esp. chs. 2–3.

45. See the much quoted editorial comments in *Spotlight* (May 1949 and October 1952).

panied by a far more radical shift toward a greater adjustment to Jamaica by the younger generation of Jamaica-born Chinese. This group now insisted on having a Western education, and later, on sending their children to the local public schools. They also established greater contact with members of the host society. In making these adjustments, they were met halfway by the less conservative members of the older and China-born generation. What emerged from their joint efforts was an attempt at formulating a segmentary Sino-Creole society which was strongly Jamaican in emphasis and which borrowed many of its institutional forms from the host society but which was directed exclusively at the Chinese community. The effort, however, came too late, and did not go far enough.

The truth is that Jamaican society had passed the stage in its development where it could tolerate, or contain, without great social risk, the existence of a segmentary Creole society, especially on the part of those members of the society who almost completely monopolized one sector of the island's economy. Starting in the 1950s it began to move into the synthetic creolization period which continues to the present.

From a more theoretical perspective, what we are suggesting is that segmentary and synthetic creolization are basically antithetical. Synthetic creolization seeks to unite all the different segmentary cultures into a unified national culture; it is, indeed, the dialectical synthesis of the various antithetical segmentary Creole cultures. Segmentary creolization, by its very nature, resists such unification. It is possible for the two types of Creole culture to exist side by side only if the group which exercises total power is not committed to synthetic creolization and is itself the supporter of a segmentary Creole culture. This was the case during the colonial period, when the British exercised power over all other groups. Once the group which assumes power is committed to synthetic creolization, however, the synthetic cultural dialectic is likely to evolve as one way of resolving the potential tensions of decolonization in a multi-ethnic society. It is sometimes possible, of course, for the new post-colonial elite to commit itself to segmentary creolization, in this way legitimizing the existence of other such Creole cultures. This, for example, is what happened in Surinam and, to some extent, in Guyana. In Jamaica, however, the new elite was firmly committed to a national synthetic Creole culture.

This clearly placed the Chinese in a dilemma. They could see that the synthetic national Creole culture was in their own interest, but unlike the other capitalist groups, whose ethnicity rested primarily on race and kinship, it meant abandoning not only the cultural exclusiveness of the period of ethnic consolidation, but the social exclusiveness and cultural distinctiveness of the hastily organized segmentary Creole culture of the post-1940 period. In other words, it was precisely because it was cultural symbols, rather than race, which formed the basis of their ethnic identification, that the Chinese found it far more difficult than the white ethnics to make any generous concessions to the emerging synthetic Creole society.

But a choice had to be made. In the end, the position of the younger generation won out by the late 1950s. The decision was a radical one. It was also the decision that was in the group's best class interests.

This rapid and near complete dismantlement of their culture was accompanied by radical intersocial as well as intrasocial changes. On the intersocial side, the Chinese chose to move both physically and interactionally into the middle and upper middle classes. They found an elite who were happy to have them. Even this change had a direct economic motivation. The native bourgeoisie had made a rapid shift in their residential and shopping patterns in both Kingston and Montego Bay. In Kingston they moved from the south, east, and center of the city to the new suburban regions of upper St. Andrews to the north of the city.[46] Prosperity and Americanization led to a demand for suburban shopping centers rather than the traditional Chinese groceries, and open markets. The Chinese were quick to adapt to these changes in residential patterns and life styles. Economically, there was a shift in emphasis from wholesaling to supermarkets. This, of course, fur-

46. Colin Clarke, "Population Pressure in Kingston, Jamaica: A Study of Unemployment and Overcrowding," *Transactions and Papers,* The Institute of British Geographers, no. 38 (1966), 174–175.

ther cut the base from under the wholesale business, since super-markets, because of their scale of operation, deal directly with the importer. The Chinese not only responded by going into the su-permarket and shopping plaza business in a big way but, for the first time, began to challenge the Middle Easterners and Jews in their traditional monopoly of the import-export business.

In response to economic developments, the Chinese moved out of Chinatown and the Chinese quarters and into the new middle-class housing and other residential areas of the main towns. At the same time, there was a shift toward the professions and toward managerial, clerical, and sales positions in non-Chinese firms. The Chinese have adopted the bourgeois life style of synthetic Creole culture with the same avidity that characterized their takeover of the retail trade system.

The Chinese, within a period of fifteen years, have ceased to be a culture group, no longer define their ethnicity in cultural terms, and have become instead an integral part of the bourgeoisie, prac-ticing, in full measure, the synthetic Creole and middle-class life style of that group.

They did not, however, cease to be an ethnic group. Rather, what they did was to change the basis of their ethnicity. While they have become culturally Jamaican, the Chinese were careful to maintain those patterns of behavior and attitudes to work and fam-ily which, on the one hand, maintain group cohesion, and, on the other hand, are congruent with those qualities which ensure high achievement in the society.[47]

The nuclear and stem families replaced the extended family. This shift in family structure meant a further move away from a distinctly Oriental pattern to one that was essentially middle-class Jamaican, but with an emphasis on strong collateral ties that en-sures the maintenance of community and kinship bonds and, at the same time, is ideal for economic success. Where the extended fam-ily was an ideal social unit for the economic success of the China-town wholesale establishments or the isolated rural grocery, the

47. Silin, "A Survey of Selected Aspects of the Chinese in Jamaica," pp. 47–48.

nuclear family ensures the flexibility the individual requires for competition in a complex modern economy.[48]

Changes in attitude, especially attitudes toward parents, the work ethic, and leisure also reflect the same balance between synthetic creolization, communal integrity, and economic achievement.[49]

There is, then, still a Chinese ethnic group in Jamaica. Somatic and generalized kinship ties and a sense of shared experience constitute their most meaningful bases of primary extrafamilial identity. However, while there is a Chinese ethnic group in the island, it would be inaccurate to say that all the Chinese in Jamaica constitute an ethnic group. Some Chinese choose not to make their somatic distinctiveness or their kinship and affinal ties their most meaningful bases of extrafamilial identification. Those who choose ethnic identification invariably make the choice, or more accurately, choose to continue to make a choice which the parental generation made for them, because it is still in their own best economic interest. Being "Chinese" gives one access to a relatively substantial pool of capital; it ensures economic "breaks" which might otherwise not have existed; it provides a wide range of contacts, both social and business; it gives one access to valuable business "intelligence"—who is on the up-and-up, who is secretly bankrupt, who has the best real estate deals, and the like—and it provides a supportive network in the otherwise harshly competitive business world. To the extent that this ethnic group continues to be a useful economic network, to that extent, and to that extent only, will the ethnic group survive.

Many Chinese Jamaicans have found, however, that their economic interests do not require, or are not best served, by this network. It is these Chinese—mainly those in the professions and who work for non-Chinese firms—who show the greatest tendency to

48. The theoretical basis of this development has been well established. See W. J. Goode, "The Role of the Family in Industrialization," and R. F. Winch and R. L. Blumberg, "Societal Complexity and Familial Organization," both in R. F. Winch and L. W. Goodman, eds., *Selected Studies in Marriage and the Family* (New York, Holt, Rinehart and Winston, 1968), pp. 64–92.

49. See Silin, "A Survey of Selected Aspects of the Chinese in Jamaica," pp. 45, 59; and Morrow, "Chinese Adaptation," pp. 50–54.

leave the ethnic group and often, though not always, seal their withdrawal from the group by marrying non-Chinese.

What of those who remain fully committed to the Chinese ethnic group? Interestingly, the Chinese have, for the first time in their history in Jamaica, begun to shift to somatic traits as the main basis for overt group identification. This shift in emphasis has been due to the erosion of what was formerly their main focus of group identity. Race is the only distinctive overt trait the group has, and by which they are recognized by other members of the society. But, of course, having said this, we must immediately add that this is the right answer to the wrong question. The real questions are: why do some Jamaican Chinese continue to maintain their ethnic ties? and how does the choice of somatic features relate to the choice of ethnicity over assimilation?

What seems to have happened and is still taking place in the Chinese ethnic group is this: choice of mate has become of vital importance for the maintenance of the continued congruence of the sets of social and economic networks which constitutes the sociological raison d'être of the ethnic group. When black women were being used to mother their children, it will be recalled that male offspring were kept in the group for cultural training and women not so chosen. Later on, as more and more Chinese colored women, as well as pure Chinese women, became available, there was a shift back to the pure Chinese racial type on the individual level, even though, on the group level, this was accompanied by a wider distribution of Negro blood. In other words, fewer and fewer Chinese were "pure" Chinese racially, while more and more individuals who were defined as Chinese were getting closer to the pure Chinese racial type.

Now when the Chinese abandoned culture as the major basis of ethnic identification, race gained in significance as a basis of group identification. This choice of emphasis was made, not because it was natural to choose race, but because an important economic factor favored the choice of race at precisely the time when culture was losing its significance. For what had happened over the years during this change in emphasis was that those Chinese who were most successful economically had been the very ones who had been most endogamous. Women have become the means whereby wealth is exchanged, shared, consolidated, and kept within the group, all this while performing the equally valuable task of perpetuating the group. As such, they have become highly valued and jealously guarded.

To summarize, then, we find that from a position where the group was defined culturally and race was a marginal factor, the Chinese have shifted from cultural and social exclusiveness to complete cultural integration into the synthetic Creole Jamaican culture and to a bourgeois life style. This shift, however, was accompanied by a consolidation of wealth accomplished through endogamy, resulting in the emergence of a tightly knit socioeconomic network which is increasingly racially homogeneous (though with fewer and fewer racially pure individuals) and which now uses racial similarity both to symbolize their distinctiveness and to sanction their all-important principle of endogamy. Jamaicans of Chinese ancestry who do not choose ethnic identification are immediately absorbed into the non-Chinese community, since there are no cultural obstacles and no reluctance on the part of non-Chinese members to marry non-ethnic Chinese.

The Chinese ethnic group, then, is likely to grow smaller with the withdrawal of those who choose to marry outside of the group and choose the nation as their most meaningful basis of extrafamilial identity. As it grows smaller, it will become more and more ethnically visible, more tightly knit, and will achieve more of the attributes of the corporate, racially defined ethnic group—a rather ominous development at a time when the overwhelming majority of the black population are themselves becoming racially conscious and are showing signs of rejecting the synthetic Creole compromise of the bourgeois elite for some, as yet unspecified, form of national "black power."

The Chinese in Guyana. In striking contrast to the pattern of development in Jamaica is the experience of the Chinese in Guyana. The Chinese were brought to Guyana to meet the same pressing labor needs that prevailed in Jamaica in the mid-nineteenth century, and, in fact, were brought under the same scheme. Those who went to Guyana also came from much the same areas of China as the Jamaican Chinese and, in some cases, were even recruited by the very same agent.[50] By 1866 Guyana had the greatest number of Chinese in its history—approximately 10,000. A year later, rapid decline in the population began.

The Chinese were brought into the colony as indentured agricultural laborers, but this scheme was abandoned in 1874 for much the same reasons that it was in Jamaica. More Chinese were to trickle into Guyana after the indenture period, but these were relatives and friends brought over by Chinese already in the colony, not by the planters. In all, approximately 700 more were to come from China after 1878. This post-indenture immigration did not reverse the seemingly irrevocable downward trend of the Chinese population. In 1879 there was a total of only 6,000 Chinese in the colony, which meant that more than half of them had either died or left the colony during the 25 years since they first arrived. The population reached its lowest point in 1911, when only 2,118 Chinese were living in the colony. Thereafter there was a slow increase until 1947 when the population was 3,528. Between then and the census year of 1960, the Chinese population had grown to a total of only 3,600, making up 0.6 percent of the total Guyana population of 600,000.

Up to the end of the nineteenth century, we have seen that there was little real difference between the pattern of adjustment of the Chinese in Guyana and their counterparts in Jamaica. Both groups refused to work on the estates, and their efforts at peasant farming were equally sporadic and unsuccessful. Both groups, too, quickly headed for the urban areas and soon became one of the most urbanized groups in their respective populations. By 1911, one third of the Chinese population in Guyana lived in the two urban centers

50. Silin, "A Survey of Selected Aspects of the Chinese in Jamaica," p. 7. Our discussion of the Chinese in Guiana will be based primarily on two published papers by Morton H. Fried, the only modern scholar to have researched the group, and an early twentieth-century work by Clementi. See M. H. Fried, "Some Observations on the Chinese of British Guiana," *Social and Economic Studies*, 5.1 (March 1956); "The Chinese in the British Caribbean," in M. H. Fried, ed., *Colloquium on Overseas Chinese* (December 29, 1957); and C. Clementi, *The Chinese in Guiana* (Georgetown, British Guiana, The Argosy Company, 1915).

of Georgetown and New Amsterdam, and at the present time over 60 percent of them live in these two urban areas.[51]

After the turn of the century, however, one begins to detect fundamental differences in the choices which the Chinese in Jamaica made from those of the Chinese in Guyana. The first difference had to do with their choice of livelihood. Where in Jamaica the Chinese were almost exclusively concerned with retail trading after rejecting agriculture, those in Guyana selected retailing as one of several means of economic survival, although it was the main one. From the start, the Guyanese Chinese showed a willingness to select a wide range of occupations.[52]

And while it remained true that up to 1943 as many as 63 percent were in the retail trade, it is of greater importance that only a small number of them made it in a big way in this industry and, as a group, they in no way monopolized either the retail or the wholesale trade as they did in Jamaica. Another ethnic group had this distinction.

A second important difference, deriving from the first, was that the Guyanese Chinese never went through a phase of ethnic consolidation; nor did they even attempt, to any great degree, to adjust through the technique of segmentary creolization. Instead, the Chinese in Guyana moved from their period of initial settlement and indenture straight into the evolving synthetic Creole culture of Guyana.

The transformation was truly remarkable. It began, in a way, the moment the Chinese landed in Guyana. From that time they broke their ties completely with the Chinese homeland. By the time Clementi studied the group in the first decade of the twentieth century, he found it possible to write that: "British Guyana possesses a Chinese society of which China knows nothing, and to which China is almost unknown." [53] Fried offers an explanation of his own, namely, that a substantial number of early migrants came during

51. L. Despres, *Cultural Pluralism and Nationalist Politics in Guiana* (New York, Rand McNally, 1967), p. 65.

52. Ibid., p. 64.

53. Clementi, *The Chinese in Guiana*, p. 359.

the Taiping Rebellion and that kinship and locality ties were already broken, as a result of this upheaval, before leaving the Mainland.[54] The explanation makes some sense, but it applies only to a part of the Guyanese Chinese community.

The real answer to the problem of the radically different adjustment of the Chinese in Jamaica and Guyana lies in Fried's almost off-hand remark: "The difficulties in making a living in British Guyana at the time." These were indeed difficult times for Guyana. It is in looking at the differences in the pattern of socioeconomic development in the two countries that we begin to understand why the Chinese chose ethnic consolidation based on cultural exclusiveness in Jamaica, and the Chinese in Guyana chose to make a total cultural break with the homeland.

After emancipation the sugar industry faced hard times in both Guyana and Jamaica, more so in the latter than in the former. In both areas the ex-slaves attempted to form a peasant sector but were more successful in Jamaica than in Guyana. In addition to this, Guyana was highly successful in recruiting indentured laborers from India after the attempt with the Chinese and the Portuguese from Madeira had failed. Thus, Guyana continued to be a monocrop, plantation-based economy with a relatively simple social and economic system, in which the mass of the population remained largely at the mercy of the planter class.

Jamaica, on the other hand, took a more complex course of development. In 1865 the Jamaican peasants, who had a strong tradition of rebellion behind them, staged an uprising against their depressed conditions which so scared the white ruling minority that it committed what Mavis Campbell called "political immolation"; that is, it voted its political constitution out of existence and asked the British government to impose direct rule.[55] There fol-

54. Fried, "Some Observations on the Chinese," p. 69.
55. Campbell, "Edward Jordan and the Free Coloureds," passim. On the changes in Jamaica before and after the upheaval of 1865, see P. Curtin, *Two Jamaicas;* G. Eisner, *Jamaica: 1830–1930* (Manchester, England, Manchester University Press, 1961); D. Hall, *Free Jamaica;* H. P. Jacobs, *Sixty Years of Change, 1806–1866* (Kingston, Institute of Jamaica, 1973); A. Hart, *The Life of George William Jordan* (Kingston, Institute of Jamaica, n.d.); V. J. Marsala, *Sir John Peter Grant* (Kingston, Institute of Jamaica, 1972).

lowed a period of relatively enlightened Crown colony government, in which basic infrastructural development took place, and the economy further diversified with the introduction of banana cultivation, mainly by the ever creative peasantry, who by now had also begun to control a sizable portion of the sugar cultivation on the island.

None of these developments took place in Guyana. The colony's economy paid a heavy price for its continued emphasis on the monocrop plantation system, especially after the British moved to free trade in sugar in 1874.[56] This prolonged crisis in the world price of sugar was reflected most tellingly in the depressing condition of the masses in Guyana.

It was to this kind of economy that the Chinese were introduced and in which they had to find a livelihood. Many of them tried retail trading and continue to do so. But here they found a major obstacle as far as any hope of quick prosperity, or even economic security in the Jamaican manner, was concerned. This took the form of another ethnic group—the Portuguese, who were recruited from Madeira in the late 1840s and '50s.[57]

In taking over the retail trade, the Portuguese were actively encouraged by the European ruling class, who gave them preferential treatment for credit over their African and Chinese competitors, partly because they were Europeans, partly because they provided a useful class and cultural buffer between the planter class and the black masses. Although thus favored, the Portuguese were kept at a distance by the British Creole planters who never saw them as being quite "white," whether racially or culturally defined; nor did the blacks ever so regard them. The fact remains, however, that they were sufficiently favored and skilled to monopolize the colony's commercial life.[58] The many Chinese who worked in the retail trade, then, had to be satisfied with the pickings left by the Portuguese traders.

56. For an excellent account of the sugar crisis in the late nineteenth century, see R. W. Beachey, *The British West Indies Sugar Industry in the Late Nineteenth Century* (Oxford, Oxford University Press, 1957).

57. K. O. Lawrence, "The Establishment of the Portuguese Community in British Guiana," *Jamaica Historical Review* 5.2 (1965), 50–74.

58. Lowenthal, *West Indian Societies*, p. 200.

What all this meant, then, was that in 1900, at a time when the Chinese in Jamaica were already economically secure and could begin to use their economic prosperity to consolidate an ethnic group through the development of institutions which supported the perpetuation of their culture, the Guyanese Chinese found it in their best economic and social interest to choose quite the opposite path.

If they were to succeed in a wide range of occupations, however, they had to creolize themselves. And here we should pause to make an important observation about the relationship between the nature and type of occupation, on the one hand, and the propensity of a culturally alien immigrant group to isolate themselves. Of all occupations, retail trading offers the best opportunity for such a group to maximize earnings while minimizing acculturation.

Where other choices have to be made, however, the cultural obstacles must be overcome. For a Guyanese Chinese to choose a career in the colonial civil service, or in the professions, or even in occupations involving a lower level of skills but a high level of ascriptive or diffuse interaction, such as barbers, chauffeurs, and so on, it was imperative that the culture of the host society be mastered. The only alternatives were manual labor and peasant farming, both of which, while they avoided the cultural problem, provided little possibility of improvement. Both alternatives were tried by the Chinese in Guyana, who tried life as indentured laborers and as pioneer farmers; both were rejected because of their limited possibilities. In rejecting these and choosing other occupations, the Chinese also chose to abandon the traditional culture and to adopt the evolving Guyanese Creole culture.

The evidence suggests that the Chinese in Guyana not only quickly and efficiently adopted the Guyanese creole culture but did it in a quite methodical and self-conscious manner. Their response to Christianity illustrates this. As early as 1875, even before they had mastered English, a Chinese language branch of the Church of England was founded by them at their insistence. Soon the Chinese had become "devout Christians." [59] This was almost forty years

59. Clementi, "The Chinese in Guiana," pp. 359–360.

before the Chinese in Jamaica had made their decision to adopt Christianity.

But note, here, another significant difference between them and the Jamaican Chinese. The latter, when they decided to adopt Christianity in the early twentieth century, went completely into the Catholic church. The Guyanese Chinese deliberately avoided the Catholic church in Guyana, although by that time it was well established there to serve the spiritual needs of the Portuguese and other Catholics, and instead became Protestants, which was the religion to choose, obviously, if creolization was the major objective. So thoroughly creolized have the Chinese become that later they began joining not just the established Anglican church, but the Pentacostal sects of the blacks, and by the 1950s were themselves "holding revival meetings in the colony . . . aimed at a general public and not specifically at other Chinese." [60]

The locally born Chinese, known as T'u-sheng, have given up even their tendency to withdraw from the total society. In the bitter ethnic fighting between blacks and Indians which preceded independence, the Chinese emerged in a new role—that of mediators between the warring ethnic groups. Significantly, a Chinese was named the first president of the newly independent nation. This was a most extraordinary appointment for a minority group that numbers less than 1 percent of the population, and it reflects as favorably on the successful creolization and broker role of the Chinese as it does unfavorably on the failure of the dominant groups to work out a genuinely multi-ethnic society in Guyana.[61] It is also an indication of the radically different responses of the two groups of Chinese that the idea of a Chinese governor-general in Jamaica is unthinkable. No Jamaican prime minister would be reckless enough to make such an appointment, and, were it made, it is unlikely that any Chinese would be foolhardy enough to accept the post.

60. Fried, "The Chinese in the British Caribbean," p. 56.

61. The Chinese are cast in the same role of conciliators between the conflicting Indian and Black groups in Trinidad, and there, too, a Chinese was appointed the first governor-general. See D. Lowenthal's remarks on the potential risks to the Chinese of overplaying this role in the East Caribbean, in his *West Indian Societies*, pp. 207–208.

In spite of the overt emphasis on endogamy, Fried also found that in practice, "There is considerable mating across ethnic lines, both with and without formal marriage." [62] Significantly, the major loss through intermarriage is through female Chinese marrying non-Chinese, quite the opposite of the present situation in Jamaica. As any student of endogamous groups knows, female outmarriage is the surest sign not only of the weakness of the endogamy principle, but the demographic decline of the group.

The second, much smaller, group consists of the China-born Chinese. These are the Chinese who migrated to the island after the indenture period. They maintain close contact with relatives back in China, quite often have wives there, and sometimes even send for brides from the Mainland or Hong Kong. Their adjustment is quite similar to that of the Jamaican Chinese during their period of ethnic consolidation—they are culturally exclusive and socially isolated. Significantly, these later migrants are among the most urban and the most concentrated in the retail trading business. They are also the most successful in the retail trade. Thus, the same factors account for the ethnic consolidation of this small group of later migrants who came at a time when economic and social conditions were such that the choice of ethnic consolidation was both possible and economically viable. It is doubtful, however, whether this group will survive. Their children are extremely ambivalent about China and their parents, and the pressure to become absorbed by the T'u-sheng group is strong—indeed, irresistible. Generally, the children of the small China-born population seem to accept this fate with resignation.[63]

CONCLUSION

I have described the development of two groups of Chinese arriving in the Caribbean, about the same time, from roughly the same region of China. Because of the structural similarities of Afro-Caribbean societies, the significant features of the two social

62. Fried, "Some Observations on the Chinese," p. 67.
63. Ibid., p. 58.

contexts which bear directly on the position of the immigrant Chinese can be isolated.

It was shown that, in the case of Jamaica, economic conditions were such that the best interests of the group were served by an exclusive concern with retail trade, and that success in this venture allowed for, and reinforced, a choice of ethnic consolidation based on cultural distinctiveness. Later, we saw how economic pressures and interests promoted a shift, first, to segmentary creolization, and soon after, a further change to a situation in which synthetic creolization was chosen but with a fundamental difference taking place between those who further chose to abandon ethnicity altogether, as opposed to those who chose to strengthen it by changing the basis of their ethnic identification from cultural to somatic and kinship ties.

On the other hand, we have seen how, in the Guyanese context, economic and social conditions were such that a wider range of occupational choices was in the best interests of the Chinese, and how, in pursuing these occupations, the choice of synthetic creolization and the abandonment of Chinese culture were the most rational courses of action. As such, ethnic consolidation was never attempted by the Guyanese T'u-sheng Chinese, who are now completely Guyanese except in their physical appearance; and even this is likely to disappear soon, given the high rate of intermarriage. At the same time, later arrivals, finding conditions closer to those existing in Jamaica, made much the same choices as the Jamaicans did in terms of ethnic identification based on cultural exclusiveness.

I wish to end on two notes: one is that my case studies, I think, have fully demonstrated the theoretical feasibility of my hypotheses. More than anything else, I hope I have demonstrated that there is no a priori reason to believe that individuals always choose ethnic identification over other forms of identification whenever the situation arises. At the same time, the primacy of economic factors over all others has been demonstrated. As far as the relationship between economic factors and ethnicity is concerned, I hope that I have at least tentatively demonstrated that people never make economic decisions on the basis of ethnic allegiance, but, on the contrary, that the strength, scope, viability, and bases of ethnic identity are determined by, and are used to serve, the economic and general class interests of individuals.

The second and final observation is this: the choices I have discussed throughout this chapter were genuine choices. What I hope I have shown, also, is that men choose their economic conditions as well, and once having chosen them, they tend in the long run to make adjustments to them which are in their own best interests. The Chinese who went to Jamaica and Guyana chose to go there, in this way choosing their contexts, their economic conditions. Once there, they tried estate labor and peasant farming and chose to abandon them. There is no inherent reason whatsoever why they could not have continued in these ventures. Certainly there was no cultural or racial predisposition not to; it is easy to show how, in neighboring Curaçao, peasant farming is exactly what the Chinese choose to remain in, and they have been quite successful at it.[64]

We have seen, too, how the Chinese changed the basis of their ethnic identity from one period to another in Jamaica, in contrast with Guyana, where the choice was never between the bases of ethnic consolidation, but whether there should or should not be an ethnic group. There is also the fact that, in both situations, individuals were free to depart from the choices which were being made by the majority of their peers. In the case of Jamaica, today, substantial numbers of Chinese are choosing between ethnic identification and national identification and are deciding on the latter. This, however, is taking place at a time when many Chinese have not only chosen ethnicity but have intensified ethnic bonds on more narrow racial lines.

The only thing guiding these choices were people's conceptions of what was in their own best economic and social interests, which is not to imply a concurrence with any vulgar economic determinism. We can fully agree with Engels' statement that "the ultimately determining element in history is the production and repro-

64. P. H. Hiss, *Netherlands America* (New York, Duell, Sloan & Pearce, 1943), p. 4.

duction of real life" and still accept the integrity, if not autonomy, of human choice. Indeed, as Engels himself goes on to add: "We make our history ourselves, but, in the first place, under very definite assumptions and conditions. Among these, the economic ones are ultimately decisive." [65]

65. Frederick Engels, "Letter to J. Bloch in Koningsberg," London 21(–22) 1890, in K. Marx and F. Engels, *Selected Works* (Moscow, Progress Publishers, 1970), III, 487.

11

FRANÇOIS BOURRICAUD
(Translated by Barbara Bray)

Indian, Mestizo and Cholo as Symbols in the Peruvian System of Stratification

The Andean countries of Peru, Ecuador, and Bolivia are all successor states to the Inca Empire. The bulk of their populations is descended from the inhabitants of that empire. They were all subjected for three centuries to the same Spanish colonial authority and since independence have followed a similar political, cultural, and social evolution. In general they have been subject to the same foreign influence, ideological, economic, and political.

In all three countries, where "racial" differences are so important, an attempt to analyze the social structure must involve an understanding of the composition of the population and of the subtle and complex relationships that have developed historically among the indigenous Indian element, the Spanish, or creole, element, and the *mestizo,* or mixed, element. Although I deal here specifically with the stratification system of Peru, in varying measure what I say would apply also to Ecuador and Bolivia.

In describing the composition of the Peruvian population, it should be understood that the census categories to which I refer do not correspond with those used in common discourse nor with those developed by sociologists. They are basically "racial" categories, although considering them as simply racial is problematic. Peru's system of social stratification was for a long time ascriptive, with status based mainly on race. In reality, however, racial criteria may be ambiguous. Peruvians often have difficulty in identifying an individual as Indian, mestizo, or *cholo* (a scornful term applied to rising mestizos). Furthermore race is neither the sole, nor necessarily the most rigorous ascriptive term. The Hindu caste system, which is based not on biological origin but on the social group into which an individual is born, results in more complete segregation than that practiced in the most racist states in the South of the United States.[1] Finally, racial discrimination leaves open, as we shall see in the case of the Peruvian Indians, the possibility of a certain upward mobility. In fact racial attributes in Peru combine physical and social characteristics in a symbolism the key to which lies at the same time in traditions of the past and in the position occupied by the group in the existing stratification system.

The Peruvian system of stratification, whether in the colonial, republican, or contemporary periods, has never made use of a strictly binary opposition between Indian and non-Indian. But neither has it been characterized by a pluralism of juxtaposed groups—that is, at once isolated from each other yet all forming part of the same economic space and subject to the same legal system, as, for example, is the case with the Jews, Italians, and Puerto Ricans of New York, despite the various kinds of discrimination they have suffered. The distinctiveness of the Peruvian stratification system resides in the ambiguity of the "racial" factor, which performs a very complex symbolic function. Membership in the native or in the creole group does not in itself determine the status of an individual, but it is largely responsible for the image the individual possesses and puts forward of himself. So the "racial factor" does not refer only to some physical attributes of an individual, but also to his social status.[2] It connects one to social status, but accord-

1. See Louis Dumont, *Homo Hierarchicus* (Paris, Gallimard, 1967).

2. The terminological ingenuity with which all the shades in the color of the skin are mentioned is adequately stressed by Magnus Mörner in *Le Métissage dans l'histoire de l'Amérique Latine* (Paris, Fayard, Librairie Arthème, 1971). When I speak of the symbolic significance of racial differences, I intend to link up status differences to some fairly ambiguous physical traits, like color of the skin, appearance of the hair, face, and so on. It is clear that not all the shades and nuances of the skin are equally significant of an individual's status. Therefore not all the categories mentioned by Magnus Mörner are relevant for our purpose. The reasons why I limit myself to only three, indio, mestizo, cholo, will be fully justified, I hope, by the following analysis.

ing to the rules of a symbolic code. To understand the position of the cholo, one must begin by realizing that the Indian, who together with the white man or creole seems to form the basic reference points of the stratification system, is himself not easy to define. It is said that an Indian may be recognized by means of a certain number of physical characteristics, but in fact the frequency of cross-breeding makes identification difficult. One might rely on the criterion of language; everyone who spoke only a native language would be regarded as an Indian. But what of those who speak a native language but also speak or understand a certain amount of Spanish? By adopting the physical criterion one reduces the size of the Indian group, while if one includes among Indians people who also have a certain amount of Spanish, the size of the group is made unduly large.

Thus one is led to introduce criteria relating to way of life—"the Indian is a peasant"—or to hierarchical status—"the Indian group occupies the lowest position in the social stratification system." This latter proposition is generally true, but only generally; certainly the converse is not true: one cannot say that all the people "at the bottom" are Indians, since many of the inhabitants of the shanty-towns are regarded as and regard themselves as cholos.

The status of Indian combines different and independent elements: race, language, way of life, hierarchical position in the process of production. If you meet a peasant who doesn't speak Spanish, chews cola, and lives in a *comunidad* or is a peon in a hacienda, you need have no fear about naming him an Indian. But it must be said that this clear-cut situation is fairly rare. Nor is there any guarantee that the brother of the person in question doesn't live in Lima, or that he himself has not spent some part of his life there, or that his son has not left the village. The Indian does not by any means constitute a "self-reproducing" group with characteristics identically repeated from generation to generation. He is subject to continuous change, and the question has been asked—and in many respects it is one of the key questions of Peruvian cultural history—whether the indigenous group is not, in the last resort, a residual category, doomed sooner or later to wither away.

According to a theory put forward both during the colonial

period and by the positivists of the nineteenth century, the "truth" of the Indian, his essential realization, the fulfillment of his individual and collective destiny, is the mestizo. But note that we say mestizo and not *criollo*. A creole is the descendant of the small minority of Spaniards born in Peru. Although this group has always been a minority and its political power has been considerably reduced since independence, it has managed to remain culturally dominant for a long time. Today the term creole no longer applies to a distinct group, but rather brings to mind a collection of individuals who possess several common cultural traits. These individuals may occupy very different levels in the social hierarchy. The term can be approving or derogatory. It describes tangible products (such as from the kitchen), activities (the dance, horsemanship, bull or cock fighting), and moral qualities (such as grace, elegance, skill, duplicity, or laziness). The common feature of this broad usage is the more or less explicit reference to a certain Spanish tradition, more Andalusian than Castillian, by which individuals recognize each other or aspire to be recognized as participating in a superior culture. For many it is above all a way of creating distance from the indigenous tradition, or more generally the provincialism of the local tradition. But the creole culture has become progressively ossified, emphasizing taste, manners, life-style. It provides little to the mobile and ambitious, especially those who are by social origin far from the genuine "Peruvian tradition"—as defined, of course, by the creoles. Today it can only provide an incomplete and imperfect identification symbolism for most Peruvians.

The mestizo as a cultural model is more acceptable in that it offers a kind of reconciliation between the two streams of the national cultural tradition. Unfortunately it is an artificial reconciliation, an intellectual compromise which never really "took." But it is in relation to the mestizo that he *can* become, that the Indian identity in the melting pot of the colonial society was formed. The colonial Indian acquired two characteristics which profoundly changed his nature: he became a Christian, and he became a subject of his Catholic Majesty, the King of Spain. The Indian of the Republic became, or rather has been promised he will become, a citizen. A mestizo is one who is neither Indian nor creole, but this description is incomplete. According to area—whether the coast or the Sierra, a big city, an average-sized provincial town, a large village (*pueblo*) or a native commune—or in other words according to contextual criteria, someone who is regarded (and regards himself) as a creole, that is, as perfectly assimilated to the values and norms of western and Hispanic tradition, may be rejected and scornfully designated a cholo.

The term cholo comprises almost all the ambiguities that can surround individual status. To start with, it has a strong negative connotation, and is usually employed in the absence of the person to whom it is applied and who would probably be offended by it. It can only be used in direct address as a sort of joke. But the message, while it tells the observer something about the relations between the two speakers, contains no information about the status of the person so designated. In order to narrow down the ambiguity surrounding the term cholo, one must compare the cholo with the traditional mestizo, the type developed by colonial society, from which he is very different. Mestizos had a whole range of occupations in colonial society, some of them comparatively distinguished, the *artes y oficios,* like those of carpenter, cabinet maker, tailor, leather worker, or saddler. Certain among them were even artists rather than craftsmen—sculptors and painters, perhaps gilding statues under the direction of a Spanish monk, or producing fine pictures to the glory of the Virgin and the saints. They also had access to jobs in the church and administration.

In some sleepy towns, like Ayacucho, in the Peruvian Sierra, the artes y oficios of the traditional mestizo have survived into our own day. José Maria Arguedas describes one of these artist-craftsmen, who carved and decorated altarpieces: "Don Joaquim Lopez Antay belongs to a family of Spanish origin, but on his mother's side, as the name Antay indicates, he is Indian—not common or vulgar Indian, but Indian smallholder. He learned his trade from his grandmother. He speaks Spanish extremely well, though with a strong accent." When a traveler from Lima—a criollo—made fun of his accent, wanting to appear a man of the world, Don Joaquim answered, Arguedas tells us, in a dignified manner: "We all have our own way of speaking, sir." [3] In fact, in his own worthy town of Ayacucho, Don Joaquim Lopez is somebody—*no es un cualquiera.* He is known and respected. When they address him, even the *vecinos* or notables, who are more or less white, and *los mistis,* the landed proprietors living on their income, often in dilapidated old town houses that preserve a porch or patio from their colonial splendor, call him *maestro* and Don Joaquim, a marked sign of deference.

Don Joaquim Lopez Antay, mestizo though he is, is by no means a cholo. Only an ignorant *Limeno,* blind to the status hierarchy of a traditional Sierra town, could make such a mistake. But no one would hesitate to use the word cholo to designate an illicit street vendor, a cattle dealer, a wool or meat salesman, a truck or taxi driver. What characterizes the cholo and distinguishes him from the traditional mestizo is that he occupies no fixed position or niche in the stratification system. He is fluid and elusive; you never find him where you expect him to be; and you never know where to place him in the stratification system. But the cholo is smart, he pushes, he can make money. He has learned a rudimentary way of managing which lays him open to the seductions of conspicuous consumption but gives him a considerable advantage over the Indians and traditional peasants. For this reason one finds him higher up, better placed, richer and more enterprising than his original status might seem to warrant. This ability to get on explains the negative reactions, the suspicion and aversion, directed against the cholo. His behavior calls in question the rigid order of old colonial society. The simple fact that, while he is neither Indian nor creole nor mestizo, he succeeds in rising demonstrates the possibilities which are open to anyone with his wits about him and which derive from what may be called the interstitial mobility of a society that is culturally very heterogeneous.

Here two sets of hypotheses become necessary, one concerning the problem of mobility in Peruvian society, the other concerning the importance of the essentially cultural factor in the mobility pro-

3. José Maria Arguedas, "El arte popular religioso y la cultura mestiza," *Revista del Museo,* 27 (Lima, 1958), 140–194.

cess. I shall try to show that Peruvian society, even during the colonial period, was, at least in certain sectors, fairly mobile. There were geographical migrations of considerable size in the first years of the conquest. But apart from the disintegration that accompanied the collapse of Inca society, the new colonial order recruited a considerable fraction of the indigenous population. In order to be eligible for employment certain characteristics were needed of many different kinds, but among them was the ability to assimilate such cultural practices as the use of Spanish or European food and clothes. The learning and mastering of these skills were as important in determining the status of an individual as was his position in the process of production. To be able to speak Spanish, dress like a misti, and eat and drink like a creole—these changed a peasant's status: he ceased to be an Indian, and could emerge from the common run to become a merchant, store clerk, peddler, or artisan. Initial cultural advantages thus largely determined the prospects of mobility, whether individual or collective. But possessing them was no more a matter of chance than, say, academic success in our own societies.

Class relations in the Marxist sense seem to me to throw little light on the Peruvian stratification system, despite the fact that in the course of the process of industrialization they have more relevance. The opposition between capitalists and workers, if the words are taken at all precisely, clearly had little importance in colonial society. It began to be felt at the end of the nineteenth century in the enclaves formed by mines and tropical sugar plantations especially. It also developed a little later in the large towns as they became at least partially industrialized and the class struggle manifested itself in the development of such organizations as unions and radical political movements.

Of course, the conflict between proletarians and capitalists is not the only form of class struggle, and if one substitutes the appropriate functional equivalents for these terms, which strictly only apply to industrial societies, one may meet with just as marked a dualism between the "exploited" Indian peasant and the "exploiting" big colonial landowner. But both the methods and the results of "exploitation" are different in a predominantly agrarian society from those in an industrial society. Wages and profit are very different from income from land. As to accumulation, its pace and dynamics are very different in an industrial economy and in an economy like that of colonial Peru. There "classes" are no more classes in the English nineteenth-century sense than, to paraphrase Spinoza, the constellation of the Dog is the same as the animal of the same name. Marxist writers have seen this and have therefore tried increasingly to place the discussion on the plane of international relations, the "center" or "metropolis" (Spain until independence, then England, and finally the United States) being supposedly dominant because of its technical, political or economic superiority, and the periphery made up of the Latin-American countries which provide raw materials and a trading preserve for the "imperialists" and are regarded as completely subjected to the "center."

But the "dependence" of a country like Peru on "world dominating centers," however indisputable that dependence may be, does not suffice to account for its own stratification system, which is a mixture of very heterogeneous elements strangely combining great rigidity with great fluidity. That is why the cholo emerges as a key character. In fact, he represents the element of mobility in a system which neither encourages nor stresses mobility. This is the central structural problem in the Peruvian stratification system. To clarify some aspects of this situation I shall follow certain historians in trying to describe how the problem of mobility presents itself to the indigenous population. I shall also try to explain why, even though the assigning of roles that are new because of modernization has not so far enabled the Indian group to attain autonomy and identity, the Indian nevertheless is tending to become an essential symbol in the legitimation system of Peruvian society.

It is important that what are now called ethnic problems should not be confused with racial problems. It seems to me that questions of ethnicity emerge only in a society in which the value system has already become oriented toward achievement, and where barriers between groups, if not broken down or overturned, have at least been eroded by a multiplicity of economic and noneconomic transactions. Thus the problem of ethnicity is a problem of so-called "post-racist societies." It is only after a certain number of rights have been won, when different "races" are placed under the same judicial system, that their identity and equality can be affirmed, that members of a minority group can be what they are and assume the fullness of their differences without endangering the cohesion of the larger group to which they belong and feel a part of.[4]

Analyzing a stratification system is such a difficult undertaking that I shall select only some of its aspects. An analysis of stratification aims at reconstructing the hierarchy a society establishes for the activities of its members and the groups specializing in these activities. An essential point in any stratification system links the hierarchy as it is, or as it is conceived of by the different groups, with the hierarchy as it would be if it conformed to the ideal prescribed by commonly held values. This tension is particularly noticeable at the level of the symbolic system: it can be detected in the images a society puts forward of itself or the motives it inculcates in its members. What I shall try to show is that neither the mestizo nor the Indian provide adequate images for the Peruvian today, at least insofar as he is trying to define his relationship not with a particular group, for example, a comunidad, but with the whole of Peruvian society in all its activities and on all its levels.

According to an image which long held sway, colonial society (and the situation changed only very slowly in the nineteenth century, long after independence) was stratified at four levels: the hacienda, the comunidad, the royal administration controlled by creoles and Spaniards, and the occupations reserved for mestizos (artes y oficios mainly). The hacienda, frequently depicted as the transplantation to America of a model of agrarian organization which developed in Spain at the end of the Middle Ages and during the period of the reconquest of the Moors, was commonly presented as a device for making the native laborer work and binding him to the land—in other words, for exploiting him. The Indians were thus transformed into serfs. Generation after generation they slaved away, using the most feeble techniques, at the poor soil of the patches of land granted them by the *hacendado* in exchange for

4. Talcott Parsons, "Full Citizenship for the Negro American?" in *Sociological Theory and Modern Society* (New York, The Free Press, 1967), pp. 422–466.

labor for which he paid no money. Scarcely able to survive at best, often in debt, they would have been unable to save, to become owners of land, to set up on their own account even if they had not been barred from doing so by legal restrictions. Those who left the hacienda only did so under duress, evicted by the master, who might wish to reduce the amount of land granted to the Indians so that he could exploit it directly himself—more "economically," by planting "profitable" crops. Or it might happen that certain hot-heads, with a grudge against the law or the administration of the hacienda, found themselves condemned to be vagabonds or brigands (*bandoleros*), obliged to swell the groups of irregulars.

The part of the indigenous population which lived outside the control of the hacienda lived in communities which had been es-tablished by the "tutelary legislation" of the crown. The real nature of the comunidad is obscured by a twofold idealization. The "in-digenists" and *hispanisantes,* the self-appointed defenders of Span-ish colonial rule, have each described it, but both accounts are un-acceptable to present-day historians. Some have pictured it as a survival of pre-Columbian agrarian organization. Common owner-ship of land was confirmed by Spanish authority, and served to "reduce" and regroup the native population in easily supervised villages (hence the name *reducciones* as applied to these Indian vil-lages). It was thought by Viceroy Toledo and his successors that the comunidad would assure Indian *comuneros* of a minimum of sub-sistence, and a balance between needs and resources would be en-sured by a periodical redistribution of land. In the early days of conquest the fields of the communities were available to the greed of Spaniards and creoles, but the colonial administration created what amounted to "reserves" or ghettoes where native traditions could survive. The preservation of the pre-Hispanic cultural model in the comunidad has called forth some very ambiguous comments. Mariategui, for example, sees the comunidad, as constituted by the protective laws of Viceroy Toledo, as a kind of abuse of Inca tradi-tion which enabled the conquerors to complete their domination of the vanquished Indians.[5] However, conservative writers like José

5. José Carlos Mariategui, *Siete Ensayos de interpretacion de la realidad peruana* (Lima, Biblioteca "Amauta," 1928).

Luis de la Riva Aguero and Victor Andres Belaunde expatiate on the solicitude of the colonial administration, which tried to limit the encroachments of the *encomenderos* and later the hacendados on the rights of the crown, and to put a stop to the violence they committed against the persons and property of the Indians.

The peninsular Spaniards and creoles—or their descendants—held most of the positions of power in the economic, administrative, and religious fields. But according to the interpretation which the early twentieth-century conservatives, in particular Riva Aguero, tried to popularize, colonial domination was justified by the good use to which the kings of Spain put their power for the benefit of the native people in their charge. "During the colonial period," writes Riva Aguero, "our people had the advantage of a paternal tutelage during its minority. There was no question of subjection to a foreign power." [6] The word Riva Aguero uses for the relations between creoles and Indians is *amparo,* which is neither exactly the French *tutelle* nor the English trusteeship, but which, as applied to the Indians, has a connotation that partakes of both. Amparo is protection, but in a much wider sense than that exercised by a tutor over his pupil. Where it differs from trusteeship is that the person affording protection, even though he does so in a disinterested, benevolent, or even philanthropic manner, does not have to account for himself to the person he has taken under his wing.

While historians may be prepared to listen to the explanations of colonial tutelage which the Peruvian conservatives seek to propose, sociologists are likely to be more wary. The tutor committed countless sins, but the image of tutelage, suspect though it may be, is informative about an attitude which still contaminates relations between creoles and mestizos on the one hand and Indians on the other: paternalism has long been, and still is, one of the paramount values in Peruvian society. At first reading, Riva Aguero's text might seem to be a eulogy of Viceroy Toledo's (and others') colonial policies from 1570 on. The author makes no reference to Fray Bartolomeo de Las Casas and the campaign of that great Domini-

6. José de la Riva Aguero, *Paisajes peruanos,* 2nd ed. with an introduction by Raul Porras Barranechea (Lima, Imprenta Santa Maria, 1955).

can against the crimes and abuses of the early conquerors, but it is instructive to compare Riva Aguero's effusions on the civilizing mission of the Spanish crown with the information provided by Las Casas. In spite of the differences in the two points of view, there are certain common elements.

As Marcel Bataillon has very convincingly shown, Las Casas' campaign on behalf of the Indians was not only directed against the encomenderos, the representative of the crown.[7] He took his appeal against the Spaniards to the king of Spain, against the conquerors to the crown. In the early years of the colony the original companions of Francisco Pizarro had been given the right to divide land and peoples among them as a reward for their services. The two mechanisms of this delegation of the power of the king of Spain were *repartimiento* and *encomienda*. Repartimiento put a number of Indians at the Spanish conqueror's disposal. Encomienda gave him various rights to the labor and services of the natives at his disposal, whom the encomendero was also supposed to convert to Christianity. There is no need to enter into the abstruse discussions which have grown up over the rights accorded to the conquerors (were these rights transmissible by inheritance, were they personal or real?), but the abuses they encouraged soon became shocking, and a passionate debate arose, with the fate of the Indians as the most obvious theme. But by calling into question the privileges of the encomenderos and more generally the status of the Spaniards in America, the discussion involved the duties of the Spanish crown toward its new subjects (his Catholic Majesty pretended that in Peru he exercised the sovereignty formerly wielded by the Inca kings), and ultimately the prerogatives of the church, whose task it was to protect the Indians against the violence done them by the conquerors.

Las Casas' attack against the institution of encomienda is characterized by the note of an ambiguous paternalism which has persisted in Peruvian tradition. "If Your Majesty gave the Indians in vassalage to the Spaniards, or gave the latter any authority or superiority over the natives . . . these same Spaniards would very soon

7. Marcel Bataillon and André Saint Lu, *Las Casas et la défense des Indiens* (Paris, Julliard, 1971).

become more independent, less submissive and less docile towards Your Majesty and his Royal Justice." Las Casas refers very clearly to the feudal threat, which was more or less contained during the colonial period but reappeared particularly strongly at the time of independence. The "feudal lords" of the colonial period were replaced by *gamonales* and *caciques*. In the early days of the Republican era, the great landed proprietors of the Sierra tended to become real lords and masters over vast areas—especially when the land was remote and inaccessible. The officials were often their own masters. In their haciendas they kept up forces of armed men, and the authority of the state was almost nonexistent. Conflict between the power of the state—or what was left of it—and the "feudal lords" of the interior was inevitable whenever the state tried to interfere in what the gamonales considered was not its business: protection of the Indians, "progressive" measures in education, and labor legislation.

The Republican state of the nineteenth century tried to remind the gamonales what the colonial administration had tried to tell the colonial lords: power over the Indians had to be exercised according to certain procedures and toward certain goals that it was the right of the administration to determine. The same values that obtained between Spaniards were to obtain between Spaniards and Indians: the Indians, since they were supposed to be Christians, were also therefore men. "All the inhabitants," wrote Las Casas, "all the peoples of this new world are free." Not content with invoking the liberty involved in the *jus gentium*, Las Casas added another strange argument which foreshadowed the champions of the social contract: "They are more free than other peoples because of particular reasons operating in their favour, for the Kings of Castile had no right over them and they belong to them neither by inheritance, purchase, exchange, nor as the result of victory in a just war." So the Indians could not just be handed over by the crown to the encomenderos. They had natural rights, in particular the freedom to dispose of themselves, to move about and to own property, and the crown had to see that these fundamental rights were respected.

Understood literally, Las Casas' text is as strictly liberal as the proclamations of the Libertadores: no power may be exercised over anyone, still less over the Indians, but that of the law—a law common to all—and in conformity with natural law. This requirement was never met during the colonial period, even by the "tutelary" legislation of Viceroy Toledo, whose main problem was to impose order in the vast territory entrusted to him. For this purpose, the Indians remained subject to a special law. As Karen Spalding says, Spanish laws defined the Indian in racial or rather quasi-racial terms.[8] In colonial Peru, individuals so designated formed a separate estate at once discriminated against and protected by distinctive laws and rules. Among the forms of discrimination of which Indians were victim are the limits set on their freedom to enter into contracts: for example, among others, their right to buy or sell, which, in connection with communal property, could only be exercised under the supervision of the administrative authority. There were other restrictions relating to their ability to go to law: their evidence did not ipso facto carry the same weight as that of a Spaniard. In some cases Indians were not fully admitted to the sacraments of the Catholic church. Last and perhaps worst—and this kind of discrimination was not completely abolished until long after independence—Indians had to pay a personal head tax. Karen Spalding lists the various restrictions, and the theme clearly running through all of them is that of minority. It is because the Indian was a child that his evidence was only of limited validity, that he could not dispose of his property as he pleased, and that he was not allowed to approach all the sacraments. For that reason too, the Indian had to be protected against the exploitation of the greedy encomendero. But because of his intrinsic weakness, he had also to be taken care of as a child under the wing of his parents.

The Indian's diminished status was supposed to be compensated for by the protection offered by the king's administration. The right to amparo, based on the precepts of natural law, could have formed the basis of a kind of universalism (all the subjects of the Catholic king are equals, at least in regard to certain fun-

8. Karen Spalding, "Social Climbers: Changing Patterns of Mobility among the Indians of Colonial Peru," *Hispanic American Historic Review* 50 (November 1970), 645–664.

damental rights). But the amparo was long interpreted as an extension of the tutelage of the Spaniard and the creole over the Indian.
True, the subordination of the Indian was to be replaced in some
vague future by a more satisfactory state of affairs in which, at the
end of the *minoria protegida,* the native would become a full-fledged
Peruvian. This prospect is referred to by Riva Aguero, but it finds
its most perfect expression in the eulogy of the mestizo (not the
cholo, of course), in whom many conservatives have seen the legit-
imization of creole power. According to Riva Aguero on the colonial period, "the three civilizing centuries par excellence" made
way for the formation in Peru of a national synthesis. "During the
long peaceful colonial gestation, our unity was silently brought into
being, the effect of the coexistence (*convivencia*) and mixture of
blood."

The two terms coexistence and mixture of blood (or physical
crossing of breeds) are not necessarily synonymous. They can stand
for two irreconcilable attitudes: on the one hand mixture and fusion, on the other separation and isolation. Convivencia can be understood as a sort of ecological juxtaposition, with a minimum of
exchanges to restrict conflict between the two groups. What I have
depicted as Toledo's policy, the concentration of a fraction of the
indigenous population in comparatively small but remote areas,
where it was placed under the protection of the crown, is a policy
of juxtaposition without mixture. In short, convivencia separates
the Indian world from the Spanish world; on the one hand the
comunidad, on the other the hacienda. But the logic of separation
could not be carried too far without contradicting the Spanish colonial aim, not only that of the conquerors but also that of the crown.
The conquerors did not come to America for charitable purposes;
they came to seek land, gold and silver. To get the minerals they
wanted they needed labor. Once the first very crude phase of confrontation between the two populations was past, the mixture
began, but it did not take place on a fair and equal basis. Moreover,
the colonial administration intervened, not in the role of a just arbiter, but as the representative of the interests of an external power
and sovereignty.

Peruvian stratification, as depicted during the colonial period by official ideology, and since independence by conservatives, is a very rigid hierarchy in which the creole is at the top, his position explained if not justified by the fact that he is the repository of higher values which are Christian, Spanish, and western; but the mestizo, in some undefined future, is supposed to take over from the creole, after a long and prudent education by the tutelary authorities. One condition was attached to this "self-liquidating mechanism": the ideal mestizo, like the famous Don Joaquim Lopez Antay of whom Arguedas speaks, and who was neither Indian nor Spanish, must *not* be a cholo. Riva Aguero shows clearly the characteristics which ought to be preserved in the "raza indigene, nuestra compañera indisoluble": frugality, tenacity, submissiveness—all these being virtues arising from the social condition of the Indian, who is and must remain a peasant and a soldier. These virtues, even if their source is really Andean, have their equivalent in the hispanic tradition.

The Indian is expected to remain a peasant, possibly an artisan, connected with occupations which give him a definite place in the stratification system. The most serious obstacle to a real fusion of races and cultures (that is, one that would be slow, peaceful, and irreversible) was that they might be too quickly and suddenly merged. According to the conservatives the thirst for gold, whether in the form of the "vile metal" or of the physical satisfaction it can buy, was primarily responsible for the worst inequities of early colonialism. It was the same greed ("the same sordid Phoenician egoism") which in the nineteenth century led the coastal oligarchy, the pseudo-creoles, who had forgotten the wise counsels of the Spanish administration and the Christian church, to turn away from the "deep Peru" of the Sierra and risk all on the exploitation of exportable raw materials like guano, cotton, sugar, and mineral ores.[9]

The immobile society Riva Aguero dreams of is not merely an ideological projection "which objectively serves the interests of the ruling class." It is a model which certainly inspired the most enlightened of the big Peruvian landowners as an ideal, especially

9. Riva Aguero, *Paisajes peruanos*, p. 118.

toward the end of the eighteenth century.[10] It seems that at any critical moment Peruvian society tends to return to this kind of organization as if by some sort of reflex. But this model, dreamed of by the most enlightened of the Spanish officials of the Toledan period and reconstructed nearly four centuries later by the Peruvian conservatives, has always met with profound and persistent resistance.

Despite the various kinds of discrimination to which they were subject, the Indians had many opportunities to emerge from their condition. Karen Spalding deserves great credit for calling attention to the "social climbers" among the indigenous population, but she may be mistaken in applying without modification, in the analysis of a culturally heterogeneous society, a concept of social mobility only valid in the framework of a society where competition is governed by criteria at once individualistic and universalist. In Peru the mobility of the indigenous population that took place is only comprehensible if one realizes the extent of the interpenetration between the creole and Spanish sectors on the one hand and the Indian sector on the other.

First, not everything Indian was relegated to the base of the colonial hierarchy. The Spanish administration confirmed, in the early days of the colonial rule, the power of the *curacas,* the Inca nobility whose collaboration it needed. The Inca officials who entered the service of the Spanish crown found themselves subjected to the conquerors' administration, and like all the other Indians they had to pay tribute—but in their case it was lighter, and the other natives still had to pay them certain dues, as in the days of the Incas. So they were part of the new power, but in a mediate and subordinate position. Some of them, like Francisco Chilche, the curaca of the Yucay valley, even managed to get hold of vast estates, especially immediately after the founding of the colony.[11]

More important for the future of Peruvian society than the "Inca nobility," whose privileges were recognized and confirmed, was the group of native worthies continually renewed throughout the

10. Jean Piel, "Terre, agriculture et société au Pérou," vol. I, pt. 1, chap. 3, unpublished thesis.

11. Nathan Wachtel, *La Vision des vaincus* (Paris, Gallimard, 1971), pp. 189 ff.

Spanish administration and after independence. The famous rebel
Gabriel Condorcangui, known as Tupac Amaru, was one of them,
although he had few imitators and followers among the Indians of
his rank. During the great periods of native unrest at the end of
the eighteenth century, these curacas or caciques remained for the
most part loyal to the crown. Rich, with large incomes, they often
owned very big estates which they ran almost like Creole haciendas.
"The curaca Choquehuanca, who sided with the Spanish administration against Tupac Amaru, owned sixteen landed estates in the
Puno area and three haciendas near Anzagaro." [12]

What emerges from the cases of both Chilche and Choquehuanca is that the wealth of the caciques, in the eighteenth as in
the sixteenth century, derived from the power they exerted as delegates of the colonial administration. They helped Spanish officials
in collecting the "tribute," and recruiting Indians to work in the
mines or in textile factories (obrajes). They also received on their
own account a number of dues in kind and free services. The question remains how far they were recognized as completely equal by
the creoles. Two criteria are especially important here. First we
need to know what chance a curaca had of marrying into the caste
of creoles or Spaniards. A few well-known examples like that of the
Inca Garcilaso de la Vega are not enough for us to say that cross-
breeding with the ruling classes was a regular practice. We also
have to ask whether the highest offices and honors in the colonial
administration were as accessible to the families of curacas as to
those of hacendados of pure Spanish origin. It appears that the indigenous nobility were limited to the middle levels of the administrative hierarchy—confined, so to speak, to positions which, while
giving them local bases of power and wealth, were definitely subordinate. From 1570 on, under Toledo, the sons of curacas attended
special schools which prepared them for administrative responsibility. They were taught Spanish; the curacas, who were generally
bilingual, could read and write (or at least sign their names in)
Spanish. During the seventeenth and eighteenth centuries this process of castellanizacion continued, but the numbers concerned re-

12. Jean Piel, "Terre, agriculture et société au Pérou."

mained few, and those who benefited from it gained only a limited education which could not endanger the creoles' and above all the Spaniards' monopoly of the highest administrative posts.[13]

Thus the position of the indigenous notables was markedly lower than that of Spanish and creole notables. But, Karen Spalding adds, "A ragged Spanish or a mestizo beggar was probably considered by other members of Spanish society to have lower status than a wealthy Indian artisan or noble." And again, "Many among the Indian colonial nobility enjoyed an economic position far above that of many Spaniards through the wealth and lands that they claimed by virtue of their descent from the pre-Conquest elite".[14] The curacas had also acquired certain cultural symbols which assimilated them to the ruling classes of colonial society. "They and their women wore European rather than Indian style clothing. They participated fully in the European money economy . . . They spent their money on expensive luxury clothing or jewellery, and even invested in the same prestige items as their Spanish contemporaries."

This interpenetration between indigenous and creole groups did not take place only at the top of colonial society. It occurred also at the bottom, which was rather more important, because of the numbers involved. First, the comunidad, which in the thinking of the Spanish colonial administrators was to be a world apart, was invaded from within by a number of creoles or Spaniards representing the administrative authority. The *corregidor*—a kind of officer for native affairs—and the *alcalde*—who represented him at the level of the native village—were assisted not only by the curacas but also by a variety of native officials of lesser rank. Viceroy Toledo decreed that in every Indian village that was the chief town of one of the new administrative areas (repartimiento), a council (*cabildo*) should be appointed. At the beginning of the seventeenth century this rule was extended to smaller places. These "small notables," unlike the curacas who dated from the days of the Incas, owed their dignity to the colonial administration. But they shared

13. See Pierre Duviols, *La Lutte contre les religions autochtones dans le Pérou contemporain* (Lima, I.F.E.A., 1971), pp. 263–270.

14. Karen Spalding, "Social Climbers," p. 649.

some privileges with the curacas, such as exemption from tribute and the right to certain free services. Close to them in status, and with the same privileges, were the lay Indians who gravitated about the church: the sacristan, the *cantor* who led the choir, and the *alguacil,* whose job it was to see that the faithful attended regularly—a kind of officer in charge of religious conformity. Last, the colonial administration appointed Indian teachers in many villages, to teach the rudiments to the young Indians: a little Spanish and the catechism.

A second point of contact between the two separate worlds that went to make up colonial society was provided by the complex mechanism of taxation. Indians had to work in the mines; they could also be requisitioned by the government for various tasks said to be in the public interest. On top of this they had to pay taxes to the encomendero and the corregidor and various other officials. They had to provide the encomendero with various kinds of workers. There were also dues in kind. Some of the dues in kind were consumed on the spot within the hacienda itself, but part was sold in small towns and went to supply the mining centers. The encomendero, and later the hacendado, thus became the center of a system of economic transactions which were at least partly monetary.

To make sure tribute was forthcoming, part of the native population was transformed into craftsmen—carpenters, weavers, and potters. In some cases they still followed native techniques. This was true of the weavers and potters, for example. But others, like the carpenters, joiners, and carvers of wood and stone, were "acculturated" to European techniques. Whatever their specialty, they had a number of advantages over the "ordinary Indians," with whom one of their later descendants, the Don Antonio Lopez Antay of José Maria Arguedas, declined to be confused. "The Toledan ordinances provide exemptions from mita service for a blacksmith, shoemaker, tailor and dyer in each Indian parish, and a decree of Charles II . . . freed all Indian artisans from the labor services." [15] (Mita was a personal and temporary service to the Inca

15. Ibid., p. 622.

state at the beginning and later to the colonial administration.) In other words, artisans were exempted both from service in the mines and from the various services due to the curacas, corregidores, alcaldes, and other notables. They were free to live where they wished and settled in towns where creoles and Spaniards became their customers.

If the term cross-breeding is used not in the limited sense of the mixing of blood, but in a wider sense, to mean the circulation of individuals belonging to two different peoples, who in spite of their differences of status exchange not merely spouses and sexual partners but also roles, jobs, goods, services, and cultural symbols, the nature of the process emerges more clearly but much less rosily than it does in Riva Aguero's phrase about a "minoria protegida." Thus we have identified several channels of cross-breeding, belonging to very different social situations. By incorporating the native nobility the Spanish colonial administration prepared the way for the merging of the highest strata of the two hierarchies, indigenous and Spanish. But the Indian nobles did not keep their original status when they entered into the ruling class, but were so to speak dissolved and dispersed. After independence, there remains no trace of the native aristocracy. As for the second-class notables, venial landgrabbers more or less created by the administration and linked to it, this cross-bred group is much larger and more in evidence, and after independence, far from disappearing, it consolidated its power and became a pool from which were drawn the "bosses" of the interior and the gamonales of the Sierra. The third opportunity for cross-breeding, in the sense in which we are using the term, came from the economic activities the Spaniards encouraged the natives to enter: the practice of the artes y oficios freed the natives from the links that bound them to village communities, made them mobile, and thus qualified them for urban employment.

As Karen Spalding points out, "By 1614, the Indian population of Lima, most of it residing in the native section of El Cercado, outside the city walls, numbered 1978 persons, many of whom practiced a trade or were apprenticed to someone who did." [16] Indians

16. Ibid., p. 646.

of this kind, even if the census called them natives, had every chance of emerging from that caste—if not they themselves, then their descendants. Not only were they exempt from the obligations that weighed on the indigenous population as a whole, but the nature of their activities brought them into physical and social contact with non-Indians, from whom they learned various Spanish and western values and symbols.

One last set of circumstances favoring cross-breeding of the kind we are speaking of was linked to what might be called wildcat mobility, as a result of the disintegration of native society caused by colonial dominance and exploitation. Forced labor in the mines, on the estates in the eastern Andes where coca was grown by Indians, on the sugar-producing haciendas on the coast, by black slaves or Chinese coolies or Indians from the interior engaged by a combination of force and guile, all these separated the Indian from his traditional roots without giving him any fixed and recognized profession, such as was practiced by the mestizo artisans. A man who was torn from his village and finally succeeded in escaping from the mines or the hacienda was no longer an Indian; but neither had he become a mestizo. He could work as a servant in the boss's house. In the old days he might be an *arriero* (muleteer); now he drives a truck. He is a jack of all trades and goes from job to job, from one place to another. This mobile, unstable, agile character, capable of seizing any chance, who reminds one of the heroes of picaresque novels, is the cholo. Clearly, the mestizo of Riva Aguero and conservative tradition is only part of the interbred population.

Since there are various kinds of cross-breeding, corresponding to different social situations, the "non-Spanish" or "non-creole" world has never had much unity: what is there in common between a cholo muleteer and a notable in a provincial town, not to mention the survivors of the Inca nobility? This lack of group unity is probably matched with very complex problems of personal identity. Without going too far into the question, we might expect, in the case of individuals particularly exposed to cross-pressures resulting from dual or multiple membership, ambivalent attitudes approaching what Kurt Lewin called "self-hatred." Karen Spalding devotes an excellent passage to the case of native notables in the seventeenth century, from among whom were drawn the ministers of native religion persecuted by the Spaniards. "At the beginning of the seventeenth century, the Spanish discovered the dual roles played by the Indian village officials . . . If we assume that the members of the Indian power group were in fact seeking higher rank and status within their own society by utilizing the power available through alliance with the Spanish officials, their participation in the native religious ceremonies becomes perfectly comprehensible. By taking part in activities that were the mark of higher status within Indian society, they might gain the recognition and prestige commensurate with their effective wealth and power." [17] By playing the game of the conquerors and behaving as their "collaborators," the curacas gained power and wealth. But while they rose socially, the native nobility of the colony—and in this respect their situation much resembled the later one of the notables of the Republic, the gamonales of the interior—ran the risk of losing the respect of the people of their own blood. To take part in the rites of the ancient Andean religions was to recover their threatened identity, and to annex the symbols that would integrate them once more into native life and cultural tradition.

The Peruvian stratification system had little chance, symbolically or in reality, of being focused around the mestizo. In the first place, at the end of the Spanish colonial rule the mass of the population was still made up of indigenous peasants, and the various cross-breed statuses we have just described involved very few persons. Moreover, insofar as the mestizo was exposed to the influence of the culturally dominant tradition and became the carrier and disseminator of these values, he was associated with the "ruling" culture. The greater part of the population remained simply Indian. Indeed, the nineteenth century is characterized by a process of "re-Indianization."

George Kubler has written a very important article on the evolution of the Peruvian population in this respect.[18] He shows that if tax statistics alone are considered, the Indian part of the population regarded as indigenous by the Spanish fiscal administration

17. Ibid., pp. 660, 661.
18. George Kubler, *The Indian Caste of Peru, 1795–1940: A Population Study Based upon the Tax Records and Census Reports* (Washington, D.C., Smithsonian Institution, 1952), p. 64.

still amounted at the end of the eighteenth century to 70 percent of the whole population of Peru, and this percentage had been shrinking continuously since the beginning of the colonial period. It dropped to 60 percent in 1854, and 55 percent in 1876. But at the time of the first national census in 1876, the actual percentage of Indians was higher than it should have been if the rate of decline observed during the colonial period had continued. Kubler concludes that at least during the first eighty years of the nineteenth century the Indian element remained stronger than would have been expected on the basis of eighteenth-century trends.

The re-Indianization of Peru due to the collapse of the colonial administration during the wars of independence and the early days of the Republic differed in scale according to area. It was most noticeable in the center and the south—with the exception of the department of Arequipa. In the coastal regions, where a capitalist export agriculture (of sugar and cotton) was growing up, the percentage of Indians declined. The causes of this process were connected with the marked stagnation that characterized Peru during the first half of the nineteenth century. Accompanying the disorders of the early republic were a shrinking of foreign trade, growing impoverishment, a "de-differentiation" of the economy during which local self-sufficiency grew, and the disruption and disappearance of state administration, which left a free hand to the military *caudillos* and the gamonales and minor gentry of the Sierra.

Kubler's data suggest that during the time of "tutelary" legislation designed to "protect" the Indian communities and their property, the process of *mestizaje* was more rapid than during the period of "liberal" land policy adopted by the libertadores, which accelerated the alienation of Indian property and its acquisition by the gamonales. At least a partial explanation lies in the fact that the new haciendas set up at the start of the Republican period on the debris of the stripped comunidades employed the same natives, who ceased to be independent comuneros and became peones, though still remaining Indians. It is also probable that the "re-ruralization" which accompanied the economic depression of the early years of independence slowed the cross-breeding stimulated by the expansion of the artisan sector.

The process of what I have called "re-Indianization" first became perceptible after the defeat in the war against Chile, both because of the role played by Indian soldiers in the resistance against the invader, especially in the famous guerrilla army led by General 'Caceres against the occupation forces, and also as the result of the *sublevaciones* (insurrections), which increasingly forced themselves on the creoles' attention. If one tried to sketch a typology of native violence from 1880 to the early 1960s, one would have to distinguish between three quite different situations. In the first place there were the *jacqueries* (peasant uprisings, in which half-breeds were usually involved), which took place in areas of the highest native density, such as for example the department of Puno, the *aymara* provinces on the borders of Bolivia, and around Lake Titicaca (Huancane, Moho, and Lampa in the north; Chucuito and Juli south of the Lake). Second was *bandolerismo,* which fed the vendettas between gamonales. This type of violence developed chiefly in the Sierra of the north, where the Indian population was less dense and the Indians were in the process of cross-breeding. Finally, in the immediately contemporary period, there is the pressure exerted by the Indian peasants to recover plundered land. The famous affair of the valley of the Convencion in the 1950s, and the strikes and sit-ins at the beginning of the presidency of Fernando Belaunde Terry (1963–1964), illustrate this third situation. I shall not deal with the second kind of agitation, chiefly linked to rivalries between gamonales, in which Indians and especially cholos play only the role of footsloggers except when they manage to win a kind of autonomy vis-à-vis their "bosses" and become sort of knights errant or "bandits d'honneur." [19]

The most famous of all the native jacqueries is that of Atusparia. It occurred in 1885, the darkest moment in Peruvian history, after the great national disaster of the Chilean war. The action unfolded in the department of Ancash north of Lima, in an inter-Andean valley with a very high Indian density. The government, at its wit's end, had tried to reintroduce the Indian capitation tax in a

---

19. See the famous rising of Eleodoro Benel in the Celendin area: Jorge Basadre, *Historia de la Republica del Peru* (Lima, Peru, Editorial Universitaria, 1968), XIII, 138–140. This situation is crystallized in the character of "fiero Vasquez" in Ciro Alegria's "El mondo es ancho y ajeno" (New York, Crofts, 1945).

disguised form but levied in quite large sums. There were also abuses on the part of the local administrative authorities, who imposed forced labor and requisitioning either for the state or for their own advantage. Trouble broke out over the building of a law court. A general uprising followed. The Indians occupied the region for several months, driving away the regular authorities and setting up their own traditional ones. The matter was settled only by the bloody reoccupation of the area by an army detachment. What gives the episode its importance is the complex yet typical way in which indios, mestizos, and criollos were related. In the chief town of the department of Ancash, a mestizo intellectual, Montestruque, put his newspaper, *El Sol de los Incas,* at Atusparia's service. Montestruque was an electoral agent for General Caceres, hero of the resistance against Chile and then leader of the opposition to the president, another general called Iglesias. The native unrest was exploited by the *politica criolla,* that is, in the interests of the political classes or part of them: in this case by the more or less liberal nationalist group which was trying to oust Iglesias. Atusparia, the leader of the rebellion, was the alcalde of a mountain village. He was a traditional notable, but can he be considered an Indian? Was he not rather a mestizo, if among the criteria for crossbreeding we include frequency of contact with and intensity of exposure to the white world and the ruling society? Beside Atusparia there emerges the figure of another leader, Uchcu Pedro, who was not an Indian notable but a miner. He had also fought with Caceres' partisans in the guerrilla war against the Chileans, and for both these reasons Uchcu was at least as "modern" as Atusparia and equally exposed, though in different ways, to the influence of the creole society he had encountered as a miner and as a soldier.

Our biographical information about the two men is too scant to take the comparison further. But one point that clearly contrasts them is the degree of radicalism with which they conducted the rebellion. Atusparia seems to have maintained contact with the administrative authorities for as long as possible, and to have remained in contact throughout with the agents of Caceres. When the army came in force to occupy the region, Atusparia was taken and surrendered. When his "boss," General Caceres, replaced Iglesias as president, he was set free. Some time later Caceres granted him an official audience in Lima. Uchcu Pedro, on the contrary, took to the maquis, was caught, and shot.

A comparison can be made between Uchcu Pedro's movement and the messianic movements which at rare intervals have characterized to some degree native resistance. Their prototype goes back to the beginning of the colonial era. Nathan Wachtel's felicitous phrase "the resurrection of the gods" well defines the millenarist hope which seems at certain times in some parts of the country to have stirred the native masses. Around the 1560s there was a widespread belief that Spanish rule was coming to an end, that the turn of the Christians' God was over, and after some cataclysm a new order, *novus rerum ordo,* would replace the old.[20] The nucleus of this native belief seems to have been not basically the idea, frequent in American cosmologies, of a series of cycles in human history, but rather the acceptance of the fact that two religious forces now controlled the development of Andean societies: the traditional gods, the *huaca,* and the God of the Christians. What the new faith announced was the end of the Christian cycle and the return—the Spanish chroniclers call it the *vuelta*—of the huaca. In fact their "return" would not be a real resurrection, for they had never been dead, only at the most sleeping. The idea of the latency of the old gods is especially noticeable in the myth of Inkari, with its image of a beheaded Inca whose body "grows in the earth" until head and body are one again and he returns.[21]

The "return of the Inca" took a more prosaic form when the leader of a native sublevacion, such as Tupuc Amaru, assumed the title of Inca. Sometimes even an official of the Peruvian Republic might take some native name, as did Teodomiro Gutierrez Cuevas, who after becoming civil and military leader of the Chucuito region at the beginning of the twentieth century assumed the native name of Rumi Maki (iron hand).

Two elements in different proportions go to make up the native

20. The movement of the Taqui Ongos, about which we are informed by various Spanish sources. See Pierre Duviols, *La Lutte contre les religions,* pp. 107–112.

21. François Bourricaud, "El mito de Inkari," *Folklore Americano,* no. 4 (1956).

sublevaciones. On the one hand there is the nativist and genuinely indigenist factor particularly evident in someone like Uchcu Pedro. On the other hand there is a clearly paternalist and ideological element observable in the more or less philanthropical and radical mestizos who offered to lead the native movement. Thus Rumi Maki, an official of the Peruvian State, who led an Indian rebellion, by origin and status belonged to the "ruling class." But since his youth he had been concerned with the Indians' lot, and in his various administrative posts he called the attention of the Lima authorities to the violence committed by the landowners against their peones, and their plundering of the comunidades.

Cuevas' indigenism was that of a mestizo motivated by moral indignation. In the same vein was la Asociacion Proindigena, founded in 1909 and dissolved in 1916, whose leaders were two young Lima intellectuals, Pedro S. Zulen, half creole and half Chinese, and his wife Dora Mayer. Its members were students, lawyers, and some professional people who though living in the provinces kept in touch with what was going on in the capital, where they had been students and had come in contact with the liberal intelligentsia. The association operated at two levels. It offered Indians, especially comunidades, the free services of the lawyers affiliated with it. When it discovered some hacendado or official guilty of scandalous abuses that would shock the enlightened public, it published their misdeeds and roused the opposition against them. The association thus brought pressure to bear on the authorities for setting up a parliamentary commission.

If one tries to define the ideology of the early indigenist movement, one is tempted to see in it a return to the principles of natural law, and in particular a reaffirmation of the old idea according to which all members of a civilized polity are equal before the law. But there was also an activist and paternalist tendency. To enable the Indian to resist violence and exploitation, it was not enough to give him comparatively formal and abstract rights. He had to be qualified, made more productive and healthier, taught to read and write—in Spanish. The "upgrading" of the Indian posed a decisive choice which the indigenist movement did not really make. Either the policy of native advancement could be to make the Indian a

Peruvian like all the rest—though then the native quality itself, the Indian "identity," would tend to be lost or at any rate become marginal. Or else, returning to the idea of amparo inherited from colonial tradition, indigenist policy might try to "protect" the Indian by strengthening its tutelary institutions. This latter view finally predominated among indigenists in the early 1920s, at the beginning of August B. Leguia's government, and even inspired certain clauses in the Peruvian constitution of 1920, stipulating that land belonging to legally recognized native communities could not be sold. Was this a return to the old Spanish colonial legislation, after a century in which the liberalism of the founders of the Republic had prevailed, at least on paper? In fact, the indigenist theorists of the 1920s, while they quoted with approval certain provisions of "las leyas de Indias," believed in a kind of evolutionist neo-positivism crossed with Durkheimian sociologism, which stressed the necessity of a long process to "equalize" the native population.[22]

Thus, the indigenism of the 1920s remained paternalistic and in fact conservative, even though the mestizo intellectuals who propagated it gave it liberal or radical expression. What I mean by indigenist conservatism has three aspects. I have already spoken of the first, the paternalist tendency. True, the indigenist "educators" meant to keep for themselves the right to "guide" the native race, and they rebelled violently against and criticized the tutelage attempted by such traditional authorities as the Catholic church. But if there was conflict about who the protectors should be, there was agreement on the need for protection. In the second place, indigenism, by stressing the originality of indigenous culture, risked making it marginal and folkloric. To be protected the Indian would have to be isolated in his communities, his language and his customs. By depicting the Indian as close to nature, wholesome,

22. The former head of the Teacher Training School at Puno and future senator José Antonio Encinas did his law thesis in 1918 on "Contribucion a una legislacion tutelar del Indigena." One of the most important proponents of this doctrine was Mariano B. Cornejo, first professor of sociology at San Marcos University, who played the role of theorist of "La Patria Nueva" during the early years of Leguia's presidency.

untouched by the corruption of gold and the evil ways of Lima and the coast, indigenism helped reinforce the dualism of traditional Peruvian culture. Finally, this dualism came to be seen as a stable desirable state. The indigenists of the twenties and thirties detected a movement toward re-Indianization in the beginnings of the great native avalanche descending from the Andes onto the coastal area. But they took for re-Indianization what was really a process of cholification, and few thought seriously that Peru would become a republic of peasants, quechua or aymara, with an Indian language and vernacular traditions that would take the place of Spanish and western traditions. What the indigenists of the 1920s and 1930s considered desirable and possible, though without seeing very clearly how it was to be brought about, was that the Indian people and culture might be preserved and become a kind of reservoir for national tradition.

I can see two reasons for this conservative tendency in Peruvian indigenism. The first reason is political. Unlike Mexico after the 1910 revolution, Peru continued to be governed by a neocolonial oligarchy, from the end of the war in the Pacific to the end of the 1960s; that oligarchy resisted the assaults of populism. Between 1930 and 1945 the APRA (Alianza Popular Revolucionaria Americana) put forward in vain the twofold slogan of "Indo-America" and "an anti-imperialist State." The Peruvian elite, helped by the army, held back the attack of the mestizo intelligentsia grouped around the Jefe Maximo, Haya de la Torre. The result was a consolidation or even strengthening of creole tradition, which went well enough with the style of development favored by the oligarchy. The indigenists of the 1920s had no very clear idea of the consequences economic development might have on Peruvian society. They limited themselves to contrasting the corruption of the "Levantine" merchants (*fenicios*) of the coast with the strictness of the traditional Indian economy, the beauties of mutual aid, and the solidarity that existed between comuneros. Haya de la Torre, with the foresight that makes the book he wrote in 1927, *El anti-imperialismo y el Apra,* still one of the main sources of the development of the ideology which in the 1950s was to become the credo of the intelligentsia, saw clearly the need for a "popular national" state (which the intellectuals who support the present military junta now call the "Estado solidario"). But the limitation of his own ideas, and the early stage that the social sciences were in at the time, apparently made it impossible for him to go beyond rather vague formulations, or to break the intense resistance that would be set up in neocolonial Peruvian society by catch-words such as "Indo-America," to which the creole conservatives' passionate reply was "El Peru es de occidente." José Carlos Mariategui might denounce the confusions and petit-bourgeois weaknesses of the anti-imperialist state, as depicted by Victor Raul, but both were stopped short by the solidity of the neocolonial Peruvian structure.

The second reason the revolutionary potentialities of the indigenist claim for fair treatment for the Indians were more than counterbalanced by the conservative element relates to the nature of the economic process in Peru after 1930, and to the scant knowledge most of the indigenist intellectuals had of economic questions. The oligarchy countered the great depression by traditional means, thus reinforcing the dualist structure which consisted of the exporting Peru of the coast on one side and the remote, sleepy Peru of the Sierra on the other. When, after the Second World War, there was a renewed and increasing demand for raw materials, ores, sugar, cotton, and fish flour, those who profited from the export boom were largely the coastal region and the urban sector. This resulted in two kinds of distortion. The distribution of profits was grossly unequal, and the traditional sector—the Indian world which the indigenists aimed at protecting—was sucked into the vacuum caused by the expansion of the exporting sector. The crisis of the old rural, provincial, indigenous society of the Sierra was aggravated, and became general. It took very different forms. In the famous case of the valley of the Convencion it was a fairly localized struggle, sometimes harsh and violent, sometimes careful and under cover, between the hacendados and the various sections of the native population temporarily united against the *patron*.[23] In other instances, like the *invasiones* of 1963–1964, there was a fron-

23. Wesley W. Craig, Jr., "Peru: The Peasant Movement of La Convencion," in Henry A. Landsberger, ed., *Latin American Peasant Investments* (Ithaca, Cornell University Press, 1969).

tal, but relatively short, attack by the native masses as a whole. But all the cases of rural unrest in the 1960s contain essential features that make them very different from the pattern dreamed up by the indigenists in the thirties. The native population was becoming economically differentiated and often contained peasants who were rich, a kind of kulak very hostile to the domination of the traditional landowner but indifferent to the communal ideal of the indigenists. This differentiation between native strata sometimes resulted in violent clashes of interest between landless and landowning Indians.

These circumstances of the 1960s were not at all conducive to a greater self-awareness on the part of the native group. The prestige of the Indian as such was becoming gradually reduced by the aura of archaism which clung to him. Archaism became attractive only to folklorizing intellectuals in search of authenticity, of *lo nuestro*. Coordination of protest movements at the national level, even though more efficient than in the twenties and thirties, was difficult because of lack of liaison. The political system tended to keep the majority of the population "on the fringe," and the mass parties themselves, the populist organizations, parties, and unions, aimed at toning down and diverting protest as much as encouraging it. So the native claim was doomed to be handled by persons and organizations which only partly endorsed it: by the notables, by the populist parties, by leftist groups using native discontent to advance their own ends. Since 1968 it has been pressed through an authoritarian state which confiscates and redistributes the estates of the hacendados and tries to organize new agricultural cooperatives over which it intends to keep close control.

It is true that since 1969 the seat of the Peruvian government has been named for Tupac Amaru. It is also true that an ambitious scheme of educational reform promises to extend the teaching of native languages to the whole of the population. These two decisions of the military government treat whatever is Indian (language, past, traditions) as a symbol of national unity and identity. *Lo indio* is supposed to express what all Peruvians have in common. This is what I would call the unifying function of lo indio. It is easy enough to see why the creole and hispanic heritage cannot fit the bill. It evokes the idea of colonial domination and by implication legitimizes the country's present dependence on the ruling world "center." But in addition to its unifying function, lo indio, like every symbolism, has an identifying function. It should enable whoever uses it, with reference either to himself or to others, to recognize himself and be recognized. But a unifying symbolism, at the collective level, may lead to an empty and abstract activism or it may dissolve into a colorful, folkloric, and regional particularism. The promotion of lo indio bears witness to the somewhat compulsive desire to create a "real" national unity, but it succeeds only very partially in the task of making apparent and recognizable the relations between different social groups. It would hardly be going too far to say that all Peruvians recognize themselves as Indians at the collective level, though none of them would accept the description entirely as applied to themselves, individually, for in this society, which might be said to be in a state of flux, differences are more strongly and genuinely felt than a national solidarity which is still abstract and artificial.

From the beginning of the 1950s until 1967, the development of Peruvian society was remarkable in the classic sense of the word: rapid urbanization, growing national product, average income, and exports (copper, fish meal), and expanding public services, such as education. This of course aggravated regional disparities and social inequality, sharply affecting the relations between Indians, metis, creoles, cholos.

The migration which brought growing numbers from the Sierra to the periphery of the large cities reflected the crisis of a traditional rural society. Apparently the old hacienda system as well as the comunidad have outlived their time, and the theme of agricultural reform, long a subversive topic, has since 1956 been on the agenda of public discussion. The *serranos* (people from mountain areas), crowded into the *barriadas* (shanty town), are exposed to a social and cultural situation which provides both shock and challenge. Richard W. Patch, a wise and informed observer, finds in his experience in the world of the barriadas and other lower-class quarters of Lima an individualistic orientation among the underprivileged: "The residents . . . believe that success is achieved by individual initiative. The person himself has control over his destiny; it is not his fate that will determine whether he will succeed or fail . . . They see success as *achieved,* not *ascribed* from birth by a transcendant God." [24]

This seems to me to be an observation of major importance. It contradicts the generally accepted view of the "traditionalist" orientation of the Andean masses. Even if we accept, as does Patch, the views attributed to the anthropologists of 1940–1950 as well founded, this traditionalism only continues to characterize that part of the population which continues—and who knows for how long?—to live in conditions which extend the colonial heritage into the second half of the twentieth century. In the second place one must note the speed with which the transformation has taken place, the remarkable efficaciousness of the barriada [25] as an agent of change. Finally, one must ask how much this transformation has been perceived by other Peruvians, and particularly by those groups which are in responsible, decision-making positions.

For many reasons, these changes have been poorly understood. The Indian stereotype, as it emerges from the indigenist literature, underlined the "collectivist" orientation of the Andean population. In the early 1950s, when the urban boom in Lima was particularly strong, anthropologists were fascinated by the persistence of the tradition of communal work. It was noted with pleasure that the serranos helped family members and others who came from their own village (*paisanos*) to build houses and participated in various groups according to their provincial origins. In short, the old *ayni* (communal work system based on exchange and reciprocity) survived. This vision was able to last because it conformed with the interests and particularly the prejudices of the intelligentsia, which under the guise of *progresismo* was ready to take a paternalistic, protective attitude toward the Indian, straight out of the colonial tradition. The Indian would continue, under the wing of the intelligentsia, his long minoria protegida, to use the phrase of the con-

24. Richard W. Patch, "La Parrada, Lima's Market: A Study of Class and Assimilation," *American Universities Field Reports,* West Coast South America Series, 14 (February 1967), 11 (my italics).
25. Today, Peruvian authorities prefer *pueblos jovenes* to the term barriada.

servative Riva Aguero. However, many Peruvian sociologists perceived the social significance of the clever, aggressive person, who even though finally defeated by adversity, broken by the battle for survival, debased by degrading conditions, seeks or at least has at one time sought to rise, as a product of social disorganization and anomie. But they tended to interpret the phenomenon in terms of anomie, rather than to pay attention to the seeds of progress which were there. The pessimistic view makes sense, of course, but Patch's rich observations show that it is one-sided. It is true that Patch's work refers only to the "marginal" sectors—not numerically, but in terms of social position—of urban society. There is good reason to believe that this individualistic orientation is spreading throughout society, in particular because of education.

As seen by those Patch has studied, Peruvian society is a jungle from which all amparo has disappeared—except, of course, for the support the urban man gets from his family and friends. But in this society where survival is so difficult, mobility initially takes the form of uncertainty and instability. Although it is necessary to rise to survive, it is not a question of rising very far: small crafts, itinerant trade for the more fortunate, precarious industrial employment. Aspirations are low, but dissatisfaction is neither strong nor widespread.

How do these individuals perceive their social universe? How do they identify each other, distinguish themselves from each other? Patch shows that the old labels—indio, serrano, cholo, criollo—acquire in the context of the barriada a strikingly rigid pattern. For those in the *parrada,* there are four categories: serrano, indio, criollo, cholo.[26] Criollo is positive; the subject refers to himself this way willingly. Serrano is slightly negative, but most often it is used to indicate geographic origin and to emphasize that he is newly arrived in Lima. Two terms are avowedly negative: indio, which implies dull or thick-headed, and cholo, which, except in a special intimate context, signifies the serrano who wants to pass as criollo. Of course, those who make these fine distinctions would never be rec-

---

26. I myself have noted two curious expressions: *el serranito,* who is no longer completely a serrano, but who is not yet a criollo, and the *criollito,* who is no longer a serrano, but who is not yet a criollo.

ognized by anyone outside their own circles as anything other than cholos.

It is clear that these different statuses may be viewed as phases in a process of acculturation related to the process of urbanization. Can one surmise that the emphasis put on these classifications only masks the emergence of a stratification system where class position replaces ethnic and cultural differences? Unlike Patch, I hesitate to respond affirmatively because of the extreme weakness of the political and economic organizations of the urban underprivileged around which class consciousness can develop.[27] What does seem clear is that neither in actuality nor symbolically is the indio or the serrano at the center of the stratification system.

It is true that even if at a conscious level the identification of serrano and indio is rejected, it does not mean that the Indian peasants may not rise to change matters in their favor. Also the military regime has increased its efforts to legitimize, even "sanctify," the Indian. Nevertheless, the agricultural reform of 1969 by the existing junta was a measure imposed by the authorities from above and in no way perceived as the result of the pressure of the masses. Even though the peasant struggles increased in the 1960s, the reform of 1969 could not be seen by the peasants as a revolutionary conquest. Clearly it was a reform granted, and granted by rulers who are as devoted to law and order as to independence and national dignity. This essential fact distinguishes the Peruvian from the Mexican or Bolivian cases.

To appreciate the effects of the law of 1969 it is essential to distinguish the intentions and objectives of its promoters from the results which are beginning to appear. The military authorities wished to put an end to a situation which appeared to them to be morally shocking and full of danger for the social fabric. The reform of 1969 appears to me to exemplify what Barrington Moore calls conservative modernization. Furthermore, during the entire period of peasant turmoil which marked the presidency of M. Belaunde, the leaders of the peasant movement never gave a nativist or indigenous character to their actions. Hugo Neira shows in a

27. As Patch himself recognizes. "La Parrado," p. 12.

convincing fashion that alongside the Indian peasants are to be found cholos from small villages, union leaders, and students who are trying to organize the indigenous masses and put them in contact with urban progressive social and political forces.[28]

It is still early to assess the results of the reform of 1969. Nevertheless I shall risk three observations. First, it does not appear, at least as of today, that the reform has noticeably slowed the rural exodus; the Sierra continues to stream into Lima and the big cities. As for the beneficiaries of governmental measures, the reform makes the peasants increasingly associated with the cooperatives based on the techniques of modern agronomy. It makes them peasants, but I doubt that it reinforces their Indian identity. The reform not only speeds the entrance of peasants into the cycle of modern economic life, but it increases their dependence on the administration, which made them proprietors ultimately dependent on it for credit, seeds, and equipment. The old minoria protegida is not on the verge of disappearing even if the mixing of strata and estates increases.

It is clear that the Peruvian stratification system is in a state of transition. Although it has been suggested that it is changing from a caste or semi-caste to a class system, I shrink from this theory. For the moment it seems to me prudent to observe that neither class nor caste structure is visible. Peruvian society is indeed being modernized and becoming industrialized, and groups are emerging, on the basis of competence and merit, in opposition to the national and foreign owners of the means of production. What I am doubtful about, however, is the speed of this transition, and what it is leading to. The Peruvian stratification system now juxtaposes elements which are more and more heterogeneous. Neither Indian nor mestizo constitutes a group around which it can crystallize. It makes no more sense to call Peru an Indian culture or society than to call it a cross-breed country. And it is clear that, given the pejorative nuances that cling to the term, no one would accept cholo and Peruvian as synonymous. On the other hand, it is true that human groups can still be found in the Andes that are stratified ac-

28. Hugo Neira, *Cuzio: Tierra o muerte* (Lima, Problemas de Hoy, 1964).

cording to the principles of colonial society, but these principles are no longer valid in an urban or industrial context and certainly cannot be applied to Peruvian society as a whole.

Despite the present uncertainty about the Peruvian stratification system, four conclusions relating to the role of the Indian can be drawn from the preceding analysis: 1. the symbolism of lo indio remains effective only in the case of small traditional groups which form isolated islands in Peruvian society; 2. it appears inadequate to express differential relations between groups in the modern sector; 3. for Peruvian society as a whole, the symbolism of lo indio expresses a desire for unity rather than an expression of identity; 4. because Peruvian society is still without a clear and definite structure it is subject to two opposing tendencies. Sometimes it tends to break up into small, isolated units; sometimes attempts are made to create an activist movement to meet the needs of the "real Peru." It is in terms of this conflict that the ambiguity of lo indio symbolism lies.

THE NEW STATES

12

MILTON J. ESMAN

Communal Conflict in Southeast Asia

Southeast Asia is ethnically the most heterogeneous of the world's regions. Centuries of large-scale migration, successive waves of religio-cultural movements, wars and trade, and most recently, colonial conquest have produced an ethnologists' paradise. Hindu, Buddhist, Confucianist, Muslim and Christian influences have been modified by mutual contact and by mixture and coexistence with indigenous practices, many of which survive. In this chapter no effort will be made to catalogue the complex and shifting ethno-linguistic map of Southeast Asia, since this is not a study in ethnology. Nor will this be a history of group differentiation and fusion in this region. Our concern is not with cultural pluralism per se or even with group interaction, but with the politicization of communal differences into issues that produce conflict and require regulation by public authority.

We shall attempt to identify some of the politically salient patterns of intercommunal relations in the contemporary post-colonial phase of Southeast Asia's history and analyze some of the problems these plural societies encounter as their elites attempt both to modernize and to create viable political systems. While many communal groups move, straddle, and transact across formal political boundaries, our unit of analysis will nevertheless be the contemporary territorial state, because at this point in history, this is the structure within which the claims of constituent communal groups are asserted and their terms of association are determined.

Each of the territorial states in Southeast Asia—Burma, Thailand, Malaysia, Singapore, Laos, Cambodia, Vietnam (North and South), Indonesia, and the Philippines—confronts major problems of pluralism. Individuals identify themselves by communal categories which antedate territorial states and these loyalties and structural solidarities compete with the claims of the latter. Thus, the communal dimension of politics is an important concern in all these countries and in some it is the chief and nagging preoccupation of political elites. Some of the latter may dream of a day in the distant future when a fully integrated or assimilated citizenry will spare their successors the political anxieties of a plural society, but for the present they must contend with this intractable reality. Yet communal solidarity is not the only line of cleavage in Southeast Asia. Class and ideology have eclipsed, though not displaced, it in the recent civil war in Vietnam, in the peasant rebellions in the Philippines, and in the long struggle between the army and the Communist party in Indonesia. Within some communal groups, particularly the larger and more modern ones, including Malays and Chinese in Malaysia, Javanese and Burmans, class cleavages would be even more intense if not for the fear that competing communal groups would benefit. A complete analysis of any of these systems would have to consider the cross-cutting consequences of ideological, class, and communal interests. I shall limit this chapter to communal cleavages because their management is critical to the maintenance of contemporary political systems in Southeast Asia.

Relations, that is, the proportion and the quality of conflict and cooperation among two or more communal groups, depend on the following factors: (1) the *relative resources* at the disposition of each group. These resources are demographic—relative numbers; organizational—degree of mobilization and capacity to put resources to political uses; economic—control of finance, means of production, or trade channels; technological—possession of modern skills; locational—control of natural resources and strategic territory; political—control or influence over the instrumentalities of the state; and ideological—the normative basis for group objectives. In addition to these objective determinants of power, the quality of intercommunal relations depends on (2) the *congruity or disparity in goals* between those who control the state apparatus and the leaders of constituent groups. If the goals are the same, for example, assimilation, then whatever the relative resources, the outcome is likely to be consensual. If, however, the goals are incompatible, one group seeking assimilation while the other demands autonomy, the consequences will be tension and conflict and outcomes will be determined by the relative resources controlled by the parties. More likely, groups may agree on some issues (for example, criteria for citizenship) and disagree on others (national language) so that outcomes may be affected by bargaining. (3) This introduces a third determining factor—the conventions, rules, procedures, and structures, the *institutions for conflict management*. Without such institutions there can be no predictability in intergroup relations and no framework for channeling group demands or for regulating outcomes.

Intercommunal relationships are not fixed. They shift over time with changes in the relative resource positions and goal perceptions of the competing parties and the institutions available for conflict management. Changes may result from factors internal to the system (election results or the impact of a local insurrection) or by external, international forces that affect the internal balance of power. The latter have been particularly prominent and destabilizing in Southeast Asia since World War II, including such events as the Indochina war, the Indonesia–Malaysia confrontation, and the incursion of Kuomintang military remnants into Northern Burma, Thailand, and Laos.

Intercommunal relations in Southeast Asia are so diverse that they cannot possibly fit a single mode of explanation. In the section that follows, I shall explore five patterns of communal politics which impose some order on this diversity, yet account for most of the empirical data. These patterns are in no way unique to Southeast Asia. In so brief a survey as this, only the gross dimensions of communal relationships can be included and much of the interesting contextual detail must be omitted.

FIVE PATTERNS OF COMMUNAL POLITICS

The first, and by far the most common and the most significant, is the *center–periphery* pattern. The center–periphery concept is straightforward: one group—in our case a communal group or communal coalition—dominates the center of the political system, the resources and the apparatus of state power, and exercises hegemonic control over other communal groups at the periphery of the system. The political center need not be located at the geographic center of the polity—though this would clarify the metaphor. In Southeast Asia, however, the two tend to coincide, with the peripheral groups located at some geographic distance from the political center. Their relative autonomy is thus affected by the ability of the center to penetrate the areas they occupy with military forces and administrative services. The communal group which controls the center need not represent a majority of the polity but is usually the largest constituent group. (See the Appendix, pages 417–418, for the demographic proportions in the Southeast Asian countries.)

The Burmans control the center in Burma. Much of the history of that troubled country since achieving independence in 1948 has resulted from the inability of the Burman political and cultural elites at the center and the peripheral peoples—Shans, Karens, Katchins, Arakanese, and Mons—to agree on terms of coexistence. Though the constitution provides for federal institutions to protect the positions of the minorities, the center generally has promoted "national unity," while the peripheral groups have claimed greater autonomy. The result has been a continuous and costly succession of insurrections, some abetted by Kuomintang remnants, others supported by the Peking government and which the Burman military has not been able to liquidate. Insurgency has become a way of life for many of the males in the peripheral groups.

The dispute between former Prime Minister U Nu and the military led by General Ne Win, which led to the ouster of the former and the army takeover in 1962, involved this very issue. The nationalistic military leadership feared that U Nu was making so many concessions to the minorities in order to gain their peaceful and voluntary participation in the political system—and incidentally to solidify his own political position—as to compromise the viability of the Burmese state. Neither repressive measures applied by the military regime during the past decade nor attempts at negotiated settlements have achieved a consensual modus vivendi

between center and periphery, nor has the center possessed sufficient coercive resources to pacify the country. On the other hand,
the minorities have not demonstrated the capacity to maintain an
effective coalition against the Burmans. So the bloodletting continues while the economy stagnates.

In neighboring Thailand, the peripheral groups are a larger
proportion of the population than in Burma, but they are less effectively mobilized. The Thai government's approach to these
groups—Malay Muslims in its four southern provinces bordering
Malaysia, Meo, Yao, and other hill tribes in the north, the large
Thai–Lao group in the depressed northeast, and the Vietnamese
enclave bordering Laos—has until recently been one of neglect,
rather than enforced assimilation, since the existence of these out-
lying peoples had not been considered a threat to the security of
the state. During the past decade, however, this situation has
changed. The Indochina war and the active support of the Thai
government for U.S. military operations has provoked the North
Vietnamese to promote insurgencies by exploiting the social and
economic grievances of the hill tribesmen, the Vietnamese refugee
settlement on the Mekong, and especially the large Lao-speaking
minority in the northeast, whom the central Thai elites have traditionally regarded as brother Thai but not favored with investments, public services, or opportunities to participate on equal
terms in the government or educational system.

The Thai government has improvised several measures for cop-
ing with these unwelcome expressions of minority discontent.
None of them is designed to encourage effective participation by
any of these groups in the political system. Their implementation
has been inhibited by the reluctance of the government to invest
heavily in these activities and the lack of enthusiasm among Thai
administrators for working with the peripheral peoples, whose language, customs and needs they do not understand, in areas remote
from Bangkok where the good life and career opportunities lie.

The most intractable case has been the Vietnamese. Originally
refugees from Laos in the pre-1954 phase of the Indochina war,
they have waxed in numbers and in relative prosperity. Now nearly
a hundred thousand strong, they sympathize with Hanoi and thus

represent a serious security problem to the Thai government. They show little interest in "returning" to Vietnam, nor has the Hanoi government, despite some repatriations in the early 1960s, demonstrated any enthusiasm to facilitate this process. The Thai government considers them unwelcome and unassimilable foreigners, will not grant them or their progeny any citizenship rights, maintains close police surveillance of their activities, and hopes for their eventual departure.

Toward the several hill tribes in the north, the government's main interest appears to be to help them achieve settled patterns of agriculture so that they can be governed in the normal Thai administrative pattern and to deny their villages as bases for antigovernment insurgent activities. Because they are small, divided, and economically backward, they will for the indefinite future be marginal to the Thai polity and economy. On the other hand, the Lao speakers in the neglected, impoverished, and underrepresented northeast have become a serious problem. Nearly as numerous as the dominant central Thai, they proved to be vulnerable to North Vietnamese-inspired subversion. In response, the Thai government with substantial U.S. assistance has mounted a large-scale counterinsurgency program combining improved public services and economic development projects with tighter security measures. The results have not been sufficient to contain the insurgency. Since the Thai government regards the Thai–Lao as ethnic Thai and because they practice a nationalistic, highly centralized and administrative style of governance oriented to assimilationist objectives, they are not inclined to consider any form of pluralism or territorial autonomy for these people.

Meanwhile, in the four southern provinces, the remnants of the defeated Chinese-manned insurgency of the Malayan Communist party have found sanctuary among the Muslims. Fifteen years after their defeat in Malaya, they have launched several guerrilla incursions from these bases across the border. At the insistence of the Malaysians, the Thai government has embarked on half-hearted and largely ineffectual efforts to curb the guerrillas but has done little to address itself to the grievances of their increasingly dissatisfied Malay minority.

Though I shall treat Malaysia as a case of balanced pluralism between Malays and Chinese, there is a center–periphery relationship in East Malaysia. In Sabah the Kadazans and in Sarawak the Iban are the largest of several indigenous ethnic groups. Since they still live in subsistence communities and are poorly educated, they are only partially mobilized politically and, especially in Sabah, do not exercise the political or cultural influence that their numbers would warrant. Politics in East Malaysia tends to replicate the West Malaysian pattern of Malay–Chinese collaboration and competition. The terms of participation for the slowly mobilizing indigenous peoples have not yet been resolved.

The Indochina states have not enjoyed sufficient peace since their formal independence in 1954 to sort out their ethnic problems. The peripheral peoples located in the mountain cordillera of Indochina occupy more than two thirds of its territory. Moving freely, often in disregard of formal state boundaries, they have been an important factor in these civil wars. Even in Cambodia, where they represent less than 2 percent of the population, it is in the eastern hills where many of them reside that the Vietcong and the North Vietnamese established their sanctuary and base of operation.

The ethnic lowland Lao at the center of that fragile polity comprise barely half its population. The several hill tribes, including the Kha (Lao-Teng) in the south, the opium-producing Meo in the center, and the Tai in the north, have made few demands on the Lao government and have enjoyed substantial autonomy. The Meo, especially, have successfully asserted the right to dispose of their profitable opium crop in international commerce, subject only to a symbolic tribute to the Lao government. During the recent war against the Pathet Lao and the North Vietnamese, the majority faction of the Meo were armed by the United States to fight the North Vietnamese invaders, and their leaders were brought into the Royal Lao government. A minority faction of the same people identified with the Pathet Lao. The ancestral territories of the Meo in Xieng Khoung province were invaded by the North Vietnamese and devastated by American bombing. Large numbers of them were displaced and forced to move as refugees into the lowland areas traditionally inhabited by the Lao. Because of the long-standing neglect and contempt of the dominant Lao for the Kha, the latter were easily subverted by the North Vietnamese who maintained the Ho Chi Minh trail and its vital logistical facilities in areas inhabited by the Kha peoples.

Both in North and in South Vietnam, the Vietnamese occupy the lowlands and control the political center, but the highlands are inhabited by indigenous tribal peoples, most of them practicing a slash and burn style of agriculture. These technologically backward peoples were protected by the French, but after 1954 they became peripheral subjects of the Vietnamese. Yet the Saigon and Hanoi regimes pursued diametrically opposite approaches to their backward, minority subjects. The Diem regime demonstrated its contempt for these people in numerous ways. It offered them a negligible role in government, denigrated their cultures, and provided few public services but attempted for security reasons to settle demobilized Vietnamese veterans and refugees from North Vietnam on lands traditionally claimed by the tribesmen. During the Vietnam war the United States provided material assistance and successfully recruited troops from these tribes in order to keep the North Vietnamese out of these territories. The hostility of these tribesmen to the Saigon government was so intense that cooperation between them would have been impossible, and indeed the Saigon government opposed the arming of its hostile tribal minorities. With the end of American participation, it appears that the Thieu government will revert to the Diem policy of racial superiority, dominance, and minimal attention to the material and symbolic needs of these tribal people. (I shall not treat the Catholic–Buddhist cleavage among the ethnic Vietnamese. During the Diem period, the highly organized Catholic minority controlled the political center of the Saigon regime and much of subsequent South Vietnamese politics has involved the relative positions of Catholics and Buddhists.)

By contrast, the Hanoi regime, profiting from Soviet minority doctrine and practice, has taken great pains to promote the dignity of the tribal peoples, to foster their language and culture, and thus to win their allegiance to the regime. They have organized two autonomous regions, the Thai–Meo and the Viet–Bac covering more than half the territory of the country. Much of the revolutionary struggle of the Vietminh against the French colonial regime was conducted from territorial bases inhabited by the tribal minorities. After their successful struggle, the Hanoi government following the Leninist policy of "national in form, socialist in content" has sponsored the use of tribal languages, provided educational and other public services, and brought tribal members into the Communist party and government. Thus the management of the center–periphery relationship by the two competing Vietnamese regimes has followed opposite policies and has produced, in the short run at least, opposite results.

From their densely populated heartland, the Javanese occupy the geographic and political center in Indonesia. An important dimension of the politics of independent Indonesia has been the struggle of the non-Javanese minorities, particularly the Sundanese in Java, the Achinese, Batak, Menangkabau and coastal Malays in Sumatra, Makassarees and Buginese in Sulewesi, and coastal Malay in Kalimantan, to resist Javanese hegemony and maintain their autonomy. The outer islands tend to be more richly endowed with natural resources, more productive economically and, allowing for very considerable linguistic and cultural diversity, more oriented to Islamic values and practices than Java. On the other hand, the Javanese dominate the overblown administrative system and the armed forces. Indonesia has oscillated between federal and unitary constitutions and has suffered major rebellions by the outer islanders against alleged political domination and economic exploitation by the Javanese. The Sukarno policy of encouraging "transmigration," to help relieve the overpopulation of Java by government-sponsored settlement of ethnic Javanese in the sparsely populated outer islands, was bitterly resented and resisted as Javanese colonialism. Indonesia's rapidly growing urban areas have become arenas of bitter conflict between communally oriented migrants competing for very scarce opportunities. These conflicts occur as frequently and as intensely among the various minorities as between any of them and Javanese. As in Burma, the peripheral peoples have no particular love for one another and do not maintain an effective coalition.

The Javanese have not attempted to impose their language or customs on their compatriots. They have accepted a version of Malay, spoken as the native language only by the Malay and Menengkabau minorities, as Bahasa Indonesia, the national lingua franca and official language of government and administration. Bahasa Indonesia seems to have been accepted both practically and symbolically by all Indonesian ethnic groups and along with the nationalist ideology and the Indonesian national army has been the chief unifying force in this large, heterogeneous country.

The management of Indonesia's pluralism has always been a major concern of the army, before 1965 when it shared power with Sukarno and since that time when it has been the governing institution of the country. Though its command structure and its enlisted ranks are dominated by Javanese, the army has attempted, with considerable success, to balance centralized control through a common nationalist and anti-Communist ideology and military discipline with considerable autonomy for its territorial commanders in administration and economic development. So long as they keep the peace and maintain effective control of their regions, the territorial commanders can serve as spokesmen for the interests of their ethnic constituents and finance their operations from the sales proceeds of regional products, often through irregular channels of commerce. The military leadership, which successfully suppressed the anti-Sukarno outer island rebellion of 1958, is aware of the importance of restraining Javanese hegemony by providing non-Javanese with some military, political, and administrative posts in the Jakarta government and guaranteeing them a measure of economic and administrative autonomy.

It is reasonable to conclude that in the polities which we have reviewed, the elites at the center fondly hope that the peripheral groups will gradually acculturate and one day assimilate into the dominant society. In this way the troublesome pluralism that afflicts their polities would eventually—and the sooner the better—be liquidated. Most of the peripheral peoples, however, have little enthusiasm for rapid acculturation and none whatever for disappearance through assimilation. Because the latter occupy large and often strategically important territories, the central governments have been compelled—albeit reluctantly—to accept the persistence of the peripheral people and to seek appropriate accommodations. The pattern of demands depends on the degree of mobilization of the peripheral groups. Their elementary demand is for territorial and cultural autonomy and freedom from colonization of their lands by the dominant group. At a more mobilized stage (for example, the Sumatran minorities in Indonesia), they are likely to demand also a fair share of political representation and positions in the central government, public services and public investments on behalf of their economic and social aspirations, and even the right to control the foreign exchange proceeds of their economic activities. The terms of accommodation depend on the ability of the peripheral groups to compel the center to take their demands seriously and of the center to accept the unwelcome necessity for autonomy and other special treatment of peripheral peoples as compatible with their conceptions of the national polity.

The second pattern of interethnic politics in Southeast Asia involves the role of the *pariah entrepreneurial minorities*. Except for the Vietnamese minority in Cambodia and the dwindling Indian community in Burma, this refers to overseas Chinese. In every Southeast Asian country there is an important and conspicuous Chinese minority which has a leading and often the dominant position in wholesale and retail distribution, finance, small industry, transport, and skilled trades. During the colonial period, many hundreds of thousands of Chinese moved into the areas of economic opportunity between the large foreign producers and traders and the native peasant populations. As the colonialists departed and the native nationalist governments assumed control, the Chinese found themselves a politically weak, foreign, but relatively prosperous, highly visible and unpopular minority concentrated primarily in urban enclaves. For the first time the Chinese, who consider themselves culturally superior to the native societies, were compelled to face the choice of retaining their Chinese nationality or of seeking integration into the indigenous polities—in those cases where this was permitted by the local authorities. Independence in Southeast Asia has generated political and cultural nationalism. This has led in every case to economic nationalism and the most vulnerable target has been the Chinese.

Except in Malaysia and Singapore, where this pattern does not apply, the post-World War II period in Southeast Asia has been one of insecurity and harassment for the overseas Chinese. They have been charged with disloyalty, as agents of foreign (both Kuomintang and Red) expansion and subversion; they have been denied citizenship in some countries, declined to accept it in some, and hold it on precarious and often second class terms in others. Their schools and cultural institutions have been harassed and frequently closed; they have been forced, at least legally, out of certain occupations and even certain geographic areas; some have "returned" to Taiwan and to mainland China. Yet despite official hostility and persecution, the overseas Chinese have demonstrated enormous resilience, resourcefulness and survival power, due in large measure to the inability of indigenous businessmen and governments to take over the crucial economic roles as middlemen, skilled tradesmen, and small-scale producers which the Chinese perform effectively and profitably. Each Southeast Asian government has improvised its own policies toward resident Chinese and has varied its policies over time. To simplify a complex reality, their approaches to the Chinese "problem" can be summarized as follows:

Assimilation. Encouraging Chinese to accept local citizenship, use the local language, espouse the local religion, intermarry—merge their identity into the dominant group. For generations, many Chinese in Southeast Asia have chosen this path voluntarily so that today many of them are fully integrated Cambodians, Filipinos, Thai, or Javanese. With assimilation—a policy being pursued actively by the current Thai government and encouraged by Cambodia and Indonesia—Chinese would be expected to give up their educational institutions and cultural identity. In return, they and their descendents would gain personal security and their economic skills would be available to the indigenous society. The outcome would not be pluralism, but the disappearance of the Chinese as a separate group.

Pariah Status. Under this pattern, Chinese are excluded from political rights, tolerated in a limited range of occupations, and subjected to petty extortion and payments for protection and services by police and other civil servants and to shakedowns by local politicians and military officers. Their schools and cultural institutions lead a shadowy and insecure existence. They are either denied citizenship, or the opportunity to acquire it is fraught with complexity, or the right, once granted, may be insecure and subject to second class treatment. Yet despite humiliation and oppression, Chinese continue to prosper economically, to enjoy significantly higher living standards than indigenous peoples, and very few opt to migrate to China. They choose to suffer pariah status as the price for higher living standards than they could expect elsewhere, hoping that conditions may improve as the early phase of nationalism recedes in their adopted countries.

Cooptation. There is a mutual attraction, a symbiosis between men of power and men of money. Many of the ruling elites in Southeast Asia, including but not limited to the generals in Thailand and Indonesia, find wealthy and commercially sophisticated Chinese to be useful partners in business ventures ranging from the marketing of Sumatran rubber to building hotels in Bangkok. In this way, enterprising Chinese, profiting from such opportunities, can enrich themselves, distribute jobs and contracts to their families and friends, and intercede with their powerful local patrons to protect Chinese interests. It is impossible to know how many Chinese benefit from business relationships of this kind where their money, economic skills, and international commerical contacts are put to mutually beneficial uses.

The hostility and envy of Southeast Asian intellectuals and politicians and the vulnerability of Chinese to xenophobic attack have been matched by the ambivalence of Chinese themselves toward the status they desire in Southeast Asia. It appears that most of them, having been born in Southeast Asia, no longer look forward to "returning" to a China they have never seen. Unlike the Kuomintang regime which claimed all ethnic overseas Chinese as subjects, the Peking government has advised Chinese in Southeast Asia to identify with and integrate into their country of residence. But on what terms? It appears that Nanyang Chinese would prefer a plural outcome with full citizenship privileges and unrestricted economic opportunity, but with the right to maintain their educational and cultural institutions and thus preserve their separate group identity. This is precisely what Southeast Asian governments are not willing to concede. At best they seem willing to permit, even encourage, Chinese to assimilate completely, as in Thailand, at the sacrifice of their continuity as a separate people. At worst, they expect that the Chinese will depart or remain a closely supervised foreign enclave. Thus, the outcome will reflect not only what native elites are willing to grant, but what Chinese in Southeast Asia are willing to accept, and both will be influenced by the pace—hitherto very slow—at which indigenous entrepreneurs and skilled personnel can displace the Chinese from their current economic roles and thus reduce the indispensability of the latter to the operation and development of Southeast Asian economies.

The third pattern of communal politics in Southeast Asia is *balanced pluralism*—a set of arrangements which recognizes the salience of communal cleavages and legitimatizes communally based social structures and political activity as essential to peaceful and consensual coexistence. The classical case is Malaysia. There communal cleavages define and dominate the political struggle. The major conflict groups are the Malays who comprise nearly half the population and the Chinese whose numbers protect them from the pariah status of their coethnics elsewhere in Southeast Asia. The country has been governed since before its independence in 1957 by a multi-ethnic elite coalition (the Alliance party) controlled by moderate English-educated Malay aristocrats and Chinese capitalists, with representatives of the smaller Indian minority also participating. The incorporation of the Borneo states of Sabah and Sarawak in 1963 to form Malaysia has not fundamentally changed this political structure. Malays are politically dominant, controlling the national parliament, the cabinet, the senior civil service, twelve of the thirteen state governments, and the expressive symbols of the polity. Non-Malays, however, enjoy the rights of citizenship, office holding, and political participation, but may not bid for political control. On the other hand, Chinese dominate those sectors of the modern economy—finance, industry, trade, and the professions—which are not still controlled by Europeans. Though there are many poor Chinese, their average per capita income is nearly double the Malays'.

While they recognize that they are better off than their brethren elsewhere in Southeast Asia, Singapore excepted, Malayan-Chinese resent their second class citizenship, the establishment of Malay as the sole official language, and educational measures which they regard as economically discriminatory and a threat to the maintenance of Chinese culture. Malays, who consider themselves the "bumiputera," the indigenous people, can demonstrate that the preferences they enjoy on land matters, scholarships, small business licenses, senior civil service, and military posts, not to mention control of the machinery and symbols of government, all of which the Chinese deplore as evidence of official discrimination, have not redressed the economic and educational gaps between the two groups. The government has therefore initiated a New Economic Policy designed, primarily through public sector enterprise, to bring 30 percent of an expanding modern economy under Malay control by 1991, but without expropriating Chinese assets or limiting their economic opportunities.

The economically conservative and communally moderate leadership of the UMNO (the United Malay National Organization) and the MCA (the Malayan-Chinese Association), the senior partners in the governing Alliance party, have had difficulty controlling their own constituencies, both of which contain important elements which demand more militant prosecution of communal interests. Every measure which compromises conflicting communal demands in the interest of mutual accommodation threatens the erosion of constituency support. The present strain in the Alliance can be traced to the inability of the MCA to maintain broad-based support among Chinese who believe that the MCA has needlessly sacrificed vital Chinese cultural, political, and even economic interests in its determination to accommodate to the politically dominant UMNO. Despite such strains as those which led to the post-election communal riots in the Kuala Lumpur area in 1969, a modified Alliance structure has survived because it seems to be essential to legitimate government, the alternative being a destabilizing and potentially oppressive one-race regime.

Malaysia is not free from bitter class cleavages within its major communal camps, yet every effort to form cross-cutting associations along economic or ideological lines has failed. The basic reality in Malaysia is plural and this is reflected in its religious, cultural, residential, occupational, and political structures. Seldom have two peoples so divided by ethnicity, religion, and life styles been fated to coexist in the same territory, yet so intermingled that regional autonomy is not available as a device for conflict management. Despite chronic strains, occasional breakdowns, continuing grievances both among Malays and Chinese, and the failure as yet to incorporate the indigenous groups in East Malaysia, the Alliance coalition has provided this plural society with a stable, effective, and reasonably responsive government. In this mutual deterrence situation where each party is capable of inflicting unacceptable damage on the other, the Alliance or its functional equivalent appears to be the sine qua non for the peaceful maintenance of this system.

Another pattern of balanced pluralism can be found in the Philippines. The Christian Philippines contain eight major ethnolinguistic groups, the largest of which comprises less than a quarter of the population. These regionally based groups have proved to be effective articulators of group interests. The organization of national political "tickets" and the distribution of political rewards take account of these ethnic factors. The failure of Tagalog to be accepted as the national language can be traced to opposition by the other seven non-Tagalog groups. The failure of the Huks in the middle 1950s to extend their insurrection beyond the Papango-speaking area in central Luzon has been traced as much to the unwillingness of non-Papango-speakers to become involved as to the effectiveness of Magsaysay's counterinsurgency efforts.

Yet among Christian Filipinos, ethnic cleavages are not as critical and ethnic solidarities do not constitute the same burden on the polity that they do in other Southeast Asia countries. There is a strong sense of national identity, class cleavages are frequently more pronounced, and the presence of as many as eight groups prevents any one of them, including the Manila-based Tagalogs, from achieving hegemony over the others. The Philippines have learned how to manage the ethnic competition among their Christian populations, who comprise 92 percent of the total. This balanced pluralism, however, has not incorporated, as we shall see, the small but geographically concentrated Muslim minority.

A fourth and less pervasive, but nevertheless important pattern in Southeast Asia is epitomized by the *irredentist* struggle of the Philippine Muslims who occupy Western Mindanao and the Sulu Archipelago adjacent to the Muslim-dominated Malaysian state of Sabah and Indonesian Borneo. Despite efforts to provide their elites with political patronage and to extend a modicum of public services, the Muslims, comprising only 4 percent of the population, have never been successfully integrated into the Philippine polity. Their alienation has been aggravated in recent years by government-sponsored migration of thousands of Christian Ilocano and Cebuano settlers into Western Mindanao, encroaching on areas which the Muslims had traditionally regarded as their own, even though they had never secured firm titles to these lands. As these lines are written, Western Mindanao is embroiled in a bloody civil war between heavily armed and well-equipped Muslim guerrillas, and Christian settlers supported by the Philippine military which has not been able to bring the situation under control. Thousands have been killed on both sides. Promises of economic development and improved public services have been ineffectual in pacifying the Muslims, well organized under young, militant leadership, because the issues to them now are the removal of the Christian intruders, control of their ancestral territories, and a degree of legal and political autonomy that the central government is not willing to concede.

The governments of Malaysia and Indonesia, sympathetic as they must be with the plight of their coreligionists, have not intervened on their behalf, though there is evidence that the militantly Muslim Chief Minister of Sabah has been much less circumspect. This is not technically an irredentist situation because Malaysia has not claimed this area. Ironically, it is the Philippines, as legatees of the Sultan of Sulu, who have asserted a highly publicized claim to Sabah as "Philippina irredenta," the successful prosecution of which would certainly aggravate both their Muslim and their Chinese minority problems.

Another latent irredentist situation is in the four southern prov-

inces of Thailand bordering Malaya where the grievances of more
than a million neglected Malay Muslims cannot be ignored by the
Malaysian government, despite their desire to maintain good relations with their more powerful northern neighbor. One reason the
Kuala Lumpur government cannot indefinitely postpone action is,
as I have previously stated, because continued neglect and deprivation have exposed the Muslims in Thailand to the blandishments of
the remnants of the Chinese guerrillas who gained sanctuary among
these people after their defeat in Malaysia fifteen years ago. They
are now attracting Muslim recruits—which they were never able to
do in Malaya—and mounting damaging raids across the border.
The neglect and incompetence of the Thai government in dealing
with this minority is producing a security problem and a potential
domestic political hot potato for the Malaysians. Hence, one can
observe an irredentist problem ripening before one's eyes.

There are other minor irredentist situations in the complex distribution of peoples in Southeast Asia. Among them are the Cam-
bodian minorities in Thailand and especially in Vietnam and the
Thai-speaking Shans in Burma. Zealots on behalf of a "Greater Indonesia," which would incorporate Malaysia into Indonesia, continue to be heard in both countries, though this appeal has declined in political significance. None of these seems likely to turn in
the near future into problems as acute as the two cases already described.

A fifth pattern occurs in *Singapore* and it is a special case. This
tiny island state at the tip of the Malayan peninsula has evolved a
distinctive pattern for managing its ethnic pluralism. Of its 2.2
million people, 75 percent are ethnic Chinese, 15 percent Malays,
the balance Indians, Eurasians, and Europeans. This Chinese enclave must establish its security in a region dominated by Malay
peoples who are deeply suspicious of foreign penetration into their
part of the world and envious of Chinese economic dynamism and
prosperity. Thus the policy of the Singapore government is to un-
derplay the Chinese theme. The national language is Malay, a symbolic gesture to the region. Four languages, Mandarin, Tamil,
Malay, and English, enjoy official status in government and education through the secondary level. Indeed, it is this model—equal

formal status for the language and culture of all constituent groups—for which Malayan Chinese have unsuccessfully struggled in their country.

But the deeper reality in Singapore is the paramountcy of the English language. The architects of the "rugged society" conceive of Singapore as the cosmopolitan and technologically sophisticated center of finance, trade, and industry in Southeast Asia. They aspire even for a world role. This requires, in their view, that the international language of finance and high technology have precedence in Singapore's educational, economic, professional, and governmental institutions. It is clear that any parent who has ambitions for his children should enroll them in an English medium school. Though higher education is available in Chinese as well as English, Nanyang University graduates must be fluent also in English if they want a fair shot at governmental or industrial employment. While at the symbolic and cultural levels, Asian languages are fostered, English is the key to personal opportunity. Thus far, as measured in employment, investment, and per capita income terms, the results have been spectacularly successful. Threatened as little as five years ago with massive unemployment and economic stagnation, Singapore has achieved full employment, is second in Asia only to Japan in per capita income, and expects to surpass the British per capita income level by 1980.

As recently as 1964, during the brief two year interval when Singapore was a state of Malaysia, there were serious communal disturbances provoked by discontents among the Malay minority and abetted by their supporters across the causeway. The relative deprivations of the Malays persist. The Singapore government's policy of providing them with equal opportunity but no special privileges has not redressed their grievances or resulted in equality of condition and falls short of the preferences which Malays enjoy in Malaysia. The Malay minority is frustrated in a Chinese-dominated, English-speaking society, but their capacity to act is limited by their economic marginality and small numbers and the disinclination of the Malaysian and Indonesian governments to intervene on their behalf.

An important longer range issue is whether a prosperous and

self-confident Chinese majority will acquiesce indefinitely in the low-profile policy of the present government which deemphasizes the Chinese dimension of Singapore life in deference to the suspicions of its neighbors and as necessary to its expanded economic development. For the moment, however, the English-first policy has met the pragmatic test and is not being successfully challenged.

PROPHECIES AND FORECASTS

What of the future of communal relations in Southeast Asia during the balance of this century?

My premise is that the present territorial states in Southeast Asia will survive without important boundary changes. The institutional pressures of the international state system are biased toward the maintenance of the territorial status quo. The recent détente between Washington and Peking reduces the prospects of major international conflict in the area. Whether it results in one Vietnam or two, the end of the Indochinese war will probably leave Cambodia and Laos territorially intact, though in the latter case weak and disorganized, with the possibility that some of the tribal minorities may seek to be annexed to their kinsmen in the adjoining autonomous areas of North Vietnam. Elsewhere, the present boundaries of territorial states are likely to hold firm, the chief pressure being Muslim dissidence in the southern Philippines and in southern Thailand.

This stability will provide opportunities for elites at the center to continue the process of consolidating control over their "national" territories and peoples. International influences which have so profoundly influenced ethnic relations during the past two decades (the KMT incursions into North Burma, the mobilization and displacement of mountain peoples during the Indochina war, the U.S. intervention on behalf of the Indonesian rebels in 1957, the Indonesian confrontation against Malaysia) are likely to diminish but not disappear. This will provide more scope for local peoples within existing territorial states to work out their differences.

The relative power of centers over peripheries is likely to grow. This is the inevitable consequence of economic and administrative development and is abetted by current international practice which distributes economic, technical, and military assistance exclusively through central governments and requires foreign investors and traders to negotiate terms of business with central government agencies. It can be expected that the centers in Southeast Asia will further penetrate their peripheries with instruments of control and public service and that the domestic economies of these countries will become increasingly integrated. Because of their mutual antipathies, it is unlikely that the peripheral peoples will be able to sustain common fronts against expanding central power, further augmenting the latter's relative strength.

There will be countervailing influences, however. With modernization, some peripheral groups will mobilize more effectively and gain economic resources which should strengthen their bargaining power. Since there is neither empirical evidence nor a priori reason to believe that any but a few of the ethnic minorities in the center–periphery states desire assimilation into the dominant groups, the issues to be sorted out are the terms of their incorporation into the polity and economy. As I have previously indicated, the terms that are worked out will depend on the relative resources available to the parties and their differential aspirations. Within the same country, therefore, the status of communal groups which are regarded as indigenous may vary greatly.

In Indonesia, the more sophisticated peripheral peoples in Sumatra will have sufficient resources to make credible claims for a degree of administrative and economic autonomy and still demand resources—jobs, representation, and public services—from the Javanese center. At the other extreme, the weak and divided peoples of West Irian will be forced to accept the status of dependency with only their geographic remoteness and inaccessibility to protect them. In Thailand, the northern hill tribes have so few resources in relation to the central government and the latter has so little interest in them, that with the winding down of the Indochina war and less prospect of external intervention on their behalf, mutually agreeable arrangements of benign neglect will probably result. By contrast, the numerically large and rapidly mobilizing Lao–Thai group in the northeast will certainly demand and receive far more in benefits from the Bangkok government than in the past, but it is

not clear whether they will claim greater regional autonomy or accept gradual assimilation and integration into the Thai political
and administrative system, which is certainly what the Thai government prefers. The peripheral minorities in Burma are likely to lose
in relative power to the central government; the cost of their insurrections will increase and they will be compelled to come to terms
with Rangoon that yield them less political and cultural autonomy
than they desire. In North Vietnam—and in all of Vietnam if the
Hanoi regime prevails—the relative congruity of objectives between the central regime and the minority highland peoples, including cultural autonomy plus opportunities for participation in
modern occupations and in the activities of the political center,
should produce a consensual modus vivendi, at least in the short
run, despite the imbalance in their resource endowments. Whatever the outcome, the ruling Lao elites will not be able to resist the
North Vietnamese precedent and will probably grant their tribal
minorities a substantial degree of formal autonomy.

Unless they are to be determined by pure imposition or by warfare, the successful management of center–periphery conflicts
requires institutional structures for bargaining and for the assertion and resolution of demands. The practice of managing intercommunal relations through normal administrative channels—the
Malaysian policy toward Sabah's Kadazans or the Thai and South
Vietnamese policy toward their hill tribes—symbolizes neglect by
the center of the claims for distinctive status and the special problems of the peripheral peoples. It compels the minorities either to
acquiesce in their subordination, to organize politically, or in ex-
tremis, to mount insurgencies in order to enhance their negotiating
position. In their aspiration for national unity, those in control of
the center prefer to treat all their subjects as individuals, following
the methods and the criteria used in relating government to the
populace within the dominant community. This, however, is seldom satisfactory to the peripheral peoples. Consensual arrangements require the establishment of formal or informal institutions
for regulating communal relations, thus legitimatizing pluralism.
These institutions, as a minimum, provide some channels for the
articulation and processing of communal interests. Concretely, they

may include communal political parties, elite coalitions, central government ministries, federal arrangements, or regional units specifically concerned with the management of communal differences. Such structures can be expected to increase as central governments in Southeast Asia, in their political development, become reconciled to the plural reality of their societies.

Among overseas Chinese, outside Singapore and Malaysia, there will be continuing tension between competing drives for assimilation and for legitimate pluralism. The latter alternative is preferred by most Nanyang Chinese, since it would permit them to retain their culture and social structures, while enjoying full political rights and economic opportunities, but it is categorically unacceptable to any of the native governments. "Return" to China is likely to be an unappealing or unrealistic prospect. Moreover, attempts to accommodate to indigenous environments by acculturation, while maintaining group identity, often leave the Chinese with the worst of both worlds: the loss of the vital elements of Chinese culture combined with continued suspicion and rejection by local peoples as an alien group.

Thus, one may expect the emerging generation of Chinese born in Southeast Asia to opt in growing numbers for assimilation through deculturation and intermarriage. Painful as it may be to their parents, many of them will follow this path, simply because a satisfactory and rewarding Chinese way of life will not be possible in Southeast Asia, there will be no salvation from China, and a more attractive personal alternative will be available. Cultural memories and practices will survive vestigially and so will some valuable local and international business links, but the solidarity structures which give vitality to Chinese as a community will wither away. The success of this policy in Thailand and Cambodia will induce elites in other countries—Indonesia, Vietnam, and perhaps even the Philippines—to adopt this approach as it promises to "solve" their Chinese problem. It will be increasingly appealing to local Chinese in the absence of opportunities for personal fulfillment or group survival on equal or even dignified terms. The most difficult problems will be encountered in the strongly Islamic areas of Indonesia where popular hostility to the Chinese is most intense and the pork-eating Chinese find Islam an unattractive way of life.

In the two systems which have legitimatized pluralism, opposite developments can be anticipated. The Philippines will have no serious problem managing the pluralism among their eight Christian ethnic communities because none of them is a serious threat to the status or survival of the others. Earlier pressure to impose the Tagalog language has been abandoned, the system is sensitive to the need to distribute benefits with some degree of equity among constituent groups, and a strong integrative national sentiment has emerged. It is even possible that in the Philippine system—a theme to which we shall return—class will supplant ethnic cleavage as the main dimension of conflict.

Malaysia, by contrast, will see not a relaxation but an intensification of the bipolar tensions between Malays and Chinese. The rising generation of politicians, especially among the Malays, is more strident than accommodative in its communal demands and the system may lack the material and political resources to satisfy both parties. Malays will use their control of government to enforce the Malay language policy and to push for substantially increased Malay participation in education and in the modern economy, while denying non-Malays the weight in government that their numbers warrant and even the legal right to argue for a "Malaysian Malaysia." Embittered Chinese will be divided between those who favor militancy and those who favor accommodative tactics within the present system, and those who would resort to revolutionary action. Chinese will be forced to defensive tactics to protect their educational and economic advantages, with little hope of realizing their aspiration for political parity. The recently expanded Alliance structure, which has provided an excellent institutional framework for managing communal conflict, will be under great strain to cope with increasingly incompatible demands for the intercommunal distribution of scarce opportunities and values. A recurrent theme in the literature on structural pluralism is the inevitability of stratification, of one communal group emerging in a dominant position. Malaysia is a concrete test of this prediction or, alternatively, of whether balanced pluralism can be sustained in a polity which was originally organized on that premise.

Marxist, liberal, and developmental theorists have been united in their inability to come to terms with the reality, the persistence, and indeed the reemergence of communal solidarities in modern societies. By definition they have identified communal solidarities with more primitive modes of human association which survive only as aberrations in universalistic, achievement-oriented, modern nation-states. They have found ideological and especially class cleavages to be the normal and legitimate dimensions of conflict in industrial and urbanizing systems. In that context, occupational and class interests are expected to cross-cut and weaken the grip of communal solidarities on modern man and ultimately to supplant them as articulators of demands and mobilizers of action. What of the relationships between class and communal solidarities in modernizing Southeast Asia?

Southeast Asia is not without its class conflicts; indeed they are intensifying. Within communal groups, among Javanese, Vietnamese, Chinese, Thai, Christian Filipinos, in rural as well as in urban areas, class tensions are growing and are eroding the patron–client lines of responsibility and deference which once integrated these societies. Every indicator points to the intensification of class conflict in these societies. With few exceptions such as Singapore, there will probably be insufficient resources to mitigate conflicts in the European and North American high-consumption, welfare-state pattern. Yet, there is no evidence in any of these polities that class solidarities within communal structures have effectively cross-cut communal cleavages where the latter retain their salience or have in any measure reduced their intensity. At all strata individuals transact for mutual advantage across communal lines. Though often quite civil, these are, nevertheless, calculated dealings. They seldom develop an affective element and they have not evolved into solidarity structures which effectively challenge the pull of communal loyalties. It would be easier to demonstrate that class conflicts can be diverted into communal hostility and violence than that ethnic conflict can be transmuted into class struggle, except where class and communal cleavages coincide. Even in the latter situation (for example, the Malays in Singapore) the struggle is likely to be articulated in communal, not in class language, because the former draws on deeper layers of identity and consciousness than the latter. Contrary to earlier expectations, urbanization, which has been regarded as a modernizing phenomenon in which traditional, particularistic, communal loyalties become irrelevant, is having the opposite effect. Rapid urbanization tends to aggravate communal antagonisms in close-quartered competition for scarce jobs, housing, educational opportunities, and political influence.

Southeast Asia will be a theatre both of class and of communal conflict during the next quarter century. Class conflict will intensify within the more modern, differentiated communal groups, but I see no evidence that one will cross-cut or supplant the other. Though some of the hundreds of small ethnic groups, which could not be treated in this chapter, may merge into more viable communal formations, most of the larger ones will retain their boundaries. Pluralism in Southeast Asia's territorial states will persist and will continue to generate important, if unwelcome, issues on the agendas of political elites.

REFERENCES

For those who wish to pursue this subject further, the following general sources are recommended:

Walker Connor. "Ethnology and the Peace of Southeast Asia." *World Politics,* 22.1 (October 1969), 52–86.
Frank Golay, Ralph Anspach, M. Ruth Pfanner, and Eliezer B. Ayal. *Underdevelopment and Economic Nationalism in Southeast Asia.* Ithaca, Cornell University Press, 1969.
George Kahin, ed. *Governments and Politics of Southeast Asia.* Ithaca, Cornell University Press, 2nd ed. 1964.
Peter Kunstadter, ed. *Southeast Asian Tribes, Minorities, and Nations.* Princeton, Princeton University Press, 1967. 2 vols.
Victor Purcell. *The Chinese in Southeast Asia.* London, Oxford University Press, 1965.

APPENDIX

A Note on Demographic Proportions

Country-by-country demographic breakdowns for Southeast Asia are useful only as gross orders of magnitude. While varying from one country to another, the reliability of these figures is limited by the following factors: inaccurate and incomplete census compilations; the omission and manipulation of data by governments which have an interest in under-reporting the numbers of their communal minorities; and the arbitrariness of classification. As an example of the latter, the Thai government considers speakers of all Thai dialects as ethnic Thai, which would yield an 80 percent "Thai" figure, while Kunstadter (whose data we use) separates the Thai into dialect groups and finds that the dominant central Thai represent only 30 percent of the total. On the other hand, Chinese, regardless of dialect group, are aggregated below in a single category. In several cases, because of incompleteness, residuals are reported under the single category "other." To repeat, the purpose of these data is to indicate general proportions, not to provide precise information.

Burma	27.5 million	Cambodia	6.7 million
Burman	55%	Khmer	85%
Shan	6	Chinese	7
Karen	7	Vietnamese	7
Katchin	7	Other	1
Mon	2		
Chin	2		
Chinese	2		
Indian	1		
Other	18		

Indonesia	124.9 million	Laos	3.0 million
Javanese	45%	Lao	50%
Sundanese	14	Tribal minorities,	
Madurese	8	including Kha, Meo,	
Coastal Malays	8	Yao, and Tai	48
Makassarese-Buginese	8	Chinese	2
Menangkabau	3	Vietnamese	1
Balinese	2		
Batak	2		

Indonesia	124.9 million	Laos	3.0 million
Achinese	1		
Chinese	3		
Other	6		
Malaysia	10.6 million	Philippines	37.9 million
Malaya	9 million	Cebuano	24%
Malays	50%	Tagalog	21
Chinese	37	Ilocano	12
Indians	11	Ilongo	10
Other	2	Bicol	8
Sabah	0.6 million	Waray-Waray	6
Kadazans	32%	Papango	3
Chinese	23	Pangasinan	3
Bejau	12	Muslim	5
Murut	4	Chinese	2
Malay	1	Other	6
Other	28		
Sarawak	1 million		
Malay	19%		
Chinese	31		
Iban	40		
Other	10		
Singapore	2.1 million	Thailand	35.3 million
Chinese	75%	Central Thai	30%
Malay	15	Lao Thai	27
Indians	9	Other Thai	23
Other	1	Chinese	10
		Malay	5
		Hill tribes	2
		Other	3
North Vietnam	21.6 million	South Vietnam	18.3 million
Vietnamese	85%	Vietnamese	88%
Chinese	1	Chinese	6
Tai	3	Khmer	2
Thai	2	Jarai, Rhade, and	
Muong	3	other hill tribes	4
Nung, Meo, Yao, and			
other hill tribes	6		

Sources: Aggregate Population Data: *U.N. Demographic Yearbook, 1972.*

Indonesia: Projections from 1930 census as reported in Leslie Palmier, *Indonesia* (London, Thames and Hudson, 1965).

Philippines: 1960 census as reported in George Kahin, ed., *Government and Politics in Southeast Asia* (Ithaca, Cornell University Press, 1964), p. 710.

Malaysia: *Government of Malaysia Statistics Bulletin* (Nov. 6, 1968).

Other figures derived from Peter Kunstadter, ed., *Southeast Asian Tribes, Minorities, and Nations* (Princeton, Princeton University Press, 1967), I, 15.

13

ALI A. MAZRUI

Ethnic Stratification and the Military-Agrarian Complex: The Uganda Case

The first successful military coup on the Nile Valley in the modern period took place in Egypt in 1952. Almost twenty years later, at the other end of the White Nile, Uganda became the latest country on the Nile Valley to be captured by its own army. The army which took over power in Egypt in 1952 was described as "solidly Egyptian and rural; its officers were of the rural middle class." General Naguib, who briefly headed the new military government in Egypt, affirmed that the officer corps of the army "was largely composed of the sons of civil servants and soldiers and the grandsons of peasants." [1]

What of the army which took over power at the other end of the Nile in Kampala? Amin's army was even more solidly "rural." If Egyptian soldiers under General Naguib were "the grandsons of peasants," Ugandan and Sudanese soldiers under General Amin were "the *sons* of peasants." There was no intermediate generation separating the great majority of Ugandan soldiers from the womb of the countryside.

What were the implications of this linkage between peasants and modern warriors? It may be understandable in a developing society that the army should recruit primarily from people with rural

1. Mohammad Naguib, *Egypt's Destiny* (Garden City: Doubleday and Company, 1955), pp. 14–15. Cited in a related context by Samuel P. Huntington, *Political Order in Changing Societies* (New Haven, Yale University Press, 1968), pp. 241–242. Huntington also cites Perlmutter on the army being "solidly Egyptian and rural."

roots, but why did the Uganda army consist so disproportionately of Nilotic and Sudanic tribesmen? How did this affect ethnic stratification in Uganda? In other words, how did political rewards and political allegiances relate to the social and ethnic origins of Ugandan soldiers?

Samuel P. Huntington, in discussing social forces pertinent to relations between the city and the countryside in certain societies, once distinguished between the brains of the intelligentsia, the guns of the military, and the numbers of the peasantry. In Huntington's view, political stability requires a coalition between at least two of these social forces. He sees a coalition of brains and guns against numbers as being rare and basically unstable. A coalition between the intelligentsia and the peasants, on the other hand, was potentially the most revolutionary. Such a coalition could destroy an existing system and then create a new and more stable arrangement.

> The third route to stable government is by the coalescence of guns and numbers against brains . . . Their rural social background often leads military regimes to give high priority to policies which benefit the more numerous elements in the countryside. In Egypt, Iraq, Turkey, Korea, Pakistan, governments born of military coups pushed land reform measures. In Burma and elsewhere military governments gave budget priority to agricultural rather than to urban programs.[2]

How relevant are these precedents for the understanding of what has been happening in Uganda? Is there indeed a military-agrarian complex underlying Uganda's experience with the soldiers?

We propose to argue that the Obote years in Uganda were basically years of a coalition between the intelligentsia and the military, between brainpower and gunpower. There was a link with the countryside to the extent that the soldiers were rurally recruited, and also because many of the most powerful members of Obote's government came from some of the least developed areas of the country. But on the whole the basic alliance was between soldiers and a large part of the country's intelligentsia. In this partnership

---

2. Samuel P. Huntington, *Political Order in Changing Societies,* pp. 241–242.

the brains were senior in status. There was genuine civilian supremacy under Milton Obote, but paradoxically that supremacy had to make considerable concessions to the military in order to survive effectively.

One significant implication of the military coup which overthrew Obote in January 1971 was, quite simply, the termination of the supremacy of the intelligentsia. The old alliance between guns and brains, with brains in control, had now been shattered. The stage was set for new alliances.

We propose to argue that there is a military-agrarian complex struggling for survival in Uganda, a fragile alliance between the soldiers and their kinsmen in the countryside. But a major problem confronting the viability of such an alliance is the simple fact that the army has been ethnically unrepresentative, recruited overwhelmingly from Nilotic and Sudanic tribes in a country with a tradition of high ethnic consciousness. The soldiers respond not merely to their rural origins, but also to their ethnic origins. The old Egyptian model of a military-agrarian complex, involving dramatic moves toward land reform and the control of the intelligentsia, is struggling in Uganda against the forces of ethnic pluralism. Egypt is ethnically homogeneous; Uganda is painfully heterogeneous. The trend toward a military-agrarian complex in Uganda is struggling against the consequences of an ethnically specialized armed force operating in a country with highly developed ethnic consciousness. But why were the soldiers of the Ugandan army recruited so selectively from Nilotic and Sudanic communities?

The present tensions in Uganda go back deep into history. And we must turn to history in the search both for explanations and for relevant definitions of critical concepts.

But in order to understand how ethnicity relates to stratification in African conditions, the concept "rural" has itself to be examined. Are there *degrees* of "ruralness"? Were the Nilotic and Sudanic tribes of Uganda particularly rural, and if so, in what sense? It is with the concept of "rural" that we must begin.

LOCATION, FUNCTION, AND STATUS

What, then, is a rural area? From a sociological point of view, three dimensions are particularly important in defining a rural area. These dimensions are *location, function,* and *status.* An area must be located in the midst of natural greenery short of a dense forest and must be some minimal distance from major centers of concentrated populations.

As regards function, a rural area earns its livelihood primarily from agriculture, and sometimes forestry and fishing if the requisite resources are near at hand.

From a political point of view, a rural area has also to be seen in terms of status. This is where stratification comes into relevance. In most societies the majority of the inhabitants of rural areas are relatively underprivileged. But there are occasions when the rural elite becomes effectively the national elite. Societies with a landed aristocracy provide such instances in history. But with industrialization and greater urbanization the shift of power has often moved toward the city, and the status of the countryside has declined. The peasants have often been relegated to a humble role in national affairs.

If location as a dimension of ruralism implies *physical* distance from major centers, status implies *social* distance from urban elites and their influence on national affairs.

Sometimes physical distance is itself a causal factor behind the social distance. In the case of Uganda, the distance separating the north from the capital city of Kampala, and the poor communications which for so long hardened this distance, were factors behind the relegation of the north to a peripheral role in national affairs. When the country at last had a northern head of government, one of the first priorities undertaken was to improve communications between the capital city of Kampala and the distant areas of Lango and Acholi. Obote converted the highroad from Kampala to Gulu into an all-weather tarmac road. He also provided a bridge to facilitate greater access to West Nile. *The Common Man's Charter,* which Obote issued in 1969 as an ideological blueprint for the new Uganda, reaffirmed the imperative of bridging the gap between the different districts of Uganda, and the necessity to pursue more equitable developmental strategies for the different parts of the country.

When Amin came into power the preoccupation with the imperative of bridging the gap between the north and the more prosperous south continued. His tribe, the Kakwa, had been even more underprivileged than, say, the Acholi. Since Amin came from West Nile, he was himself particularly keen to ensure easy access to West Nile. His interest in having an airport built near Arua, the main town of West Nile, was in part a quest to reduce the isolation of West Nile. That isolation had a good deal to do with the status of West Nile as a particularly rural area sociologically. Amin employed Israelis to help him build that airport. By the time he expelled the Israelis, the airport was not yet complete. But the ambition to reduce the implications of physical distance, as well as reduce the social distance between the north and the more prosperous south of the country, continued to be a lingering feature of Amin's ambition.

For a while he even entertained the idea of a second university of Uganda, with a campus in Gulu and Arua, but his hopes for considerable support from the French government toward realizing this goal were not fulfilled. The idea of a second university, with special locational preference given to northern areas, was part of Amin's strategy to deruralize the Nilotic and Sudanic areas of the country.

It is certainly clear from Uganda's experience that the dimension of *status* in the definition of a rural area is in turn intimately connected with both location and function. Certainly from a political point of view the status of rural areas in national affairs is what gives rural location and rural function their most salient meaning.

We should now turn more fully to this concept of rural status, explore its ideological implications, and apply it to the analysis of both geographical location and cultural functions in Uganda's historical experience.

A Maoist interpretation of the Third World is that of a global countryside, neglected and sometimes exploited by the city folk of the affluent countries of the world. This approach looks upon the division between the developed and the less developed countries as being basically similar to the division between the city and the rural areas. A pattern of differential development, social and cultural distance, and asymmetrical political and economic interaction between these diverse geographical areas, together find a basis for such a functional definition of city versus country.

A related radical approach uses the categories of center and pe-riphery instead of city and country. The Norwegian scholar Johan Galtung has perhaps gone furthest in linking imperialism to the dichotomy between center and periphery, and working out an en-tire theory of dominance based on that dichotomy.[3]

Applying these concepts to a single society, instead of the world as a whole, could yield important insights of its own. In the history of Uganda the role of Buganda looms large. (Buganda is the terri-torial home of the Ganda community and the name of the East Af-rican kingdom. Baganda is the name applied to members of the Ganda community. Muganda is the singular of Baganda, that is, one member of the community. Ganda, the root word, is also used as an adjective.)

Using Galtungian terms, Buganda had long been the center of the society, while northern Uganda was clearly part of the periph-ery. Using Maoist terms, Buganda was the city writ large, while much of the rest of the country was functionally rural in this spe-cial sense of differential development, imbalance in the distribution of industries, and exploitative relationships. The Baganda were at the top of the emerging system of ethnic stratification.

For a while in its history Buganda even entered the role of a subimperial power, collaborating with the British in controlling and ruling significant parts of the rest of the country. Buganda provided many of the administrators for British rule assigned to different parts of the country. And through much of the colonial period the Baganda were clearly the heartland community of the country, displaying an impressive responsiveness to the stimulus of the new educational and cultural skills which came with the impe-rial power and European missionaries. The region became the best developed economically, the best educated, the best integrated through a network of communications, and the most influential po-litically. As Kampala evolved into the capital city, Buganda devel-oped into the capital region.

As Buganda became more urbanized and consolidated its central-ity in national affairs, it also became demilitarized. At the time that the British arrived in this part of the world, the Buganda

3. See, for example, Johan Galtung, "A Structural Theory of Imperialism," *Journal of Peace Research*, 2.2 (1971), 81–117.

kingdom had been militarily one of the most powerful in East Africa as a whole. The kingdom had evolved impressive political and social institutions and had developed systems of collective organization which converted Buganda into an impressive military force.

The 1900 Agreement concluded between Buganda and Britain inaugurated a new era. The agreement itself put special limitations on the numbers and types of arms which the king of the Baganda could acquire or keep for the protection of the palace. But beyond that the process of demilitarizing the Baganda had got under way. The military profession which had been one of honor and commitment began to lose over time some of its luster. With the 1900 Agreement the Baganda shifted from a conception of national autonomy based on military might to a conception of their autonomy based on contractual rights. Over time they learned how to exploit effectively the terms and implications of the 1900 Agreement. They learned how to use the courts with sophistication in pursuit of their rights against the British. Militarily they were of course no match for British military technology. The Baganda now realized that their ultimate weapons against the British were legal and political. The profession of arms was left to "lesser" ethnic communities.

The British themselves had in addition a vested interest in the demilitarization of Buganda. British policies for military recruitment turned to other areas, reinforcing the Baganda's own increasing inclination to look for alternative avenues of honor, income, and achievement.

But if Buganda was becoming a less promising area of recruitment for the King's African rifles, where else should the British turn for those recruits? There was a large number of alternative areas. The British could have turned to other Bantu areas of the country. To some extent the British did turn to those. But the Bantu areas were specially susceptible to the demonstration effect of Buganda's ways. Buganda's system of administration and cultural styles were to some extent emulated in the other Bantu areas of the country. Certainly the other areas of kingdoms in Uganda, all basically Bantu, displayed a marked tendency to use Buganda as a reference point, if not as a model. The demilitarization of Buganda was followed by a demilitarization of the other kingdoms.

Once again the British themselves had a vested interest in helping the demilitarization of the kingdoms. There was in British calculations an assumption that those African societies which were politically organized as states before the British came were a greater military risk once subjugated by the British than those African societies which were segmentary and politically acephalous. Buganda and Bunyoro, as kingdoms which had been particularly strong upon the arrival of the British, were regarded by the British for a while as potential military risks of a specially ominous kind.

The northern tribes of Uganda, to the extent that they were less centralized in their political organization, emerged as safer areas for military recruitment into the colonial armed forces. In reality the British had encountered upon arrival some resistance in parts of the north. And the record of northerners as fighters and warriors was already established. But the nature of northern political organization was such that the societies had collections of individual warriors, rather than units of organized armies. The two factors together increased the attractiveness of the north as a recruiting area for the British colonial armed forces. The *individuals* so recruited were believed to have good martial qualities, but the societies from which they sprang were often not centralized enough to raise the threat of organized armies of resistance under the banner of a single political authority.

The relatively segmentary Nilotic and Sudanic communities of the north were already becoming politically peripheral in Uganda. But their very status as a political periphery made them attractive for military recruitment into the imperial armed forces. What had happened was once again an interplay between political and economic factors in converting the rural areas of northern Uganda into a preeminently suitable source of recruits into the Ugandan army. The foundations of a fundamentally different system of ethnic stratification in the future were being laid. But behind the historical developments were also some salient cultural differences between ethnic groups. What were originally factors primarily of interest to anthropologists carried implications of long-term consequences. Let us now turn more closely to these cultural variations among Uganda's ethnic groups.

ON CULTURE AND COMBAT

African traditional societies which lacked the structures of state organization had by necessity to develop alternative structures of political and military stability. Many evolved the tradition of "neighborhood defense," based on the principle of constructing settlements in a manner which provided neighborhood self-reliance in military matters.

In addition a number of societies evolved age-grade systems providing for functional specialization. G. P. Murdock may have exaggerated the Cushite derivative nature of age-grade systems, but he was surely right in seeing the system as being designed to compensate for political decentralization. In the words of Murdock:

> The Nilotes unquestionably acquired their age-grade systems through fusion with, or imitation of, the Eastern Cushites. The reason for the spread of these systems must lie in their survival value. They clearly promoted military strength and social integration and thus doubtless served to offset in large measure the disadvantages inherent in a minimal development of political organization.[4]

The special arrangements of settlements, and the age-grade systems, were in turn connected among the Nilotes to pastoralism as a way of life. In both the Sudan and Uganda pastoralism is often a major, and in some cases the dominant, factor in the economic style of the tribes which have produced soldiers for national armies. The tradition of protecting mobile animals, and the quest for new pastures, might have resulted in certain *athletic* qualities pertinent to the military profession. Recruitment into colonial armies sometimes equated athletic qualities with martial qualities. The stamina of the man who walks dozens of miles with his cattle, the stamina of the "long distance runner," could so easily be seen as relevant also for military performance.

In addition pastoralism as an economic way of life produces a

4. George Peter Murdock, *Africa: Its Peoples and Their Culture History* (New York, McGraw-Hill, 1959), p. 339.

"world view" of its own which encompasses martial values. In this sense one might even distinguish between personal valor and military honor. Personal valor is invoked when the individual herdsman is protecting his own cattle or his own wives and children against raiders. Military honor in this sense comes into play in *collective* combat against a collective external enemy.

Pastoralism may sharpen concepts of personal valor—self-defense in the old sense of the rugged and isolated frontier. Each family had to be its own "army," each man his own warrior.

On the other hand, societies which combine pastoralism with cultivation, but without a tradition of centralized authority structures, may have concepts which are a little nearer to those of collective military honor.

In more elaborate state systems like those of traditional Buganda and Bunyoro, fighting for the king could become an even bigger measure of valor than fighting to protect one's cattle or one's private settlement. Military service was elaborately interlinked with political organization. The contrast between the northern tribes and the kingdoms of Uganda struck the foreign observers quite early, though sometimes they misunderstood the implications of what they were observing. Baker wrote in 1874:

The order and organization of Unyoro were a great contrast to the want of cohesion of the northern tribes. Every district throughout the [Nyoro] country was governed by a chief, who was responsible to the king for the states of the province. This system was extended to sub-government and a series of lower officials in every district, who were bound to obey the orders of the lord-lieutenant . . . In the event of war, every governor could appear, together with his contingent of armed men, at short notice. These were the rules of government that had been established for many generations throughout Unyoro.[5]

By the time the British came to Uganda, Bunyoro was beginning to evolve a kind of standing army round the nucleus of the King's or Mukama's bodyguard.

Until King Kabarega, Bunyoro did not traditionally have a permanent standing army. In time of war the chiefs sometimes became military leaders and were responsible for making available

5. S. Baker, *Ismailia* (London, Macmillan, 1874), II, 212–213.

able-bodied men under their jurisdiction. Political and military leadership were often completely fused. There were chiefs who gained great national reputation as war leaders—"and crowns (*Makondo*) had been awarded to successful generals." [6] During the reign of Kabarega, the *Barusura,* or king's bodyguard, developed into an effective military force. Bunyoro was about to institutionalize its warriors and make them a standing army. But the British were at last at hand, and Kabarega's reign signified both the climax of the Nyoro military organization and the beginning of the demilitarization of Bunyoro.

Ganda political culture also emphasized military honor rather than personal valor. In the course of the nineteenth century Buganda was developing a special Royal Guard Corps as the basis of a gradually evolving regular army. The bulk of the army was still recruited from peasant militia, but the capacity for mobilizing that army was considerably facilitated by the relative political centralization of the system. Behind it all was an ethos of militarism which had become extra militant by this period. Once again political and military organization were substantially fused. In the words of Lloyd Fallers:

Organizationally . . . warfare represented the clearest working-out of the pattern towards which the whole polity was moving: an institutional system in which positions of honor were open to challenge, in which ability and diligence were quickly rewarded and failure was quickly punished . . . War was thus the focus of what had perhaps become, in the nineteenth century, the master value in Ganda culture—the aggrandizement of the nation and the king.[7]

These were the organizational factors which made the Bantu kingdom such a striking contrast to the relatively acephalous political arrangements of the northern tribes.

Yet the northern tribes after colonial annexation could still be

6. See John Beattie, *The Nyoro State* (Oxford, The Clarendon Press, 1971), pp. 128–129.

7. L. A. Fallers, assisted by F. K. Kamoga and S. B. K. Musoke, "Social Stratification in Traditional Buganda," chap. 2, in L. A. Fallers, ed., *The King's Men: Leadership and Status in Buganda on the Eve of Independence* (London, Oxford University Press, on behalf of the East African Institute of Social Research, 1964), pp. 111–130.

deemed to produce some of the best *individual* warriors. Just as the British had made assumptions about extra martial prowess among the Gurkhas and Punjabis, so they made assumptions about such prowess among the Nilotic and Sudanic peoples of northern Uganda.

Additional cultural factors included the interplay between food culture and physical anthropology. Eastern and western Nilotes and Sudanic tribes produced a disproportionate number of men who were tall and slim. This particular kind of physique was interpreted in the colonial period as additional evidence of military suitability. The "tall and lean" were regarded as "good drill material."

Food culture over generations could have influenced the emergence of lean physical specimens, especially among communities which were truly pastoral. Reliance on milk and meat as the staple food, with periods when almost nothing else was added to the diet, had its impact on physical anthropology. Millet among other Nilotes was interpreted by the communities themselves as a diet fundamentally more relevant to physical strength than the *matoke* (plantain bananas) of some of the Bantu tribes.

But whatever the relevance of food culture for physique, there is little doubt that the recruitment officers of the imperial power in Uganda came to look at Nilotic and Sudanic communities as being *physically* better "drill material" than most of the people of the Bantu kingdoms. In Ankole the ruling elite was sufficiently pastoral in its origin and culture that specimens of similar physique were available. But as Ankole was a kingdom, and as the new criteria of prestige in colonial Uganda moved away from military symbolism, and since in any case Buganda was an important model for the other kingdoms, Ankole's representation in the Ugandan armed forces was as modest as the representation of the other kingdoms.

An ethnic separation of powers seemed to be underway in Uganda. There was a disproportionate presence of the Bantu in administration and the economy. But there was also developing a disproportionate Nilotic and Sudanic presence within the armed forces of the new Uganda.

Buganda itself remained the most privileged part of the Bantu areas. It was indeed a city writ large. The Nilotic and Sudanic areas were virtually the most peripheral in the new national entity. The soldiers were coming from a part of the country which was rural in location, function, and status. The stage was set for the beginnings of a military-agrarian complex.[8]

THE MILITARIZATION OF THE COUNTRYSIDE

With both the disadvantages of physical and social distance and the presumed advantages of rural culture for military performance, peasant warriors began to join the army in significant numbers. For some villages the army was second only to agriculture as a major source of livelihood and income for the local community. For some peasants a military career was their first introduction to Uganda as a national entity. What was once said of young Turkish farm lads was also true of raw recruits from rural Uganda. These recruits "from isolated villages now suddenly felt themselves to be part of the larger society. The connection between their private life and public role became vivid to them—and this sense of their new personality they diffused around them when they returned to their villages." [9]

In some important sense the country boys became conscious of their membership in the Ugandan nation. Hundreds acquired some technical training relevant to some aspect of their military functions. Some were helped to become literate. All had to learn or improve their Swahili as a medium of interaction with lads from other ethnic areas. Those areas had indeed become partially militarized when they became converted into major grounds for recruitment into the armed forces. But the recruits themselves also became partially nationalized in their perspectives, though still retaining serious rural handicaps.

8. Consult also Mazrui, "The Lumpen Proletariat and Lumpen Militariat: African Soldiers as a New Political Class," *Political Studies,* 21.1 (March 1973), and Mazrui, "The Militarization of Charisma: An African Case Study," paper presented at the 9th World Congress of the International Political Science Association, Montreal, August 20–25, 1973.

9. See Daniel Lerner and Richard D. Robinson, "Swords and Ploughshares: The Turkish Army as a Modernizing Force," *World Politics,* 12 (October 1960), 26–29.

The theme of rural status retained a critical relevance. As in many developing societies, the reduced opportunities in the rural areas tended to inflate the value of a military career to many in those areas. In the words of Marion J. Levy,

> . . . insofar as membership in the armed forces is generally open to members of the society, the vast majority of the members of a given society are likely to be individuals of a single class, and hence if the armed force organizations are large scale, most recruitment is likely to come from people of more or less common origins. This is especially true, of course, of relatively nonmodernized societies. In such societies armed force organizations are frequently elite organizations whose members are likely to come from representatives of a single elite class. If they are not elite organizations and recruitment is open class, the vast majority of individuals concerned are likely to come from agrarian social backgrounds.[10]

In Uganda's experience the military did not recruit from an elite class. On the contrary, it had considerable difficulty in recruiting from the new educated elite. The overwhelming majority of the soldiers were therefore drawn from what Levy called "people of more or less common origins . . . from agrarian social backgrounds."

But were these people in sympathy with their rural origin and peasant compatriots? Their prejudices and predispositions were certainly considerably influenced by their social backgrounds. What Robert Scalapino said of the military rulers of Korea in the early 1960s has also been true to some extent of the majority of the officers and men of the Ugandan army. These were young men "who came from rural backgrounds and who, in many cases, have known poverty at close range. It is natural for these men to have a rural orientation—to feel an empathy with the farmer. Such men must always regard urbanism with a certain ambivalence." [11]

But there is one important difference in Uganda's conditions as compared with either Turkey or Korea. Uganda is a *polyethnic* society, deeply divided along these primordial lines. Lugbara peasants

10. Marion J. Levy Jr., "Armed Force Organizations," *The Military and Modernization*, ed. Henry Biemen (Chicago, Aldine-Atherton, 1971), p. 63.

11. Robert A. Scalapino, "Which Route for Korea?" *Asian Survey*, 2 (September 1962), 11.

in the armed forces may have a bond of affinity with Lugbara peasants in the villages, but there is no guarantee that they would have a bond of sympathy with Kakwa or Acholi peasants inside or outside the army. The bonds of shared social origins are sometimes in conflict with the tensions of differing ethnic origins. In such conditions, a military-agrarian complex is seldom either neat or stable. Conflicting loyalties—partly ethnic, partly in terms of social origin, and partly arising from the pulls of occupational allegiance—would periodically shake what might otherwise have been a bond of empathy between soldiers and rural folk.

OBOTE'S MILITARY-INTELLECTUAL COMPLEX

But while the army in Uganda was being recruited so overwhelmingly from semi-literate and rustic sectors of the population, politics as a profession was recruiting from the new educated elite. The colonial experience had put a special premium on certain verbal and literary skills. The aspiring politician had to have among his credentials some of the symbols of modern education as defined by the conquering imperial culture. If the legislature was to be the central recruitment mechanism for the new political elite, then entry into the legislature required competence in the English language. Oratory as a political skill at the national level also required an effective utilization of the imperial language. Uganda had to choose its national leaders from among those who put across their views in the imported language of the European metropole.

As political parties were formed in the late 1950s and the early 1960s, aspiring intellectuals left some of their older professions to join the mainstream of political ambition. Schools especially lost a number of able teachers to the new profession of politics. In the 1961 elections in Uganda the Democratic party "poached" many a teacher from Catholic schools in different parts of the country to stand as candidates in the parliamentary elections. Obote's own party also "poached" on the schools, but to a lesser degree. What the whole experience did indicate was, quite simply, the need in politics for skills which were also associated with the teaching profession.

The imperial heritage and its prestige, the adoption of English as a national language, the requirement of competence in English for parliamentarians in a situation where people learned English from schools and not from the home and marketplace, all prepared the ground for the rise of the intelligentsia as the dominant force in at least the first few years of Uganda's independence. In the Uganda situation we define the intelligentsia in educational and occupational terms—a group with at least twelve years of formal education and constituting a white-collar stratum.

Milton Obote himself was preeminently an intellectual, not only in his education but also in the sense of being someone capable of being fascinated by ideas and with skills for handling those ideas effectively. But at first his alliance was not between the intelligentsia and the military but mainly between the modern intelligentsia under his leadership and the indigenous traditionalists, especially those who followed Kabaka Mutesa II of Buganda. Following the 1962 election Obote's Uganda People's Congress and Buganda's Kabaka Yekka party formed a coalition government, with the Democratic party in opposition. The Democratic party had always had its own share of Uganda's intellectuals, but before long it began to lose some of its best people in parliament to the Uganda People's Congress.

The basic alliance between the intelligentsia and the traditionalists, especially the traditional aristocracies in the kingdoms of Uganda, came to an end in 1964. That year was also the beginning of a military-intellectual coalition under Obote's leadership. The military mutiny which had taken place in January 1964 had ended with a number of concessions to the armed forces, and a new basis of partnership was created between Obote's government and what was now increasingly Obote's army. The armed forces at the time of the achievement of independence had been underestimated as a political force, but by 1964 Milton Obote was quite clear in his determination to maintain a workable alliance with the armed forces against the traditionalist forces of the country.

In 1966, following Obote's military confrontation with the Kabaka of Buganda, another stage was reached in the evolution of the new military-intellectual complex. As head of the army Obote replaced Brigadier Opolot with Brigadier Idi Amin. The intellectual gulf between Amin and Obote emphasized in symbolic terms the supremacy of the intelligentsia in that partnership. It was indeed to be Obote's brain behind Amin's gun. Idi Amin, grossly underestimated by Obote himself and by many people since then, appeared to be a jovial but ignorant warrior capable of being manipulated in different ways. Many regarded Amin as no more than a buffoon, though potentially a dangerous buffoon. With Obote's astuteness to control and manipulate him, the intelligentsia seemed assured of remaining senior partners in their coalition with the military.

Obote recruited intellectuals from other parts of the country to his support. Among the Baganda the position was less neat. Ganda intelligentsia were sometimes torn between the demands of traditionalist loyalties within their own ethnic group and the lure of modern reforms as symbolized by the Uganda People's Congress. Had Obote not humiliated the Baganda so continuously from 1966 onwards after he defeated their king, he might have recruited many Baganda intellectuals to some of his reforms.

In 1969 there started a new phase in the fortunes of the coalition between the military and Obote's intelligentsia. Milton Obote started his "strategy of the move to the left." He began to define new socialistic goals. He entered the stream of documentary radicalism with his series of documents indicating new political policies and ideological directions.[12] The ideological content of most of the documents of Obote's move to the left implied a concern for the peasantry. The arguments against the injustices of "feudalism," especially in the former kingdoms of Uganda, reaffirmed sympathy with the "oppressed" common folk. The egalitarian theme of the move to the left strategy seemed to be a clarion call for a new

12. Documentary radicalism as a strategy of capturing in documents a vision of a new society to be created is discussed more fully in Mazrui, *Cultural Engineering and Nation-Building in East Africa* (Evanston, Northwestern University Press, 1972), chap. 5. See also Mazrui, "Leadership in Africa: Obote of Uganda," *International Journal* 25.3 (June 1970). Consult also D. L. Cohen and J. Parson, "The Uganda People's Congress Branch and Constituency Elections of 1970," *Journal of Commonwealth Political Studies* 11.1 (1973), 46–66.

partnership between the peasantry and the intelligentsia. Such a partnership between brains and numbers constituted, as Huntington has reminded us, preeminently the catalyst for revolution.

With Obote's Document No. 5 concerning new methods of elections came the idea of linking the political intelligentsia with peasants in all four corners of the country. A member of parliament could no longer stand for one constituency in one particular area, usually his ethnic home. Document No. 5 required every parliamentary candidate to stand for election simultaneously in four constituencies—one constituency in the north, one in the south, one in the west, and one in the east. Each candidate would therefore have to woo large numbers of ordinary folk in parts of the country distant from his own. And between elections each parliamentarian would have had to nurse constituencies consisting of communities ethnically diverse and regionally disparate. If parliamentarians, including ministers within parliament, constituted the cream of the political intelligentsia, the members of this political elite were now to be nationally interlinked with the voting peasantry in all the four corners of the nation.

Did the army intervene in Uganda in January 1971 in order to prevent this partnership between the peasantry and the political intelligentsia? The military coup of January 1971 had a number of causes, some personal to the relations between Amin and Obote, others structural to the situation. But if the army did not intervene to stop a partnership between the intelligentsia and the peasantry, it did intervene partly to stop the demotion of the military to an even more junior position in its own partnership with the educated elite. In the preceding twelve months Obote had started making decisions about the army without consulting its head or even discussing it with the defense counsel. Promotions were made behind Amin's back, responsibilities were distributed within the armed forces without the pretense of giving the armed forces an adequate say in determining these matters. There might have been very strong political reasons why Obote had to bypass the normal decision-making machinery for the armed forces in matters like promotion, allocation of duties, and potentially even recruitment. But

Obote's increasing tendency to bypass normal channels gave Amin and that part of the army which supported Amin a growing feeling of ominous political demotion.

There is little evidence that Amin feared an alliance between the rural masses and the educated elite under Milton Obote. But he did fear the increasing autonomy of the political intelligentsia, partly signified by Obote's new style of rule, and partly by a concern for the implications of the new elections under Document No. 5 which were scheduled to take place early in 1971. Under the provisions of his Document No. 5 Obote had done nothing to reduce the dominance of the educated class in the political process. All the evidence seemed to suggest that triumphant parliamentarians would be basically drawn from the same stratum of society as in 1961 and 1962, even if they were now ideologically converted to other goals. There was no rethinking about the official language for parliament, which was to continue to be the hub of the nation's political life. Since parliamentarians still had to have a competence in the English language and English was a language obtained through an educational process, a deep-seated preference for the educated class of parliamentarians was bound to remain part of the system.

The linguistic problem could have been handled by shifting the main emphasis of decision making into the party away from parliament and making the party more responsive to the pressures of the peasantry. An alternative way of handling the linguistic problem in a country like Uganda in a manner which would give greater political influence to people who did not speak English would have been to choose experimentally two or more African languages as "parliamentary languages" with provision for simultaneous translation. This would have been similar to the experiment conducted in colonial Tanganyika with regard to the role of English and Swahili as parliamentary languages.

If a social revolution was what Milton Obote was after, the first alternative of shifting ultimate power from parliament to the *party*, and reorganizing the party in a manner which would increase its responsiveness to the peasantry, would have made greater revolutionary sense. But in reality Obote's move to the left remained basically a game being played by the intellectuals of Uganda. Many intellectuals found a new sense of purpose in this vision, and a new opportunity for verbal enthusiasm. Obote himself was probably sincere, but he did not pursue the logic of his revolutionary ideas. The image which was emerging was not one of a budding partnership between the peasantry and intelligentsia, but one of an increasingly self-righteous and uncompromising group of intellectuals in power in an African country. Obote's military-intellectual complex was cracking without an adequate substitute. Peasants in Obote's revolutionary strategy were still objects; they were not as yet participating subjects in a major social transformation.

On January 25, 1971, Milton Obote fell from power.[13]

AMIN: PANGAS AND PLOUGHSHARES

What sorts of changes did Obote's successor, General Idi Amin, seek to introduce? At first it seemed as if this would be another kind of military-intellectual coalition. Amin seemed to feel considerable deference toward the educated in his society. He created the most technocratic and best educated cabinet in the history of Uganda. He recruited from the ranks of the highly educated civil service, from the legal profession, and even from Makerere University in Kampala. Amin's original cabinet had a range of expertise which included engineering as well as law, zoology as well as economics. The country seemed to be set on a new approach to that old partnership between guns and brains.

Yet one fundamental difference soon asserted itself. Whereas Obote's military-intellectual complex gave the intelligentsia the status of the senior partner, Amin's temporary partnership with the intelligentsia soon revealed that it was the guns which were enjoying seniority. The technocrats in the cabinet and the civil service responded to the moods of the general himself. There were reports of a minister being physically slapped across the face by the general. There were certainly reports of cabinet ministers being shouted down and silenced on matters that the general did not

13. For related issues consult Selwyn Ryan, "Uganda: Balance Sheet of the Revolution," *Mawazo* 3.1 (June 1971), and Ryan, "Electoral Engineering in Uganda," *Mawazo* 2.4 (December 1970).

want to hear about. An important partnership did indeed exist between these technocrats and the new military government, but the military was now clearly and indisputably the senior partner. The tables had been turned on the intelligentsia.

But would Amin more effectively create a partnership with the peasantry than Milton Obote had done? Would the agrarian social origins of Uganda soldiers establish at least informal links between the barracks and the countryside?

Amin's response to his position in power had a deep agrarian factor from the start. The idea of consulting elders from district to district as a way of getting rural consensus was revived by the general quite early. Amin moved from one group of elders to another, from one district to another, vigorously pursuing a primordial system of oral consultation which had already been dying under the weight of political modernization in Uganda. Within the first few months of his rule Amin covered more square miles of Ugandan territory, addressing meetings and listening to elders, than Obote covered in all his eight years in office. Amin converted even Makerere professors at one stage into a group of elders and came to the university to *listen* rather than to talk. The peripatetic nature of Amin's initial style of rule was itself profoundly influenced by the political culture of rural areas in Uganda.

Amin has brought other cultural inputs, derived from his peasant origins, into the political process in Uganda. His entire style of diplomacy is striking for its lack of middle-class "refinements." The world of international relations is dominated in its norms by the values of the middle classes and the international intelligentsia. International law itself was a product of the thinking of European middle and upper classes on how diplomacy was to be conducted and relations between states organized and controlled. There are subtleties and refinements in embassies throughout the world, and in the corridors of international organizations, which are distant from some of the bluntness and relative spontaneity of rural folk. The peasants in all countries of the world are among the least sensitized to international issues. They are often the most obstinately parochial in their view of the universe. And because of that, this whole phenomenon of relations between states has remained something shaped, organized, and controlled by the values of the middle and upper classes and their respective intellectual wings.

Idi Amin, like Nikita Khrushchev before him, has brought to the refined diplomatic banquet of the middle and upper classes of the world the rustic embarrassment of inadequate inhibition. Like Russia's Nikita Khrushchev in the 1950s and early 1960s, Idi Amin is today a peasant bull in the china shop of diplomatic history. In peasant areas one visits friends without being invited. The necessity of an invitation is a middle-class and upper-class phenomenon. Amin came into power and proceeded to treat diplomatic visits in a similar manner. Israel, Britain, and France had claimed to be friends of his regime. He visited each of those at his own initiative. He also visited West Germany with the casualness of one peasant knocking on the door of his rural friend. Of course in reality arrangements had to be made to receive the president of Uganda, security had to be ensured, major diplomatic banquets had to be held. The refinements of European diplomacy, so dominant in the world as a whole today, had to be extended to this visiting rural dignitary from Uganda. But the spontaneity of going there without invitation had all the bearing of the cumulative rural socialization which Amin and his kind often manifest without thinking.

Most presidents would not give interviews to the press on matters of state wearing nothing but a swimming costume. But Amin has been known to expose himself to the ridicule of international photographic journalism by doing precisely that. Some of the pictures that have hit the international magazines were calculated to portray a naked African in political power. Most presidents would prepare carefully for their press conferences. Amin has learned to do a little of that more recently, but there is still a wide area of spontaneity in the way in which he addresses the world at large. Almost any idea that occurs to him on the spur of the moment could be given articulation. Peasants do not normally send telegrams to each other. Amin has learned to use this particular medium but with some rustic bluntness. And his messages have ranged from wishing Richard Nixon a quick recovery from Watergate to a reaffirmation of deep, and even romantic affection for Julius Nyerere "though your hair is grey."

Some of these tendencies are personal to Amin rather than to his social origins. But the very fact that he lets his personal tendencies have such free play while occupying the top office of his nation might have been influenced by the relative spontaneity of rural upbringing among the Kakwa.

His attitude toward the Asians of Uganda was a feeling widely shared among ordinary people in the country. By the time Amin came into power Indophobia, or negative response to people of Indian origin, had become a gut peasant response in the country. Indophobia was not unique to the peasants. On the contrary, many members of Obote's ruling intelligentsia were strongly anti-Asian. But Obote's government would never have handled the Asian issue in quite that manner. The normal diplomatic inhibitions that operate in matters affecting other nations would—under Obote— have been allowed to moderate the fate of the Asians.

Even humanitarian arguments quite often are arguments steeped in middle-class assumptions and are therefore more likely to impress an African intellectual than an African peasant who remembers having been insulted over the years by Asian shopkeepers or Asian employers. The style of Amin's expulsion of the Asians was in this sense an aspect of his peasant origins.

A related factor might well have been derived from the tensions of rural-urban dichotomies. The great majority of the Asians of Uganda were urban people. Those Asians that opened up shop in isolated rural areas often signified an urban presence in the countryside. Much of the resentment of the Asians was racial and economic, but there might also have been a residual symbolic factor signifying rural-urban tensions. These tensions focused on this alien group partly because it could be hated without the complications of cross-cutting kinship ties. But after they were expelled what was to happen? Their shops became available to a wide range of categories of Ugandans. These included Ugandans who would not have stood a chance of moving into this level of economic endeavor in the old days under Obote. Apart from the soldiers themselves, there have been new shopkeepers in Uganda whose origins range from the northern peasantry to the Buganda aristocracy. It is too early to be sure how successful the experiment of indigenization of commerce in Uganda in the wake of the expulsion of the Asians will be. But if the experiment does emerge triumphant, it could be interpreted as one of the first steps toward a coalition between the peasant warriors under General Amin and the aspiring masses in *both* town and country in Uganda.

One obstacle continues to loom large. The heritage of ethnicity in the country carries its own record of mutual atrocities. That heritage also implies a pull of favoritism and differential rewards. A grand alliance between the soldiers and the peasantry falls short of conclusive consummation in the shadow of the nation's genealogical history.

ETHNICITY AND THE MILITARY

When Dwight Eisenhower warned his countrymen about the military-*industrial* complex of the United States he was reminding his countrymen of the political weight of military establishments even in mature liberal democracies. Eisenhower's concern was not with the social origins of members of the military establishment in the United States but with the political consequences of interlocking elites of industry and the armed forces. That section of industry which catered to the whole area of military technology was, of course, the most intimately related to the military elites. But the interplay between industry and the armed forces in a country like the United States is wider than that, and is related especially to the interplay between technology, commerce, and war.

In Uganda, on the other hand, it is precisely the social origins of soldiers that provide the basis of political allegiances. In colonial conditions this was so in part because of the ethnic basis for the recruitment of soldiers. The colonial authorities in some cases avoided certain communities in any effort to recruit for the armed forces. The exclusion of those communities was motivated by considerations which ranged from a presumption that members of certain communities did not have either the valor or the physique to be soldiers, to an imperial calculation that such communities when equipped with arms might create problems for the colonial order. Persistent in the imperial mentality was the simple assumption that martial prowess was ethnically distributed. Some tribes were simply better warriors than others.

In the course of World War II, an attempt was made in different parts of Africa by the colonial powers to assess the martial qualities of different communities, partly with a view to determining priorities in recruitment for their armies against Germany, Italy, and Japan. In East Africa research was conducted for this purpose. The chief native commissioner of Kenya asked that a census be undertaken to determine "the soldierly qualities of the members of the various tribes composing the East African Force." The issue was referred to a Conference of Governors of the East African colony, and a questionnaire was sent to each commanding officer in 1941. "Each of the countries in East Africa was to furnish the Native Commissioner with names of tribes, giving provinces, districts. A similar survey, but a hasty one, had been carried out in 1932 in order that opinions of K. A. R. Officers might be obtained with a view to deciding which tribes were likely to make the best soldiers." [14]

Tarsis Kabwegyere reminds us of the specific qualities which were looked for. These included adaptability, reaction to discipline, steadiness under bombing, stamina and staying power, powers of leadership, intelligence, esprit de corps, cleanliness, capacity for hard living, general health, ability to fraternize, fighting qualities, and certain other special qualities and skills. Each ethnic group was assessed, and a ranking system was devised.

But soldierly qualities had to be balanced against other considerations. Although in the early days of the colonial presence in Uganda the Baganda was still regarded as a martial community, there was an understandable reluctance among colonial administrators to recruit disproportionately from the Baganda into the armed forces. The Baganda were already becoming among the best organized and most politically conscious of the communities in the country, and the imperial power naturally hesitated to militarize the Baganda.

Thus, both those who were excluded from the armies and those

14. Cited by Tarsis B. Kabwegyere, *The Politics of State Formation: The Nature and Effects of Colonialism in Uganda* (Nairobi, East African Literature Bureau, 1974), pp. 115–117.

who provided the bulk of the army were chosen substantially in terms of ethnic categories. This basis of recruitment was to have repercussions in the relations between soldiers and civilians after independence.

The different communities and tribes themselves had stereotyped ideas of each other, sometimes influenced by considerations of which community was capable of providing better soldiers. In Nigeria, although the armed forces were recruited from both the north and the south, within the armed forces mutual ethnic stereotypes conditioned interaction between different sections and ranks.[15] With this background of ethnic basis for the recruitment of soldiers into the armed forces and the persistence of ethnic stereotypes, the actual composition of the military at the time of independence in many African countries carried all the potentialities for an ethnic resurgence.

Some scholars have argued that colonialism did not simply create new potential nation states; it also created the tribes themselves. Groups that never before considered themselves as a cohesive political community were converted into such a community by colonial methods of administration. Kabwegyere cites some examples, including that of the Acholi in Uganda, who were later to be regarded as a particularly martial community and provided a disproportionate number of soldiers for the Uganda army in the days of Apolo Milton Obote.[16] Administrative convenience in the colonial period helped bring together into the Acholi District clans that previously had never engaged in collective action nor been subject to the same collective administrative authority. The Acholi began to see themselves as an amalgamated community, although tensions between clans continued, and divisions between East Acholi and West Acholi have persisted. A broad new Acholi political consciousness was superimposed over the narrower parochialisms of the subunits of the Acholi.

By the time Obote was overthrown the Acholi constituted the

15. M. J. Dent, "The Military and Politics: A Study of the Relation between the Army and the Political Process in Nigeria," in Robert Melson and Howard Wolpe, eds., *Nigeria: Modernization and the Politics of Communalism* (East Lansing, Michigan State University Press, 1971), p. 373.

16. Kabwegyere, *The Politics of State Formation*, pp. 43–45.

largest single group within the armed forces of Uganda, although they were clearly one of the smaller groups in the total population of Uganda. Between a third and a half of the Ugandan army consisted of Acholi. Their preponderance was partly due to their categorization as a tribal unit in the colonial period, and partly to their presumed martial qualities.

This second presumption was related to physical height. As an ethnic community the Acholi and other northern tribes of Uganda had produced a disproportionate number of tall people. Since recruitment into the Uganda armed forces gave preference to candidates who were 5′ 8″ or over, the northern communities, especially the Acholi, had an edge.

By the time Amin captured power from Obote, he was all too aware of the preponderance of the Acholi within the armed forces. Would they be loyal to the new regime under Amin or would they retain their earlier loyalty to Milton Obote? In his early announcements explaining why the coup had taken place, Amin asserted that the Acholi, in alliance with Obote's own tribe, the Langi, had plotted to disarm all other soldiers and assert a complete ethnic monopoly of military power in Uganda. Thus, tensions against these two communities began in the early days of Amin's assumption of power. Since then thousands of Acholi and Langi have perished as a result of Amin's political and military insecurity. Almost every year since he took power in 1971, issues of ethnicity have been profoundly interlinked with issues of domestic balance of power. In July 1972, the Acholi and the Langi were once again singled out by spokesmen of the Amin regime as plotters against his government. It was asserted that they were waiting for an invasion of pro-Obote refugees from Tanzania and would provide internal support as the refugees from across the border sought to undermine and then overthrow the government of Idi Amin. In the wake of these renewed accusations many Acholi and Langi in Uganda decided to flee the country. Ethnicity in Uganda had worn once again the ominous face of militarized revenge and brutality. Among those Ugandans in exile in Tanzania, ethnic factors were also at play. Even as they plotted to invade the country and overthrow Idi Amin's government, the Ugandan exiles were sometimes torn by their own ethnic cleavages, with the Langi at variance with the Acholi over traditional war ceremonies in preparation for this collective enterprise.[17]

Is this kind of militarized situation more bedeviled by ethnic factors than civilian politics? The answer varies somewhat from one African country to another. But, to the extent that in most African countries recruitment into the armed forces has been more ethnically specialized than participation in civilian politics, the military situation carries graver risks of ethnic conflict than does the civilian political system. Certainly in Uganda, politics in the first eight years of independence was more ethnically representative than was access to military careers. Parliament, the cabinet under Obote, and increasingly the civil service provided more of a cross-section of the different communities of Uganda than the armed forces could ever claim. Political mobility, in the sense of different regions and tribes having access to effective political participation and representation at some level, was greater when political power depended on the interplay of civilian pressures than when it came to depend upon the balance of ethnic factions within the armed forces.

Those who blame both tribalism and the creation of nation states on colonialism may have a point, but what is often overlooked is that tribalism may be an outcome of the creation of the nation state. Bringing together divergent linguistic and cultural groups within the boundaries of a new state has generated new levels of ethnic consciousness. Even if the British had not explicitly bracketed different clans into a new community called Acholi, the forces of competition within the national system of Uganda would have led to the discovery by the Acholi of a shared culture and language. This ethnic consciousness was bound to be sharpened in the scramble for a share of what independent Uganda as a new politi-

17. David Martin refers to the irritation of the younger exiles over the Acholi war dance and song in the preparation for the invasion of Uganda. Martin seems to suggest that it was the younger, modernized or westernized soldiers in exile who were particularly unhappy about such a ceremony. In fact, in addition to the reservations of the more modernized or westernized of the exiles, there were also reservations on the part of those who belonged to other ethnic communities. For Martin's allusion to this episode consult his *General Amin* (London, Faber and Faber, 1974), p. 189.

cal community had to offer to its constituent parts. In Uganda, as elsewhere in Africa, it was not simply a case of the new nation-state lacking a transethnic identity and legitimacy of its own. It was a case of the very presence of such a nation-state lending legitimacy and purpose to the ethnic sub-units and strengthening parochial loyalties.

In some African countries under military rule the extent of retribalization might for a while be disguised by the appearance of a firm political order with "iron discipline." But ethnic resurgence begins to take place as soon as the iron military grip begins to loosen, or when civilian rule is restored after a period of military control. For example, Ghana under Kofi Busia witnessed a resurgence of ethnic particularism following the rule by the National Liberation Council. At best, a military regime succeeds in putting ethnic cleavages in a society in "cold storage." At worst, military rule, partly because of the pattern of recruitment into the armed forces and partly because of the nature of army rule itself, simply degenerates into eruptions of militarized ethnicity with periodic violent confrontations.

But why is the level of brutalization in some African societies so high? Why does retribalization under military conditions carry such a heavy risk of violence? As already suggested one part of the answer is that the different ethnic groups in an African country seek to control or at least to share political power. Those who actually do possess the scarce resource of central political power find themselves strongly tempted not to share it except on the basis of special alliances. Favoritism, ethnic nepotism, and ethnic competitiveness play their roles in creating inequalities and disequilibrium in the distribution of political goals.

But the old warrior tradition also intrudes, conditioning attitudes, especially in situations where soldiers attempt to monopolize the central institutions of power. In many African societies the old warrior tradition was based not simply on the ambition to maintain collective security but also on the ambition to foster collective prosperity. The warrior was not simply a person who waited until his cattle or his women were attacked before using his military skills for defensive purposes. On the contrary, the warrior considered economic competition not primarily as rivalry between individuals or subgroups within the same society, as it is considered to be in western capitalist countries, but more as a continuing dialectic of rivalry with alien or semi-alien societies nearby.

If rustic soldiers are in power today, soldiers who retain some of the warrior tradition, the gap between the national center and the rural periphery may be narrowed, and once again Amin's Uganda may be merely an example of a more widespread phenomenon.[18]

CONCLUSIONS

Something like a military-agrarian complex seems to be in the making in Uganda. But the process drips in blood partly because of the very nature of Uganda's history. Ethnic competitiveness, going back to the days when Buganda was the powerful province while West Nile was among the poorest of the areas, has left a deep mark on the behavior of the polity. Some of the spontaneity of Uganda peasantry has a violent theme within it. Just as villagers might spontaneously rise, chase a thief, and beat him to death in response to a hue and cry, so the warriors in modern barracks may sometimes brutalize their compatriots in a fit of either insecurity or arrogance. The military-agrarian complex has its costs in a country of many tribal groupings, especially if the military is disproportionately enlisted from only a few of those groupings.

The theme of ethnic rivalry continues to bedevil Uganda under Amin. If Egypt is the most culturally homogeneous of all the countries of the Nile Valley, Uganda may well be the least culturally homogeneous along that valley. It remains to be seen whether rustic warriors in control of a modern state will have greater success in transforming the fortunes of the countryside than other coalitions of social forces have had before. If Amin has now planted the seeds of a new partnership between the soldiers and the masses, Uganda is not yet ready to celebrate the harvest. Politics, like nature, takes its time.

18. A particularly perceptive paper on the long-term consequences of ethnically selective recruitment into the armed forces is Hilary B. Ng'weno, "Tribes, Armies and Political Instability in Africa," unpublished manuscript, Center for International Affairs, Harvard University, March 1969.

THE OLD EMPIRES

14

RICHARD PIPES

Reflections on the Nationality Problems in the Soviet Union

Twenty-five years ago, when as a graduate student looking for a dissertation subject, I first interested myself in the Soviet nationality problem, the field of study was virtually uninhabited. Indeed, it was considered uninhabitable. My Russian friends thought that whatever national antagonisms there were in their country had been stimulated by hostile powers interested in dismembering Russia. American specialists, even some of the most knowledgeable ones, regarded nationalism in the Soviet Union as a relic of the past, doomed to dissolve—as would ethnic differences in the United States—in the acid bath of "modernization." Both tended to regard nationalism as a retrograde phenomenon and therefore, by a mental shortcircuit to which intellectuals are prone whenever reality impinges on their ideals, to treat its investigation as reactionary too. Now, in the 1970s, the situation looks quite different. Not that we have seen much overt stirring of nationalism in the USSR. Basically, the national minorities of the Soviet Union are as firmly in hand as they were in the 1940s, and they are kept in this condition by the same means as in Stalin's day. What has changed is the climate in the West. The easy assumptions about the inevitable disappearance of nationalism have faded away as in country after country ethnic differences, thought to have been neutralized long ago, began to raise their ugly heads. In a world where one can seriously contemplate independence for Quebec, where the Ulster Catholics and Protestants are waging civil war against one another,

where 100,000 Ibos have been massacred for the crime of being
born Ibos, it is difficult to maintain that in the Soviet Union, where
more than one half the population consists of minorities, ethnic
differences can be reduced to culinary or sartorial trivia. In the
past fifteen years a veritable flood of "minoritological" studies has
saturated the market, to the point where it is difficult to keep track
of the titles of books on the subject of Soviet nationalities, let alone
of their contents.

This chapter is to deal with ethnic differences and conflicts in the
contemporary Soviet Union and not with the problem of ethnicity
in general; but before proceeding further, I cannot resist making
some more general observations insofar as these shed light on the
assumptions with which I approach Russia.

In primitive and isolated societies ethnic self-consciousness does
not emerge because there exists (in theory, at any rate) full homogeneity of race, language, and culture. A community which enters
into no contact whatever with other races, languages, and cultures
thinks of itself as representing the human species rather than any
of its branches. This fact is reflected in the ethnic names which
primitive peoples like to give themselves when asked who they are:
"men." On first contact with people of another breed, the initial reaction is to treat them as ancestors. As O. Mannoni has shown in
his *Prospero and Caliban: The Psychology of Colonization,* the natives of
Madagascar immediately became dependent on their colonial conquerors, regarding them, because they were immune to magic, as
ancestors come to save and protect them. The cargo cults of the Pacific illustrate the same point. It is only after protracted contact and
as a result of friction which inevitably develops when two cultures
establish a permanent relationship that ethnic awareness arises.

These anthropological observations are not intended as revela-
tions. They are meant to stress something that is taken for granted
when dealing with primitive societies but that is usually left out in
the modern context, namely that communication between civiliza-
tions *increases* their self-awareness, that it makes their members
more, not less, conscious of representing a particular branch of humanity rather than humanity itself; and, further, that in an age of
ideologies such communication creates an environment favorable

to the spread of nationalism. In investigating nationalist movements, it is therefore always essential to focus attention on the intensity of contact between peoples of various races, languages, and cultures, and on the nature of these contacts, paying particular attention to various forms of competition which may result from them. Once this is done, it becomes apparent why modern life aggravates national animosities rather than, as nineteenth-century liberals and socialists liked to believe, commits them to oblivion.

The first thing that must be said about the nationality problem in the Soviet Union is that it bears very little resemblance to the American or Indian nationality problems and a great deal to those experienced by the classic empires of the West, most of which had dissolved after World War II. The Soviet Union is not a country (as is the United States) which has been significantly colonized by foreigners or whose ethnic composition has become diversified as a result of immigration; nor is it a state (like India) voluntarily put together by different ethnic groups and regions. It is the product of conquest carried out by one dominant nationality—the Great Russian—in the course of an expansion from its original homeland, the Volga–Oka mesopotamia, that began in the fourteenth century, and has never really stopped. The primary impetus to this expansion has been the insatiable need for fresh land and other resources to support a population which kept on exhausting them so fast that it has had no choice but to pull up its stakes and move. V. O. Kliuchevsky, the greatest of Russian historians, put the matter succinctly in the second chapter of his *Course* when he said that Russian history is the history of a country that "colonizes itself." Of course, "itself" is not quite correct because from the beginning the Russians, whose earliest identifiable home had been in Central Europe, invaded and settled land populated by others: first the Finns of the taiga, next the Turks of both the forest zone and steppe, and then scores of other peoples. This process of migration always brought the Russians in contact and often in conflict with peoples of entirely different ethnic backgrounds: so much so that the processes of nation building and empire building are, in the case of Russia, hopelessly intertwined. In the eighteenth and nine-

teenth centuries the course of imperial conquest was more consciously pursued; but even then, the rapidity with which Russian
peasants and other colonists poured overland into areas gained by
force of arms tended to blur the lines which in the case of Western
overseas empires so neatly separated colony from metropolis.

The chronological and geographic inseparability in Russia of the
processes leading to the building of the nation-state and the empire
has had the effect of making Russians remarkably insensitive to
ethnic problems. Before the Revolution, even liberal and democratic political groups, normally so alert to all forms of oppression,
were inclined to ignore ethnic problems, and to react to demands
of the nationalities for a greater role in self-government as "reactionary." The consensus of political parties of the center and to the
left of it was that the elimination of autocracy and introduction of
democratic institutions would of themselves solve all that ailed the
country, national frustrations included. This attitude no longer
prevails, if only because the formal structure of the Soviet Union—
its pseudo-federal state system—marks a constitutional recognition
of national differences as genuine. Still, when pressed, Great Russians tend to sneer at the national minorities and not to take their
complaints seriously. It is probably true that today a large part of
the Great Russian population believes the minorities to be better
off than themselves because they enjoy the benefits of Russian investments, Russian technology, and Russian military protection
without giving much in return.

Russian leaders, past and present, have followed what may be
called the French model of colonial rule. In contrast to the British,
the French have traditionally striven to extend to their colonial
peoples full rights of native Frenchmen as a means of assuring
their ultimate assimilation. Muscovite and Imperial Russia have
pursued a like policy by opening the ranks of the privileged elite—
the *dvorianstvo*—to the land-owning and educated groups among
the conquered minorities.[1] The Soviet regime has followed suit in

1. Tsarist policy was most successful in regard to those nations whose nobility
had not enjoyed the same privileges as its Russian counterpart. It was a failure
when applied to the extremely privileged nobilities of the western provinces of the
empire, such as those of Poland.

this as in so many other respects by allowing the minority elites in the Soviet Union and countries of Eastern Europe access to the Communist party apparatus and all the benefits and privileges that membership in these bodies entails. However, this time-tested policy which enabled tsarist Russia to siphon off into safe channels of personal self-seeking much of the potential nationalist resistance no longer works quite as well today. The trouble is that whereas in Eastern Europe before the twentieth century primary allegiance focused on one's social estate, in the present century, because of the breakdown of the estate structure and spread of egalitarianism, the individual's primary allegiance has shifted toward the nation. The Tatar or Georgian prince who in Imperial Russia might have felt closer affinity for his Russian equivalent than for the peasant or tradesman of his own nationality no longer exists. His "democratized" descendant, a party apparatchik functioning in Kazan or Tiflis, has become a kind of wardheeler who has no choice but to identify with the Tatar and Georgian nation. Whereas the status and prestige of a noble depended in part on heredity and wealth and in part on favor of the crown, that of a Communist official depends partly on favor of the party hierarchy and partly on his ability to administer the population over which that party places him. We have here a clear example how bureaucratization and the social leveling that accompanies it intensify the national loyalties of the elite.

It is customary to think of the Soviet Union as a living ethnic museum inhabited by hundreds of quaint ethnic groups. Now while it is true that there are in the USSR well over one hundred officially recognized ethnic groups (the 1970 census identifies by name 103) a high proportion of them are so small as to be of interest only to the anthropologist or ethnographer. For the student of the political and sociological sides of the national problem, there exist only a dozen or so significant national minorities, grouped into the following categories:

1. The Ukrainians and Belorussians, who are racially and linguistically close to the Great Russians, and share with them the same religion. If nevertheless they are regarded as distinct nationalities, it is because for a period of five centuries (c. 1300 to c. 1800)

they lived under Lithuanian and Polish rule, during which time they came under strong Western influence channeled through Poland and its Catholic church.

2. The Muslims, most of them Turkis by race and nearly all of the Sunni persuasion. These had come under Russian rule over a long period which began with the conquest of Kazan in 1552 and ended in the 1880s with the conquest of Turkmenia. In the 1920s, the Soviet government, frightened by the spectre of a Pan-Islamic and Pan-Turanian movement, split these Muslims under its rule into numerous nationalities with their own "republics" and "autonomous regions."

3. The two major Caucasian groups, the Georgians and Armenians, both of Middle Eastern stock but Orthodox Christian by religion. They came under Russian rule around 1800.

4. The Jews who constitute a problem *sui generis* because they lack a specific territory and administrative organs of their own. They also are not given the educational or other cultural outlets allowed even the smallest and culturally most backward ethnic minorities, although numerically they constitute the twelfth largest ethnic group in the country. Jews are identified as an ethnic group (in their internal passports) largely for the purpose of discrimination: they are kept out of sensitive jobs and are subjected to restrictive quotas in institutions of higher learning.

5. The three Baltic nationalities, independent between 1918 and 1939, and incorporated into the Soviet Union as a result of the Nazi-Soviet Pact.

6. West European groups, descendants of one-time immigrants and colonists, of whom the 1.6 million Germans are the most numerous.

From the point of the Soviet regime, which is dominated by Great Russians, it is troubling that in recent decades the demographic trend has begun unmistakably to favor the minorities. The Great Russians no longer enjoy the highest birth rate in Europe, as they did prior to the Revolution. The traumatic experiences of the 1930s and 1940s, combined with a steady movement of Russian peasants from the impoverished countryside into the somewhat better stocked cities, has caused this birth rate to drop precipitously.

In this respect, the results of the 1970 census must cause Soviet leaders deep concern; indeed, they may engender among them a sense of racial anxiety not unlike that which seized German Austrians in the late nineteenth century and Germans proper after World War I and which played a major role in the rise of National Socialism with its racist hysteria. In the brief interval which elapsed between the last two censuses (1959–1970), the Russian population of the USSR had increased by 14.9 million or 13 percent, whereas the rest of the population had grown by 18.0 million or 18 percent. The "oriental" component of the non-Russian population particularly has demonstrated a spectacular rate of growth, the number of Kazakhs increasing by 46 percent, of Uzbeks by 52 percent, and of Tajiks by 53 percent. This more rapid reproduction rate of the non-Russians has whittled down in eleven years the proportion of Russians in the total population of the USSR from 54.5 to 53.5 percent. How embarrassing this development is to the regime can be deduced from the fact that, in contrast to the case with previous censuses, the compilers of the 1970 census have not been allowed to provide the percentage figure of Russians in the total population, although, of course, they provide all the data which enable the reader to calculate this himself.[2] This is very much in line with the persistent belief of the Soviet bureaucracy that as long as one does not talk of things they will disappear.

Are the national minorities being assimilated? Is it likely that even as their numbers increase relative to the dominant Great Russian nationality they will succumb to Great Russian culture and lose their ethnic identity? Such certainly is the hope of the Soviet authorities who for many years have been advancing a theory of gradual *sblizhenie* (rapprochement) of the various nationalities inhabiting the country, ultimately leading to the creation of a common "Soviet" nation. The evidence, such as it is, does not point in this direction.

A good way to test the resilience of the ethnic minorities to the assimilatory process, so strongly encouraged by the regime, is to

2. Tsentral'noe Statisticheskoe Upravlenie pri Sovete Ministrov SSSR, *Itogi Vsesoiuznoi Perepisi Naseleniia 1970 goda* (Moscow, 1973), IV, 9.

look at the figures provided by the censuses bearing on linguistic loyalties.[3] In 1926 Russians constituted 54.0 percent of the population of the USSR by nationality but 58.5 percent by language. In other words, at that time 4.5 percent of the country's population was linguistically—and probably also in other respects—Russified. In 1959 the corresponding figures were 54.5 percent and 59.3 percent, giving 4.8 percent for those linguistically assimilated. This represented a net gain of 0.3 percent or about 600,000 citizens. It is not an impressive figure, especially if one bears in mind two facts: that the 1930s and 1940s were a period of intense Russification carried out through the Soviet school system, and that during World War II the Germans had massacred on Soviet territory virtually the whole Yiddish-speaking population, which, had it survived, would have weighed the balance in favor of non-Russian-speaking groups. If we now look at the 1970 census we find that the proportion of Soviet citizens who regard Russian as their "mother tongue" has actually decreased. In 1970, out of 241.7 million inhabitants of the USSR, 141.8 million or 58.7 percent declared Russian to be their mother tongue—0.6 percent fewer than in 1959.[4] Certainly, a major factor in this decline has been the more rapid growth of the non-Russian ethnic groups: the 0.6 percent drop in native Russian-speakers has to be matched against an 1.0 percent drop in ethnic Russians. But no matter what the reason, it is a fact and one which argues against the thesis of linguistic assimilation. As one runs one's eyes down the statistical tables listing the principal nationalities and their linguistic preferences, one notes that among the major groups, especially those with their own republics (and therefore a certain degree of control over the educational system), some 96 to 98 percent of the population remain loyal to their native languages. The process of linguistic assimilation is most pronounced among the smaller ethnic groups. But even

3. In the Soviet Union, one's national attribution, as stated in the internal passport, is fixed. The census takers ask, in addition, which language one considers the "mother tongue" and, in the case of citizens who speak more than one language, which is their second best.

4. Ibid., table 4, pp. 20–22. The computation is mine because this, too, the editors have failed to provide.

among them, it need not be taken for granted that abandonment of the native language necessarily and automatically leads to the adoption of Russian. While this is indeed the case with nationalities of European origin, the others usually assimilate to that major ethnic group with which they have the closest ethnic and cultural affinity: thus the 34 percent Bashkirs who no longer regard Bashkir their mother tongue almost certainly have adopted the Tatar language.

The 1970 census makes a great deal of the fact that for most of the non-Russian nationalities, Russian is far and away the leading second language. The emphasis is intended to suggest that a subtle shift of linguistic habits is taking place, and that in time what is now the second language will become the first. Nothing in the experience of other imperial systems suggests that this is likely to happen. Russian is certainly becoming the *lingua franca* of a vast region extending from the Baltic to the Pacific, and it is likely to retain this status even if the Soviet Union follows the path of other Western empires and dissolves. But surely the fact that English has been for a long time the common language of Indian intellectuals, and since independence has become the official language of India's Parliament, did not and does not indicate a progressive *sblizhenie* of the English and the Indians. The same holds true of French-speakers in northwest Africa, or of English-speakers in Ireland.

Additional evidence attesting to the survival of strong ethnic bonds could be drawn from the *samizdat* literature published in the borderlands. The Ukrainians have been especially active in demanding by means of underground publications full rights for themselves and the other ethnic groups inhabiting the Soviet Union. In response, Soviet security organs have carried out in the past decade massive arrests and deportations of Ukrainian intellectuals. Because of the greater interest of Western media in Russian and Jewish dissidents, the facts bearing on these repressions have not been adequately reported. It is probably true (though there is no way of demonstrating the fact) that in proportion to the population more dissidents have been arrested in the Ukraine than in the Russian Republic. Even in the literature published in the USSR with the censor's imprimatur an experienced eye can often detect nationalist sentiments expressed in a circuitous or "aesopian" manner.

If one were to seek a single cause of the persistence of national self-awareness and nationalist sentiment among the Soviet minorities, one would have to single out a demographic factor, namely the steady encroachment of Russians on non-Russian territories. The outward movement from the center of the forest, to which allusion has been made above, marks one of the continuities of Russian and Soviet history which neither changes in administration nor the government's official policies toward the minorities have been able significantly to alter. Traditionally, the movement of the Russian population has proceeded in a southern and southeastern direction, from the forest to the black earth belt. In more recent years, Russians have also begun to move west and southwest. This shift is probably due to the opportunities opened up by conquest after 1939 of the relatively richer territories of what had once been eastern Poland and the three independent Baltic republics as well as the growth of military industries and troop concentrations in areas facing NATO. The following table indicates the increase in the proportion of Russian residents between 1959 and 1970 in the principal republics lying on the western periphery of the USSR: [5]

Republic	1959	1970
Ukrainian SSR	16.9	19.4
Belorussian SSR	8.2	10.4
Lithuanian SSR	8.5	8.6
Latvian SSR	26.6	29.8
Estonian SSR	20.1	24.7

Overall, however, the main thrust of the population movement still points, as it has over the past five hundred years, to the south and southeast.

Now these borderlands, unlike the American West before the Civil War, are not a sparsely populated no-man's-land. They are

5. Ibid. table 2, pp. 12–15.

the homelands of major nationalities, many of them with cultures entirely different from the Russian, some with traditions of statehood reaching back to the pre-Christian era. The steady influx of Russians engenders vicious conflicts over land, housing, and jobs with the indigenous population. It is a daily irritant in relations between Russians and the minorities which even the best of will could not eliminate. Such rivalry would produce tensions and animosities even in affluent societies. In the Soviet Union, where there is a severe shortage of goods and services, it assumes highly explosive forms. The growing contact between nationalities in the Soviet Union thus occurs under the worst possible circumstances, creating a situation potentially not unlike that which led in the 1950s in Algeria to a bloody civil war.

Among other sources of friction, the following deserve mention:

1. The frustration of the native elites resulting from the fact that they possess many of the paraphernalia of statehood but almost no effective power. They are annoyed at the control exercised over them by personnel, almost invariably Russian, sent from Moscow and concealed behind the camouflage of insignificant jobs in the state or party apparatus. This annoyance is aggravated by the knowledge that in the ex-colonial possessions of the West there has occurred a genuine transfer of power.

2. Competition over investment capital and resources. In its economic planning, Moscow tends to ignore national frontiers, treating the USSR as an entity in which regional allocations are made on the basis of administrative or economic considerations but almost never ethnic ones. There is a widespread belief in the borderlands—how justified one cannot tell—that they are being bilked by the Russians, and that if they were truly independent their standards of living would go up. The issue may become even more acute should the minorities with high reproduction rates come to expect that in the future capital investments be made proportionate to the population increase in order to ensure jobs for their numerous offspring.

3. Annoyance of the minority intelligentsia with the proscription placed on minority nationalism, which becomes instantly labeled a "bourgeois deviation," and with the free rein given Russian chau-

vinism in its crassest forms. Here control over the educational system plays an important role. Why is it that only 3 percent of Russians speak a second language, which (if one excepts the 8,000
Beludzhis) is the *lowest* percentage of any ethnic group in the USSR
to do so, whereas among the minorities the percentage of Russian-
speakers is typically15–30 percent, and often exceeds 50 percent?
In Lenin's time pressure was applied on Russians living in non-
Russian areas to master the local languages, and officials in the administration were required to do so. Of this policy nothing remains
but a memory. In 1970, 29 million Russians lived in areas set aside
for national minorities (21 million in the union republics, and 8
million in the autonomous republics of the Russian Republic or
RSFSR). Of this 29 million at the very most 870,000 bothered to
learn the language of the population among whom they regularly
resided. This figure is a better commentary on the attitude of Russians toward non-Russians than any dozen treatises on Soviet nationality policy.

The coincidence of existing demographic, economic, and ideological factors creates an explosive situation which on a number of
occasions has already led to violent outbursts against the Russians
(for example, the riots in Tiflis, the capital of Georgia, in 1957, and
acts of self-immolation in Vilnius, the capital of Soviet Lithuania, in
1972).

The Soviet government is undoubtedly aware of what the facts
and figures portend and it is visibly conscious of the danger of minority nationalism, for it represses it with an even greater show of
force than it does dissent in Russia proper. It could, of course, try
to attenuate the tension by genuinely enforcing the provisions of its
constitution and transform what is now a Soviet empire into a
Commonwealth of Soviet Communist states. By so doing, it would
eliminate some of the worst abuses of the present system, since
under a looser confederation the native elite would have some say
about the number of Russian immigrants, the distribution of jobs,
the allocation of local resources, and the nature of education. But
in reality the Soviet government cannot do so. In the first place, since
its power in large measure rests on the support of the Great Rus-

sian population, it must convince this population that its interests are identical with the interests of the Communist regime. This has been Soviet practice since the early 1930s. There is no alternative to it because the Communist ideology has long ceased to hold whatever attraction it may have once exerted. Second, the regime is afraid that if it ever began to decentralize it would be unable to control the process; in other words, that even moderate administrative concessions to the union and autonomous republics would inevitably lead to their demanding complete independence. The history of other imperial systems, notably the British, suggests that this fear is not groundless. And so the Soviet government temporizes, fostering a vague ideal of ultimate national unification and in the meantime relying on the police to keep the nationalities in hand.

15

JYOTIRINDRA DAS GUPTA

Ethnicity, Language Demands, and National Development in India

Recent reexamination of the role of ethnicity in developed as well as in underdeveloped political processes has led to extensive discussions on the meaning, function, and contribution of ethnic groups. Until recently many social observers, including scholars of most colors, confidently pronounced ethnicity to be a legacy of primordial social relations which deserves a bleaching treatment by appropriate modern social action. In this sense, ethnicity was viewed not merely as a categoric marker of collectivity differentiation but mostly as a pejorative property of unwanted persistence. Thus social analysis and moral premise were conveniently blended into a sophisticated package under the appealing title of sociology of modernization and development.[1] Then, suddenly in the sixties, the explosive demonstration of ethnic politics in the very home of mature modernity shocked these theorists into the recognition that the salience of ethnic action can hardly be inferred from the standard aggregate indices of modernity.

Note: I am grateful to the Institute of International Studies at Berkeley for supporting my research on ethnicity and integration in India. For helpful comments I would like to thank Charles Ferguson of Stanford University and Ralph Retzlaff at the University of California at Berkeley.

1. Most theories of modernization and development either ignore ethnicity or treat it as an unfortunate survival which will be taken care of as modernization proceeds. One recent survey of the place of ethnicity in the literature on development produced by the political scientists demonstrates how the latter have consistently ignored the relevance of the ethnic factors. See Walker Connor, "Nation-Building or Nation-Destroying" in *World Politics* (April 1972), esp. pp. 319–321.

The gains resulting from this recognition are likely to be many. It is likely that the study of ethnicity will be more informed by scholarly curiosity than intellectual indignation. Developmental studies can now afford to consider the ethnic dimensions of the politics of poor countries with less impatience.[2] Once ethnicity is given the serious attention it deserves, theories of development may become more sensitive to the commonalities of problem sets facing the backward and the mature countries alike. This will augur a better appreciation of the complexity of the developmental tasks and thereby a more realistic evaluation of the products of developmental policies.

ETHNIC ENCLOSURES

Ethnicity may be regarded as an enclosing device which carves out a recognizable social collectivity based on certain shared perceptions of distinctive commonness often augmented by diachronic continuity.[3] Viewed in this way, ethnicity would refer to a class of social collectivity which may be divided into types based on particular marks of distinction like race, caste, religion, language, culture, or some composites of these items.[4] These types may be ranked in terms of their degree of proximity to the principle of genetic closure. For example, ideally, a racial grouping works out its enclosure by the principle of birth ascription, but a proselytizing religious community is unlikely to close its doors to prospective entrants from various racial groups.

A close look at the variety of ethnicity in different points of time and space would indicate that, conceptually, the category of eth-

2. A recent attempt in this direction is Cynthia H. Enloe, *Ethnic Conflict and Political Development* (Boston, Little, Brown, 1973). See also Michael Hechter, "Towards a Theory of Ethnic Change," in *Politics and Society* (Fall 1971), pp. 21–45.

3. Frederik Barth emphasizes the notion of ethnic boundary as the critical element in the concept of ethnicity. See his *Ethnic Groups and Boundaries* (London, Allen and Unwin, 1969), p. 15.

4. For a discussion of comparison among classes of social collectivities see Gerald D. Berreman, "Race, Caste, and Other Invidious Distinctions in Social Stratification," *Race* (April 1972), pp. 385–414. Also Pierre L. van den Berghe, *Race and Ethnicity* (New York, Basic Books, 1970), esp. part 1, and R. A. Schermerhorn, *Comparative Ethnic Relations* (New York, Random House, 1970).

nicity covers so wide a ground that it can be useful mostly at a broad, though significant, level of abstraction. At this level, several points are worth noting. The pervasiveness of ethnicity should not blind us to the differential attributes of various kinds of ethnic groups. Second, the same social collectivity may simultaneously subscribe to a multiplicity of ethnic identifications. Given this possibility of multiplicity of identifications, collectivities may work out their ordering of the relative importance of identifications. This ordering is likely to be fluid and not necessarily determined by some innate preferences of the members. Third, the stability of ethnic groups may be deceptive. The lines of enclosure of such groups may be extended, or there may be internal segmentation within a group eventually leading to fragmentation. Fourth, the extension of ethnic groups rarely tells us anything about the intensity of commitment existing within the group. Intensity, again, can be considered from the perspective of the members' sense of affinity to each other, their degree of affiliation to its presumed norms, and their degree of investment in the maintenance or expansion of the group. Finally, one should note the difference between an ethnic group as a categoric group and its transition to purposive action or its transformation into an active community.

POLITICS OF ETHNIC GROUPS

Ethnic groups, though pervasive, are not necessarily interesting for political analysis. If they choose to remain close to the level of categoric groups, implying that ethnicity in such a case merely refers to a description of some individuals into a presumed ethnic collectivity, it will provide little that is interesting to a student of politics. Ethnicity, however, becomes a relevant political question when ethnic divisions tend to create solidarities affecting political thinking and action. By itself, ethnic division may or may not lead to political division. Some form of political translation of the ethnic interests is necessary to move ethnic groups from a social space to a political space. This transition is usually achieved through the mediation of political commitment and organization.[5] The form of

5. See Harry Eckstein, *Division and Cohesion in Democracy: A Study of Norway* (Princeton, Princeton University Press, 1966), pp. 33–36.

this organization may range from ad hoc to institutionalized associations just as the duration may vary from intermittence to permanence. In terms of scope, they may opt for exclusive action or they may find it profitable to share authority in multi-ethnic coalitions or aggregative organizations.

Between the existence of multiple ethnic groups and competitive ethnic politics, there lies a series of transformations, the success or failure of which tends to determine the extent and the nature of political consequences in a particular political society. Also, whether the end product is likely to be divisive or cohesive or integrationally neutral will depend on how those transformations are worked out in particular contexts of resource, culture, rules, organization, and statesmanship. This is not to say that the politics of ethnicity should be judged exclusively in terms of the norm of integration. There are other competing values in politics that may be equally relevant, such as autonomy, authority, liberty, productivity, justice, and the like. However, we have stressed here the case of integration because most of the recent discoveries of the importance of ethnicity in the social sciences have been obsessed by an equation implying that ethnicity is primordial, and that primordial divisions are politically disintegrative in consequence.[6] The notion of primordiality as an attribute of a social group is relatively uninformative about its state of being and uninstructive about its contribution to political action.[7] Its reference to origin is historically apt up to a point but analytically useless so far as one seeks to understand a group's relative position in social and political space and its relative capability in the society. It prods us to construct imprecise time dualities in terms of modern-primordial or style dualities in terms of civil-primordial, neither of which serves any useful purpose in understanding the significant processes of the role of ethnicity in contemporary society and politics. Specifically, it blocks our view

6. See Clifford Geertz, "The Integrative Revolution, Primordial Sentiments and Civil Politics in the New States," in his edited volume *Old Societies and New States* (Glencoe, The Free Press, 1963), p. 111.

7. An interesting case study that shows the integrational possibilities of primordial groups is R. William Liddle, *Ethnicity, Party, and National Integration* (New Haven, Yale University Press, 1970), esp. pp. 205–230.

from the substantial role of ethnic politics in modern societies like the United States, Canada, Italy, Ireland, Belgium, Yugoslavia, and the USSR, just as it obliterates our understanding of the complexity of new politics of ethnicity in the context of political development of new nations.

LANGUAGE, ETHNICITY, AND POLITICAL COMMUNITY

Among many marks of ethnicity, language has assumed an important place in the history of past political evolution and present political situation. Language provides a bond of unity among its speakers and defines a line of separation marking off one speech community from another.[8] The bond of unity marked by language may be one of chance or choice, depending on whether the linkage is attained through mother tongue or a second language. In this sense, ethnic bond based on language can be viewed as either an evolved bond based on mother tongue or a deliberately created unity founded on a language other than mother tongue. Even the case of evolved bond is less self-evident than is sometimes assumed. Communities may alter both the name of their language and the extension of their speech community for a variety of reasons in different historical situations. On the other hand, it is difficult to imagine how and in what useful sense the mother tongue speakers of the English language ranging from Englishmen, Americans, Canadians, Australians, to the Eurasian community in India can be conceived of either as a categorical ethnic community or a politically relevant community.

For a moment, if we assume that language helps us identify some ethnic groups, it still remains problematic as to how and when such groups acquire a consciousness of kind. Once this is known, the question remains under what conditions such a consciousness of kind is brought to bear on the political sphere of a society and what patterning of political activity emerges from the politicization of language loyalty. The consequences of such political transformation of language-based ethnicity would seem to depend on a multiplicity of factors and their particular interactions, none of which

8. See T. Shibutani and K. M. Kwan, *Ethnic Stratification* (New York, Macmillan, 1965), pp. 75–76.

can be inferred from the character of the ethnic group considered merely in terms of its origin, composition, or social distinctiveness.

LANGUAGE SALIENCE IN SOUTH ASIA

Language, like religion, constitutes one of the most important marks of identification in South Asia. It was in 1947 that politics based on religion divided the subcontinent into India and Pakistan. In 1972, however, a second partition of the subcontinent took place whereby East Pakistan became Bangladesh on the basis of the linguistic claim of Bengali self-determination.[9] East Pakistan constituted the numerically larger part of Pakistan, and in 1947 the people of East Pakistan saw themselves as Pakistanis first and Bengalis secondarily. At that time their greatest perceived enemy was the Bengali-speaking Hindus of East Bengal. Language served as no bond at all. In two decades the same people of East Pakistan were locked in a mortal battle with their fellow Muslims of West Pakistan and in the process lost three million lives.

Which ethnic identification is more authentic for the people of East Bengal, Muslim or Bengali? Immediately after the independence of Bangladesh, violent riots rocked Pakistan. Later all of West Pakistan accused the East Pakistanis of being bad Muslims because they were out to challenge the unity of the Muslim Pakistani ethnic authenticity. But soon West Pakistan's language groups staged their own movements of autonomy: Sindhi speakers, Baluchi speakers, and Pashto speakers attacked the authority of the Punjabi speakers.[10] What is more interesting is that, though the Punjabi speakers now constitute the largest single group, they have never tried to impose their own language on Pakistan. Rather, they have championed the status of Urdu which was generally accepted in West Pakistan as the symbol of Muslim nationalism. All this would imply that the speakers of Sindhi language identify with

9. A standard survey of language movements preceding the formation of the new state of Bangladesh is Badruddin Umar, *Purba Banglar Bhasha Andolan O Tatkalin Rajniti* (Dacca, Masla Brothers, 1970), and A. K. Fazlul Haq, *Mukti Sangram* (Dacca, Dacca University, 1972). (Both are in Bengali.)

10. The complicated ethnic diversity in Pakistan based on language and other factors is presented in Yu. V. Gankovsky, *The Peoples of Pakistan: An Ethnic History* (Lahore, Peoples Publishing House, n.d.), esp. pp. 163–208.

Urdu when they need a West Pakistan coalition against East Pakistan, but when the threat of East Pakistan disappears they discover their Sindhi identification against the Punjabi domination within (West) Pakistan. This is a typical case of fluidity of linguistic identification and language demands stemming from such identification.

In South Asia, as in many other parts of the world, social groups belong to a variety of ethnic circles. On occasions these circles coincide and may mutually reenforce each other; at other times they cut across each other. Even when they coincide, they do not necessarily reenforce, rather they may be deliberately separated for selectively accentuating one and muting the others. It is, as it were, a process of choice among alternative markers of identification which apparently depends on the decisions of the articulators of the particular group's interest. What the articulators decide is not endogenously determined by the nature of the ethnic group. In other words, there is no readily recognizable primordially given set of interests of an ethnic group; just as after the formulation of a set of interests, there is no unique way of activating the pursuit of such interests in the arenas of social or political competition.

EMERGENCE OF LANGUAGE DEMANDS IN INDIA

A careful study of language demands expressed by various language communities of India, the interplay of these demands in the political arena, and the responses by the public authorities to these demands may clarify some of the complex relationships between language and ethnicity, especially when these are considered in the context of the process of national development. By language demands we refer to publicly expressed demands on the political authorities made by organized groups claiming to represent categoric ethnic collectivities based on language loyalties. It may be noted here that in India separate ethnic collectivities based on distinctively different languages have existed for centuries, but the emergence of language demands on public authorities is of relatively recent origin. Only recently, with the progress of social change and the attendant increase of political opportunities in the context of expanding public space, have these demands been generated and pursued to an extent that they have become salient facts of national political life.

Language demands in modern India have been expressed at several levels. During the period of British colonial rule, the nationalist demand for freedom was associated with a demand for the replacement of the colonial language of administration by a national language as a unifying symbol of nationalism. This demand was made at the more visible level of the nationalist politics, and it appeared to represent the aspiration of an inter-ethnic national coalition. However, there were other levels of language demands where the relation between ethnicity and language was more direct and visible. One of these levels can be identified as the demand for the recognition of the regional languages as the media of education, administrative transaction, and judicial proceedings at the relatively lower levels of the operation of law courts. The demand for elevating the status of regional languages to a level of functional importance and prestige ran parallel to sustained efforts made by regional leaders to standardize the regional languages.[11]

The regionalization of language demands represented a move to bring together segmental social groups such as tribes, castes, dialectal speech groups, and religious communities within the relatively wider unity of regional communities defined by linguistic affinity and closure.[12] Systematic attempts to create such wider ethnic entities out of particular collections of segmental ethnicities proceeded in different parts of India along with the development of the still wider nationalist movement. The duality of these two processes of mobilization and integration sometimes led to convergence but relatively often this created a tension and conflict between them. For example, the emergence of Tamil nationalism in the south around the turn of this century can be seen as a story of success in cementing various lower caste groups into a united Davidian movement including diverse religious and other groups within it, but at the

11. A detailed account of language politics in India is contained in Jyotirindra Das Gupta, *Language Conflict and National Development* (Berkeley, University of California Press, 1970).

12. See Joan V. Bondurant, *Regionalism Versus Provincialism* (Berkeley, University of California, Indian Press Digest Monograph, 1958), pp. 21–54.

same time one may detect in the same process a challenge to Indian nationalism. Whether to interpret this challenge as a device for exerting pressure for the promotion of the perceived interests of a regional community or as a threat to national unity is a question which will be discussed later.

JOB COMPETITION AND LANGUAGE RIVALRY

One feature of the regional level of language demands was the creation of a movement for reservation of employment opportunities for the "sons of the soil." This demand was especially strident in those regions of India where migrants from other regions were employed in the upper sector of the job structure. For example, in the province of Bihar a persistent movement was launched during the thirties of this century to reserve jobs of these regions for "the sons of the Bihar soil." It should be noted that what was proposed in Bihar in an open declaration was pretty close to what was being suggested, whether loudly or in organized whispers, in almost all the regions of India.[13] The case of Bihar is particularly interesting because the identity of Bihar was not defined primarily in linguistic terms. Bihar happened to be a part of the Hindi language area if the concept of Hindi is extended to include the major Bihari dialects, the educated speakers of which often claim an affinity to standard Hindi.[14] In any event, though not claiming to represent a self-enclosed language area, many leaders of Bihar used the argument of language with a negative thrust. Thus a large part of the movement was directed against the Bengali speakers, for they were perceived to have occupied "an excessive number of offices in Bihar." Similar moves were made in Orissa, Assam, and other areas. Unlike Bihar, the regionalist leaders of both Orissa and Assam claimed to represent self-contained language communities,

13. See Nirwal Kumar Bose, *Problems of National Integration* (Simla, Indian Institute of Advanced Study, 1967), pp. 47–50.

14. Some of the major dialect speakers in Bihar are assumed to be Hindi speakers by the Hindi leaders, but these dialect speakers refuse to be enumerated as Hindi speakers. This is true even now (as of the time of the 1971 census enumeration). In fact, a major Bihari dialect, Maithili, has been the symbol of an autonomy movement in recent history.

though it was doubtful to what extent such claims were actually endorsed by the lower sectors of these provinces' population, many of whom had little use for the standard languages that the leaders were urging them to believe to be their own standard language.

As the later events indicate, in many cases the political leaders have succeeded in fashioning relatively larger language-based ethnic communities out of a mass of disparate segmental ethnicities. The creation of these language communities was sometimes facilitated by the system of the administrative division of India into provinces as carved by the colonial rulers. Also, it is worth noting that the leaders of the nationalist movement endorsed the formation of such communities,[15] and many of them actively helped the particularist pursuits of these movements in their own regions. In this sense, many of the regional language communities in India have been far from natural in their growth; rather, their creation and maintenance have been a result of deliberate political processes. It will be unrealistic to characterize these regional political processes as inherently opposed to the national political processes. The nationalist movement assumed these regional movements to be an appropriate part of integrating the nation in a two-step process: unifying the segmental small groups in viable regional communities and then integrating these regions into a multi-ethnic national community. This is not to deny that many of them were at times worried about the possible strains likely to arise along this sequential path. However, given the size and diversity of the country and given their faith in democratic politics, it is understandable why they were unwilling to consider regional integration through created ethnic ties as necessarily opposed to the logic of developing a national community.

15. A report prepared by Rajendra Prasad for the Working Committee of the Indian National Congress presents an extensive survey of the Bihar situation as of 1938. This report endorsed by the Indian National Congress uses the term provincials to refer to the sons of the soil and declares that their "desire to seek employment in their own locality is natural . . . and rules providing for such employment to them are not inconsistent with the high ideals of the Congress, particularly when they exist in all provinces." A.I.C.C. Papers, 1938, Nehru Museum Collection, G 60, p. 18.

ORGANIZATIONAL CONTEXT OF LANGUAGE DEMANDS

We have stressed the role of the language leaders in creating ethnic consciousness based on language loyalty. Around the turn of this century, in different parts of India, small groups of intellectuals began forming literary societies, cultural groups, and political associations to articulate the "cause" of their respective languages. These voluntary associations served as the common platform for uniting literary writers, scholars, political leaders, and other persons of eminence around the common purpose of promoting the interests of their language community.[16] In some areas of India, where a sense of language community had not yet clearly evolved, these leaders offered a definition of their community by advancing a theory of proper enclosure of speech groups within the language community and through elaborate prescriptions of linguistic propriety, dispensable contaminations from impure influences, and boundary markers to identify potential intruders from the gray zone of adjacence. One example would be the role of the voluntary associations in north India which began as literary societies for developing Hindi. Beginning at the end of the nineteenth century, the leaders of the Hindi associations succeeded in establishing a definition of proper Hindi and the authentic Hindi language community. It is interesting that the first move on the part of the associational leaders was to promote the use of one standard script, that is, the Nagari script, among various dialect groups of north India. Along with this effort to make many speech groups of some linguistic affinity converge toward a common writing system, exhortations were made to standardize and modernize the written and the spoken forms of this new Hindi. The success of these efforts also assured the gradual divergence of the new Hindi from Urdu. These two categories were previously used to refer to two styles of the same language. But from the beginning of the first decade of this century they came to refer to two distinctly different languages.

This divergence was facilitated by the political rivalry between

16. For an elaboration of the structure and role of voluntary associations see J. Das Gupta, *Language Conflict and National Development*, chaps. 6 and 7.

certain Hindu and Muslim leaders who by emphasizing the supposedly religious rationale for Sanskritizing Hindi and Persianizing Urdu, respectively, consistently helped widen the rift. Hindi and Urdu voluntary associations thus succeeded in creating two language communities out of one. At the same time each of these language communities sought to expand its size by gradually absorbing peripheral dialectal communities through political persuasion, using literary, cultural, and religious appeals as convenience demanded. These associations have been described in some detail because their activities were also associated with the question of selecting national languages, Hindi for composite Indian nationalism and Urdu for separatist Muslim nationalism. They operated simultaneously at the regional and multi-regional national levels, seeking to define language communities of narrower and wider range at the same time.

No such dual demand and its attendant paradoxical implications constrained the language associations which operated at single regional levels. Thus the ethnic promotional tasks of the language associations concerned with Assamese, Bengali, Oriya, Telugu, Tamil, Marathi, Gujarati, and other languages proceeded to define their own communities, interests, and objectives at their regional level. The process of organizational development was similar to the cases of the Hindi and Urdu associations. All of them began as societies with a literature, constantly recalling the greatness of their exclusive heritage and exhorting the need to expand the sphere of their glory by strengthening their communities. Each had a ready list of enemies and intruders, and usually their adjacent communities occupied the top ranks in such lists. However, it would be a mistake to assume that the leaders of these associations were merely interested in the promotion of their own communities. Most of them were at the same time involved in the nationalist movement. None of them imagined their community to be potentially self-sufficient. Though their basic aim was to strengthen their own communities in the national competition for investment, employment, income, status, and glory, they also realized that unless they helped the national movement for independence and development, their long-term objectives would remain unfulfilled. It is in this context that one can appreciate the apparent paradox of the Indian nationalist movement that most of its participants were regionalists and nationalists, ethnicists and cosmopolitans, localitarians and centeritarians, depending on issues discussed, levels relatively emphasized, and particular audiences responded to.

LANGUAGE DEMANDS AFTER INDEPENDENCE

Before independence, language demands were expressed either as long-range aspirations or as short-term limited appeals to and pressures on the colonial administration. Independence changed the pattern of the political system, altered the rules of making and meeting demands, and assured the demand groups of substantial access to political authorities. At this point it may be noted that the system of government introduced in independent India has been a parliamentary democracy with a federal structure. The basic framework of the government is elaborated in the constitution which was enacted in 1950 and, unlike many new states, has maintained its authoritativeness without interruption. As the most authoritative and elaborate document defining not merely the structure of government but also the objectives of the national political community, the constitution was expected to reflect the basic outlines of the language policies of the nation.[17] Since there was no consensus on the content of national language policy, what the constitution offers represents a compromise. This compromise, naturally, has faced subsequent challenges, and a considerable part of the history of language politics of the decades following the adoption of the constitution is concerned with either the problems of

17. Unlike most constitutions, the Indian constitution goes into an unusual elaboration of social objectives and safeguards perhaps to register assurance that the changing majorities in the legislatures at the center and the states will not frivolously affect the distribution of balance in the national community. It is also important to note that the constitution defines the structure and purpose of government both for the federal level and the state level at the same time. For a brief analysis of the logic and content of this complicated document and its working see Durga Das Basu, *Introduction to the Constitution of India* (Calcutta, S. C. Sarkar, 5th ed., 1971). The provisions of the constitution specially relating to language questions and ethnic balance of interest are discussed in pp. 332–340. See also G. N. Srivastava, *The Language Controversy and the Minorities* (Delhi, Atma Ram, 1970), esp. pp. 1–19.

implementation of the language provisions or their redefinition.

Language demands in independent India have been concerned with many issues, of which the most important are the following: the official language of the federal government; the reorganization of the states of the federation along regional linguistic lines; official language of the states of the federation; and language policies relating to education, public employment, and general communication. Though some of these issues are related to each other, they can be clearly distinguished and placed at different levels in terms of their salience in national politics, their claims on national resources, the extent of the national community affected, the degree of urgency and intensity perceived by the participants in relevant political action, and their relation to national development.

The federal language question has generally been identified as the national language question partly because the federal government is a major coordinator of the nation and also because it was related to replacement of English by an Indian language. The nationalist sentiments characteristic of independence movements generally invest a sense of urgency on the replacement of the symbols of colonial domination by authentic national symbols. The Indian nationalist movement, long before independence, had settled that Hindi should replace English.[18] The constitution translated this aspiration into a legal provision and directed the federal government to effectively implement it within a fifteen-year time schedule.

18. The nationalist rhetoric left some questions unclarified, perhaps deliberately. By Hindi it sometimes meant literary Hindi of a Sanskritized variety, sometimes the commonly spoken variety that hardly distinguished between Hindi and Urdu, and often as expressed by Gandhi and Nehru a form known as Hindustani, which legitimated the two varieties as one composite language written in either Nagari or Persian script. The stylistic controversy is reflected in a key provision of the Indian constitution, which instructs the national government "to promote the spread of the Hindi language, to develop it so that it may serve as a medium of expression for all the elements of the *composite culture of India* and to secure its enrichment by *assimilating* without interfering with its genius, the forms, style and expressions used in *Hindustani and in the other languages of India* specified in the Eighth Schedule and by drawing, wherever necessary or desirable, for its vocabulary *primarily on Sanskrit* and secondarily on other languages" (article 351, italics added). For an analysis of this question see J. Das Gupta, *Language Conflict and National Development,* pp. 137 ff.

The choice of Hindi as an authentic national symbol, despite the fact that it neither had the prestige associated with some other Indian languages, nor was it spoken as mother tongue by more than a third of the national population, reflected an agreement among most language groups to reach a viable compromise. It is interesting to recall that some of the strongest advocates of Hindi during the nationalist movement, including leaders like Mahatma Gandhi, were non-Hindi speakers. Their objective was to create a composite national community where the people would be at least bilingual using Hindi as a language of national linkage and honor while using their regional language for most transactions.[19] This linguistic dualism was related to their conception of India as a coordinate community of multi-ethnic justice and balance where the promotion of Hindi would not make any non-Hindi ethnic community worse off.

However, when the British threat disappeared and the Constituent Assembly began to deliberate on the framework of a national constitution, many non-Hindi-speaking nationalists perceived that in case Hindi replaced English, the Hindi speakers would enjoy a natural advantage in dominating the economic institutions and political authorities of the nation.[20] The degree in which this Hindi threat was perceived was greater in the southern states than the other states of the federation, and, of the southern states, Madras was thought to be considerably more threatened than Mysore and Kerala. On the other hand, some non-Hindi states supported the Hindi policy. In fact, a compromise policy was resolved whereby Hindi became the language of official use for the federal government, with English serving as an associate language. This was possible because most language groups were willing to consider the language question in the context of the other equally important national questions. Hindi leaders, for example, were also political

19. In the process they rarely brought out the differences between the concepts of official language of administration, common language of communication, and national language for the limited use of interregional linkage purposes.

20. A detailed examination of the politics of constitution making in India with special reference to inter-group conflict and compromise is presented in Ralph H. Retzlaff, "The Constituent Assembly and the Problem of Indian Unity," Ph.D. dissertation, Cornell University, 1960.

leaders competing for other values besides the status of their language, and, in this competition, by conceding a little on the language issue, they were closer to attaining other values. Besides, Hindi speakers were divided among themselves, and some of them were either pro-English or uncommitted to a policy of alienating the other language groups of the nation.

CONSTRAINTS AND DETERMINANTS

A particular set of situational constraints prevented the Hindi leaders from an extremist pursuit of Hindi policy. As stated earlier, in spite of Hindi's attaining single-group numerical language majority within the nation (30 percent), the combined coalition strength of the other language groups (Tamil, Telugu, Marathi, Gujarati, Bengali, and so on) could be ignored only at its peril. Also, the Hindi language was not perceived to be prestigious by most non-Hindi speakers, if not even by most of the English-educated Hindi speakers. At the same time, the Hindi area in India has consistently ranked lower than many other language areas in terms of literacy and income. This factor makes Hindi less attractive in comparison with some other Indian languages. The advantages of Hindi would seem to be restricted to relative number and a limited currency of a corrupt form of Hindi in some Indian non-Hindi states for limited sets of transactions. But these advantages are far from overwhelming.

Along with these situational constraints, a set of political factors influenced the outcome of language demands in the sector of national language policy. In the first place, the legacy of the political culture of the national movement contributed a sense of the value of democratic political competition within a national frame of politics. Second, the organizational legacy of the national movement left a relatively dense layer of associational activities in which a number of language associations remained active participants for about half a century and continued after independence. These language associations derived basic support from their respective language groups, but their doors were also open to outsiders. Thus Hindi organizations recruited members from non-Hindi areas which accepted Hindi as their second language and were willing to elevate Hindi to a status of either national or official language. Third, the democratic political structure of the country appeared to put a premium on compromise, adjustment, and negotiated settlement. There were occasions when language politics assumed violent form, but these reflected moments of impatience and tactics of opening doors of discussion rather than an exclusively pursued strategy of action. Finally, one may note the acts of statesmanship discernible in the top leadership of the country. To cite one example, all the prime ministers of India, so far, have come from the Hindi area, but all of them eventually succeeded in evoking the trust of the non-Hindi politicians by assuming a stance of moderation, negotiation, compromise, and coordination.

STATE-LEVEL DEMANDS

If inter-ethnic coordination is a required foundation of successful and durable political leadership and authority at the national level, the rules of success seem to take a different turn when one considers the patterns of state-level politics. At this level integral ethnicity rather than ethnic pluralism appears to supply the dominant premise of language demands and language politics. Initially, the states of the Indian federation inherited the territorial boundaries of the provinces of the colonial administration. The lines of boundary of these provinces were drawn according to the criterion of colonial convenience of administration. The nationalist movement encouraged instead the criterion of linguistic coherence as the basis of states in independent India. Long before independence, the organization of the Indian National Congress followed the linguistic criterion in charting the location of its regional organizational units. Regional leaders and people thus naturally expected that the advent of independence would initiate a restructuring of the old provinces into new linguistic states.

The regional expectation of reorganization of provinces remained unfulfilled in some areas even after some years had elapsed since independence. In fact, immediately after independence, the national leadership sought to put the question of regional reorganization on linguistic lines on a low order of priority and urgency in order to concentrate on the reorganization of the national economy and other pressing issues facing a fragile new state based on an extremely underdeveloped economy and desperate poverty.[21] However, the priority ordering of the national authority was rejected by the leaders of several states, especially of those states which contained more than one large language community with distinctly identifiable ethnic enclosure. The state of Madras, for example, contained Tamil- and Telugu-speaking communities. Marathi and Gujarati communities were administratively juxtaposed in Bombay just as Punjab continued an uneasy coexistence of Punjabi and Hindi speakers.

It was in Madras that the Telugu leadership refused to remain in the combined state and demanded a separate state in the federation.[22] The center hesitated, and the Telugu region grew restless. The failure of the national leadership to respond to the sensitivity of the regional leadership and the refusal of the former to negotiate with the latter led to extensive popular movement and violence. In 1952 the formation of Andhra Pradesh was conceded and the Andhra State Act of 1953 legalized the construction of this ethnic home of the Telugu speakers. This event set a precedent which strengthened the movements for a separate state for the Marathi, Gujarati, and the Punjabi speakers, and later for the hill population in Assam.[23] The Report of the States Reorganization Commission adopted in a modified form by the States Reorganization Act of 1956 seemed to provide a systematic formula for reconciling the

21. The political strategy of the national political authority, dominantly shared by the Indian National Congress at the level of government and party organization, was one of subjecting the linguistic reorganization issue to a series of studies by expert commissions like the Dar Commission of 1948 appointed by the Constituent Assembly and the J. V. P. Committee of 1949 set up by the Congress party. These studies opposed the formation of linguistic states, and the national government, armed with this expert opinion, proceeded to treat the regional demands from the perspective of administrative rationality rather than political rationality and prudence. For a summary of the controversies of this period, the first decade following the adoption of the constitution, see B. L. Sukhwal, *India: A Political Geography* (Bombay, Allied Publishers, 1971), pp. 83–86.

22. For the complicated context of the evolution of Telugu language demands see Selig S. Harrison, *India: The Most Dangerous Decades* (Madras, Oxford University Press, 1960), pp. 220–237.

23. See B. L. Sukhwal, *India: A Political Geography,* pp. 87–98.

interests of the regional movements with those of national unity. As later events demonstrated, no such formula could satisfy the language demands of all kinds with equal success. By trial, pressure, and occasional violence, regional language politics of the first two decades led to the emergence of Maharashtra, Gujarat, Haryana, Punjab, and the hill states of Assam, in addition to Andhra Pradesh. Apart from the creation of linguistic states, regional reorganization also involved approximate ethnic homogenization of states in another manner. In many areas, parts of states were transferred to others in order to make the existing states more linguistically coherent and ethnically congruent than they were before. Because many of the demands for linguistic states were associated with occasional violence, many national leaders, intellectuals, and external observers became afraid of the reorganization issue as a whole; and their attitude toward ethnic demands were inevitably colored by this sense of alarm. This alarmist attitude has failed to recognize the constructive role of ethnic reorganization of states and its contribution to long-range integration of the Indian nation on the basis of a sense of coordinate mutuality. Compared to the earlier system of provinces, the linguistic states of India have not proved to be administratively irrational at all.[24] It is difficult to dismiss the significance of the fact that most of the newly carved linguistic states have also been the most developmentally dynamic states of India, as, for example, Maharashtra, Gujarat, Punjab, and Haryana. By separating them from one another, each has undeniably gained on the point of ethnic pride and autonomy, but these are also the states which have rarely created problems of coordination with the national plan of development.

It is also important that with the creation of linguistic states the salience of language demands tends to decline and the energies of these states are channeled to more productive competition and cooperation. Within each state, language competition tends to be replaced by other modes of competition. Thus, in the south, the

24. Most observers have tended to compare the prospects of linguistic division of India with those of an idealized portrait of integration. If only they could turn their attention to a realistic comparison, their conclusions might be very different.

movement for Andhra Pradesh during the fifties assumed such an intensity that it was unimaginable that within a decade language as a marker would have to contend with other claims. Telugu nationalism's very success in gaining a state made it obsolete. In the sixties the Telugu speakers became more interested in competing among themselves in class terms (witness the peasant movements), caste terms (Kamma and Reddi conflicts), or regional terms (the Telengana movement).[25] In Maharashtra, similarly, Marathi unity evoked a less responsive chord in politics than the question of regional, class, or caste disparity within the state. With some variations, the same story pertains in the cases of the Tamil state of Madras, the Punjabi state of Punjab and the Hindi state of Haryana. The success of language demands eroded the appeal of language politics and yielded the ground to other forms and symbols of competitive and cooperative politics.

STATE LANGUAGE AND MINORITY DEMANDS

The third level of language demands is concerned with the problem of the selection of an official language of the states for their own population. Since the states are based on the language loyalty of their own people, the choice of their official language has not posed much of a political problem except in one major respect. Even after linguistic reorganization, each state contains sizable numbers of people who speak other languages. When these minorities speak the language of a neighboring state and if they are clustered in an area contiguous to the borders of that state, they tend to raise problems of inter-state adjustment that are often difficult to solve. The Mysore–Maharashtra dispute, for example, has dragged on for years, and it has yet to find a compromise mutually acceptable to both these states. However, disputes of this kind rarely affect the course of either national life or the significant affairs of these states.

The intra-state minority demands concerned with the language

25. For details of Andhra politics see Hugh Gray, "Andhra Pradesh," in Myron Weiner, ed., *State Politics in India* (Princeton, Princeton University Press, 1968), pp. 399–431. The same volume also has an excellent chapter on the development of Maharashtrian politics prepared by Ram Joshi in pp. 177–214.

of administration, instruction, and judicial proceedings usually involve claims to grant acceptance of minority language for these purposes. Again, if the particular minority language claiming functional recognition happens to be a majority language of a neighboring state and if the size of this minority is substantial, it raises difficult political problems of inter-ethnic rivalry, including violence. The chain of violence over the years intermittently continuing in Assam over the rights of the Bengali minority may be cited as one example.[26] The politics of Urdu demands in various states provides another example.

In general, however, language demands of these minorities are usually directed to securing facilities of instruction in their own languages at various levels of education, with a special emphasis on the school level. Usually, these demands are advocated by organized associations and most often one target of these associations is the state administration. Since they claim a small part of the respective state's resources, it has not been difficult to reach a negotiated settlement. Only in cases of persistent denials, minorities seek the intervention of the national government. As it worked out in the case of the Urdu demands in Uttar Pradesh, federal intervention produced the desired result.

This solution is interesting because language demands are normally expected to emerge from large language communities who direct such demands to the national political authority. The burden of satisfying these demands is on the latter. It is natural that in the process of negotiation, language communities assume the stance of defenders of autonomy and language rights. But when the same communities attain autonomy and authority, they carry the burden of satisfying the language demands of minorities in their own states. On occasions when they prove to be unresponsive to these demands, the minorities look to the national authorities for reminding the states of their need to be responsive.

---

26. The language riots in Assam in 1973 and earlier have not been subjected to serious scholarly examination. One recent account analyzes the Assam situation in an extremely perceptive way: Annadashankar Ray, "Chira Chenehi Mor Bhasha Janani," in *Desh* (April 28, 1973), pp. 1277–1284 (in Bengali).

LANGUAGE DEMANDS AND NATIONAL DEVELOPMENT

The levels of language demands discussed above [27] imply that the ethnic source of language demands tells us very little about the course and consequence of such demands. Language demands, especially in developing nations, cannot be inferred from the nature of language groups. These groups tend to make demands only when social mobilization offers competitive opportunities and values. In this sense language demands are a function of economic, social, and political development. Similarly, the public authorities to whom these demands are addressed are products of similar developmental processes. How these demands will be processed depends largely on the relative negotiability of the demands, the style and organization of demand articulation, and the willingness and capability of the developing authorities to process them.

It is often argued that the new states are incapable of processing language demands because these demands are not cast in negotiable terms and also because these states are so fragile to start with. Hence, either these states should suppress such demands or these demands will devour the state. This notion is suggested by the premise that language demands are inherently divisive, if not disintegrative. As we have seen in this discussion, this is an oversimplification derived from a false opposition between ethnicity and the logic of national integration. If, on the other hand, we assume the variable possibilities of expression, organization, and processing of such demands, we can work out a threshold where given certain conditions, language demands can strengthen the fabric of a new nation and its structures of authority and participation. Of course, there is a possibility that language demands can outweigh the processing capability of the national authority and thus threaten a nation. But this may be true equally of demands derived

27. I have not discussed in this paper the fourth level of language demands, except implicitly as they are meshed in with the other levels, because the language demands concerning education, employment, and communication require a separate study which cannot be incorporated within the scope of this paper. A forthcoming paper will be devoted to this level.

from non-ethnic bases as well. The labels of language or ethnicity do not necessarily invest any particularly divisive or disintegrative property on demands. When disintegrative consequences emerge, chances are they are determined by a variety of systemic and processual variables of politics causally unrelated to either ethnicity or primordiality. The ethnic basis of language demands is less significant than the particular definition of language interest selected and promoted by organized leadership, their success in mobilizing members of their community, their interaction with other groups, the nature of the rules of politics, the structures of authority, participation, and negotiation, and the capability of the political authority to process demands. Careful and systematic studies of these factors will help us discern the complexities associated with language demands and their probable consequences on national development.

16

LUCIAN W. PYE

China: Ethnic Minorities and National Security

Among all the varied cases of the relationship of ethnicity and politics China is unique because of the degree to which national security considerations have transformed once tolerable relations into delicate and potentially explosive matters. Elsewhere in the world societies have either long lived with ethnic tensions or the process of modernization has brought to light new tensions as demands for justice and equity magnify all lingering differences. In the past in China the minorities were either overwhelmed by the Han majority, which had its own significant regional and dialect differences, or strong enough in their geographical isolation, as in Tibet and Outer Mongolia, to be left alone by weak Chinese governments.

As the Communists began governing the issue of the "national minorities" had to yield to the spirit of Chinese nationalism, first during the Japanese war and second during the confrontation with the Soviet Union. For reasons which spring from deep within the Chinese spirit and which were reinforced during the era of Western encroachment and of the "Unequal Treaties," the Han Chinese have developed a powerful sense of their territorial identity, which, some might say, overrides their sense of cultural identity. The concentration of minorities in border territories is at the heart of this linkage of ethnic and national security questions.

It has been considerations of national security which have forced the Chinese to vacillate in their minorities policies. Security policies have been for the Chinese the functional equivalent of industrialization for other societies in elevating the importance of assimilation and the desirability of having a more homogeneous culture. The Chinese Communists have moved from espousing the right of self-determination to tolerating only surface cultural differences.

But before I analyze these current developments a few words about the traditional Chinese minorities problem are in order. Historically all who lived beyond the pale of Chinese civilization tended to assume that the Chinese were blessed with a homogeneous culture and a common racial stock. The Chinese themselves, in their reverence for their ancestors and their reference to their multitudes as being of the "old hundred surnames," seemed to stress their common biological ties. As knowledge of China grew, foreigners began to discover that behind the Chinese posture to the world there were in fact important internal divisions.

Divisions of significance, however, did not seem to challenge the biological unity of the Han people. In the modern era outsiders learned about regional differences, particularly between the rice-growing south and the wheat-growing north, and further, between the more cosmopolitan, urban coastal peoples and the more parochial and rural interior peoples. Finally, modern Chinese politics was increasingly seen in terms of clashes between classes: of peasant against landlord, of soldiers against scholars, of modernized professions against traditional interests. An extensive literature has analyzed the divisions which have played so important a role in the "Chinese revolution" of the last hundred years, but among them one did not find ethnic problems. Cursed by a thousand problems on its road to modernization, China seemed to have been spared that ultimate challenge to national unity, ethnic division and conflict.

It is true that almost as soon as the Chinese moved out of their national homeland and established overseas communities, especially in Southeast Asia, it became apparent to all that there were differences among the Chinese. As the Chinese sorted themselves out among benevolent associations and secret societies, observers were left groping for the right words to describe the differences among them. The British in Malaya and the Dutch in the Indies tried for a while to use such terms as "tribe" and "lineage" before settling on "dialect group" and "community." [1] To this day considerable confusion remains as to whether there is any legitimate basis for classifying different Chinese in Malaysia and Singapore.

It is therefore appropriate in beginning our analysis of "national" minorities in China to note briefly the problem of classifying the differences among the Chinese immigrants from Amoy as Hokkiens, from Swatow as Tiechius, from Hainan as Hailams, and the Kheds from Kwangtung and Fukien as Hakkas, and so forth. For Westerners through the generation of Victor Purcell these distinctions caused no trouble for all could be equally treated as tribes. Subsequent scholars, however, have severe problems. The various groups have all the social attributes usually associated with ethnic differences: they have different spoken languages, they marry among themselves, they pursue different skills and occupations, they trust those of like identification over others, and finally and above all, they accept as a basic feature of their personal identification their ties with a distinctive community.

However outsiders, and especially the British, may have been making too much of the parochialism of Chinese who, in spite of all being Han, have their local differences in language and custom. But the problem cannot be so easily dismissed because among the different communities there are some, specifically the Hakkas or Kheds, that historians and anthropologists would say are indeed ethnographically "more different" from the Central Han Chinese than others. More important, all Chinese in a subtle manner know that the Hakkas are a special minority group. Only the very highly trained outside observer, and any insider, can tell that the Hakkas are distinctive.

In a strange fashion this peculiar character of the Hakkas in Malaysia is typical of the more general problem of minorities in China. From one perspective many of them do not seem that distinctive: from another there is no question of their being of a different category. Pushing further the model of the Hakkas, this has

1. It is noteworthy that the Englishman most closely identified with the aspirations of the Chinese in Malaya immediately after World War II, Victor Purcell, still used the designation of "tribes." See Victor Purcell, *The Chinese in Southeast Asia* (London, Oxford University Press, 1951).

meant that under some conditions it has been easy for the Hakkas to assimilate under the general label of overseas Chinese, while under others they have maintained their distinctive identities. Similarly, with the minorities in the home country it has at times seemed as though assimilation into the larger community was a natural process, while at other times the technically non-Han people have seemed to be distinct ethnic communities with more than just the customary regional and dialect differences.

These considerations have meant that in modern times Chinese governments have been somewhat ambivalent over the question of whether in fact they do or do not have peculiar problems with ethnic minorities. On the one hand, the major divisions of Chinese society involving region and dialect have so threatened the unity of the country that until the Communist regime there was little time left over for worrying about ethnic minorities. On the other hand, whenever Chinese officials did have to confront the fact of such minorities they accepted their non-Han character and felt the need for special policies.

During the period when the Nationalist government was able to set policies, the assumption was that most minorities, and most particularly those in the southwest, were historical remnants, living with backward cultures, who would soon be assimilated into Han civilization once China as a whole had regained its rightful claim to greatness in the international arena. Such aborigines as the Miao, Pai, T'ung, and the Yi or Lolo, who had for thousands of years resisted assimilation into Chinese civilization, would be, it was believed, easy to assimilate if only the government could get its policies focused. The larger minorities such as the Tibetan, Uighurs, and Mongols were recognized as being more difficult to assimilate but ultimately they too would come to recognize the superiorities of Chinese culture.

The confidence of Chinese Nationalist officials in the all enveloping powers of assimilation was fully the match of the faith of European colonialists in the ultimate victory of their more "advanced" civilization, or the once undaunted confidence of Americans in the assimilating powers of American society. When the Chinese Nationalists introduced Han language and sought to spread Han

Chinese schooling they were acting with the not surprising expectations of those who are better off materially that those who are less well off will welcome change. Evidence of resistance to Han culture was ignored, or at least not publicized, and the argument was made that simply more time and more resources would be necessary to accomplish the inevitable.

The Nationalists' goal of Sinicizing the minorities was frustratingly similar to that of many other colonial efforts, in spite of the fact that it all occurred within the acknowledged territories of China. As in many colonial situations the Nanking government's first insoluble problem was that of finding an administrative handle with which to apply leverage in order to influence and organize the different minorities. Historically the Chinese had usually followed policies of various forms of "indirect rule," in the sense of relying upon minority leadership and their own institutions of power. When the Nationalists followed such methods they discovered that the minority leaders usually displayed great skills in building their own powers while obstructing the Chinese policies they opposed. When the Nationalists sought to ignore or break down traditional minority authority systems they usually could find no one to cooperate with them.

Just as in the case of colonial authorities, the Nationalists fell back upon the hope that by offering desirable, if not desired, services they might win over to inevitable assimilation the stubborn minorities. Hence they introduced into minority areas hospitals and schools and sought quite explicitly to emulate the practices of Western missionaries.[2]

With respect to the larger minorities, the Nationalists had, as might be expected, even less success in their goals of assimilation. While they were in power, the Nanking government had to accept the de facto autonomy of Tibet.[3] In 1928, when the Nationalists were establishing their regime, they sent a mission to Tibet which

2. David M. Deal, "Peking's Policies towards Ethnic Minorities in Southwest China, 1927 to 1965," mimeographed paper given at Northwest Regional Seminar on China, University of Washington, April 28–29, 1972.

3. Alfred P. Rubin, "The Position of Tibet in International Law," *China Quarterly*, no. 35 (July–September 1968), 110–154.

failed to convince the Lhasa authorities of the merits of joining the Chinese Republic; and on the eve of the Kuomintang departure from the mainland they failed to obtain the consent of Tibetan officials to the application to Tibet of the new Chinese constitution. The Nationalists never gave up the claim that Tibet belonged to China; they were simply incapable of deploying enough force to compel the Tibetans to acknowledge Chinese rule.

A more conspicuous failure of the Nationalists was their inability to uphold Chinese claims to Outer Mongolia. Here failure meant the loss of territory and thus a dramatic indication that minority problems might be linked to security considerations, a matter that has become increasingly a central concern in Chinese "national minorities" policies. But before coming to the present we should chart briefly the high points in Chinese Communist policies toward minority people.

FROM IDEOLOGY TO SECURITY CALCULATIONS

From the inception of their party, the Chinese Communists adopted Lenin's views that "national minorities" should have the right of secession, but the "proletariat" should seek to consolidate ever larger units of rule and hence should work to diminish any desire for separation. At the Second Party Congress, when they were in close contact with the Cominform, the Chinese for no reason relating to local issues proclaimed the doctrine of regional autonomy for "national minorities." This Leninist concept was later sanctified in the 1931 constitution of the Kiangsi Soviet, which proclaimed "the right of self-determination of the national minorities in China, their right to complete separation from China, and the formation of an independent state for each minority nationality." [4]

As a result of the Long March, which carried the Red Army through several minority populated territories, the Chinese Communists discovered that the politics of minority interests was com-

4. Brandt, Schwartz, and Fairbank, *A Documentary History of Chinese Communism* (New York, Atheneum, 1966), p. 217, as quoted by June Dreyer, "China's Minority Nationalists in the Cultural Revolution," *China Quarterly,* no. 35 (July–September, 1968), 97.

plicated and that ideological proclamations were not enough to win over people with deep historic distrust of Han power. First they had to bribe their way through Lolo territory,[5] and then they had to make their way through Eastern Tibet against a completely hostile population.[6] Experience as contrasted to ideology was such that by the time the Communists came to power their earlier ideal of a federated state had given way to an appreciation of the value of a unitary state. After 1949 the Chinese stopped speaking of the rights of secession and recognized only the possibility of "autonomous regions."

It was possibly in the area of the "national question" that the Chinese made the first explicit break from the Leninist tradition in that they openly rejected Lenin's principle of "self-determination" and the right of secession. The Chinese argued that the experience of the Japanese war had united all elements in support of the Chinese revolution and therefore, "It was in accord with this noble wish of the people of all nationalities that the Chinese Communist Party advocated the carrying out of the principle of nationalistic equality and national regional autonomy within the unity of the great family of the motherland and discontinued emphasizing the slogan of national self-determination and federalism. Consequently, the question of national division or national separation does not even arise in present-day circumstances: such schemes would inevitably meet with the violent opposition of the broad masses of nationalists . . . Anyone wishing to advance [the slogan of national separation] could only expect to find himself completely isolated." [7]

Once the Communists had the responsibility for ruling all of China, their policies toward the minorities took up from where the Nationalists had left off. With even greater vigor than their predecessors the Communists sought to bring the "benefits of progress" to all minorities. It was acknowledged, at least initially, that minor-

---

5. Nym Wales, *Red Dust* (Stanford, Stanford University Press, 1952), p. 71.

6. Edgar Snow, *Red Star over China* (New York, Random House), p. 204.

7. Chang Chih-i, *A Discussion of the National Question in the Chinese Revolution,* trans. in George Mosely, *The Party and the National Question in China* (Cambridge, M.I.T. Press, 1966), pp. 68–69.

ity peoples would have to be treated according to a slower timeta-
ble than Han people, but as the confidence of the Communists
grew, before the failures of the Great Leap became apparent, they
became convinced that in a matter of a few years they should be
able to assimilate the smaller minority peoples into the mainstream
of Chinese life. During this period, men who had studied and
worked with the national minorities, most notably the famous anthropologist Fei Hsiao-t'ung, were accused of having failed before
"liberation" both to show respect for minority customs and to facilitate minority progress. First these scholars and later the Communist government were confronted with the awkward task of finding
a clear path between these two contradictory policy requirements.
How was it possible to respect the minorities and avoid the evils of
"Han chauvinism" while at the same time seeking to revolutionize
the minorities and bring them into the world of socialism?

With the Great Leap, and during succeeding years of the early
1960s, the pressures for assimilation increased and concern over
manifestations of "Han chauvinism" declined. In part the attitude
of the regime changed because of the shock of discovery that the
mere act of spreading the word of the New Socialist China was not
enough to cause the minorities to drop their "feudal" ways and en-
thusiastically join in the workers' and peasants' revolution. To win
over the smaller minorities would require the vigorous application
of more explicitly assimilationist policies which, although more effectively implemented, represented the logical and historical continuity of the program of the Nationalists and previous Chinese governments.

In part, however, the Peking authorities had to change their
approach toward the national minorities because of the dramatic
resistance of the Tibetans.[8] Once the decision was taken to assert
Chinese authority in Tibet, it became necessary to deploy military
force and this in turn left the Chinese with no alternative to breaking down traditional forms of authority and imposing Han leadership over the Tibetans. Inexorably the goal of spreading revolu-

8. For an account of the Tibetan revolt which is sympathetic to the Tibetans
and based on interviews with their leaders, see George N. Patterson, *Tibet in Revolt*
(London, Faber and Faber, 1960).

tionary progress to all within the domain of what Peking considered China raised tensions between the niceties of forms and the realities of power. In 1962 the Chinese established the Tibetan Autonomous Region, which in practice meant the introduction of Han cadres to provide the steel framework of administration. The pattern was the same as that in 1947 when the Inner Mongolian Autonomous Region was established and in 1955 when the Sinkiang Uighur Autonomous Region was recognized.

In these areas to the north and west the form of "indirect rule" was accompanied by policies of encouraging the in-migration of Han settlers, the expansion of central administrative authority, and ceaseless efforts to point out that the future lay unambiguously with the road of progress defined by Peking. That is to say, even though on the surface the Communists appeared to give greater legitimacy to the "autonomy" of the largest minorities than had the Nationalists, in practice their objective was to strengthen China's territorial claims, in part by stimulating Sinification. Communist capabilities ensured a more complete penetration by the Han of the Tibetan, Uighur, and Mongol societies and raised the prospect that even if assimilation were not at hand, administrative integration was.

Earlier Chinese governments had sought to encourage the migration of Han peoples especially into Sinkiang and Inner Mongolia, but only the Communists have had the mobilization capacity to implement effectively such a policy. In 1947 when the Inner Mongolian Autonomous Region was established the ratio of Chinese to Mongols was 3 to 1, but by 1971 the ratio was 15 to 1.[9] The Sinkiang immigration raised the Han proportion from 5.5 percent in 1949 to 20.5 percent in 1962 and 45 percent in 1966.[10] A belief that has deeply depressed the Tibetan refugee colonies in both India and the United States is their understanding that Han migration into Tibet has now reached the point at which Hans now outnumber by possibly 2 to 1 the native Tibetans. Most dramatic of all

9. William Heaton, "Inner Mongolia: Aftermath of the Revolution," *Current Science*, 9.9 (April 1971), 13.

10. Amrit Tal, "Sinification of Ethnic Minorities in China," *Current Science*, 8.4 (February 1970), 15.

was the upsurge in migrations after the border incidents with the Soviet Union. In 1969 and 1970 over one million Han settlers were moved into Inner Mongolia.[11]

It is thus possible to observe a steady change in the attitudes of the Chinese Communists toward the ethnic minorities in China. They began by accepting the extreme Leninist view of the right to separation but by the time they came to power they had rejected this right and spoke of the need for all peoples in China to be "liberated" from feudalism and share in the common unity of revolutionary participation. After scarcely a decade in power the somewhat romantic view that all differences between Han and non-Han might dissolve in the camaraderie of working together to shed "feudal thoughts and customs" and gain proletarian insights and dedication had to give way to a new appreciation of how hard it would be to break down the differences between Han and non-Han. The shock of the Tibetan revolt and the widespread defections of nationality cadres during the Great Leap period forced the Chinese to take a more sober and less trusting view of their minorities problem.[12]

Then came the decisive break with the Soviet Union and the discovery that the problem of national minorities was directly linked to the larger problem of China's national defense. Possibly the event which most traumatically shocked the Chinese was the dramatic exodus in the summer of 1962 of some 50,000 Kazakhs and other non-Han Chinese from Ili-chou in Sinkiang across the border to the Soviet Union and the Kazakh SSR.[13] There is still no resolution of the conflicting Chinese and Soviet accounts of precisely what triggered this huge out-flowing of nomadic peoples from Mao's China, but the general historical situation is unambiguous. By the time the Communists came to power in 1949, Chinese rule in the border area of Sinkiang was so weak that Soviet influence

11. Heaton, "Inner Mongolia."

12. For a discussion of the disaffection of the first classes of Tibetan cadres during the strains related to the Great Leap, see Mosely, *The Party and the National Question in China,* introduction.

13. For a detailed analysis of these events see George Moseley, *A Sino-Soviet Cultural Frontier: The Ili Kazakh Autonomous Chou* (Cambridge, East Asian Research Center, Harvard University, 1966).

had completely penetrated in particular the Ili district.[14] Under the policy of "leaning to one side" and in the spirit of socialist brotherhood it was impossible for the new Chinese Communist ruler to seek to counter Soviet influences. However, as the Sino-Soviet rift intensified and particularly after the break came into the open in 1960, it became necessary for the Chinese to assert their sovereign claims. The Chinese were not in a sound political position to do this because the previous years of the Great Leap had involved numerous attempts elsewhere in Sinkiang to introduce communes and alter the nomadic habits of other minorities. The Kazakhs were aware of these threats to their traditional ways, and the Soviets had been vigorously spreading reports about the dangers of Peking's policies. Thus by 1962 when relatively mild initiatives by the Chinese were combined with Soviet horror propaganda, near panic seized the Kazakh community. The fact that such numbers would leave China demonstrated not only the failure of what Peking considered to be conciliatory policies toward minorities but also the vulnerability of China's borders. In the subsequent years the Chinese have increasingly seen the "nationalities problem" as one of guarding the sacred territory of the Chinese motherland.

THE REALITIES OF GUARDING THE BORDERS

From this review of the ethnic minority problem in Communist China it is apparent that the Chinese case is distinctive because it is

14. The Ili area was a source of dispute between Russia and China since the Ch'ing dynasty. Indeed, it was the subject of a rather celebrated case in Western versus Chinese styles of international law and also the first occasion for Yalta to become an infamous name in Chinese foreign relations. Briefly, the Chinese negotiator at a conference held in Yalta made concessions about China's claim to suzerainty over Ili which infuriated the Chinese emperor, who immediately ordered the diplomat recalled and beheaded. This act created consternation among the Western diplomats in Peking who had been trying to teach the Chinese the principle of diplomatic immunity, for their own safety, but who now realized that they would also have to insist that the principle be applied by the Chinese government to its own diplomats. As the doyen of the fledgling diplomatic corps said, "How can one outwit a Chinese negotiator if one knows he is to lose his head for it?" For a good general account of the Ili controversy see: Hosea Ballou Morse, *The International Relations of the Chinese Empire* (London, Longman, Green, 1910, 1918).

so intimately tied to basic issues of national security. In the past Chinese problems of cultural diffusion and assimilation were not significantly different from problems of ethnic integration in other societies. What is special in the Chinese case is that a society which historically was hardly prepared to admit to having minorities and whose sense of cultural homogeneity helped create a strong feeling for the historically immutable territory of "China" should suddenly discover that its basic security is now threatened because its border territories are populated mainly by ethnic minorities.

A few facts can help explain the basis of this growing sense of Chinese anxiety. The basic contradiction of China is that while only 6 percent of the population is non-Han, this minority makes up in fact the majority peoples of nearly 60 percent of the territory in China. Furthermore, over 90 percent of the border with her neighbors is inhabited by non-Han peoples. The only significant border area occupied by Han population is along the Amur and Ussuri rivers, the boundary where the Chinese have had their most severe border fights with the Russians.[15] The fact that they have had problems in this Han populated area must have made the Chinese more aware of the populations on most of their other borders.

In the past the Chinese took comfort in the fact that only 6 percent of their people were non-Han, but now officials in Peking have become acutely conscious that this percentage represents in absolute terms some 52 million people. Similarly, in the past the Chinese minimized their minority problem because the national minorities were divided among 52 or possibly even 54 communities,[16] several with less than 10,000 members. Now, however, Peking officials emphasize to Western visitors the fact that at least 10 and possibly 11 national minority groups number over one million. Also disturbing is the fact that as the Chinese have learned more

15. For an excellent analysis of these incidents see Thomas W. Robinson, "The Sino-Soviet Border Dispute: Background Development, and the March 1968 Clashes," *American Political Science Review*, 66.4 (December 1972), 1175–1202.

16. The Chinese Communists have varied in their official count of national minorities between 52, which was used in most of the earlier reports, and 54, which is the number now cited by the Central Institute of National Minorities. This change is another indication of rising Chinese concern over and sensitivity toward their minorities problems.

about some of their larger national minorities, they have had to raise quite significantly their estimates of the size of these populations.[17]

Thus in 1969 when the Chinese became involved in serious border clashes with the Russians, Peking had to recognize that it has a far more serious national minority problem than any Chinese government had ever previously acknowledged. Circumstances which had once seemed favorable to Chinese interests now had to be revised. In particular, the many minorities who straddled China's borders and were once seen as providing the basis for a possible Chinese forward policy of subversion in Southeast Asia were now seen as a potentially subversive element in China. The exodus of the Kazakhs, who once numbered over half a million, raised questions about the Uighurs' loyalty, and they represented at least four million people with kinfolk also on the Soviet side. On the southern border the Chuang, whose population may have reached ten million, had been perceived for years as Thai speakers capable of supporting a Free Thai movement against the influence of Bangkok in the north and northwest of Thailand, were suddenly seen as requiring special attention because of their potential vulnerability to anti-Chinese appeals. In Peking doubts began to arise also as precisely to whom the minorities along the Burmese and Lao borders were likely to be loyal, particularly since only the Chinese had been harassing them to make them participate in any national system. Thus, by the end of the 1960s, when the overseas Chinese were seen as less threatening to Southeast Asian governments, and when the Cultural Revolution had weakened somewhat Peking's administrative influence over its minorities, questions arose about the balance of loyalties of some groups who straddled China's borders.

These changes in Chinese attitudes were part of a more fun-

17. The Chinese, for example, for a long time thought of the Tibetans as totaling fewer than two million, but by the late 1950s they spoke of about three million Tibetans. Nobody has better than the roughest approximation of how many Tibetans there are. George Patterson reports careful estimates based on calculations of numbers of monks and the size of monasteries lead to figures as high as five to ten or even twenty million. Patterson, *Tibet in Revolt*, p. 35.

damental alteration in basic Chinese views about Chinese security. For the last hundred-odd years the Chinese had lived with a world view in which military danger was likely to come from the sea. First in the form of British and European sea power, then from Japan, and most recently in the threat of American power. During this period China had been fortunate in being able to leave relatively unguarded the longest border in the world. Chinese military power was thus deployed in the eastern and southern regions where the Han population was concentrated. Indeed in modern times the Chinese evolved a unique pattern of civil-military relations in which armies—from those of the warlords, through the Nationalists and down to the Communists—participated to a great extent in civil administration and were concentrated where the Chinese population was the most dense. The combination of living off local resources and helping civil rule seemed to reduce the burden of the military.

The break in Sino-Soviet relations which reached a climax in the border fighting of 1969 brought to an end that era and reestablished the historic and tragic Chinese security problem of having to station troops along a huge underpopulated border. Suddenly China was back to the problem which was as old as the Great Wall and which was an ingredient in the collapse of all her great dynasties: that is, the problem of extracting resources and manpower from the densely populated Han regions in order to establish lonely garrisons in the non-Han territories.

Harrison E. Salisbury has described the almost pathological and racist fears of the Russians of the "Mongol hordes" of long ago and hence of the Chinese today.[18] What is often overlooked is that the Chinese on their side have an equally powerful historic fear of tribal peoples moving down into their agricultural domains. The Great Wall of China is a monument to this fear, and now that the Chinese are reacting again to a threat from the north it is understandable that the historic imagery of the dangerous "barbarians" of the border regions, that is, some of their national minorities, has again come alive in the Chinese imagination.

18. Harrison E. Salisbury, *War between Russia and China* (New York, W. W. Norton, 1969).

We have evidence of the Chinese anxiety about the minority peoples along the northern border from some unpublicized changes which the Chinese have been making with respect to the boundaries of provinces and autonomous regions along the border of China. Until these changes came in 1970, the Inner Mongolian Autonomous Region extended along the southern border of the Mongolian People's Republic and on up in the east until it shared a border with the Soviet Union. The territory of the Autonomous Region did in fact coincide with the area of Mongol settlement. After the troubles with the Russians, the territory of Heilungkiang, the Han populated province along the Amur and Ussuri rivers, was extended to the west so as to include the entire boundary with the USSR. The Inner Mongolian Autonomous Region was further cut in size when Kirin province, also Han populated, was extended to the west to the border of the Mongolian People's Republic. Presumably, Mongol herdsmen are still able to move into these new areas of Kirin and Heilungkiang to graze their flocks in the summer, but administrative and military control of the area is now firmly in Han hands.

Similarly, recent changes in the internal map of China have apparently cut down the size of the Ningsia Hui Autonomous Region and the Sinkiang Uighur Autonomous Region. Furthermore since 1969 there has been a significant step up in the rate of Han people moving into Sinkiang and Kansu. Such influxes of Han peoples in the past have always been accompanied by increased ethnic tensions as the Han tended to monopolize the better farming lands, government offices, and the better paid jobs in the railroads, industries, and the servicing of the military.

The combination of internal tensions and the external security threats has convinced the Chinese to reinvestigate their political policies of winning over, or at least controlling, national minorities. The seriousness with which they take this task can be seen from activities at the Central Institute of Nationalities.

THE CENTRAL INSTITUTE OF NATIONALITIES

Current Chinese policies toward the national minorities are vividly manifest at the Central Nationalities Institute, which is located on the western side of Peking, near the Academy of Sciences and on the route to where Peking National University (Peita) is now located on the old Yenching University campus.[19] The purpose of the institute, which was established on June 11, 1951, is to train revolutionary cadres, from each minority community, who are expected to return to their people and provide appropriate leadership. Since its founding the institute has turned out nearly ten thousand trained propagandists and party members.

Before the Cultural Revolution the training course could last as long as five years for most students who were being prepared for key leadership roles. At that time the average enrollment was about 2,800 students. From 1966 to 1970 the institute was closed by the Cultural Revolution, and new classes of students were only again brought to Peking for training when classes began on January 3, 1972. At the present the institute has 1,200 students, 30 percent of whom are members of the Chinese Communist party and 70 percent of whom are Communist Youth League members. The People's Liberation Army has 90 students at the institute. In addition there are some 70 to 80 Han Chinese being trained in minority languages and culture.

Physically, the institute is conspicuously better endowed and funded than even the leading Chinese universities. Its buildings are well maintained, its museum is brightly lighted with colorfully painted signs, its athletic fields are more extensive and have more equipment than those of even the elite universities and middle schools. The dormitory rooms seem more comfortable than the quarters associated not only with universities and the military but also the rest houses of government bureaus. Special care is given to providing from time to time food for some of the different dietary traditions. There is a special kitchen for the Muslims, and the dancers from all groups, who are seen as needing more energy, have their special training tables.

The contrast between the very heavy investment in the institute and the slowness with which the training program is picking up since the Cultural Revolution suggest some of the frustrations the

19. I visited the institute in December 1972, during a 26-day trip to China.

Chinese have had in arriving at appropriate policies for the national minorities at a time of crisis in national security. Officials at the institute insist that national minority policies are based solely on Marx and the thoughts of Mao Tse-tung (no mention of Lenin) and that there has been no change in content since before the Cultural Revolution. On the other hand they do admit that it is still impossible to teach history and that daily sessions of "struggle, criticism, and transformation" are still going on to arrive at an appropriate curriculum for teaching about the proper relations between Han and non-Han traditions. Trained anthropologists who once staffed the department of history and customs are currently not allowed to teach.

Officials suggest that the cause of the crisis has been in part the dropping of the old pre-Cultural Revolution practice of recruiting influential people in terms of the traditional cultures and instead recruiting workers, peasants, and soldiers who have little standing in their home communities. Reports indicate that in the past many "students" at the institute were from the "tribal" or "feudal" leading families—one Tibetan prince brought to this "workers' " revolutionary training ground a bevy of personal servants to look after his needs. During the Cultural Revolution many of these earlier trained cadres displayed distaste and even stubborn resistance, instead of enthusiasm, for the Red Guards and Mao's revolutionary officials.

Although current recruits have supposedly far better revolutionary class backgrounds, the very humble nature of their origins, combined with the expectation that they are moving swiftly to positions of power, makes them appear in the eyes of just about everyone as suspiciously opportunistic individuals. The Chinese dilemma is how precisely to take the young people from the minority groups, who on the face of it would seem not to be destined for leadership, and put them into key positions without leaving them hopelessly tainted with the brush of Uncle Tomism. Officials are quite frank about this problem. First they admit that among more "feudalistically" inclined peoples, as they see most of their minority nationals, there is not enough appreciation of revolutionary virtues to understand that people from lowly peasant and worker backgrounds are appropriately the leaders of the future and not just rude social climbers. Second, the officials at the institute concede that the students they are training are expected to go back to their communities and spread the word of Mao, which regretfully makes them appear to be agents of Han domination.

The principal solution the Chinese have found for their dilemma has been to emphasize the training of the nationalist cadres in their own folkways so that they can return to their communities and appear to be more knowledgeable about traditional customs than even their elders or those who have not been contaminated by close associations with Han Chinese. Thus the major emphasis in the cadre curriculum is in the fine arts and handicrafts. Traditional songs are practiced which are only slightly modified, usually near the end of the verses, to give way to propaganda themes and the praise of Chairman Mao. The object is to ensure that the cadre will be as skilled as anyone in his community in traditional music, dance, and costume.

To the consternation of Han officials it has turned out that the post-Cultural Revolution recruits from more humble class backgrounds have tended to be "culturally disadvantaged," not just in normal educational skills but also in their ethnic cultures. Lower class Tibetans, Mongols, and Uighurs lack understanding of the social niceties associated with images of leadership in their respective cultures. Many are also illiterate in their own language and do not know a word of Chinese. Thus the burdens of language and cultural training are much greater than in the past when better educated cadres had five years of training. Now the short-term course for cadres is only two to three years. The uneven cultural background of the current students has also required extensive subdividing of classes into smaller and more homogeneous groups according to levels of talent and knowledge, all of which further complicates the program.

A second major problem of cadre training has been in the area of language education. Cadres have to be, on the one hand, fully capable of carrying to their people the ideas, slogans, and "thought" of Mao and his revolution and thus they do require extensive training as translators. On the other hand, it is desirable that they not appear to be people who have lost their roots in their own culture and been completely assimilated into the Han world. The very distinctiveness of revolutionary language and the Communist concern over the "correctness of thoughts" work to dramatize the distance of Han culture from traditional ways and hence to spotlight the moral and cultural issue of assimilation. All the efforts at teaching traditional songs and dances are designed to mask the issue of assimilation and to demonstrate the cadre's identification with his cultural origins. On the other hand his need to perform his basic revolutionary role compels him to speak in terms which make him appear to be a running dog of the Hans.

At present representatives of 51 out of 54 "recognized" minorities attend the institute. During the 1950s the emphasis was particularly on dealing with Tibetans in the light of Peking's difficulties in extending its rule in Tibet. At present the Tibetans are still the largest group, consisting of some 400 cadres, and 90 out of 100 in the short course. There has, however, been a rise in the number of Uighurs to over 150.

The daily regime at the institute is what one might expect at a party cadre training center. Early morning exercises are followed by 50 minute classes from 8 A.M. to noon; then a rest break and then further drills from 1:30 to 3:30, followed by sports, and then evening homework from 7:30 to 10:30 and "lights out." The classes seek to blend language training, propaganda and political education, and song and dance performances. The institute does have a library of 600,000 volumes, 10 percent of which are in minority languages, and the most valuable are local chronicles in Chinese. At present, however, there is no research of a scholarly nature taking place, and there will not be any until they have resolved the issue of how to treat "history." [20] Academically trained anthropologists are also not at present teaching. Instruction is entirely in the hands of party cadres and PLA representatives.

It is impossible to judge how effective the Central Institute will

20. Before the Cultural Revolution the Central Institute did facilitate field research under the guidance of such recognized anthropologists as Wu Wen-tsuo, who trained at Dartmouth and Columbia before teaching at Yenching, and the world famous Fei Hsiao-t'ung, but now these men are not in leadership roles. Fei Hsiao-t'ung during the Cultural Revolution spent two years and three months at a "May Seventh School" working at farming. He is now elderly but of quick mind and publicly accepts the current trends in China.

be in building loyalty to Peking among minority elements. The approach is determined, the investment is high; but one is left with the feeling that, as sincere as the attempt is, the policy is slightly artificial. Possibly this is an inevitable characteristic of any policy that strives to accelerate inter-ethnic relations not for its own sake but for some extraneous political end. Although the analogy is not entirely apt, the Chinese policy, if transferred to America, would be similar to the United States government's sponsoring the "Black Power movement," monopolizing the teaching of "Afro-American studies," and directing those who are thus trained to be more "knowledgeable" about a somewhat synthetic "black culture" to make all their "cultural performances" climax in uninhibited praise of the President.

FUTURE PROSPECTS

While it is difficult to forecast the likely effects of current Chinese policies toward the national minorities, it is not hard to discern certain trends.

First, as the Chinese accept the prospect of a long-term security threat along their inner borders, the historic Chinese distrust of the once nomadic, non-Han peoples is likely to rise. The obsession of the Chinese over protecting their "territories," which was heightened by their "losses" through the "unequal treaties" of the nineteenth century, will make them even more hypersensitive to the vulnerability of their borders, which lie almost entirely in minority dominated regions. The compulsions of national security are thus likely to heighten anxieties and stimulate the desire of Han authorities to eliminate any differences in underlying values and loyalties among the minorities, while tolerating differences only in the matter of forms, such as dress and folk dances.

The reactions of minorities to this increased pressure for political conformity is likely to be uneven. Power relationships within each minority community may shift as a consequence of Han pressures, and the result is likely to be greater internal ethnic tension. Those minorities who straddle the border with the Soviet Union will certainly find themselves in a complex situation. As both targets of suspicion and subjects of courting, these minorities have leverage with Peking but are also highly vulnerable.

In this situation it is hard to predict the balance of advantage or danger for each or all the minorities, but it does seem highly likely that the uniqueness of their circumstances will tend to heighten their ethnic awareness and make them feel not just culturally but also politically distinct.

The speed with which increased Han Chinese security anxieties can stimulate minority political awareness has already been demonstrated by the reactions of Tibetans to Chinese policies not just since the revolt of 1969 but more significantly since the Sino-Indian border fighting of 1962. As the PLA came to dominate more and more administration in Tibet, the Tibetans became increasingly sensitive to their separate identities. Even though younger Tibetans did not have as deep attachments to Buddhism as did their elders, they have shown a new sense of ethnic awareness as they have been forced to recognize that they are different from the Han troops who appear to be manifestly a foreign occupation force.[21]

In more sociological terms it seems highly likely that as the processes of social change proceed in China and as more members of the national minorities come closer to the Han in cultural and economic circumstances, the greater will be their concern about their ethnic identities and the power status of their communities. During the last twenty years individual members of various national minorities have been welcomed into representational roles in a form of "tokenism." At the same time as increasing numbers of the minorities have been trained to play party cadre roles and convey the wishes of Peking in return for power and status advantages they have become vulnerable to the charge of being opportunistic. In time, however, as the numbers of better educated increase, these representational and agent roles are likely to decline and be replaced by roles based on the genuine autonomy of the national minority.

There is a certain irony in this prospect, for in its early enthusi-

21. For a report on Tibetan attitudes as acknowledged in the Chinese press see "National Minorities," *China News Analysis,* no. 720 (August 9, 1968), 3–5.

asms and before the rise of fears for national security on the land frontiers, the Chinese Communist party did genuinely favor precisely such a development toward greater autonomy. In its very first years the CCP would have welcomed the idea that the national minorities were increasing in both cultural development and a sense of autonomy and self-identification. The paradox has been that with the need to maintain the territorial integrity of China the Communists have moved toward more and more aggressive assimilationist policies. In order to facilitate penetration for spreading their control they have also helped maintain cultural forms and thus the basis for separate identity. Consequently they may have arrived at precisely the right policy mix for both advancing a minority and making it feel more self-conscious of its separate identity.

In sum, we come to the final conclusion that paradoxically as economic and cultural differences break down the Chinese are likely to find that they still have national minority problems, which will possibly be even more acute than in the past. When the cultural patterns between Han and non-Han were quite different and they each lived in relatively separate worlds, and when the Han Chinese had other pressing concerns and ignored those they considered their inferiors, the national minorities were able in practice to realize considerable autonomy. That is to say, in the past when the policy of the Chinese government was assimilationist, practical factors led to the realities of autonomy. The drift of Tibet and Outer Mongolia toward independence was only the most conspicuous assertion of autonomy by national minorities against weak Chinese authorities. Then came the Communists with their policy of praising autonomy for the national minorities but introducing practices which were more threatening to the autonomy of minorities. Moreover, Peking's increased capacity to penetrate the national minorities has made Chinese authorities more effective in supporting assimilation policies, particularly as they have become more anxious about their security problems.

Yet we know from the experiences of more industrial countries, the leveling of cultural differences can lead to greater ethnic tensions as economic and political power considerations are elevated in relative importance. In China we are not seeing the cultural leveling between Han and non-Han because of industrialization but rather as the result of a combination of ideological commitment and national security concerns on the part of the government. Therefore China may shortly be confronted with the types of ethnic divisions typical of advanced industrial societies while remaining in a pre-industrial state and lacking the material resources that more affluent countries may have for ameliorating their ethnic divisions.

In China ideology and national security considerations may be serving as the functional equivalent of the social forces associated with industrialization in breaking down the significance of cultural uniqueness and in elevating the importance of political and economic differences in ethnic relations. These considerations have a compelling quality which will force the Chinese authorities to press for the solution of national minority problems and to feel that they cannot afford to allow time to work to reduce distrust. As long as the minorities are seen as linked to the vital question of the nation's safety, Peking will find it hard to maintain a relaxed and sympathetic posture. More important, the security factor means that, whereas in industrializing societies it is possible to diffuse power toward ethnic groups as they become more assimilated, in China it may be hard to yield significant power to the minorities as they can hardly be trusted as the ultimate guardians on the borders.

In speculating about the possibility that national security considerations in China can produce effects comparable to advanced industrialization in other societies with respect to ethnic divisions, we have gone beyond current realities. Recent events in China do, however, point in the direction of these speculations, and more important, we can already note that the Chinese case seems to support a general law of ethnic relations which holds that substantive differences in cultural practices and values are less important than the realities of power and economic relationships in determining the intensity of ethnic tensions. As the cultures of the non-Han come closer to that of the Han, the ethnic identities of the non-Han will be increasingly defined by their sense of political efficacy and well-being as compared to the Han majority.

Thus the Chinese, like so many people, are learning that as they reduce differences and encourage the ideals of equality the remaining irreducible differences will come to be seen as the cause of even greater injustices than were associated with the earlier gross cultural differences.[22] Whatever the Chinese policies to cope with these problems, it is certain that there will not be a return to the original ideal of encouraging national autonomy because any minorities policy in China will certainly be subordinated to the higher issues of national security.

22. Chinese appreciation of the delicacies of policies toward minorities and of the issue of "genocide" associated with some assimilationist policies was most recently revealed in the Chinese delegate's speech at the United Nations Economic Commission for Asia and the Far East (E.C.A.F.E.) when in dismissing as imperialist propaganda the Malthusian specter, Chi Lung said that in China "population increase in a planned way" was a part of overall economic planning and that, "In national minority areas and other sparsely populated areas, we adopt appropriate measures to help increase population." *Peking Review,* no. 17 (April 27, 1973), 17. By merely mentioning the issue the Chinese delegate attracted attention to Peking's ambivalence about whether minorities should be treated differently or be assimilated and treated like all other Chinese.

Contributors

Daniel Bell, Professor of Sociology, Harvard University

François Bourricaud, Professor, Université René Descartes, Paris

Jyotirindra Das Gupta, Associate Professor of Political Science, University of California, Berkeley

Milton J. Esman, John S. Knight Professor and Director, Center for International Studies, Cornell University

Nathan Glazer, Professor of Education and Social Structure, Harvard University

Milton M. Gordon, Professor of Sociology, University of Massachusetts, Amherst

Andrew M. Greeley, Director, Center for the Study of American Pluralism, at National Opinion Research Center, Chicago

Donald L. Horowitz, Research Associate, The Brookings Institution, Washington, D.C.

Harold R. Isaacs, Professor of Political Science, Massachusetts Institute of Technology

Martin Kilson, Professor of Government, Harvard University

Ali A. Mazrui, Professor of Political Science, University of Michigan

William C. McCready, Senior Study Director, National Opinion Research Center, Chicago

Daniel P. Moynihan, Professor of Government, Harvard University

Talcott Parsons, Professor of Sociology, Emeritus, Harvard University

Orlando Patterson, Professor of Sociology, Harvard University

William Petersen, Robert Lazarus Professor of Social Demography, Ohio State University

Richard Pipes, Professor of History, Harvard University

John Porter, Professor of Sociology, Carleton University, Ottawa, Canada

Lucian W. Pye, Ford Professor of Political Science, Massachusetts Institute of Technology

Index

Absorption, 16, 293

Academic freedom, 62

Acculturation, 84, 85, 293; and assimilation, 124; earning and, 344; in Indonesia, 401; urbanization and, 385

Achievement: personal, 77; and technical competence, 170; value of, 294, 295, 357

Achievement groups, 157

Achinese, in Sumatra, 399

Acholi (Uganda tribe), 424, 434, 445, 446, 447

Action Committee on Arab-American Relations, 24

Activism, white, 259

Adjustment, pattern of, 340

Affirmative action, 70, 146, 307

Africa, 143; ethnicity in, 172n; Subsaharan, 74

Africans, 13, 34

Afro-Americans, 71, 72n, 243; culture indigène of, 251; social status of, 240

Afro-Caribbean societies, 313-322, 346

Afro-West Indians, 318, 319

Age-grade systems, 428

Aggression, 36, 95

Agriculture, 317, 398

Alcohol, consumption of, 214, 219

Algeria, 150

Alienation, 68, 260

Allegiances, 311; class, 313; ethnic, 312; special, 66

"Allemanic," 191

Allport, Gordon, 120

Alsace, 55

Amalgamation, 115, 116, 124, 126, 138; West Indian example of, 129

Americanism, 114

Americanization, 335

Americans: black, 72 (see also Blacks); Negro, 16; neo-ethnicity of Negroes, 236 (see also Negroes); white, 72. See also Whites

Amin, Gen. Idi, 420, 423, 424, 436, 439-443

Amish quincentennial, in Canada, 287

Amparo, 360, 363, 384

Ancestry, common, 121, 490

Andhra Pradesh, 483, 484, 485

Andhra State Act, Indian, 483

Anglo-Indians, in India, 41

Anglophones, in Canada, 268

Anglo-Saxons: and democratic process, 220-222; on moral issues, 220t; political participation of, 218t

Ankole, elite of, 431

Anomie, 184

Anthropologists, 73, 93, 303; Chinese, 505, 507

Anthropology, 155n, 222, 310

Anti-imperialism, 150

Anti-Semitism, 68, 108

Anxiety, 215t, 230

APRA (Alianza Popular Revolucionaria Americana), 279

Arab countries, 143, 151

Archaeology, 299

Archaism, in Peru, 381

Arensberg, C., 211

Arguedas, José Maria, 354